Cultural Trauma and Collective Identity

# Cultural Trauma
# and Collective Identity

JEFFREY C. ALEXANDER

RON EYERMAN

BERNHARD GIESEN

NEIL J. SMELSER

PIOTR SZTOMPKA

UNIVERSITY OF CALIFORNIA PRESS

*Berkeley* • *Los Angeles* • *London*

An earlier version of Chapter 6, Jeffrey Alexander,
"On the Social Construction of Moral Universals:
The 'Holocaust' from War Crime to Trauma Drama,"
originally appeared in *European Journal of Social
Theory*. Reprinted by permission of Sage Publications,
Ltd.

University of California Press
Berkeley, California

University of California Press, Ltd.
London, England

Library of Congress Cataloging-in-Publication Data

Cultural trauma and collective identity / Jeffrey C.
Alexander . . . [et al.].
p. cm.
Includes bibliographical references and index.
ISBN 978-0-520-23595-3 (pbk. : alk. paper)
1. Social problems—Psychological aspects.
2. Psychic trauma—Social aspects. 3. Crises—
Psychological aspects. I. Alexander, Jeffrey C.

HN13 .C845 2004
361.1—dc21 2003012762

Manufactured in the United States of America
13 12 11 10 09 08
10 9 8 7 6 5 4 3

The paper used in this publication is both acid-free and
totally chlorine-free (TCF). It meets the minimum
requirements of ANSI/NISO Z39.48–1992 (R 1997)
*(Permanence of Paper)*. ⊚

# Contents

# Preface

The idea of "cultural trauma" developed over the course of an intensive year-long dialogue among the coauthors.

The opportunity to engage in such a dialogue was provided by a generous grant from the William and Flora Hewlett Foundation to the Center for Advanced Studies in the Behavioral Sciences under the title of "Values and Social Process." Neil J. Smelser, the CASBS Center Director, and I took joint responsibility for directing the earlier phases of this project. The results of our two earlier initiatives were published in Neil J. Smelser and Jeffrey C. Alexander, eds., *Diversity and Its Discontents: Cultural Conflict and Common Ground in Contemporary America* (Princeton: Princeton University Press, 1999) and in a special edition devoted to "The Public Representation of Culture and History" of the *American Behavioral Scientist* 42 (6), March 1999. It was my special privilege to direct the third phase of this funded research as a "Special Project" during the 1998–99 academic year at the center, to which I invited the contributors to this volume as collaborators. It was our great fortune that Neil Smelser chose to participate fully in our discussions despite his administrative responsibilities. Smelser exercised a powerful influence on the proceedings. We would like to record our gratitude not only to the Hewlett Foundation and the library and administrative staff of CASBS but to Neil Smelser as well. We would also like to publicly acknowledge the contributions to this project of Bjorn Wittrock, the sixth member of our special project at the center and a full-time participant in the seminar. We are indebted to him for his precise and imaginative contributions to conceptualizing cultural trauma and for his critical comments on our chapters as they developed. To our regret, pressing commitments made it impossible for Bjorn to make an independent contribution to this volume.

Although this book was initially launched as an investigation into "common values and social polarization," the authors soon realized that it was cultural trauma that we were really talking about, and the more we explored this concept, the more we came to believe that it possessed compelling theoretical importance and empirical power.[1] We found that in the disciplines of the humanities there had already emerged a rapidly growing literature on trauma, and we analyzed these contributions alongside the century-long discussion of trauma in psychological thought.[2] We realized that we could build upon both these discussions to study social phenomena. We also realized that, in order to do so, we would need to create a new, more distinctively sociological approach.

We developed this approach both discursively and empirically. We read through other literatures and invited researchers in the humanities and psychological sciences to make presentations of their own research.[3] We processed this information collectively in the course of hard-nosed, sometimes contentious weekly discussions among ourselves. Over the same period of time, we made use of the emerging cultural trauma concept to pursue our own case studies, reporting back to the group as our understandings developed, responding to criticism and revising our approach in turn. We made step-by-step comparisons, created provisional models, went back to the case studies, and revised our models again. We did not aim to produce an ostensibly complete set of formally elegant propositions. What we wanted, rather, was to create a model open-ended and robust enough to sustain revision and reformulation. What we created is a vigorous heuristic that allows us to "see" and understand our empirical topics in a new way.

In the introduction to this book, I present the background of the approach that we have taken and outline my own version of the model we have employed. In the chapters following, my colleagues and I present a series of theoretically informed empirical studies that elaborate and emphasize different dimensions of our common approach. By taking on such vastly contrasting empirical phenomenon, these chapters demonstrate the potential that "cultural trauma" has for new explanation, for taking events and social processes that have long been familiar and marking them in new ways.

I would personally like to thank Ann Fitzpatrick, assistant to the chair, for her patient and creative help in coordinating the details of this project, and Isaac Reed, coordinator for the Center for Cultural Sociology, for his enthusiastic and always astute editorial assistance.

*Jeffrey C. Alexander*
*Yale University*

## NOTES

1. Piotr Sztompka brought our attention to "trauma" after the first day of discussion. In the course of the second day we added the crucial adjective "cultural." The balance between the "social" and "cultural" elements of trauma remains an issue of some disagreement between Sztompka and the other authors of this book.

2. Neil Smelser provides an overview of the developments in this psychological discussion in relation to the themes of the present volume in chapter 2.

3. We would particularly like to recognize, in this connection, Norman Naimark and Hilda Sabato, who were also fellows at CASBS, and Kenneth Thompson, professor at the Open University, who made very helpful presentations to our group. During the course of our project at the Center, we also benfited from less formal discussions with Eduardo Cadava, Nancy Cott, and Arie Kuglanski, also fellows at the Center.

# CHAPTER I

# Toward a Theory of Cultural Trauma

JEFFREY C. ALEXANDER

Cultural trauma occurs when members of a collectivity feel they have been subjected to a horrendous event that leaves indelible marks upon their group consciousness, marking their memories forever and changing their future identity in fundamental and irrevocable ways.

As we develop it here, cultural trauma is first of all an empirical, scientific concept, suggesting new meaningful and causal relationships between previously unrelated events, structures, perceptions, and actions. But this new scientific concept also illuminates an emerging domain of social responsibility and political action. It is by constructing cultural traumas that social groups, national societies, and sometimes even entire civilizations not only cognitively identify the existence and source of human suffering but "take on board" some significant responsibility for it. Insofar as they identify the cause of trauma, and thereby assume such moral responsibility, members of collectivities define their solidary relationships in ways that, in principle, allow them to share the sufferings of others. Is the suffering of others also our own? In thinking that it might in fact be, societies expand the circle of the we. By the same token, social groups can, and often do, refuse to recognize the existence of others' trauma, and because of their failure they cannot achieve a moral stance. By denying the reality of others' suffering, people not only diffuse their own responsibility for the suffering but often project the responsibility for their own suffering on these others. In other words, by refusing to participate in what I will describe as the process of trauma creation, social groups restrict solidarity, leaving others to suffer alone.

*pull collectivities together*

## ORDINARY LANGUAGE AND REFLEXIVITY

One of the great advantages of this new theoretical concept is that it partakes so deeply of everyday life. Throughout the twentieth century, first in Western societies and then, soon after, throughout the rest of the world, people have spoken continually about being traumatized by an experience, by an event, by an act of violence or harassment, or even, simply, by an abrupt and unexpected, and sometimes not even particularly malevolent, experience of social transformation and change.[1] People also have continually employed the language of trauma to explain what happens, not only to themselves, but to the collectivities to which they belong as well. We often speak of an organization being traumatized when a leader departs or dies, when a governing regime falls, when an organization suffers an unexpected reversal of fortune. Actors describe themselves as traumatized when the environment of an individual or a collectivity suddenly shifts in an unforeseen and unwelcome manner.

We know from ordinary language, in other words, that we are onto something widely experienced and intuitively understood. Such rootedness in the life-world is the soil that nourishes every social scientific concept. The trick is to gain reflexivity, to move from the sense of something commonly experienced to the sense of strangeness that allows us to think sociologically. For trauma is not something naturally existing; it is something constructed by society. It is this construction that the coauthors of this volume have set themselves the task of trying to understand.

In this task of making trauma strange, its embeddedness in everyday life and language, so important for providing an initial intuitive understanding, now presents itself as a challenge to be overcome. We have come to believe, in fact, that the scholarly approaches to trauma developed thus far actually have been distorted by the powerful, commonsense understandings of trauma that have emerged in everyday life. Indeed, it might be said that these commonsense understandings constitute a kind of "lay trauma theory" in contrast to which a more theoretically reflexive approach to trauma must be erected.

### Lay Trauma Theory

According to lay theory, traumas are naturally occurring events that shatter an individual or collective actor's sense of well-being. In other words, the power to shatter—the "trauma"—is thought to emerge from events themselves. The reaction to such shattering events—"being traumatized"—is felt and thought to be an immediate and unreflexive response. According to the lay perspective, the trauma experience occurs when the traumatizing event interacts with human nature. Human beings need security, order, love, and connection. If something happens that sharply undermines these needs, it hardly seems surprising, according to the lay theory, that people will be traumatized as a result.[2]

### Enlightenment Thinking

There are "enlightenment" and "psychoanalytic" versions of this lay trauma theory. The enlightenment understanding suggests that trauma is a kind of rational response to abrupt change, whether at the individual or social level. The objects or events that trigger trauma are perceived clearly by actors, their responses are lucid, and the effects of these responses are problem solving and progressive. When bad things happen to good people, they become shocked, outraged, indignant. From an enlightenment perspective, it seems obvious, perhaps even unremarkable, that political scandals are cause for indignation; that economic depressions are cause for despair; that lost wars create a sense of anger and aimlessness; that disasters in the physical environment lead to panic; that assaults on the human body lead to intense anxiety; that technological disasters create concerns, even phobias, about risk. The responses to such traumas will be efforts to alter the circumstances that caused them. Memories about the past guide this thinking about the future. Programs for action will be developed, individual and collective environments will be reconstructed, and eventually the feelings of trauma will subside.

This enlightenment version of lay trauma theory has recently been exemplified by Arthur Neal in his *National Trauma and Collective Memory*. In explaining whether or not a collectivity is traumatized, Neal points to the quality of the event itself. National traumas have been created, he argues, by "individual and collective reactions to a volcano-like event that shook the foundations of the social world" (Neal 1998, ix). An event traumatizes a collectivity because it is "an extraordinary event," an event that has such "an explosive quality" that it creates "disruption" and "radical change . . . within a short period of time" (Neal 1998, 3, 9–10). These objective empirical qualities "command the attention of all major subgroups of the population," triggering emotional response and public attention because rational people simply cannot react in any other way (Neal 1998, 9–10). "Dismissing or ignoring the traumatic experience is not a reasonable option," nor is "holding an attitude of benign neglect" or "cynical indifference" (Neal 1998, 4, 9–10). It is precisely because actors are reasonable that traumatic events typically lead to progress: "The very fact that a disruptive event has occurred" means that "new opportunities emerge for innovation and change" (Neal 1998, 18). It is hardly surprising, in other words, that "permanent changes were introduced into the [American] nation as a result of the Civil War, the Great Depression, and the trauma of World War II" (Neal 1998, 5).

Despite what I will later call the naturalistic limitations of such an Enlightenment understanding of trauma, what remains singularly important about Neal's approach is its emphasis on the collectivity rather than the individual, an emphasis that sets it apart from the more individually oriented psychoanalytically informed approaches discussed below. In focusing on events that create trauma for national, not individual, identity, Neal follows the path-breaking sociological model developed by Kai Erikson in his widely influential book *Everything in Its Path*. While this heart-wrenching account of the effects on a small Appalachian community of a devastating flood is likewise constrained by a naturalistic perspective, it established the groundwork for the distinctively sociological approach we adopt in this volume. Erikson's theoretical innovation was to conceptualize the difference between collective and individual trauma. Both the attention to collectively emergent properties and the naturalism with which such collective traumas are conceived are evident in the following passage.

> By individual trauma I mean a *blow* to the psyche that *breaks through* one's defenses *so suddenly and with such brutal force that one cannot react to it effectively* . . . By collective trauma, on the other hand, I mean a *blow* to the basic tissues of social life that *damages* the bonds attaching people together and impairs the prevailing sense of communality. The collective trauma works its way slowly and even insidiously into the awareness of those who suffer from it, so it does not have the quality of suddenness normally associated with "trauma." *But it is a form of shock all the same,* a gradual realization that the community *no longer exists* as an effective source of support and that *an important part of the self has disappeared* . . . "We" no longer exist as a connected pair or as linked cells in a larger communal body. (Erikson 1976, 153–54, italics added)

As Smelser suggests in chapter 2, following, lay trauma theory began to enter ordinary language and scholarly discussions alike in the efforts to understand the kind of "shell shock" that affected so many soldiers during World War I, and it became expanded and elaborated in relation to other wars that followed in the course of the twentieth century. When

Glen Elder created "life course analysis" to trace the cohort effects on individual identity of these and other cataclysmic social events in the twentieth century, he and his students adopted a similar enlightenment mode of trauma (Elder 1974). Similar understandings have long informed approaches in other disciplines, for example, the vast historiography devoted to the far-reaching effects on nineteenth-century Europe and the United States of the "trauma" of the French Revolution. Elements of the lay enlightenment perspective have also informed contemporary thinking about the Holocaust and responses to other episodes of mass murder in the twentieth century, as Eyerman and I suggest in our respective discussions of "progressive narratives" in this volume.

## Psychoanalytic Thinking

Such realist thinking continues to permeate everyday life and scholarly thought alike. Increasingly, however, it has come to be filtered through a psychoanalytic perspective that has become central to both contemporary lay common sense and academic thinking. This approach places a model of unconscious emotional fears and cognitively distorting mechanisms of psychological defense between the external shattering event and the actor's internal traumatic response. When bad things happen to good people, according to this academic version of lay theory, they can become so frightened that they can actually repress the experience of trauma itself. Rather than activating direct cognition and rational understanding, the traumatizing event becomes distorted in the actor's imagination and memory. The effort to accurately attribute responsibility for the event and the progressive effort to develop an ameliorating response are undermined by displacement. This psychoanalytically mediated perspective continues to maintain a naturalistic approach to traumatic events, but it suggests a more complex understanding about the human ability consciously to perceive them. The truth about the experience is perceived, but only unconsciously. In effect, truth goes underground, and accurate memory and responsible action are its victims. Traumatic feelings and perceptions, then, come not only from the originating event but from the anxiety of keeping it repressed. Trauma will be resolved, not only by setting things right in the world, but by setting things right in the self.[3] According to this perspective, the truth can be recovered, and psychological equanimity restored, only, as the Holocaust historian Saul Friedlander once put it, "when memory comes."

This phrase actually provides the title of Friedlander's memoir about his childhood during the Holocaust years in Germany and France. Recounting, in evocative literary language, his earlier experiences of persecution and displacement, Friedlander suggests that conscious perception of highly traumatic events can emerge only after psychological introspection and "working through" allows actors to recover their full capacities for agency (Freidlander 1979, 1992). Emblematic of the intellectual framework that has emerged over the last three decades in response to the Holocaust experience, this psychoanalytically informed theorizing particularly illuminated the role of collective memory, insisting on the importance of working backward through the symbolic residues that the originating event has left upon contemporary recollection.[4]

Much as these memory residues surface through free association in psychoanalytic treatment, they appear in public life through the creation of literature. It should not be surprising, then, that literary interpretation, with its hermeneutic approach to symbolic patterns, has been offered as a kind of academic counterpart to the psychoanalytic intervention. In fact, the major theoretical and empirical statements of the psychoanalytic version of lay trauma theory have been produced by scholars in the various disciplines of the humanities. Because within the psychoanalytic tradition it has been Lacan who has emphasized the importance of language in emotional formation, it has been Lacanian theory, often in combination with Derridean deconstruction, that has informed these humanities based studies of trauma.

Perhaps the most influential scholar in shaping this approach has been Cathy Caruth, in her own collection of essays, *Unclaimed Experience: Trauma, Narrative, and History* and in her edited collection, *Trauma: Explorations in Memory* (Caruth 1995, 1996).[5] Caruth focuses on the complex permutations that unconscious emotions impose on traumatic reactions, and her approach has certainly been helpful in our own thinking about cultural trauma.[6] In keeping with the psychoanalytic tradition, however, Caruth roots her analysis in the power and objectivity of the originating traumatic event, explaining that "Freud's intuition of, and his passionate fascination with, traumatic experiences" related traumatic reactions to "the unwitting reenactment of an event that one cannot simply leave behind" (Caruth 1995, 2). The event cannot be left behind because "the breach in the mind's experience," according to Caruth, "is experienced too soon." This abruptness prevents the mind from fully cognizing the event. It is experienced "too unexpectedly . . . to be fully known and is therefore not available to consciousness." Buried in the unconscious, the event is experienced irrationally, "in the nightmares and repetitive actions of the survivor." This shows how the psychoanalytic version of lay trauma theory goes beyond the Enlightenment one: "Trauma is not locatable in the simple violent or original event in an individual's past, but rather in the way its very unassimilated nature— the way it was precisely *not known* in the first instance—returns to haunt the survivor later on." When Caruth describes these traumatic symptoms, however, she returns to the theme of objectivity, suggesting that they "tell us of a reality or truth that is not otherwise available" (Caruth 1995, 3–4, italics added).[7]

The enormous influence of this psychoanalytic version of lay trauma theory can be seen in the manner in which it has informed the recent efforts by Latin American scholars to come to terms with the traumatic brutalities of their recent dictatorships. Many of these discussions, of course, are purely empirical investigations of the extent of repression and/or normative arguments that assign responsibilities and demand reparations. Yet there is an increasing body of literature that addresses the effects of the repression in terms of the traumas it caused.

The aim is to restore collective psychological health by lifting societal repression and restoring memory. To achieve this, social scientists stress the importance of finding—through public acts of commemoration, cultural representation, and public political struggle—some collective means for undoing repression and allowing the pent-up emotions of loss and mourning to be expressed. While thoroughly laudable in moral terms, and without doubt also very helpful in terms of promoting public discourse and enhancing self-esteem, this advocacy literature typically is limited by the constraints of lay common sense. The traumatized feelings of the victims, and the actions that should be taken in response, are both treated as the unmediated, commonsense reactions to the repression itself. Elizabeth Jelin and Susana Kaufman, for example, directed a large-scale project on "Memory and Narrativity" sponsored by the Ford Foundation, involving a team of investigators from different South American countries. In their powerful report on their initial findings, "Layers of Memories: Twenty Years After in Argentina,"[8] they contrast the victims' insistence on recognizing the reality of traumatizing events and experiences with the denials of the perpetrators and their conservative supporters, denials that insist on looking to the future and forgetting the past: "The confrontation is between the voices of those who call for commemoration, for remembrance of the disappearances and the torment, for denunciation of the repressors, and those who make it their business to act as if nothing has happened here." Jelin and Kaufman call these conservative forces the "bystanders of horror" who claim they "did not know" and "did not see." But because the event—the traumatizing repression—was real, these denials will not work: "The personalized memory of people cannot be erased or destroyed by decree or by force." The efforts to memorialize the victims of the repression are presented as efforts to restore the objective reality of the brutal events, to separate them from the unconscious distortions of memory: "Monuments, museums and memorials are . . . attempts to make statements and affirmations [to create] a materiality with a political, collective, public meaning [and] a physical reminder of a conflictive political past" (5–7).

### The Naturalistic Fallacy

It is through these Enlightenment and psychoanalytic approaches that trauma has been translated from an idea in ordinary language into an intellectual concept in the academic languages of diverse disciplines. Both perspectives, however, share the "naturalistic fallacy" of the lay understanding from which they derive. It is upon the rejection of this naturalistic fallacy that our own approach rests. First and foremost, we maintain that events do not, in and of themselves, create collective trauma. Events are not inherently traumatic. Trauma is a socially mediated attribution. The attribution may be made in real time, as an event unfolds; it may also be made before the event occurs, as an adumbration, or after the event has concluded, as a post-hoc reconstruction. Sometimes, in fact, events that are deeply traumatizing may not actually have occurred at all; such imagined events, however, can be as traumatizing as events that have actually occurred.

This notion of an "imagined" traumatic event seems to suggest the kind of process that Benedict Anderson describes in *Imagined Communities* (Anderson 1991). Anderson's concern, of course, is not with trauma per se, but with the kinds of self-consciously ideological narratives of nationalist history. Yet these collective beliefs often assert the existence of some national trauma. In the course of defining national identity, national histories are constructed around injuries that cry out for revenge. The twentieth century was replete with examples of angry nationalist groups and their intellectual and media representatives, asserting that they were injured or traumatized by agents of some putatively antagonistic ethnic and political group, which must then be battled against in turn. The

Serbians inside Serbia, for example, contended that ethnic Albanians in Kosovar did them traumatic injury, thus providing justification for their own "defensive" invasion and ethnic cleansing. The type case of such militarist construction of primordial national trauma was Adolph Hitler's grotesque assertion that the international Jewish conspiracy had been responsible for Germany's traumatic loss in World War I.

But what Anderson means by "imagined" is not, in fact, exactly what we have in mind here. For he makes use of this concept to point to the completely illusory, nonempirical, nonexistent quality of the original event. Anderson is horrified by the ideology of nationalism, and his analysis of imagined national communities partakes of "ideology critique." As such, it applies the kind of Enlightenment perspective that mars lay trauma theory, which we are criticizing here. It is not that traumas are never constructed from nonexistent events. Certainly they are. But it is too easy to accept the imagined dimension of trauma when the reference is primarily to claims like these, which point to events that either never did occur or to events whose representation involve exaggerations that serve obviously aggressive and harmful political forces. Our approach to the idea of "imagined" is more like what Durkheim meant in *The Elementary Forms of Religious Life* when he wrote of the "religious imagination." Imagination is intrinsic to the very process of representation. It seizes upon an inchoate experience from life, and forms it, through association, condensation, and aesthetic creation, into some specific shape.

Imagination informs trauma construction just as much when the reference is to something that has actually occurred as to something that has not. It is only through the imaginative process of representation that actors have the sense of experience. Even when claims of victimhood are morally justifiable, politically democratic, and socially progressive, these claims still cannot be seen as automatic, or natural, responses to the actual nature of an event itself. To accept the constructivist position in such cases may be difficult, for the claim to verisimilitude is fundamental to the very sense that a trauma has occurred. Yet, while every argument about trauma claims ontological reality, as cultural sociologists we are not primarily concerned with the accuracy of social actors' claims, much less with evaluating their moral justification. We are concerned only with how and under what conditions the claims are made, and with what results. It is neither ontology nor morality, but epistemology, with which we are concerned.

Traumatic status is attributed to real or imagined phenomena, not because of their actual harmfulness or their objective abruptness, but because these phenomena are believed to have abruptly, and harmfully, affected collective identity. Individual security is anchored in structures of emotional and cultural expectations that provide a sense of security and capability. These expectations and capabilities, in turn, are rooted in the sturdiness of the collectivities of which individuals are a part. At issue is not the stability of a collectivity in the material or behavioral sense, although this certainly plays a part. What is at stake, rather, is the collectivity's identity, its stability in terms of meaning, not action.

Identity involves a cultural reference. Only if the patterned meanings of the collectivity are abruptly dislodged is traumatic status attributed to an event. It is the meanings that provide the sense of shock and fear, not the events in themselves. Whether or not the structures of meaning are destabilized and shocked is not the result of an event but the effect of a sociocultural process. It is the result of an exercise of human agency, of the successful imposition of a new system of cultural classification. This cultural process is deeply affected by power structures and by the contingent skills of reflexive social agents.

## THE SOCIAL PROCESS OF CULTURAL TRAUMA

At the level of the social system, societies can experience massive disruptions that do not become traumatic. Institutions can fail to perform. Schools may fail to educate, failing miserably even to provide basic skills. Governments may be unable to secure basic protections and may undergo severe crises of delegitimation. Economic systems may be profoundly disrupted, to the extent that their allocative functions fail even to provide basic goods. Such problems are real and fundamental, but they are not, by any means, necessarily traumatic for members of the affected collectivities, much less for the society at large. For traumas to emerge at the level of the collectivity, social crises must become cultural crises. Events are one thing, representations of these events quite another. Trauma is not the result of a group experiencing pain. It is the result of this acute discomfort entering into the core of the collectivity's sense of its own identity. Collective actors "decide" to represent social pain as a fundamental threat to their sense of who they are, where they came from, and where they want to go. In this section, I lay out the processes that form the nature of these collective actions and the cultural and institutional processes that mediate them.

### Claim Making: The Spiral of Signification

The gap between event and representation can be conceived as the "trauma process." Collectivities do not make decisions as such; rather, it is agents who do (Sztompka 1991a, 1993a; Alexander 1987; Alexander, Giesen, Munch, and Smelser 1987).[9] The persons who compose collectivities broadcast symbolic representations—characterizations—of ongoing social events, past, present, and future. They broadcast these representations as members of a social group. These group representations can be seen as "claims" about the shape of social reality, its causes, and the responsibilities for action such causes imply. The cultural construction of trauma begins with such a claim (Thompson 1998).[10] It is a claim to some fundamental injury, an exclamation of the terrifying profanation of some sacred value, a narrative about a horribly destructive social process, and a demand for emotional, institutional, and symbolic reparation and reconstitution.

### Carrier Groups

Such claims are made by what Max Weber, in his sociology of religion, called "carrier groups" (Weber 1968, 468–517).[11] Carrier groups are the collective agents of the trauma process. Carrier groups have both ideal and material interests, they are situated in particular places in the social structure, and they have particular discursive talents for articulating their claims—for what might be called "meaning making"—in the public sphere. Carrier groups may be elites, but they may also be denigrated and marginalized classes. They may be prestigious religious leaders or groups whom the majority has designated as spiritual pariahs. A carrier group can be generational, representing the perspectives and interests of a younger generation against an older one. It can be national, pitting one's own nation against a putative enemy. It can be institutional, representing one particular social sector or organization against others in a fragmented and polarized social order.

### Audience and Situation: Speech Act Theory

The trauma process can be likened, in this sense, to a speech act (Austin 1962; Searle 1969; Habermas 1984; Lara 1999).[12] Traumas, like speech acts, have the following elements:

Speaker: the carrier group

Audience: the public, putatively homogeneous but sociologically
   fragmented

Situation: the historical, cultural, and institutional environment
   within which the speech act occurs

The goal of the speaker is persuasively to project the trauma claim to the
audience-public. In doing so, the carrier group makes use of the particularities of the historical situation, the symbolic resources at hand, and the
constraints and opportunities provided by institutional structures. In the
first place, of course, the speaker's audience must be members of the carrier group itself. If there is illocutionary success, the members of this originating collectivity become convinced that they have been traumatized by
a singular event. Only with this success can the audience for the traumatic claim be broadened to include other publics within the "society at
large."

### Cultural Classification: The Creation of Trauma as a New Master Narrative

Bridging the gap between event and representation depends upon what
Kenneth Thompson has called, in reference to the topic of moral panics,
a "spiral of signification" (Thompson 1998, 20–24).[13] Representation of
trauma depends on constructing a compelling framework of cultural
classification. In one sense, this is simply telling a new story. Yet this storytelling is, at the same time, a complex and multivalent symbolic process
that is contingent, highly contested, and sometimes highly polarizing. For
the wider audience to become persuaded that they, too, have become
traumatized by an experience or an event, the carrier group needs to
engage in successful meaning work.

Four critical representations are essential to the creation of a new
master narrative. While I will place these four dimensions of representations into an analytical sequence, I do not mean to suggest temporal-
ity. In social reality, these representations unfold in an interlarded manner that is continuously cross-referential. The causality is symbolic and
aesthetic, not sequential or developmental, but "value-added" (Smelser
1962).

These are the questions to which a successful process of collective
representation must provide compelling answers:

A. *The nature of the pain.* What actually happened—to the particular group and to the wider collectivity of which it is a part?

- Did the denouncement of the Vietnam War leave a festering wound on the American psyche, or was it incorporated in a more or less routine way? If there was a shattering wound, in what exactly did it consist? Did the American military lose the Vietnam War, or did the Vietnam trauma consist of the pain of having the nation's hands "tied behind its back"?[14]

- Did hundreds of ethnic Albanians die in Kosovo, or was it tens and possibly even hundreds of thousands? Did they die because of starvation or displacement in the course of a civil war, or were they deliberately murdered?

- Was slavery a trauma for African Americans? Or was it, as some revisionist historians have claimed, merely a coercive, and highly profitable, mode of economic production? If the latter, then slavery did not produce traumatic pain. If the former, it involved brutal and traumatizing physical domination.

- Was the internecine ethnic and religious conflict in Northern Ireland, these last thirty years, "civil unrest and terrorism," as Queen Elizabeth once described it, or a "bloody war," as claimed by the IRA (quoted in Maillot 2000).

- Were there less than a hundred persons who died at the hands of Japanese soldiers in Nanking, China, in 1938, or were there 300,000 victims? Did these deaths result from a one-sided "massacre" or a "fierce contest" between opposing armies? (Chang 1997, 206)

B. *The nature of the victim.* What group of persons was affected by this traumatizing pain? Were they particular individuals or groups, or "the people" in general? Did a singular and delimited group receive the brunt of the pain, or were several groups involved?

- Were the German Jews the primary victims of the Holocaust, or did the victim group extend to the Jews of the Pale, European Jewry, or the Jewish people as a whole? Were the millions of Polish people who died at the hands of German Nazis also victims of the Holocaust? Were Communists, socialists, homosexuals, and handicapped persons also victims of the Nazi Holocaust?

- Were Kosovar Albanians the primary victims of ethnic cleansing, or were Kosovar Serbs also significantly, or even equally victimized?

- Are African Americans the victims of the brutal, traumatizing conditions in the desolate inner cities of the United States, or are the victims of these conditions members of an economically defined "underclass"?

- Were North American Indians the victims of European colonizers, or were the victims particularly situated, and particularly "aggressive," Indian nations?

- Are non-Western or third world nations the victims of globalization, or is it only the least developed, or least equipped, among them?

C. *Relation of the trauma victim to the wider audience.*   Even when the nature of the pain has been crystallized and the identity of the victim established, there remains the highly significant question of the relation of the victim to the wider audience. To what extent do the members of the audience for trauma representations experience an identity with the immediately victimized group? Typically, at the beginning of the trauma process, most audience members see little if any relation between themselves and the victimized group. Only if the victims are represented in terms of valued qualities shared by the larger collective identity will the audience be able to symbolically participate in the experience of the originating trauma.[15]

- Gypsies are acknowledged by contemporary Central Europeans as trauma victims, the bearers of a tragic history. Yet insofar as large numbers of Central Europeans represent the "Roman people" as deviant and uncivilized, they have not made that tragic past their own.

- Influential groups of German and Polish people have acknowledged that Jews were victims of mass murder, but they have often refused to experience their own national collective identities as being affected by the Jews' tragic fate.

- Did the police brutality that traumatized black civil rights activists in Selma, Alabama, in 1965, create identification among the white Americans who watched the events on their televisions in the safety of the nonsegregated North? Is the history of white American racial domination relegated to an entirely separate time, or is it conceived, by virtue of the reconstruction of collective memory, as a contemporary issue?[16]

*D. Attribution of responsibility.*  In creating a compelling trauma narrative, it is critical to establish the identity of the perpetrator, the "antagonist." Who actually injured the victim? Who caused the trauma? This issue is always a matter of symbolic and social construction.

- Did "Germany" create the Holocaust, or was it the Nazi regime? Was the crime restricted to special SS forces, or was the Werhmacht, the entire Nazi army, also deeply involved? Did the crime extend to ordinary soldiers, to ordinary citizens, to Catholic as well as Protestant Germans? Was it only the older generation of Germans who were responsible, or were later generations responsible as well?[17]

## Institutional Arenas

This representational process creates a new master narrative of social suffering. Such cultural (re)classification is critical to the process by which a collectivity becomes traumatized.[18] But it does not unfold in what Habermas would call a transparent speech situation (Habermas 1984).[19] The notion of transparency is posited by Habermas as a normative ideal essential to the democratic functioning of the public sphere, not as an empirical description. In actual social practice, speech acts never unfold in an unmediated way. Linguistic action is powerfully mediated by the nature of the institutional arenas and stratification hierarchies within which it occurs.

*Religious.* If the trauma process unfolds inside the religious arena, its concern will be to link trauma to theodicy. The Torah's story of Job, for example, asks, "Why did God allow this evil?" The answers to such questions will generate searching discussions about whether and how human beings strayed from divinely inspired ethics and sacred law, or whether the existence of evil means that God does not exist.

*Aesthetic.* Insofar as meaning work takes place in the aesthetic realm, it will be channeled by specific genres and narratives that aim to produce imaginative identification and emotional catharsis.

- In the early representations of the Holocaust, for example, *The Diary of Anne Frank* played a vital role, and in later years an entirely new genre called "survivor literature" developed (Hayes 1999). In the aftermath of ethnocide in Guatemala, in which 200,000 Mayan Indians were killed and entire villages destroyed, an ethnographer recorded how, in the town of Santa Maria Tzeja, theater was "used to publicly confront the past":

> A group of teenagers and . . . a North American teacher and direc-tor of the community's school write a play that documents what Santa Maria Tzeja has experienced. They call the play "There Is Nothing Concealed That Will Not Be Disclosed (Matthew 10:26)," and the villagers themselves perform it. The play not only recalls what happened in the village in a stark, unflinching manner but also didactically lays out the laws and rights that the military vio-lated. The play pointedly and precisely cites articles of the Guate-malan constitution that were trampled on, not normally the text of great drama. But, in Guatemala, reading the constitution can be a profoundly dramatic act. Peformances inevitably led to moving, at times heated, discussions. [The production] had a cathartic impact on the village. (Manz 2002)

As this example suggests, mass media are significant, but not neces-sary, in the aesthetic arena. In the aftermath of the eighty-day NATO bombing that forced Yugoslavian Serbs to abandon their violent, decade-long domination of Albanian Kosovo, Serbian films provided mass chan-nels for reexperiencing the period of suffering even while they narrated the protagonists, victims, and the very nature of the trauma in strikingly different ways.

> It is hard to see why anyone who survived 78 traumatic days of air-strikes in 1999 would want to relive the experience in a theater, bringing back memo-ries as well of a murderous decade that ended in October with the fall of President Slobadan Milosevic. Yet Yugoslavia's feature film industry has done little else in the past year but turn out NATO war movies [some of which] have begun to cut through the national façade that Milosevic's pro-pagandists had more than 10 years to build. [In one movie, the protagonist recounts that] "it is dead easy to kill . . . They stare at you, weep and wail, and you shoot 'em and that's the end—end of story. Later, of course, they all come back and you want to set things right, but it's too late. That's why the truth is always returning to judge men." (Watson 2001, A1–6)

*Legal.* When the cultural classification enters the legal realm, it will be disciplined by the demand to issue a definitive judgment of legally binding responsibilities and to distribute punishments and material reparations. Such a demonstration may have nothing at all to do with the perpetrators themselves accepting responsibility or a broader audience identifying with those who suffered as the trauma drama plays out.

- In regard to binding definitions of war crimes and crimes against humanity, the 1945 Nuremberg Trials were critical. They created revolutionary new law and resulted in dozens of successful prosecutions, yet they did not, by any means, succeed in compelling the German people themselves to recognize the existence of Nazi traumas, much less their responsibilities for them.[20] Nonetheless, the legal statutes developed at Nuremberg were elaborated in the decades following, laying the basis for dozens of highly publicized lawsuits that in recent years have created significant dramaturgy and unleashed profound moral effects. These trials for "crimes against humanity" have implicated not only individuals but national organizations.

Because neither postwar Japanese governments nor the most influential Japanese publics have recognized the war crimes committed by Japan's Imperial war policies, much less taken moral responsibility for them, no suit seeking damages for Imperial atrocities has, until recently, ever made any substantial headway in Japan's courts. In explaining why one suit against the Imperial government's biological warfare unit has finally made substantial progress, observers have pointed to the specificity and autonomy of the legal arena.

> As a member of the Japanese biological warfare outfit, known as United 731, Mr. Shinozuka was told that if he ever faced capture by the Chinese, his duty to Emperor Hirohito was to kill himself rather than compromise the secrecy of a program that so clearly violated international law . . . Now, 55 years later, he is a hale 77-year old. But still haunted by remorse, he has spoken—providing the first account before a Japanese court by a veteran about the workings of the notorious unit . . . That this case, now in its final stages, has not been dismissed like so many others is due in part to painstaking legal research and to cooperation over strategy by some of Japan's leading lawyers. Lawyers who have sued the government say the fact that this case has become the first in which a judge has allowed the extensive introduction of evidence instead of handing down a quick dismissal may also attest to an important shift under way on the issue of reparations. (French 2000, A3)

*Scientific.* When the trauma process enters the scientific world, it becomes subject to evidentiary stipulations of an altogether different kind, creating scholarly controversies, "revelations," and "revisions." When historians endeavor to define a historical event as traumatic, they must document, by acceptable scholarly methods, the nature of the pain, the victims, and responsibility. In doing so, the cultural classification process often triggers explosive methodological controversies.

- What were the causes of World War I? Who was responsible for initiating it? Who were its victims?
- Did the Japanese intend to launch a "sneak" attack on Pearl Harbor, or was the late-arriving message to Washington, D.C., by the Japanese Imperial government delayed by inadvertence and diplomatic confusion?
- The German "Historichstreit" controversy captured international attention in the 1980s, questioning the new scholarly conservatives' emphasis on anticommunism as a motivation for the Nazi seizure of power and its anti-Jewish policies. In the 1990s, Daniel Goldhagen's *Hitler's Willing Executioners* was attacked by mainstream historians for overemphasizing the uniqueness of German antisemitism.

*Mass media.* When the trauma process enters the mass media, it gains opportunities and at the same time becomes subject to distinctive kinds of restrictions. Mediated mass communication allows traumas to be expressively dramatized and permits some of the competing interpretations to gain enormous persuasive power over others. At the same time, however, these representational processes become subject to the restrictions of news reporting, with their demands for concision, ethical neutrality, and perspectival balance. Finally, there is the competition for readership that often inspires the sometimes exaggerated and distorted production of "news" in mass circulation newspapers and magazines. As an event comes to be reported as a trauma, a particular group as "traumatized," and another group as the perpetrators, politicians and other elites may attack the media, its owners, and often the journalists whose reporting established the trauma facts.

- During the traumas of the late 1960s, American television news brought evocative images of terrible civilian suffering from the Vietnam War into the living rooms of American citizens. These images were seized upon by antiwar critics. The conservative American politician Vice-President Spiro Agnew initiated virulent attacks against the "liberal" and "Jewish dominated" media for their insistence that the Vietnamese civilian population was being traumatized by the American-dominated war.

*State bureaucracy.* When the trauma process enters into the state bureaucracy, it can draw upon the governmental power to channel the representational process. Decisions by the executive branches of governments to create national commissions of inquiry, votes by parliaments to establish investigative committees, the creation of state-directed police investigations and new directives about national priorities—all such actions can have decisive effects on handling and channeling the spiral of signification that marks the trauma process (Smelser 1963).[21] In the last decade, blue ribbon commissions have become a favored state vehicle for such involvement. By arranging and balancing the participation on such panels, forcing the appearance of witnesses, and creating carefully choreographed public dramaturgy, such panels tilt the interpretative process in powerful ways, expanding and narrowing solidarity, creating or denying the factual and moral basis for reparations and civic repair.

- Referring to hundreds of thousands of Mayan Indians who died at the hands of Guatemalan counterinsurgency forces between 1981 and 1983, an ethnographer of the region asserts that, "without question, the army's horrific actions ripped deep psychological wounds into the consciousness of the inhabitants of this village [who were also] involved in a far larger trauma" (Manz 2002, 293–94). Despite the objective status of the trauma, however, and the pain and suffering it had caused, the ability to collectively recognize and process it was inhibited because the village was "a place hammered into silence and accustomed to impunity" (ibid.). In 1994, as part of the negotiation between the Guatemalan government and the umbrella group of insurgent forces, a Commission for Historical Clarification (CEH) was created to hear testimony from the affected parties and to present an interpretation. Five years later, its published conclusion declared that "agents of the State of Guatemala . . . committed acts of genocide against groups of Mayan people" (ibid.). According to the ethnographer, the report "stunned the country." By publicly representing the nature of the pain, defining victim and perpetrator, and assigning responsibility, the trauma process was enacted within the governmental arena: "It was as if the whole country burst into tears, tears that had been repressed for decades and tears of vindication" (ibid.).

- In the middle 1990s, the postapartheid South African government established a Truth and Reconciliation Commission. Composed of widely respected blacks and whites, the group called witnesses and conducted widely broadcast hearings about the suffering created by the repression that marked the preceding Afrikaner government. The effort succeeded to a significant degree in generalizing the trauma process beyond racially polarized audiences, making it into a shared experience of the new, more solidary, and more democratic South African society. Such a commission could not have been created until blacks became enfranchised and became the dominant racial power.

- By contrast, the postfascist Japanese government has never been willing to create official commissions to investigate the war crimes committed by its imperial leaders and soldiers against non-Japanese during World War II. In regard to the Japanese enslavement of tens and possibly hundreds of thousands of "comfort women," primarily Korean, who provided sexual services for imperial soldiers, the Japanese government finally agreed in the late 1990s to disperse token monetary reparation to the Korean women still alive. Critics have continued to demand that an officially sanctioned commission hold public hearings regarding the trauma, a dramaturgical and legally binding process that the Japanese government, despite its ambiguous and brief public apology to the "comfort women," has never been willing to allow. It is revealing of the significance of such a governmental arena that these critics eventually mounted an unofficial tribunal themselves.

> Last week in Tokyo, private Japanese and international organizations convened a war tribunal that found Japan's military leaders, including Emperor Hirohito, guilty of crimes against humanity for the sexual slavery imposed on tens of thousands of women in countries controlled by Japan during World War II. The tribunal has no legal power to exact reparations for the survivors among those so-called comfort women. But with its judges and lawyers drawn from official international tribunals for the countries that once were part of Yugoslavia and for Rwanda, it brought unparal-

leled moral authority to an issue scarcely discussed or taught about in Japan. (French 2000, A3)

## Stratificational Hierarchies

The constraints imposed by institutional arenas are mediated by the uneven distribution of material resources and the social networks that provide differential access to them. The following questions illustrate this problem.

Who owns the newspapers? To what degree are journalists independent of political and financial control?

Who controls the religious orders? Are they internally authoritarian, or can congregants exercise independent influence?

Are courts independent? What is the scope of action available to entrepreneurial legal advocates?

Are educational policies subject to mass movements of public opinion, or are they insulated by bureaucratic procedures at more centralized levels?

Who exercises controls over the government?

As I have indicated in my earlier reference to the governmental arena, local, provincial, and national governments deploy significant power over the trauma process. What must be considered here is that these bodies might occupy a position of dominance over the traumatized parties themselves. In these cases, the commissions might whitewash the perpetrators' actions rather than dramatize them.

- In the 1980s, the conservative American and British governments of Ronald Reagan and Margaret Thatcher initially did little to dramatize the dangers of the virulent AIDS epidemic because they did not wish to create sympathy or identification with the homosexual practices their ideologies so stigmatized. This failure allowed the epidemics to spread more rapidly. Finally, the Thatcher government launched a massive public education campaign about the dangers of HIV. The effort quickly took the steam out of the moral panic over the AIDS epidemic that had swept through British society and helped launch appropriate public health measures (Thompson 1998).

- In 2000, reports surfaced in American media about a massacre of several hundreds of Korean civilians by American soldiers at No Gun Ri early in the Korean War. Statements from Korean witnesses, and newfound testimony from some American soldiers, suggested the possibility that the firings had been intentional, and allegations about racism and war crimes were made. In response, President Clinton assigned the U.S. Army itself to convene its own official, in-house investigation. While a senior army official claimed that "we have worked closely with the Korean government to investigate the circumstances surrounding No Gun Ri," the power to investigate and interpret the evidence clearly rested with the perpetrators of the trauma alone. Not surprisingly, when its findings were announced several months later, the U.S. Army declared itself innocent of the charges that had threatened its good name:

  > We do not believe it is appropriate to issue an apology in this matter. [While] some of those civilian casualties were at the hand of American solider[s] , that conclusion is very different from the allegation that was made that this was a massacre in the classic sense that we lined up innocent people and gunned them down. (*New York Times* 2000, A5)

## Identity Revision, Memory, and Routinization

"Experiencing trauma" can be understood as a sociological process that defines a painful injury to the collectivity, establishes the victim, attributes responsibility, and distributes the ideal and material consequences. Insofar as traumas are so experienced, and thus imagined and represented, the collective identity will become significantly revised. This identity revision means that there will be a searching re-remembering of the collective past, for memory is not only social and fluid but deeply connected to the contemporary sense of the self. Identities are continuously constructed and secured not only by facing the present and future but also by reconstructing the collectivity's earlier life.

Once the collective identity has been so reconstructed, there will eventually emerge a period of "calming down." The spiral of signification flattens out, affect and emotion become less inflamed, preoccupation with sacrality and pollution fades. Charisma becomes routinized, effervescence evaporates, and liminality gives way to reaggregation. As the heightened and powerfully affecting discourse of trauma disappears, the "lessons" of the trauma become objectified in monuments, museums, and collections of historical artifacts.[22] The new collective identity will be rooted in sacred places and structured in ritual routines. In the late 1970s, the ultra-Maoist Khmer Rouge (DK) government was responsible for the deaths of more than one-third of Cambodia's citizens. The murderous regime was deposed in 1979. While fragmentation, instability, and authoritarianism in the decades following prevented the trauma process from fully playing itself out, the processes of reconstruction, representation, and working through produced significant commemoration, ritual, and reconstruction of national identity.

> Vivid reminders of the DK's [Khmer Rouge] horrors are displayed in photographs of victims, paintings of killings, and implements used for torture at the Tuol Sleng Museum of Genocidal Crimes, a former school that had become a deadly interrogation center . . . as well as in a monumental display of skulls and bones at Bhhoeung Ek, a former killing field where one can still see bits of bone and cloth in the soil of what had been mass graves. The PRK [the new Cambodian government] also instituted an annual observance called The Day of Hate, in which people were gathered at various locales to hear invectives heaped on the Khmer Rouge. State propaganda played on this theme with such slogans as: "We must absolutely prevent the return of this former black darkness" and "We must struggle ceaselessly to protect against the return of the . . . genocidal clique." These formulaic and state-sanctioned expressions were genuine and often expressed in conversations among ordinary folk. (Ebihara and Ledgerwood 2002, 282–83)

In this routinization process, the trauma process, once so vivid, can become subject to the technical, sometimes desiccating attention of specialists who detach affect from meaning. This triumph of the mundane is often noted with regret by audiences that had been mobilized by the trauma process, and it is sometimes forcefully opposed by carrier groups. Often, however, it is welcomed with a sense of public and private relief. Intended to remember and commemorate the trauma process, efforts to institutionalize the lessons of the trauma will eventually prove unable to evoke the strong emotions, the sentiments of betrayal, and the affirmations of sacrality that once were so powerfully associated with it. No longer deeply preoccupying, the reconstructed collective identity remains, nevertheless, a fundamental resource for resolving future social problems and disturbances of collective consciousness.

The inevitability of such routinization processes by no means neutralizes the extraordinary social significance of cultural traumas. Their creation and routinization have, to the contrary, the most profound normative implications for the conduct of social life. By allowing members of wider publics to participate in the pain of others, cultural traumas broaden the realm of social understanding and sympathy, and they pro-vide powerful avenues for new forms of social incorporation.[23]

The elements of the trauma process I have outlined in this section can be thought of as social structures, if we think of this term in something other than its materialist sense. Each element plays a role in the social construction and deconstruction of a traumatic event. Whether any or all of these structures actually come into play is not itself a matter of structural determination. It is subject to the unstructured, unforeseeable contingencies of historical time. A war is lost or won. A new regime has entered into power or a discredited regime remains stubbornly in place. Hegemonic or counter publics may be empowered and enthusiastic or undermined and exhausted by social conflict and stalemate. Such contingent historical factors exercise powerful influence on whether a consensus will be generated that allows the cultural classification of trauma to be set firmly in place.

## TRAUMA CREATION AND PRACTICAL-MORAL ACTION: THE NON-WESTERN RELEVANCE

In the preceding pages, I have elaborated the middle-range theory that informs the case studies in this book. In doing so, I have modeled the complex causes propelling the trauma process. In illustrating this analytical argument, I have referred to traumatic situations in Western and non-Western, developed and less developed societies—in Northern Ireland and Poland, the United Kingdom and Cambodia, Japan and Yugoslavia, South Africa, Guatemala, and Korea.

It would be a serious misunderstanding if trauma theory were restricted in its reference to Western social life. True, it has been Western societies that have recently provided the most dramatic apologias for traumatic episodes in their national histories. But it has been the non-Western regions of the world, and the most defenseless segments of the world's population, that have recently been subjected to the most terrifying traumatic injuries. The victims of Western traumas have disproportionately been members of subaltern and marginalized groups. The empirical case studies that follow deal with the legacies of annihilated Jews, enslaved African Americans, defeated German nationals, and dominated and impoverished Poles. It should hardly be surprising, in other words, that the theory developed in relation to these empirical cases can so fluidly be extended to the experiences of trauma outside of Western societies. In the course of this introduction, I have mentioned also Gypsies, Mayan Indians, American Indians, Kosovar Albanians, Chinese city dwellers, and Cambodian peasants.

The anthropologist Alexander Hinton has suggested that, "while the behaviors it references have an ancient pedigree, the concept of genocide . . . is thoroughly modern" (Hinton 2002, 25). Indeed, it is the very premise of the contributions he and his fellow anthropologists make to their collective work, that by the latter half of the twentieth century this modern framework had thoroughly penetrated non-Western societies. "On the conceptual level," Hinton writes, "terms like 'trauma,' 'suffering,' and 'cruelty' are linked to the discourses of modernity."

> In the mass media, the victims of genocide are frequently condensed into an essentialized portrait of the *universal* sufferer, an image that can be . . . (re)broadcast to *global* audiences who see their own potential trauma reflected in this simulation of the modern subject. Refugees frequently epitomize this modern trope of human suffering; silent and anonymous, they signify both a *universal humanity* and the threat of the pre-modern and uncivilized, which they have supposedly barely survived . . . Particularly in the *global* present, as such diverse populations and images flow rapidly across national borders, genocide . . . creates diasporic communities that threaten to undermine its culminating political incarnation. (Hinton 2002, 21–22; italics added)

There is no more excruciating example of the universal relevance of trauma theory than the way it can help illuminate the tragic difficulties that non-Western societies have often experienced in coming to terms with genocide. Because genocide is more likely to occur in collective arenas that are neither legally regulated, democratic, nor formally egalitarian (Kuper 1981),[24] it is hardly surprising that, in the last half century, the most dramatic and horrifying examples of mass murder have emerged from within the more fragmented and impoverished areas of the non-Western world: the Hutu massacre of more than 500,000 Tutsis in less than three weeks in Rwanda, the Guatemalan military's ethnocide of 200,000 Mayan Indians during the dirty civil war in the early 1980s, the Maoist Khmer Rouge's elimination of almost a third of Cambodia's entire population in its revolutionary purges in the late 1970s.

The tragic reasons for these recent outpourings of mass murder in the non-Western world cannot be our concern here. A growing body of social scientific work is devoted to this question, although a great deal more needs to be done (Kleinman, Das, and Lock 1997). What cultural trauma theory helps us understand, instead, is a central paradox, not about the causes of genocide but its aftereffects: Why have these genocidal actions, so traumatic to their millions of immediate victims, so rarely branded themselves on the consciousness of the wider populations? Why have these horrendous phenomena of mass suffering not become compelling, publicly available narratives of collective suffering to their respective nations, let alone to the world at large? The reasons, I suggest, can be found in the complex patterns of the trauma process I have outlined here.

In fact, several years before the Nazi massacre of the Jews, which eventually branded Western modernity as the distinctive bearer of collective trauma in the twentieth century, the most developed society outside the West had itself already engaged in systematic atrocities. In early December 1938, invading Japanese soldiers slaughtered as many as 300,000 Chinese residents of Nanking, China. Under orders from the highest levels of the Imperial government, they carried out this massacre in six of the bloodiest weeks of modern history, without the technological aids later developed by the Nazis in their mass extermination of the Jews. By contrast with the Nazi massacre, this Japanese atrocity was not hidden from the rest of the world. To the contrary, it was carried out under the eyes of critical and highly articulate Western observers and reported upon massively by respected members of the world's press. Yet, in the sixty years that have transpired since that time, the memorialization of the "rape of Nanking" has never extended beyond the regional confines of China, and in fact barely beyond the confines of Nanking itself. The trauma contributed scarcely at all to the collective identity of the People's Republic of China, let alone to the self-conception of the postwar democratic government of Japan. As the most recent narrator of the massacre puts it, "Even by the standards of history's most destructive war, the Rape of Nanking represents one of the worst instances of mass extermination" (Chang 1997, 5). Yet, though extraordinarily traumatic for the contemporary residents of Nanking, it became "the forgotten Holocaust of World War II," and it remains an "obscure incident" today (ibid., 6), the very existence of which is routinely and successfully denied by some of Japan's most powerful and esteemed public officials.

As I have suggested in this introduction, such failures to recognize collective traumas, much less to incorporate their lessons into collective identity, do not result from the intrinsic nature of the original suffering. This is the naturalistic fallacy that follows from lay trauma theory. The failure stems, rather, from an inability to carry through what I have called here the *trauma process*. In Japan and China, just as in Rwanda, Cambodia, and Guatemala, claims have certainly been made for the central relevance of these "distant sufferings" (Boltanski 1999).[25] But for both social structural and culture reasons, carrier groups have not emerged with the resources, authority, or interpretive competence to powerfully disseminate these trauma claims. Sufficiently persuasive narratives have not been created, or they have not been successfully broadcast to wider audiences. Because of these failures, the perpetrators of these collective sufferings have not been compelled to accept moral responsibility, and the lessons of these social traumas have been neither memorialized nor ritualized. New definitions of moral responsibility have not been generated. Social solidarities have not been extended. More primordial and more particularistic collective identities have not been changed.

In this concluding section, I have tried to underscore my earlier contention that the theory presented here is not merely technical and scientific. It is normatively relevant, and significantly illuminates processes of moral-practical action. However tortuous the trauma process, it allows collectivities to define new forms of moral responsibility and to redirect the course of political action. This open-ended and contingent process of trauma creation and the assigning of collective responsibility that goes along with it are as relevant to non-Western as to Western societies. Collective traumas have no geographical or cultural limitations. The theory of cultural trauma applies, without prejudice, to any and all instances when societies have, or have not, constructed and experienced cultural traumatic events, and to their efforts to draw, or not to draw, the moral lessons that can be said to emanate from them.

NOTES

1. Whether the lay perception of events as "traumatic" was at some point in historical time confined to the West, or whether the language was also intrinsic to the preglobalization cultural discourse of non-Western societies, is an issue that merits further investigation. It does not, however, concern us directly here. The premise of this book is that, in the context of modern globalization, members of both Western and non-Western collectivities do employ such a framework. The claim, then, is that the theory of cultural trauma presented here is universal in a postfoundational sense, and throughout this introductory exposition I will illustrate the model with examples from both Western and non-Western societies.

The notion that this theory of cultural trauma is universally applicable does not suggest, however, that different regions of the globe—Eastern and Western,

Northern and Southern—share the same traumatic memories. This is far from
the case, as I remark upon in chapter 6.

2. The ultimate example of such naturalization is the recent effort to locate
trauma in a specific part of the brain through P.E.T. scanning, the brain color
imaging that has become a research tool of neurology. Such images are taken as
proof that trauma "really exists" because it has a physical, material dimension.
We would not wish to suggest that trauma does not, in fact, have a material component. Every component of social life exists on multifold levels. What we object
to is reduction, that trauma is a symptom produced by a physical or natural base.
In this sense, trauma theory bears marked resemblance to another naturalistic
understanding that has permeated contemporary social life, namely the notion of
"stress." According to contemporary lingo, persons are "placed under stress," i.e.,
it is a matter of their environments, not of the mediation of actors who construct
an environment as stressful according to their social position and cultural frame.

3. A more distinctively sociological representation of the psychoanalytic
approach to trauma is Jeffrey Prager's (1998) study of repression and displacement in the case of a patient who claimed sexual harassment by her father. Prager
goes beyond lay trauma theory by demonstrating how the individual's memory of
trauma was the product, not only of her actual experience, but also of the contemporary cultural milieu, which by its emphasis on "lost memory syndrome"
actually presented the possibility of trauma to her.

4. For a nonpsychoanalytic, emphatically sociological approach to memory,
derived from the Durkheimian tradition, see the important statement by Paul
Connerton, *How Societies Remember* (1989).

5. For an analysis of Lacan in the psychoanalytically informed humanities,
see specifically Caruth's "Traumatic Awakenings: Freud, Lacan, and the Ethics of
Memory," 91–112 in Caruth 1996.

6. See particularly Giesen, chapter 3, in this volume.

7. For another illuminating and influential work in this tradition, see
Dominick LaCapra, *Representing the Holocaust: History, Theory, Trauma*
(1994).

8. All quotations are from pp. 5–7.

9. Piotr Sztompka emphasizes the importance of "agency" for theorizing
social change in *Sociology in Action: The Theory of Social Becoming* (1991) and
in *The Sociology of Social Change* (1993). See also Alexander 1987 and Alexander, Giesen, Munch, and Smelser 1987.

10. The concept of "claims" is drawn from the sociological literature on
moral panics. See Kenneth Thompson 1998.

11. In relation to issues of cultural change and conflict, Weber's concept has
been developed further by S. N. Eisenstadt in "The Axial Age: The Emergence of
Transcendental Visions and the Rise of Clerics" (1982), and, most recently, Bernhard Giesen in *Intellectuals and the Nation* (1998). Claim-making groups correspond also to the concept of "movement intellectuals" developed, in a different
context, by Ron Eyerman and Andrew Jamison in *Social Movements: A Cognitive Approach* (1994). Smelser (1974) illuminated the group basis for claim making in his reformulation of Tocqueville's notion of "estate." See also Bjorn Wittrock 1991.

12. The foundation of speech act theory can be found in the pragmatically inspired interpretation and extension of Wittgenstein carried out by J. L. Austin in *How to Do Things with Words* (1962). In that now classic work, Austin developed the notion that speech is not only directed to symbolic understanding but to achieving what he called "illocutionary force," that is, to having a pragmatic effect on social interaction. The model achieved its most detailed elaboration in John Searle's *Speech Acts* (1969). In contemporary philosophy, it has been Jurgen Habermas who has demonstrated how speech act theory is relevant to social action and social structure, beginning with his *Theory of Communicative Action* (1984). For a culturally oriented application of this Habermasian perspective to social movements, see Maria Pia Lara, *Feminist Narratives in the Public Sphere* (1999).

13. He also speaks of a "representational process." Stuart Hall develops a similar notion, but he means by it something more specific than what I have in mind here, namely the articulation of discourses that have not been linked before the panic began.

14. For the contingency of this process of establishing the nature of the pain, the nature of the victim, and the appropriate response in the aftermath of the "trauma" created by the Vietnam war, see J. William Gibson 1994.

15. This thesis is developed in chapter 6 in this volume.

16. See chapter 4 in this volume.

17. See chapter 3, following.

18. Maillot's representation of the difficulties of the Northern Ireland peace process combines these different aspects of the classifying process:

None of the "agents of violence" would agree on the reasons for the violence and on its nature. In fact, only the supporters of the IRA and, to a much less extent, part of the nationalist community, would agree that there was an actual "war" going on. For a substantial section of the Unionist community, the IRA is entirely to blame. "Our whole community, indeed our whole country, has been the victim of the IRA for over 30 years," said Ian Paisley Jr. . . . As all the other issues discussed in the run-up to the signing of the Good Friday Agreement, the question of victims proved highly emotional and controversial . . . one that enabled all participants to vent their frustration and their anger, and one that revealed the different approaches each side was to take. Indeed, the very term *victims* proved controversial, as participants disagreed on the people who constituted this group.

19. The notion of transparency, so necessary for creating a normative, or philosophical, theory of what Habermas has called his "discourse ethics," is debilitating for creating a sociological one.

20. See Giesen's chapter, this volume.

21. Smelser described how state agencies and other agents of social control make efforts to "handle and channel" what we are here calling the trauma process.

22. Insofar as such memorializations are not created, the traumatic suffering has either not been persuasively narrated or has not been generalized beyond the immediately affected population. This is markedly the case, for example, with the 350-year enslavement of Africans in the United States. In chapter 3, Ron Eyer-

man demonstrates how this experience came to form the traumatic basis for
black identity in the United States. However, despite the fact that white Americans initiated what has been called the "second Reconstruction" in the 1960s and
1970s, and despite the permeation among not only black but white American
publics of fictional and factual media representations of slavery and postslavery
trauma, white power centers in American society have not dedicated themselves
to creating museums to memorialize the slavery trauma. A recent letter to the editor in the *New York Times* points eloquently to this absence and to the lack of
black-white solidarity it implies:

> To the Editor: The worthy suggestion that the Tweed Courthouse in Lower Manhat-
> tan be used as a museum to memorialize New York City's slave history . . . evokes a
> broader question: Why is there no *national* museum dedicated to the history of slav-
> ery? One can only imagine the profound educational and emotional effect a major in-
> stitution recounting this period of our history would have on *all* Americans. Perhaps
> President-elect George W. Bush, in striving to be a uniter of people, would consider
> promoting such a project in our capital? (*New York Times*, December 19, 2000,
> sec. 1).

23. There are, in other words, not only empirical but also moral consequences of this theoretical disagreement about the nature of institutionalization.
For example, the routinization of recent trauma processes—those concerned
with the democratic transitions of the last decade—has produced a body of specialists who, far from being desiccated and instrumental, have worked to spread
a new message of moral responsibility and inclusion. As this book went into edit-
ing, the *New York Times* published the following report under the headline "For
Nations Traumatized by the Past, New Remedies."

> From temporary offices on Wall Street, a new international human rights group
> has plunged into work with 14 countries, helping them come to terms with the
> oppressions that mark their recent past. The International Center for Transitional
> Justice opened its doors on March 1, incubated by the Ford Foundation and led by
> Alex Boraine, an architect of South Africa's Truth and Reconciliation Commission.
> The South African commission was the first to hold public hearings where both
> victims and perpetrators told their stories of human rights abuses in the era of
> apartheid. With a growing number of countries turning to truth commissions to
> heal the wounds of their past, many governments and human rights groups in Asia,
> South America, Africa and Europe are now asking for advice, information and techni-
> cal assistance from those that have been through the process . . . The foundation . . .
> asked Mr. Boraine . . . to develop a proposal for a center that would conduct research
> in the field and help countries emerging from state sponsored terrorism or civil
> war . . . "The day we got our funds, we were actually in Peru, and it has been a
> deluge ever since." (July 29, 2001, A5)

24. For one of the first and still best sociological statements, see Kuper 1981.
25. This insightful work, by one of the most important contemporary French
sociologists, develops a strong case for the moral relevance of mediated global
images of mass suffering, but does not present a complex causal explanation for
why and where such images might be compelling, and where not.

# CHAPTER 2

# Psychological Trauma and Cultural Trauma

NEIL J. SMELSER

The objective of this chapter can be appreciated only by keeping in mind the context in which it appears—in a book on cultural trauma. I will focus on psychological trauma (and to a lesser extent on its sister idea, psychological stress) not so much as a phenomenon in itself, but as one that has relevance for and generates insights about cultural traumas. Several implications follow from this emphasis:

- My treatment of psychological trauma will be selective, not exhaustive. Part of this strategy is out of self-defense on my part, because the study of trauma is by now an industry and its literature is mountainous. In addition, however, not all aspects of psychological trauma (strategies for clinical treatment, for instance) are relevant; I will concentrate on what has theoretical and empirical value for the analysis of cultural trauma.

- Some conceptual muddiness in the concepts of trauma and stress must be noted at the outset. On the surface, trauma seems to connote a sudden overwhelming experience and stress a more prolonged aggravating condition. However, both concepts suffer from multiple definitions and they overlap, as suggested by the ideas of "acute stress," "traumatic stress" (van der Kolk et al. 1996), and "successions of partial trauma" (Freud and Breuer 1955 [1893–95], 288). Indeed, the currently reigning clinical classification—Posttraumatic Stress Disorder (PTSD)—includes both terms. Given this confusion, I will have to deal with selected aspects of the range of phenomena rather than search for "true" definitions and empirical referents.

- Of necessity I will stress both the promise and the limitations of theory and research at the psychological level for understanding at the cultural level. Above all, it is essential to avoid psychological reductionism (via which the cultural level evaporates) and uncritical analogizing (a sin that recalls ancient fallacies associated with biological models of society and conceptions of the group mind).

- The most promising avenues of insight appear to be in the definition of trauma; its status as negotiated process; the roles of affect, cognition, and memory in traumas; and the roles of defense against, coping with, and working through traumas.

- At the end of the chapter I will step back from the idea of trauma, "objectify" it as a social and political process, and comment on both the scientific evolution and scientific degeneration of the concept.

These qualifications observed, I add unashamedly that this exercise has been intellectually profitable for me, and I hope that readers may be persuaded of its value.

## ISSUES OF DEFINITION AND CONCEPTUALIZATION

The starting point of this section will be Sigmund Freud's writings between 1888 and 1898, when he and Breuer focused so intently on psychical trauma and its relation to hysteria. This focus is admittedly arbitrary; work on trauma predated Freud, notably in the French psychiatric tradition, and Freud subsequently altered his views, notably in the dramatic reformulation that assigned childhood fantasy such an important etiological role. The focus is justified, however, in that it yields the needed fruit for discussing implications for cultural trauma.

Working within the scientific/medical model that was so important in his thinking in the 1890s (Freud 1956 [1895]), Freud conceived of hysteria as having a definite cause, course of development, outcome, and cure. With respect to cause, he identified "a passive sexual experience before puberty" (Freud 1962a [1896], 152), usually molestation or seduction by a father, sibling, or household servant. The memory and affect associated with the event are subsequently repressed from consciousness and consigned to a status of prolonged latency or incubation. Freud characterized the memory of the trauma as "a foreign body which long after its entry must continue to be regarded as an agent that is still at work" (Freud and Breuer 1955 [1893–95], 6). Sometime after puberty, and with appropriate precipitating conditions or events, the affect associated with the trauma—usually fright—returns, is defended against, and ultimately is converted into an organic symptom such as the paralysis of a limb, the loss of a function such as eyesight, or an inhibition. Freud went to special pains in emphasizing the importance of affect: "In traumatic neuroses the operative cause of the illness is not the trifling physical injury but the affect of fright" (Freud and Breuer 1955 [1893–95], 5–6). The putative cure, effected through the psychotherapeutic techniques used at the time, was the disappearance of the symptom after "we [Freud and Breuer] had succeeded in bringing clearly to light the memory of the event by which it was provoked and in arousing its accompanying affect, and when the patient had described that event in the greatest possible detail and had put the affect into words" (Freud and Breuer 1955 [1893–95], 6). The occurrence of the disorder results from "an accretion of excitation" (Freud 1956 [1887–88], 137) caused by the trauma, first blocked by repression, stored up, expressed in a symptom, and then relieved by catharsis and verbal working through. We note that even this skeletal account involves reference to event, memory, affect, and a cognitive process ("putting the affect into words").

A close reading of Freud's texts indicates that even at this early phase of formulation he was struggling toward a more complex account of trauma-induced disorders. He noted that the traumas of childhood "are all the more momentous because they occur in times of incomplete development and are for that reason liable to have traumatic effects" (Freud  1963, 361)—implying that at a later developmental stage, that is, in a different context, the traumas would not be so severe. Moreover, as early as 1888, he doubted that an event (trauma) in itself constituted a sufficient causal condition for the development of hysterical symptoms. True, he said that a particularly intense psychical assault would be traumatic, but he added immediately that it might also be "an event which, *owing to occurrence at a particular moment,* has become a trauma" (Freud 1963, 361, italics added). Later he noted that the memories produced by the patient were often those "which we should not have judged worthy in themselves of constituting traumas" (1956 [1892]). This qualifying language constitutes an implicit though important confession that a trauma can be event plus context. To put the point blankly, Freud was beginning a journey that would lead to the conclusion that a trauma is not a thing in itself but becomes a thing by virtue of the context in which it is implanted. (Freud's subsequent modification concerning sexual fantasies as content of traumas went further and suggested that trauma could be a nonevent, but instead all context [i.e., general infantile sexuality]). More recently, de Vries (1996) has reminded us that individuals in different cultures (for example, those with fatalistic religious traditions) may be less susceptible to "traumas" as they are understood in Western countries.

Freud again evoked the logic of context in referring to the appearance of hysterical symptoms when he took note of concurrent (or auxiliary) causes. Among them he mentioned "emotional disturbance, physical exhaustion, acute illness, intoxications, traumatic accidents, intellectual overwork, etc." These are not the primary causes; those are the traumatic assaults. At the same time,

> fairly frequently they fill the function of agents provocateurs which render manifest a neurosis that has previously been latent; and practical interest attaches to them, for a consideration of these stock causes may offer lines of approach to which a therapy which does not aim at a radical cure and is content with repressing the illness to a former state of latency. (Freud 1962b [1896], 148)

Elsewhere he identified "precipitating events" as playing a role. For a person with a latent neurosis, an adult experience such as "actual sexual violation to mere sexual overtures or the witnessing of sexual acts in other people, or . . . receiving information about sexual processes" (1962b [1896], 166) will trigger the outbreak of symptoms.

Within a decade after these formulations, Freud had moved even further from the "cause-effect" (i.e., infantile sexual trauma-hysterical neurosis) by developing his theories of drive and defense. On the one hand, he began to treat hysterical symptoms not merely as a "breaking through" of excitation but being—"like other psychical structures"— (Freud 1959 [1908], 163), the expression of a wish fulfillment. In addition, he recognized that symptoms constitute compromises "between two opposite affective and instinctual impulses, one of which is attempting to bring to expression a component instinct or a constituent of the sexual constitution, and the other is attempting to suppress it" (Freud 1959 [1908], 164).

By this time, Freud had arrived at a scientific point where he was employing identical psychic dynamics to account for almost everything of interest to him—dreams, parapraxes, jokes, neurotic symptoms, character traits. These dynamics were conflict over impulse expression, strong associated affect, defenses against both impulse and affect, and outcome. Noting this, one can appreciate the inner tension in his theory that would drive him in the direction of developing a more complex theory of the defense mechanisms, constituting as they would the key factors in determining the choice of symptoms or behavior patterns. To focus on defenses would prevent his theory from degenerating, as it was in danger of doing, into a common explanation of everything.

The sure conclusion arising from the above line of reasoning is that, even in Freud's preliminary formulations, the idea of trauma is not to be conceived so much as a discrete casual event as a part of a process-in-system. To put the conclusion in its briefest form, trauma entails some conception of system. As Freud proceeded to include one qualification after another—most of them apparently suggested by the ongoing accumulation of clinical information—this system came to include the idea of drives (mainly sexual at this stage) located in a psychological structure at some stage of less-than-complete development (prepubertal in the theory of hysteria), affected over time by a diversity of external and internal causes (primary traumatizing event, concurrent causes including the general health of the organism, precipitating events), all playing out in the context of a continuing struggle between an instinctive apparatus versus a defensive apparatus. This idea of system was further informed by a number of postulates including hydraulic (economic) assumptions about the flow of psychic excitation and the conversion of psychic conflict into both psychic and motoric symptoms.

## IMPLICATIONS FOR THE STUDY OF CULTURAL TRAUMAS

### Historical Indeterminacy

I begin with a radical proposition, one that follows from the discussion of context above. The proposition: No discrete historical event or situation automatically or necessarily qualifies in itself as a cultural trauma, and the range of events or situations that may become cultural traumas is enormous. In his essay for this volume, Sztompka, tying cultural traumas to the effects of processes of social change, is able to produce a formidable list (pp. 00–00) that includes mass migrations, wars, mass unemployment, and dislocations associated with rapid social change. This list is helpful, but both Sztompka and we acknowledge that not all of them necessarily constitute cultural traumas and that it would be possible to add more to his list. The radical aspect of this proposition rests on the fact that we are normally accustomed to think of some events—catastrophic natural disasters, massive population depletion, and genocide, for example—as in, by, and of themselves traumatic. They are nearly certain candidates for trauma, to be sure, but even they do not qualify automatically.

Several corollary observations follow from the proposition:

- The theoretical basis for the proposition is that the status of trauma as trauma is dependent on the sociocultural context of the affected society at the time the historical event or situation arises. A society emerging from a major war, suffering from diminished economic resources, experiencing rampant internal conflict, or having shaky social solidarity is more trauma prone than others that are more solid in these respects. Historical events that may not be traumatic for other societies are more likely to be traumas in afflicted societies.

- Several definitional accomplishments must be made before an event can qualify as a cultural trauma. It must be remembered, or made to be remembered. Furthermore, the memory must be made culturally relevant, that is, represented as obliterating, damaging, or rendering problematic something sacred—usually a value or outlook felt to be essential for the integrity of the affected society. Finally, the memory must be associated with a strong negative affect, usually disgust, shame, or guilt. Looking at the sweep of American history, the memory of the institution of slavery appears to qualify most unequivocally as a cultural trauma, because it comes close to meeting these three conditions. The seizure of Native Americans' lands and the partial extermination of their populations is another example, but at the present time its status as trauma is not as secured as is slavery.

- A given historical event or situation may qualify as a trauma at one moment in a society's history but not in another. Without doubt the regicides of Charles I in England in the mid-seventeenth century and Louis XVI in the French Revolution constituted major cultural traumas for decades afterward but are no longer dealt with in contemporary political or social discourse. Even so catastrophic a phenomenon as the black death, fully traumatic for decades after it occurred, is not currently regarded as traumatic for the societies it affected, even though historians are fully aware of its traumatic consequences at the time.

We conclude, then, that cultural traumas are for the most part historically made, not born. This fundamental point leads us to the issue of the mechanisms and agencies involved in the process of making, to which we will turn presently.

### System

If the definition of a cultural trauma—like a psychological trauma—depends above all on context, what kind of context is this? In the example above, taken from Freud's early writing, the personality system is represented as an environmentally open system (i.e., capable of being damaged from outside), possessing the capacity to internalize (through memory) this damage, capable of defending against it by a partially successful repression, but ultimately vulnerable to its impact.

What kind of system is a culture? I do not want to tread on the shaky analytic ground of comparing personality, social, and cultural systems—a common enterprise in the 1950s (Parsons and Shils 1951; Sorokin 1962) but one that is all but defunct nowadays—but a few words can be said. A social system refers to the organization of social relations in society; its main units are social roles and institutions, and these are normally classified along functional lines—economic institutions, legal institutions, medical institutions, educational institutions, family institutions—though the idea frequently includes systems of ranking (stratification) into social classes, racial and ethic groups, and so on.

It is possible to describe social dislocations and catastrophes as social traumas if they massively disrupt organized social life. Common examples would be decimation through disease, famine, and war. The Great Depression of the 1930s can also be regarded as a social trauma, because it crippled the functioning economic institutions of those societies it affected, and it often led to strains or even breakdowns in their political and legal systems. The important defining characteristic of social traumas is that the affected arenas are society's social structures.

As a system, a culture can be defined as a grouping of elements—values, norms, outlooks, beliefs, ideologies, knowledge, and empirical assertions (not always verified), linked with one another to some degree as a meaning-system (logico-meaningful connections, in Sorokin's words).

For a national society—my main reference point in this essay—we expect that there exists a culture with national reference that manifests variable degrees of unity and coherence. By unity I refer to the degree to which there is general consensus about the culture in the society, and the degree to which subcultures, countercultures and cultural conflicts compromise that consensus. By coherence I refer to the tightness or looseness of the meaningful relations among the elements of the cultural system.

A cultural trauma refers to an invasive and overwhelming event that is believed to undermine or overwhelm one or several essential ingredients of a culture or the culture as a whole. The Protestant Reformation qualifies as a cultural trauma because of the fundamental threat it posed to the integrity and dominance of the Catholic cultural worldview. The imposition of Western values on colonial societies in the nineteenth and twentieth centuries provides additional examples. The exposure of migrating groups to the cultures of the host societies into which they migrate provides still more.

Some historical events qualify as both socially and culturally traumatic. I mentioned the case of the Great Depression as a social trauma. In addition to its disruptive social effects, it also constituted a crisis for the culture of capitalism (free enterprise, the private property system, the profit system, and ideology of progress and material plenty) and shook the faith of those committed to it as an ideological system.

Several other points about the concept of cultural trauma can be advanced. National cultures in complex societies are typically problematic with respect to unity and loose with respect to coherence. It follows that a claim of traumatic cultural damage (i.e., destruction of or threat to cultural values, outlooks, norms, or, for that matter, the culture as a whole), must be established by deliberate efforts on the part of cultural carriers—cultural specialists such as priests, politicians, intellectuals, journalists, moral entrepreneurs, and leaders of social movements. In most cases the process of establishing is a contested process, with different political groups divided with respect to whether a trauma occurred (historical contestation), how its meaning should be regarded (contestation over interpretation), and what kinds of feelings—pride, neutrality, rage, guilt—it should arouse (affective contestation). Furthermore, once a historical memory is established as a national trauma for which the society has to be held in some way responsible, its status as trauma has to be continuously and actively sustained and reproduced in order to continue in that status. These features mean that a cultural trauma differs greatly from a psychological trauma in terms of the mechanisms that establish and sustain it. The mechanisms associated with psychological trauma are the intrapsychic dynamics of defense, adaptation, coping, and working through; the mechanisms at the cultural level are mainly those of social agents and contending groups.

## The Salience of Affect

At the psychological level, the active elements in both the traumatic situation and the process of coping with are negative affects. Freud ultimately came to focus on anxiety as the key emotional response to danger and threat (Freud 1959 [1926 {1925}]; Freud 1955 [1923{1922}], 236), but one could easily expand this to include guilt, shame, humiliation, disgust, anger, and other negative affects. For Freud, anxiety (and affects more generally) is an inner language that serves to communicate between the perceptual apparatus (which recognizes both internal and external dangers) and the organism's adaptive apparatus. It is the motive force for mobilizing both ideational and motoric responses to the threat.

Generalizing this principle, we may conceptualize both negative and positive affects as having mainly a "readying" function with respect to purposive behavior. Contrary to utilitarian formulations that regard actors as seeking pleasure and avoiding pain as end states, both pain (threat) and pleasure (gratification) are best regarded not as accompanying ideational and motoric activity, but, rather, as anticipating that activity and mobilizing the organism to participate in it or avoid it.

Furthermore, because every human being, from the beginning of life, maneuvers his or her way through a world that is actually and potentially both threatening and gratifying, every human being also experiences every variety of anticipatory negative and positive affect. By virtue of this, affects constitute a kind of universal language, the symbolic representations of which operate as effective means of communicating among individuals. Unlike other language structures, however, the language of affect involves fewer difficulties of translation from one language to another, because it is a product of universal experience. As Epstein observes:

> Much of everyday social intercourse involves the expression of affect: we must be alert to the feelings of others just as we are careful what we disclose of our own. In negotiating these encounters we also come to recognize, if only subliminally, that how and what we feel is transmitted not just verbally but by nonverbal cues as well, cues that may indeed carry the more vital information: in a given "message" tone of voice, a raising of the eyebrows or some other involuntary movement of the body may count as much as,

or even more than, verbal content. Nor of course is it only in the context
of such personal interaction that the important role of affect is to be seen:
it is indeed difficult to think of any human activity or social event that is not
ordinarily accompanied by some degree of emotional expression. (Epstein
1992, 1–2)

A further implication of this theoretical representation is that affects,
once experienced, can generalize and endow meaning to events and situations that need not necessarily have occurred or existed. One telling
range of relevant evidence on this score is the finding (McCann and
Pearlman 1990; Pearlman and MacIan 1995) that trauma therapists
(that is, psychotherapists who specialize in dealing with patients with
posttraumatic stress disorder) often themselves experience traumatic
affects and symptoms in the course of therapy. This has been called
"vicarious traumatization." These effects are experienced more vividly
among therapists who have themselves had traumatic experiences in
their own backgrounds, but the self-esteem of those who have not had a
personal history of trauma is also adversely affected. This principle also
explains why individuals who are passively watching or reading thrilling,
gripping, or frightening movies or books can be temporarily "traumatized" by them even though they are completely fictional. They attach the
affects that would have been excited by actual events to fictional situations. This implies further that trauma can be experienced by attaching
appropriate affects to imagined situations.

Affect also occupies a position of centrality in our understanding of
cultural trauma. A cultural trauma is, above all, a threat to a culture with
which individuals in that society presumably have an identification. To
put it differently, a cultural trauma is a threat to some part of their personal identities. As such, this threat, if experienced, arouses negative
affects. We may go further: if a potentially traumatizing event cannot be
endowed with negative affect (e.g., a national tragedy, a national shame,
a national catastrophe), then it cannot qualify as being traumatic.

The language of affect thus provides a notable link and continuity
between the cultural and psychological levels. In a not-well-known passage, Parsons described "affect" as a symbolic medium of interchange
and argued that for that reason "affect is not in the first instance primarily a psychological medium but rather one whose primary functional
significance is social and cultural" (Parsons 1978 [1974], 316). Not surprisingly, Parsons focused on love and other positive affects as they relate
to social solidarity; but negative affects can readily be included in this
formulation. I would not, however, go so far as Parsons has. Affects are

significant at both the psychological and psychocultural levels; they constitute a language that links those levels.

To conclude this line of reasoning: those interested in establishing a historical event or situation as traumatic must speak in a language that will reach individual people. And since affect plays such a salient role in alerting individuals to threatening and traumatizing phenomena, experiencing the language of negative affect is a necessary condition for believing that a cultural trauma exists or is threatening. This is not to reduce affect-laden cultural representation to individual psychological experiences, or vice versa, but to point out that it is the medium that links the two levels.

*Embeddedness in Personality*

A notable feature of a psychological trauma is its embeddedness or indelibility in the structure of personality. Once lodged, it will not go away. More than a century ago, Charcot (1887) described traumatic memories as "parasites of the mind." Freud spoke of the traumatic memory as a "an indelible imprint" (Freud 1962a [1896], 153), as a "foreign body . . . an agent that is still at work" (Freud and Breuer 1955 [1893–95], 6), as something which the nervous system "has been unable to dispose of" (Freud 1956 [1887–88], 137), and as producing "permanent effects" (Freud 1956 [1893], 153). Caruth referred to trauma as a wound that is "not healable" (Caruth 1996, 4). In a more detailed description, van der Kolk described this fixation as follows:

> When the trauma fails to be integrated into the totality of a person's life experiences, the victim remains fixated on the trauma. Despite avoidance of emotional involvement, traumatic memories cannot be avoided; even when pushed out of waking consciousness, they come back in the form of reenactments, nightmares, or feelings related to the trauma. . . . Recurrences may continue throughout life during periods of stress. (van der Kolk 1996, 5)

This characterization must be regarded as relative. The degree of indelibility varies according to the severity of trauma, the helplessness of the victim, and whether the traumatic event is experienced as one of "human design." Nonetheless there is general consensus on the issue of long-lastingness in the clinical literature.

Students of collective trauma have stressed its indelibility at the sociocultural level as well. According to Neal's account:

> The enduring effects of a trauma in the memories of an individual resemble the enduring effects of a national trauma in collective consciousness. Dismis-

sing or ignoring the traumatic experience is not a reasonable option. The conditions surrounding a trauma are played and replayed in consciousness through an attempt to extract some sense of coherence from a meaningless experience. When the event is dismissed from consciousness, it resurfaces in feelings of anxiety and despair. Just as the rape victim becomes permanently changed as a result of the trauma, the nation becomes permanently changed as a result of a trauma in the social realm. (Neal 1998, 4)

Confirming examples of this indelibility can be easily produced—the memories of the Nazi Holocaust, American slavery, the nuclear explosions at Hiroshima and Nagasaki. However, other traumalike events mentioned by Neal himself, such as the Challenger explosion, the Watergate affair, and the Cuban missile crisis do not seem to qualify quite so readily or completely. We should say more precisely that in the case of a collective trauma, there is often an interest in representing the trauma as indelible (a national shame, a permanent scar, etc.), and if this representation is successfully established, the memory does in fact take on the characteristics of indelibility and unshakeability.

If the element of indelibility becomes fixed in the cultural definition of a trauma, it then becomes difficult to imagine that it will be "worked through" in any once-and-for-all way. The psychological literature on trauma sometimes suggests the possibility of virtual disappearance through cure or psychic work. Freud's formula of cure through catharsis plus putting the affect into words is described as a "cure," and the idea of "grief work" after traumatic loss of a loved one through death suggests returning to normal functioning and reconstituting a new social world. In the case of full-blown cultural traumas, however, a more appropriate model would be one of constant, recurrent struggle—moments of quiescence perhaps, when some convincing formula for coming to terms with it takes root, but flarings-up when new constellations of new social forces and agents stir up the troubling memory again.

### Claim on Psychic Energy

Being indelible in important ways, a psychological trauma has an insistent claim on the person's psychic energy. It becomes a part of the psyche. However, as we will stress later, one of the major patterns of defensive or adaptive activity on the part of the person is to deny, to become numb, to avoid situations that might reactivate the memory of the trauma, and to develop dissociational symptoms (Horowitz 1976, 4–5). These reactions might be regarded as efforts—never completely successful, because of the indelibility principle—to remove the traumatic memory from the psychic system.

The counterpart of these reactions at the collective level is collective denial or collective forgetting, though we should take care not to suggest that this formulation involves some kind of "group mind" at work when the fact is that many individuals in a collectivity, as individuals, deny a historical event. A better way of expressing the idea is to say that in order for a historical event or situation to become established as a collective memory, there must be assumed or established, as a logically prior condition, a claim for common membership in a collectivity—for example, a nation or a solidary subnational population such as an ethnic or religious minority. For example, to establish the Nazi Holocaust as a relevant cultural trauma for Germany and Germans, there must be a meaningful membership group recognized as Germans. To say this may appear to be announcing the trivial or obvious, because, with the commanding power of the idea of the nation as membership group, to use the word "German" almost automatically implies a meaningful cultural reference and membership group. However, it should not be forgotten that the link between trauma and national membership can be a contested one. For example, for several decades the East German communist regime adopted a more or less official ideological policy that the Holocaust was a product of the workings of capitalist bourgeois forces, and that they, as Germans to be sure, but as Germans disassociated from and inimical to those forces, were not called upon to bear responsibility for the trauma. According to that story, the Holocaust was not their memory, even though they were Germans.

### Collective Trauma and Identity

A further corollary, following immediately from the preceding, is that a collective trauma, affecting a group with definable membership, will, of necessity, also be associated with that group's collective identity. Put simply, a meaningful cultural membership implies a name or category of membership, and the social-psychological representation of that category produces a sense of psychological identity with varying degrees of salience, articulation, and elaboration:

> All collective traumas have some bearing on national identity. While in some cases national trauma results in enhancing a sense of unity within a society, there are other cases in which collective traumas have fragmenting effects. . . . Through the epic struggles of the American Revolution and the

American Civil War we came to recognize more clearly what it means to be an American. . . . The social heritage provides us with an everyday blueprint and a sense of social continuity. A serious crisis of meaning surfaces when we can no longer make assumptions about the continuity of social life as it is known and understood. (Neal 1998, 31)

Any given trauma may be community- and identity-disrupting or community- and identity-solidifying—usually some mixture of both (Erikson 1994). In any event, this line of reasoning suggests why the ideas of collective trauma, collective memory, and collective (e.g., national) identity are so frequently associated with one another in the literature on sociocultural trauma.

We may now advance a formal definition of cultural trauma: a memory accepted and publicly given credence by a relevant membership group and evoking an event or situation which is a) laden with negative affect, b) represented as indelible, and c) regarded as threatening a society's existence or violating one or more of its fundamental cultural presuppositions.

The obvious observation to add at this point of transition is that if a historical event or situation succeeds in becoming publicly identified as a cultural trauma, then this certainly imparts an air of urgency—a demand for those who acknowledge it as such to come to grips with it. This leads us immediately to the topic of defense.

## DEFENSE, SYMPTOMS, AND COPING

One standard word used in characterizing a psychological trauma is that it is an "overwhelming" experience (Prince 1998, 44). A more detailed version of this idea is found in McCann and Pearlman (1990, 10), which lists the following identifying ingredients: [a trauma] "(1) is sudden, unexpected, or non-normative, (2) exceeds the individual's perceived ability to meet its demands, and (3) disrupts the individual's frame of reference and other central psychological needs and related schemas." This is an accurate characterization of many of the events that constitute trauma (near-death on the battlefield, rape, witnessed murder of a parent), but this definition must always be considered a beginning. While it is possible to conceive a situation that is completely overwhelming, it is almost always the case that an exposed individual "fights back" against the experience and its effects, however primitively. This reactive ingredient was present in Freud's earliest formulations and leads directly to the notions of defense and coping.

Some years ago I attempted a systematic classification of the psychological mechanisms of defense (Smelser 1987), the literature on which was plagued by vagueness, overlapping, repetition, and confusion of different levels of generality. In the first instance, and consistent with the psychoanalytic tradition, I classified these defenses as reactions against an internal threat, that is, instinctual arousal. This model, based on Freud's representation and formalized later by Rapoport (1951), constructs a highly generalized sequence, beginning with mounting drive tension, which, when its gratification is delayed, gives rise to psychic drive representations, characteristic discharges of affect associated with these representations, and characteristic hallucinatory representations of potentially gratifying objects. The tension is reduced when the drive is gratified by some kind of motor activity leading to a change in the state of the organism.

One principle of defense mechanisms is that they can be activated at different stages in this process, beginning with instinctual arousal and ending with behavior (motor activity). That is to say, the drive representation can be defended against (e.g., repression), the associated affect may be defended against (e.g., suppression of affect), the object of gratification can be distorted (e.g., displacement), and the gratifying behavior can be defended against (e.g., inhibition).

Furthermore, I identified four separate modes of defense:

1. to block the threatening intrusion (e.g., denial),

2. to reverse the threatening intrusion into its opposite (e.g., to convert contempt into awe),

3. to shift the reference of the threatening intrusion (e.g., projection), and

4. to insulate the threatening intrusion from its associative connections (e.g., depersonalization).

Combining the four "stages" of gratification and the four "modes" of defense into a single grid produces the classification of defense mechanisms found in Table 1. The table represents a more or less exhaustive "repertoire" of defenses available to an individual in fending off threatening internal intrusions. In any struggle against an unwanted intrusion, the individual typically employs a multiplicity of defenses, a "layering" (Gill 1961). With respect to trauma in particular, clinical evidence reveals that a victim of trauma may more or less simultaneously rely on, for example, denial, blaming or scapegoating others (projection), avoidance, defining the trauma as a "valuable" experience (reversal), displacing the

TABLE I. THE MECHANISMS OF DEFENSE CLASSIFIED IN TERMS OF BASIC MODES
AND DEVELOPMENT PHASES OF BEHAVIOR

| Stages | 1 | 2 | 3 Psychic Representation (Hallucination) of Gratification Situation | | | 4 Behavioral Outcome |
| | | | 3a. Cognitive representation drive | 3b. Relevant affect | 3c. Relevant object | |
| Modes | Libidinal tension | Delay of gratification | | | | |
| Blocking | | | Repression | Suppression of affect | Withdrawal, denial | Inhibition |
| Reversal into opposite | | | Change of instinctual aim | Reversal of affect | Reversal from other to self as object | Reaction formation; undoing |
| Shift in reference of | | | Projection of impulse | Projection of affect | Displacement; identification; rationalization | "Acting out" |
| Insulation from associative connective | | | "Splitting" or isolation of impulse | Isolation of affect | Depersonalization of experience | Isolation of behavioral event |

threat to another source, and rationalizing. Speaking of an unwanted memory of a trauma, Freud described this complexity: "[The precocious event (i.e., trauma)] is represented . . . by a host of symptoms and of special features, . . . subtle but solid interconnections of the intrinsic structure of the neurosis . . . the memory must be extracted from [resistances] piece by piece" (1962 [1986], 153).

The next step in my analysis was to suggest that this repertoire of coping strategies is not limited to fending off internal threats (the dominant approach to defenses in psychoanalysis) but can apply to external threats as well. Thus, in the face of danger (for example, environmental toxicity), the individual can resort to denial (the threat does not exist), to suppression of affect (it may exist, but there is nothing to worry about), to displacement of threat (it is a threat only in Third World countries), "acting out" (engaging in ritual protections against the threat), and so on.

At this moment I should confess that, in the light of the foregoing passages, I am not altogether happy with the terms "defense," "defensive," and "defense mechanisms," even though I will continue to use the terms for reasons of consistency with past usage. The term "defensive" has the connotation that the user of defenses is on the run, or has his or her back against the wall, in the face of threats. The statement "don't be defensive" certainly suggests that. Because, however, to employ these strategies as often as not involves active adaptation and mastery—even exploitation—of one's situation, I prefer the more neutral term of "coping mechanisms," or even the awkward "ways of coming to terms with external and internal threats and intrusions."

It is a part of the human condition that life is a continuous struggle, in the sense that any individual is forever experiencing, defending against, capitalizing on, and coming to terms with both external and internal dangers and threats of danger. For that reason it is possible to treat the repertoire of coping strategies, like affect, as a kind of universally—certainly generally—recognized language that can be communicated and shared by individuals and in collectivities. Everyone knows what it is to deny, to blame, to accuse (project), and to love what one has previously hated and vice versa (reversal), because these modes of coping are part of everyone's experience—even though every individual has a distinctive and preferred pattern of modes in his or her individual armory. This postulate of generality and shareability is—as in the case of affect—a necessary one if we are to be able to speak of collective coping as an ingredient of cultural traumas. Representations, in order to be collective, must be mutually understood and shared.

I now turn to a number of specific observations about coming to terms with cultural traumas as such.

## Mass Coping Versus Collective Coping

It stands to reason that a historical event with penetrating if not over-whelming significance for a society will also constitute a major situation to be coped with on the part of many individuals in the society, even if it does not constitute a personal trauma for them. I have in mind the imposition—by virtue their very occurrence—of a need to give defini-tion to Nazism and the Holocaust in Germany, the ending of slavery in the United States, the imposition of Soviet-dominated communist rule in Poland—to choose examples included in this volume. Many (though not all) Americans were similarly called upon to come to terms—in dif-ferent ways and at different times—with major events such as Pearl Harbor in 1941, the internment of Japanese-Americans in 1942, the dropping of the atomic bombs on Japanese cities in 1945, and the Cuban missile crisis of 1962. Under the pressure of such events, more-over, many people in the respective populations coped with the same or similar reactions—such as fighting off their anxiety, dismissing or deny-ing the significance of the event, depersonalizing, and so on. We call this aggregation of individual responses a mass phenomenon because it involved many people having the same reactions and assigning the same meaning.

However, we should be careful not to refer to such mass responses as a collective response or defense. To bring them into the latter category, some or all of the following ingredients of "collective memory work" have to be accomplished.

- The response must be highlighted as a response to a trauma that affects all members of the relevant collectivity. In his speech fol-lowing the Japanese attack on Pearl Harbor, President Roosevelt announced that the treacherous assault established "a date that will live in infamy"—a statement that proclaimed indelibility, an assault on the whole of the American people, and an outrage to be feared and detested. The speech worked to crystallize the sea of mass responses to the event into a collective response. The cho-rus of utterances by national leaders, black and white, proclaim-ing the assassination of Martin Luther King Jr. in 1968 as a national shame, worked toward the same end.

- The collectivization of coping responses is rarely, however, achieved by a proclamation by political leaders. It frequently involves these, of course, but it is more often a prolonged process of collective groping, negotiation, and contestation over the proper historical meaning to be assigned, the proper affective stance to be adopted, the proper focus of responsibility, and the proper forms of commemoration. For example, the initial response to the death of President Roosevelt in 1945 was a mixture of mass sadness on the part of those who loved the president, guilt on the part of those who were secretly pleased to be rid of the hated man, and confusion on the part of those who were apprehensive about the loss of leadership amid the uncertainties of the war and the peace to follow (de Grazia 1948). This initial confusion and groping was channeled into a semiofficial national response of mourning, carried in the words of leaders such as Vice President Truman and Eleanor Roosevelt, by the highly publicized solemn journey of the train bearing Roosevelt's coffin from Warm Springs to Washington, and by the official conferring of presidential power on Truman ("the king is dead, long live the king").

- Most often the establishment of a collectivity's responses to a trauma is a matter of bitter contestation among groups, sometimes over long periods of time and often without definitive settlement. The issue of how to remember slavery and the American Civil War has never been completely resolved among groups of African Americans who continue to come to terms with its meaning for their cultural identity, among many in the North who want to remember it as a heroic obliteration of a national curse, and among many southerners who want to remember it as a simultaneously heroic and tragic end to a distinctive southern way of life. To choose another example, the post–World War II years have involved continuous and sometimes bitter debates among those who regard the dropping of the A-bomb on Japan as a military triumph, as a fully justified way of saving American lives in the war, as a regrettable necessity, as a savage act, and as a national travesty (Linenthal 1989). Those involved in such debates often have specific interests to promote or protect (the armed forces, political parties, social movements for peace and countermovements against them, and so on). Insofar as these contests are chronic and never come to a point of consensus over meaning, appropriate affect, and preferred coping strategy, we do not have a completely official version of a collective trauma, but rather a continuing counterpoint of interested and opposing voices.

- Many contestations can thus be regarded as largely symbolic struggles over different ways in which historical events should be remembered and what affective stance (positive or negative) ought to be assumed. This is certainly true with respect to struggles over commemorative rituals, monuments, and museums. The nature of these struggles, moreover, will change over time, as different constellations of interested groups with different agendas emerge on the scene. In many cases, of course, public insistences on how events and situations should be remembered are at the same time thinly disguised claims for improving a group's economic position, political recognition, and social status. For example, veterans of quasi wars and military actions short of wars have an interest in being remembered as veterans of heroic struggle because of the array of legal privileges and material benefits available to them. As we will note below, certain advantages also accrue to individuals and groups who succeed in having themselves diagnosed (remembered) as victims of traumas.

- Symbolic struggles over the proper remembering of traumas often have a generational dimension. Giesen's treatment of Holocaust memories reveal an accusatory stance (mainly in the 1960s) by children who had not experienced the Holocaust but whose parents had. Many hawks in the Vietnam war period were older citizens who bitterly "remembered" Chamberlain's appeasement strategies before World War II (and were convinced that the same mistakes should not be made again); whereas many doves were younger persons who had not had that generational memory imprinted on them or who "remembered" it differently from the older generation.

## The Issue of Collective Repression

Freud regarded repression as a special defense mechanism in coping with trauma, and, in his later writings, with neurotic conflict more generally. It was an initial, general response of the prepubertal child (presumably not equipped with a full repertoire of defenses at that developmental phase) in dealing with trauma. In principle, repression is an extremely effective defense in dealing with threats, because, if successful, it banishes the threat and obviates the need for additional defensive activity. For Freud, however, repression was typically not successful. It only succeeded in incubating, not obliterating the threat. The occasion for new and heightened adult defense against the memory of trauma was the failure of repression, the breakthrough of anxiety, and the mobilization of a whole array of other defenses, including in the last analysis, symptom as defense. In current diagnoses the phenomena of defensive repression, denial, and avoidance are typically included in the diagnosis of posttraumatic stress disorders.

It seems inadvisable to seek any precise sociocultural analogy for the psychological repression of trauma. Certainly one dominant response to a trauma can be mass denial, unwillingness to remember, and forgetting—as demonstrated by the situation in West Germany immediately after the Holocaust and the case of slavery among blacks in the immediate postemancipation period (see Giesen and Eyerman, this volume). It is difficult to imagine anything like the complete success of an organized political effort to ban a major historical event or situation from memory, largely because it is impossible to control, even with extreme efforts, private oral intercommunication among citizens, between parents and children, and so on. Thus the idea of "cultural repression" in any full sense does not make social-psychological sense, even though determined totalitarian governments (Hitler's Germany, Stalin's Soviet Union, and Mao's China) have made massive attempts to cover up and rewrite history.

By the same token, it does not seem advisable to seek a precise analogy for the idea of psychological incubation—the notion of a repressed, highly charged, under-the-surface force ready to break into the open at all times. The reason this "smoldering volcano" imagery seems unsatisfactory is that the "active" or "inactive" status of cultural trauma is so contingent on forever changing and ongoing social and political conditions and on ongoing processes of negotiation and contestation among groups. I make this assertion in full knowledge of the fact that interested groups (including governments) often represent cultural traumas as indelible marks or scars, forever nagging at the body social and the body politic. The very status of "indelibility," however, is itself subject to constantly changing historical circumstances.

## The Universality of Blame and Scapegoating

At the psychological level this mechanism is an obvious one. It involves both displacement and projection—assigning responsibility and blame on others for unwanted internal or external intrusions, especially if these intrusions evoke the possibility of self-blame or guilt (including survivor guilt). If extreme enough, these reactions crystallize into a solidly established paranoia that defies considerations of empirical reality and logic.

Similarly, when any kind of accident, disaster, shock, public disgrace, or breakdown of social control occurs, an almost inevitable first (and even continuing) response is to assign responsibility and blame. Sometimes this reaction is more or less institutionalized—the firing of the manager of an athletic team during or after a losing season, the cashiering of the captain of a naval vessel after a navigational failure (no matter whose fault it actually was), the firing of a chief executive officer when corporate profits fall or the company founders. With respect to unanticipated failures or disasters, the tendency to seek responsibility and blame is nearly automatic. It is virtually assured if there is any indication that the failure is "man-made" as opposed to natural (earthquakes, floods, hurricanes, natural forest fires). Even the latter produce hostile reactions toward agents who were supposed to forecast or prevent it or who are responsible for reacting to it once it occurs (Smelser 1962). The same scapegoating effect is a regular feature of "moral panics"—collective hysteria in response to uncertainty and threat—in which some inimical agent is identified as attacking something held sacred (Thompson 1998).

Cultural traumas, when defined and accepted as such, do not escape this tendency. In every one of the case studies of cultural trauma detailed in this volume, the assignment of responsibility is salient. Who is at fault? Some hated group in our midst? Conspirators? Political leaders? The military? Capitalists? A foreign power? We ourselves as a group or nation? Earlier I noted that the very effort to establish a cultural trauma is a disputed process, as are debates and conflicts over "preferred defenses." Perhaps even more divisive ingredients of the cultural-trauma complex are finger-pointing, mutual blame, and demonization. Furthermore, when these conflictual consequences appear on the scene, they themselves become potential sources of trauma, and typically result in the mobilization of efforts, mainly on the part of political authorities, to calm the scene—whether by publicly proclaiming a responsible agent and joining in the attack, by launching "impartial" investigating commissions to settle questions of responsibility in a cooler and more neutral way, or otherwise attempting to calm the waters by "working through" the issues of blame and responsibility.

### Attraction and Repulsion and the Establishment of Ambivalence

One of the peculiarities that has been noticed in connection with acute psychological traumas is a very strong dual tendency: to avoid and to relive (Freud 1964 [1939 {1834–38}], 35–63). At the ideational level one main defense is some form of amnesia (numbing, emotional paralysis [Krystal 1978] actual forgetting, denial, difficulty in recalling, or unwillingness to contemplate or dwell on the traumatic event). At the same time, the trauma has a way of intruding itself into the mind, in the form of unwanted thoughts, nightmares, or flashbacks. These apparently antagonistic tendencies have presented themselves to some as a paradox (Caruth 1995, 152). At the behavioral level the same double tendency has been observed: a compulsive tendency to avoid situations that resemble the traumatic scene or remind the victim of it, but at the same time an equally strong compulsion to repeat the trauma or to relive some aspect of it (van der Kolk 1996, 199–201).

When seeking an analogy at the sociocultural level, we discover such dual tendencies—mass forgetting and collective campaigns on the part of groups to downplay or "put behind us," if not actually to deny a cultural trauma on the one hand, and a compulsive preoccupation with the event, as well as group efforts to keep it in the public consciousness as a reminder that "we must remember," or "lest we forget," on the other. A memorial to an event, it has been pointed out, has elements of both reactions: to memorialize is to force a memory on us by the conspicuous and continuous physical presence of a monument; at the same time a memorial also conveys the message that now that we have paid our respects to a trauma, we are now justified in forgetting about it. These two reactions are most vivid in Giesen's account of the array of attempts to come to terms with the Holocaust in postwar West Germany. The preoccupation with and controversies over memorials of the Holocaust continue to be conspicuous phenomena in Germany and to a lesser extent in the United States. The great public controversy over memorials to the Vietnam war, especially the one in Washington, D.C., reveals the same dynamic of double memory—the compulsion to remember and the compulsion to forget (Scruggs and Swerdlow 1985; Wager-Pacifici and Schwarz 1991; Glazer 1996). One major qualification on psychological analogizing, however, should be stressed. At the psychological level the battle between the two tendencies goes on within the psyche; at the cultural level, there may be instances of alternating between compulsive avoidance and compulsive attraction in some individuals and groups, but the major manifestation is a conflict among different groups, some oriented toward playing down the trauma and others in keeping it alive (Geyer 1996).

A closely related defense against trauma is to convert a negative event into a positive one. In some cases this is relatively unproblematic. The American Revolution, potentially if not actually a trauma in American history (and certainly a trauma if it had failed), has been almost universally remembered as a positive, heroic myth of origin for the American nation (Neal 1998, 22–23). In other cases the shift is more problematical. Some Poles remember some aspects of the Communist era (e.g., security of income) with nostalgia, particularly in the context of unemployment and other costs of a market economy (see Sztompka, in this volume; see also Wnuk-Lipinski 1990). Eyerman's chapter demonstrates decisively that many African American intellectuals in the late nineteenth century revived the memory of slavery as a historical blessing in the sense that, even though a trauma, it gave black Americans a positive basis for identity in a world that had revoked the postslavery promise of full citizenship by the imposition of Jim Crowism in the South and discrimination in the North. Even the German remembering of the Holocaust, in which it seems almost impossible to find anything positive, shows a glimmer of this element: to remember it strengthens our resolve not to permit it to happen again.

In all events, this double tendency, once it appears in the memory and memorializing of traumas, firmly establishes one of their most remarkable characteristics: ambivalence toward them. Like psychological ambivalence, its manifestation at the sociocultural level sets the stage for the frequently observed tendency for generation after generation to engage in compulsive examining and reexamining, bringing up new aspects of the trauma, reinterpreting, reevaluating, and battling over symbolic significance. These are the ingredients of what might variously be called cultural play, cultural fussing, even culture wars. Ambivalence lends strength to the assertion of indelibility: cultural traumas can never be solved and never go away. Over time the repeated and relived cultural activity yields a reservoir of hundreds of different renditions of the memory—some dead, some latent, some still active, some "hot," but in all events many that are available for resuscitation. This produces a fascinating type of cultural accumulation—a nonending, always-expanding repository consisting of multiple precipitates (both negative and positive) of a continuous and pulsating process of remembering, coping, negotiating, and engaging in conflict.

Once thus endowed with status of ambivalence, finally, cultural traumas manifest a tendency toward producing political polarization and sharply divided debates. All the elements necessary for this characteristic have by now been mentioned—a threatening if not overwhelming assault on cultural integrity and an event or situation endowed with powerful, ambivalent affects. This combination produces the familiar effect of "splitting," whereby one side of the ambivalence is more or less completely denied, negated, or repressed and the other side made to be the whole story. Political polarization results when two or more political groups—each having adopted rigid, opposing modes of splitting—confront one another and have at it in either-or struggles over the meaning and assessment of the trauma.

## EXCURSUS: THE SCIENTIFIC EVOLUTION AND DEVOLUTION OF TRAUMA

It is of interest, in concluding, to call attention to an engaging theoretical/methodological/ideological observation about the century-long scientific history of the notion of psychological trauma. This observation is not meant to be an exhaustive survey of conceptualization and research on the topic, but rather a general commentary on the fate of a scientific concept.

From a medical point of view the idea of trauma, both for adults and for children, traces to the labors of psychiatrists in nineteenth-century Europe, and the explanation-sketches developed by the French pioneers Janet and Charcot (van der Kolk, Weisaeth, and van der Hart, 1996, 52–53; Kahn 1998, 4–5). Freud's work on hysteria crystallized this interest and offered several new elements. In his formulations during the 1890s, summarized at the beginning of this chapter, Freud developed a scientifically precise proposition: a distinctive event (passive sexual experience in childhood) occasions repression of both affect and memory, a period of incubation, and subsequently the appearance of specific conversion symptoms. This formulation soon proved limited and inadequate for Freud himself. Early he distinguished between the "actual neuroses," created by an objective, overwhelming physical experience, and "psychoneuroses," arising from the infantile sexual experiences. Subsequently, he developed two separate models of trauma, one the "unbearable situation" model, derived from his work on the war neuroses of World War I, and the "unacceptable impulse" model, arising from his increasing stress on the role of infantile sexual fantasies in the development of the psychoneuroses (van der Kolk, Weisaeth, and van der Hart 1996, 55).

The feature of Freud's work I wish to take as a starting point in this excursus is his formulation of trauma and symptom in conversion hysteria. It was a precise formulation, however unsatisfactory and fleeting it proved to be. The subsequent history of both trauma and its consequences can be told as a vast multiplication of events regarded as traumatic, a corresponding multiplication of symptoms associated with trauma, and a curious politicization of the phenomenon. The results of his history yield a paradoxical mix of scientific advance and scientific degeneration.

The concern with "shell shock" in particular and the war neuroses in general during World War I firmly established battlefield experiences as a species of trauma. World War II added new interest and knowledge (Grinker and Spiegel 1945). After World War II much attention focused on the traumatic experiences of both child and adult survivors of concentration camps (Krystal 1988). The Korean War yielded the "brainwashing" experiences of prisoners of war (Hyde 1977), the Vietnam war a prolonged concern with battle-related traumas (Lifton 1973; Dean 1992). Traumas arising from death and loss have been a continuing concern in psychoanalysis (Freud 1957 [1917]; Klein 1986 [1940]; Loewald 1980 [1962]) and psychiatry (Lindemann 1944), and these figure significantly in the literature on trauma. Also of relevance are the psychological impacts of natural catastrophes such as earthquakes, floods, and accidents (Erikson 1976). More recently, and associated with the increasing recognition of domestic violence as a social problem, traumas of child abuse, application of extreme discipline, spousal battering, incest, rape, and traumatic sexual mistreatment—and the witnessing of all of these (Pynoos and Eth 1985)—have been added.

The accumulation of clinical and psychological knowledge resulted in the naming of a disorder and its formal inclusion in 1980 as "posttraumatic stress disorder"—a subclass of anxiety disorders—in the American Psychiatric Association's Diagnostic and Statistical Manual of Mental Disorders. This gave rise to an "explosion of scientific research" (van der Kolk 1996, 62) on PTSD of industry proportions, producing thousands of research reports, new journals such as *Journal of Traumatic Stress, Dissociation,* and *Child Abuse and Neglect,* as well as handbooks (e.g., van der Kolk, McFarlane, and Weisaeth 1996; Yehuda 1998), and entire books on the methodology of measurement, assessment, epidemiology, and treatment (Wilson and Keane 1997). The National Institute of Mental Health founded a Violence and Traumatic Stress branch.

To indicate how far the idea of anxiety disorders has penetrated into the conditions of everyday life, I reproduce an e-mail directed to faculty and staff at the University of California, Berkeley, at the time I was drafting this chapter:

> FREE SCREENINGS FOR ANXIETY DISORDERS. May 6, 11 a.m.-2 p.m., 3rd floor of the Martin Luther King Student Union. Faculty or staff members who feel they may have symptoms of an anxiety disorder can participate in this free, confidential screening program. The screening program will include viewing a short video, completing a screening questionnaire and discussing the results with a mental health professional. Referral for follow-up evaluation and treatment will be available.
>
> This screening is being sponsored by the Alameda County Psychological Association and UC Berkeley's University Health Services and the Association of Psychology Undergraduates.

As might be expected, the recent official definition of posttraumatic stress disorders is very inclusive:

> The development of characteristic symptoms following exposure to an extreme traumatic stressor involving direct personal experience of an event that involves actual or threatened death or serious injury, or other threat to one's physical integrity; or witnessing an event that involves death, injury or a threat to the physical integrity of another person; or learning about unexpected or violent death, serious harm, or threat of death or injury experienced by a family member or other close associate (American Psychiatric Association 1994, 424).

The number of potentially traumatic events involved is even more comprehensive, including but not limited to:

> military combat, violent personal assault (sexual assault, physical attack, robbery, mugging), being kidnapped, being taken hostage, terrorist attack, torture, incarceration as a prisoner of war or in a concentration camp, natural or manmade disasters, severe automobile accidents, or being diagnosed with a life-threatening illness. For children, sexually traumatic events may include developmentally inappropriate sexual experienced events without threatened or actual violence or injury. Witnessed events include, but are not limited to, observing the serious injury or unnatural death of another person due to violent assault, accident, war, or disaster or unexpectedly witnessing a dead body or body parts. Events experienced by others that are learned about include, but are not limited to, violent personal assault, serious accident, or serious injury experienced by a family member or a close friend; learning about the sudden unexpected death of a family member or close friend; or learning that one's child has a life-threatening disease. The disorder may be especially severe or long lasting when he stressor is of human design (e.g., torture, rape). The likelihood of developing this disorder may increase as the intensity of any physical proximity to the stressor increase. (American Psychiatric Association 1994, 424)

With respect to level of intensity and complexity, Early has suggested a nine-category system of levels ranging from invasive events in a defense-less state to "a state of cataclysm which would overcome everyone" (e.g., atomic explosions) (Early 1993).

The scientific research on symptoms associated with posttraumatic stress disorder has also produced an impressive array:

> recurrent and intrusive recollections of the event, . . . recurrent distressing dreams during which the event is replayed . . . dissociative states . . . [i]ntense psychological distress, . . . physiological reactivity which occurs when the person is exposed to triggering events that resemble or symbolize an aspect of the traumatic event (e.g., anniversaries of the traumatic event; cold, snowy weather or uniformed guards for survivors of death camps in cold climates; hot, humid weather for combat veterans of the South Pacific; entering any elevator for a woman who was raped in an elevator) . . . [avoiding] thoughts, feelings, or conversations about the traumatic event . . . [avoiding] activities, situations, or people who arouse recollections of it . . . amnesia for an important aspect of the traumatic event . . . [d]iminished responsiveness to the external world ("psychic numbing" or "emotional anesthesia") . . . diminished participation in previously enjoyed activities . . . feeling detached or estranged from other people . . . markedly reduced abil-ity to feel emotions . . . a sense of a foreshortened future . . . persistent symp-toms of increased anxiety . . . difficulty falling or staying asleep . . . exagger-ated startle response . . . outbursts of anger . . . difficulty concentrating or completing tasks. (American Psychiatric Association 1994, 424–25)

If we regard the history of the concept of trauma in this constructed journey, we note a progression from the simple (and as it turned out, erroneous) causal connection contained in Freud's theory of conversion hysteria to a vast number of possible (not necessary) traumatic events and situations all funneling into a single clinical entity (posttraumatic stress disorder), which is manifested in an equally vast number of possi-ble (not necessary) symptoms. The overall result is an enormous gain in recognition of comprehension and complexity, but a loss of formal sci-entific precision. The progression of conceptualization, research results, and treatment has produced a classificatory jumble, and as a conse-quence, a formal degeneration in the status of scientific thinking about the concept. At the very least, this sprawl calls for a disaggregation of subtypes and a search for processes specific to each.

In discussing trauma in cultural perspective, de Vries took notice of the fact that the appearance of posttraumatic stress in the diagnostic manuals of the American Psychiatric Association amounted to a legitimization of the phenomena, in that it categorized it as an "exogenous event," that is, one that "happens" to an individual in such a way that he or she is not responsible for it, or is a "victim" of it. This observation raises the larger social—economic, political and moral—aspects of that symptomatology. Let us consider first the war neuroses. To label combat stress as a disorder, or a medical phenomenon, is not only a diagnostic act, but also a decision that entitles the veteran to treatment (usually free of charge) in a Veteran's Administration Hospital. At the very least this diagnosis creates an economic incentive for the veteran to possess that label (perhaps even outweighing the psychic cost of the stigma of being labeled mentally disturbed). Such diagnoses, considered in the aggregate, may also constitute an important cost consideration for the providing hospitals.

The traumatic disorders emanating from domestic violence pose even more complexities. While not passing judgment on the actual traumatic status of exposure to child abuse, rape, and battering, it is important to point out that the medical, legal, and social status of their effects has been an object of interest and political activity on the part of victims' groups organized on behalf of the victims. (Many of these groups have been offshoots of the more general feminist movement.) In the process the effects have taken on additional significance. If they are classifiable as a medical symptom, the victims acquire a real or potential claim on physicians, insurance companies, and other payment systems for compensation of treatment. If defined as sufficiently serious, these effects may also be the occasion for lawsuits on the part of victims against parents and other perpetrators. Finally, they may become the basis for individuals and groups to claim that they are in a wronged category, thus establishing a certain—though often ambivalently regarded—claim for moral recognition and status as victims. In this connection, we have even witnessed the growth of a national group of parents wronged by falsely accusing children. Numerous related controversies have sprung up, such as that concerning the legal status of recovered memories, and the debate about the moral legitimacy or nonlegitimacy to be accorded to the psychoanalytically derived claim that experiences of being wronged may be the product of fantasy, not real experience.

The process involved in making a symptomatology (trauma) into a political resource is an interesting subject in and of itself, and deserving of scientific understanding. The point I wish to make, in concluding this excursus, is that the tendency for the notion of trauma to sprawl and include ever-new ranges of phenomena—plus the economization, politicization, and moralization of trauma—has, from a scientific standpoint, created a jungle that defies attempts at scientific formulation and understanding.

# CHAPTER 3

# Cultural Trauma

*Slavery and the Formation*
*of African American Identity*

RON EYERMAN

In this chapter I explore the notion of cultural trauma in the formation of African American identity from the end of the Civil War to the Civil Rights movement. The trauma in question is slavery, not as institution or even experience, but as collective memory, a form of remembrance that grounded the identity-formation of a people. As has been discussed elsewhere in this volume and as will be further developed here, there is a difference between trauma as it affects individuals and as a cultural process. As cultural process, trauma is linked to the formation of collective identity and the construction of collective memory. The notion of a unique African American identity emerged in the post–Civil War period, after slavery had been abolished. The trauma of forced servitude and of nearly complete subordination to the will and whims of another was thus not necessarily something directly experienced by many of the subjects of this study, but came to be central to their attempts to forge a collective identity out of its remembrance. In this sense, slavery was traumatic in retrospect, and formed a "primal scene" that could, potentially, unite all "African Americans" in the United States, whether or not they had themselves been slaves or had any knowledge of or feeling for Africa. Slavery formed the root of an emergent collective identity through an equally emergent collective memory, one that signified and distinguished a "race," a people, or a community, depending on the level of abstraction and point of view being put forward. It is this discourse on the collective and its representation that is my focus.

That slavery was traumatic can be thought to be obvious, and for those who experienced it directly, it must certainly have been. In a recent attempt to trace the effects of slavery on contemporary African American behavior patterns, Orlando Patterson (1998, 40) writes, "Another feature of slave childhood was the added psychological trauma of witnessing the daily degradation of their parents at the hands of slaveholders . . . to the trauma of observing their parents' humiliation was later added that of being sexually exploited by Euro-Americans on and off the estate, as the children grew older." While this may be an appropriate use of the concept of trauma, it is not what I have in mind here. The notion of an African American identity, however, was articulated in the latter decades of the nineteenth century by a generation of blacks for whom slavery was a thing of the past, not the present. It was the memory of slavery and its representation through speech and art works that grounded African American identity and permitted its institutionalization in organizations such as the National Association for the Advancement of Colored People (NAACP), founded in 1909–10. If slavery was traumatic for this generation, it was so in retrospect, mediated through recollection and reflection, and, for some black leaders and intellectuals, tinged with a bit of strategic, practical and political, interest.

While exploring the meaning of cultural trauma is part of the aim of this and other chapters, some notion of the parameters of its usage should be stated here. As opposed to psychological or physical trauma, which involves a wound and the experience of great emotional anguish by an individual, cultural trauma refers to a dramatic loss of identity and meaning, a tear in the social fabric, affecting a group of people that has achieved some degree of cohesion. In this sense, the trauma need not necessarily be felt by everyone in a community or experienced directly by any or all. While some event may be necessary to establish as the significant cause, its meaning as traumatic must be established and accepted, and this requires time to occur, as well as mediation and representation. Arthur Neal (1998) defines a "national trauma" according to its "enduring effects," and as relating to events "which cannot be easily dismissed, which will be played over again and again in individual consciousness" and which then become "ingrained in collective memory." In this account, a national trauma must be understood, explained, and made coherent through public reflection and discourse. Here mass media and their representations play a decisive role. This is also the case in what we have called cultural trauma. In his chapter, Neil Smelser offers a formal definition of cultural trauma that is worth repeating: "a memory accepted and publicly given credence by a relevant membership group and evoking an event or situation that is a) laden with negative affect, b) represented as indelible, and c) regarded as threatening a society's existence or violating one or more of its fundamental cultural presuppositions." In the current case, the phrase "or group's identity" could be added to the sentence. It is the collective memory of slavery that defines an individual as a "race member," as Maya Angelou (1976) puts it.

In Cathy Caruth's (1995, 17, and Caruth 1996) psychoanalytic theory of trauma, it is not the experience itself that produces traumatic effect, but rather the remembrance of it. In her account there is always a time lapse, a period of latency, in which forgetting is characteristic, between an event and the experience of trauma. As reflective process, trauma links past to present through representations and imagination. In such psychological accounts, this can lead to a distorted identity-formation, in which "certain subject-positions may become especially prominent or even overwhelming, for example, those of victim or perpetrator . . . wherein one is possessed by the past and tends to repeat it compulsively as if it were fully present" (LaCapra 1994, 12).

Allowing for the centrality of mediation and imaginative reconstruction, one should perhaps not speak of traumatic events, but rather of traumatic effects (Sztompka in this volume). While trauma necessarily refers to something experienced in psychological accounts, calling this experience *traumatic* requires interpretation. National or cultural trauma (the difference is minimal at the theoretical level) is also rooted in an event or series of events, but not necessarily their direct experience. Such experience is mediated, through newspapers, radio, or television, for example, which involve a spatial as well as temporal distance between the event and its experience. Mass-mediated experience always involves selective construction and representation, since what is visualized is the result of the actions and decisions of professionals as to what is significant and how it should be presented. Thus, national or cultural trauma always engages a "meaning struggle," a grappling with an event that involves identifying the "nature of the pain and the nature of the victim and the attribution of responsibility" (Alexander in this volume). Alexander calls this the *trauma process* when the collective experience of massive disruption, a social crisis, becomes a crisis of meaning and identity. In this trauma process "carrier groups" are central in articulating claims, representing the interests and desires of the affected to a wider public. Here intellectuals, in the term's widest meaning (Eyerman and Jamison 1994), play a significant role. *Intellectual,* as used here, refers to a socially constructed, historically conditioned role rather than to a structurally determined position or a personality type. Although bound up with particular individuals, the concept refers more to what individuals do than who they are. Generally speaking, intellectuals mediate between the cultural and political spheres that characterize modern society, representing and giving voice not so much to their own ideas and interests, but rather articulating ideas to and for others. Intellectuals are mediators and translators, between spheres of activity and differently situated groups, including the situatedness of time and space. In this sense, intellectuals can be film directors, singers of song, as well as college professors. In addition, social movements produce "movement intellectuals" who may lack the formal education usually attributed to intellectuals, but whose role in articulating the aims and values of a movement allow one to call them by that name.

As with physical or psychic trauma, the articulating discourse surrounding cultural trauma is a process of mediation involving alternative strategies and alternative voices. It is a process that aims to reconstitute or reconfigure a collective identity, as in repairing a tear in the social fabric. A traumatic tear evokes the need to "narrate new foundations" (Hale 1998, 6), which includes reinterpreting the past as a means toward reconciling present/future needs. There may be several or many possible responses to cultural trauma that emerge in a specific historical context, but all of them in some way or another involve identity and memory. To anticipate, the appellation "African American," which may seem more or less obvious and natural today, was one of several paths or reactions to the failure of reconstruction to integrate former slaves and their offspring as Americans, and to the new consensus concerning the past in the dominant culture in which slavery was depicted as benign and civilizing. Among the alternatives, the idea of returning to Africa had been a constant theme among blacks almost from the first landing of slaves on the American continent. Another alternative, later in its development, also involved emigration, but to the north to Canada or the free states and territories like Oklahoma, rather than to Africa. Such a move, which was discussed and realized in the later decades of the 1800s did not necessarily exclude a new identity as an African American, but did not necessarily include it either. This alternative, however, did involve an openness to new forms of identification and the attempt to leave others behind.

Developing what W. E. B. Du Bois would describe as a "double consciousness," African *and* American, offered another possibility, one that implied loyalty to a nation but not necessarily to its dominant culture or way of life. In 1897 Du Bois posed the question, "What, after all, am I? Am I an American or a Negro? Can I be both? Or is it my duty to cease to be a Negro as soon as possible and be an American?" (Du Bois 1999, 16–17). However this dilemma, as an aspect of the process of cultural trauma, is resolved, the interpretation and representation of the past and the constitution of collective memory is central. The meaning of slavery was a focal point of reference. A similar process, under way among whites and black attempts to negotiate cultural trauma, was intimately intertwined with this national project. By the mid-1880s the Civil War had become the "civilized war" and "a space both for sectional reconciliation and for the creation of modern southern whiteness" (Hale 1998, 67). As the nation was re-membered through a new narration of the war, blacks were at once made invisible and punished. Reconstruction and blacks in general were made the objects of hate, an Other against which the two sides in the war could reunite. The memory of slavery was recast as benign and civilizing, a white man's project around which North and South could reconcile.

## COLLECTIVE MEMORY

The history of the study of memory is a tale of the
search for a faculty, a quest for the way in which the
mind-brain codes, stores and retrieves information.
Only with the recent interest in language and in cultural
aspects of thinking has there emerged the wider view
of remembering as something that people do together,
reminding themselves of and commemorating
experiences which they have jointly undertaken.

                                        Alan Radley (1990)

Memory is usually conceived as individually based, something that goes on "inside the heads" of individual human beings. "Memory has three meanings: the mental *capacity* to retrieve stored information and to perform learned mental operations, such as long division; the semantic, imagistic, or sensory *content* of recollections; and the *location* where these recollections are stored" (Young 1995). Theories of identity formation or socialization tend to conceptualize memory as part of the development of the self or personality and to locate that process within an individual, with the aim of understanding human actions and their emotional basis. In such accounts, the past becomes present through the embodied reactions of individuals as they carry out their daily lives. In this way, memory helps account for human behavior. Notions of collective identity built on this model, such as those within the collective behavior school, theorize a "loss of self" and the formation of new, collectively based, identities as the outcome of participation in forms of collective behavior like social movements. Here memory, as far as it relates to the individual participant's biography, tends to be downplayed, because it is thought to act as a barrier to forms of collective behavior that transcend the normal routines of daily life. The barrier of memory once crossed, the new collective identity is created sui generis, with the collective, rather than the individual, as its basis. The question of whether this collective may develop a memory has, as far as we know, rarely been addressed by this school.

Alongside these individually focused accounts of memory have existed a concern with collective identity and with "how societies remember," with roots in Durkheim's notion of collective consciousness (Connerton 1989). Here collective memory is defined as recollections of a shared past "that are retained by members of a group, large or small, that experienced it" (Schuman and Scott 1989, 361–62). Such memories are retained and passed on either as part of an ongoing process of what might be called public commemoration, in which officially sanctioned rituals are engaged to establish a shared past, or through discourses more specific to a particular group or collective. This socially constructed, historically rooted collective memory functions to create social solidarity in the present. As developed by followers of Durkheim such as Maurice Halbwachs (1992), memory is collective in that it is supra-individual, and individual memory is always conceived in relation to a group, be this geographical, positional, ideological, political, or generationally based. In Halbwachs' classical account, memory is always group memory, both because the individual is derivative of some collectivity, family, and community, and also because a group is solidified and becomes aware of itself through continuous reflection upon and re-creation of a distinctive, shared memory. Individual identity is said to be negotiated within this collectively shared past. Thus while there is always a unique, biographical memory to draw upon, it is described as being rooted in a collective history. Here collective memory provides the individual with a cognitive map within which to orient present behavior. In this sense, collective memory is a social necessity; neither an individual nor a society can do without it. As Bernhard Giesen (in this volume) points out, collective

memory provides both individual and society with a temporal map, unifying a nation or community through time as well as space. Collective
memory specifies the temporal parameters of past and future, where we
came from and where we are going, and also why we are here now.
Within the narrative provided by this collective memory, individual identities are shaped as experiential frameworks formed out of, as they are
embedded within, narratives of past, present, and future.

The shift in emphasis in the social sciences and humanities toward lan-
guage-based, text-oriented analysis and to the effects of "visual culture"
on identity formation has brought new developments to the study of
memory. In the field of comparative literature, for example, more attention is being paid to the importance of collective memory in the formation of ethnic identity and the role of literary works in this reflective
process. With the cultural turn to focus on the centrality of cognitive
framing and the emphasis on language and intertextuality, memory is
located not inside the heads of individual actors, but rather "within the
discourse of people talking together about the past" (Radley 1990, 46).
This is a development that has its roots in forms of analysis often called
"poststructuralism" and in feminist theory and practice. In the 1970s
feminists developed techniques of "consciousness raising" that attempted
to make the personal political, to theorize the development of the self
within a politically as well as symbolically structured social context.
Armed with theories of socialization that combined Marx and Freud
(and sometimes G. H. Mead), feminists developed techniques for liberating individuals from the distorted identity formation of male-dominated
society. Like the collective behavior school mentioned above, with whom
they shared many theoretical assumptions, some feminists viewed individual memory as a barrier to collective political action. "Memory
work" was one technique developed by feminists after the women's
movement moved into the academy, as a way of recalling faded or
repressed images of domination.

A more recent development concerns the idea of collective memory
itself. The editors of a volume concerning developments in literary theory
(Singh, Skerrett, and Hogan 1994) define collective memory as "the combined discourses of self: sexual, racial, historical, regional, ethnic, cultural, national, familial, which intersect in an individual." These form a
net of language, a metanarrative, which a community shares and within
which individual biographies are oriented. Here Foucault and poststructuralism unite with the Durkheimian tradition referred to above.
Collective memory is conceived as the outcome of interaction, a conver-

sational process within which individuals locate themselves, where identities are described as the different ways individuals and collectives are positioned by, and position themselves, within narratives. This dialogic process is one of negotiation for both individuals and for the collective itself. It is never arbitrary.

From this perspective, the past is a collectively articulated, if not collectively experienced, temporal reference point that shapes the individual more than it is reshaped to fit generational or individual needs. This is a necessary addendum, especially where political motivation is concerned. In response to what he calls the "interest theory" of memory construction, where the past is thought to be entirely malleable to present needs, Michael Schudson (1989) suggests several ways in which the past is resistant to total manipulation, not least of which is that some parts of the past have been recorded and thus obtain at least a degree of objectivity. Supporting this, Barry Schwartz (1982, 398) writes that "given the constraints of a recorded history, the past cannot be literally constructed; it can only be selectively exploited." In this context a distinction between collective memory and recorded and transcribed history is useful. If, as Halbwachs suggests, collective memory is always group memory, always the negotiated and selective recollections of a specific group, then collective memory is similar to myth. This, in fact, is how Arthur Neal (1998) conceives of it in his work on national trauma. From Halbwachs's "presentist" perspective, collective memory is essential to a group's notion of itself and thus must continually be made over to fit historical circumstance. While this collective memory makes reference to historical events, that is, events that are recorded and known to others, the meaning of such events is interpreted from the perspective of the group's needs and interests, within limits of course. History, especially as a profession and academic discipline, aims at something wider, more objective, and more universal than group memory. Of course, history is always written from some point of view and can be more or less ethnocentric, but as an academic discipline, even within the constraints of nationally based institutions, its aims and, especially, its rules of evidence, are of a different sort from the collective memory of a group. At the very least, professional historical accounts can be criticized for their ethnocentricism.

An overheard conversation between a historian and a Holocaust victim can perhaps illustrate what I mean. In this conversation the victim was recalling his memories of an infamous Jewish guard in a Polish ghetto. He vividly recalled his personal experience of this man. The historian pointed out that this could not have occurred, as this guard was in another camp at that particular time and could document that claim. The victim remained skeptical, but, perhaps because he was also a scientist, was willing to consider the claim. Later, the historian, who specializes in atrocities such as the Holocaust, recounted that he often faces this problem of the difference between memory and documented history.

While the focus on language and ways of speaking has had many liberating effects on the study of collective memory and identity, there are limitations as well. According to Alan Radley, "This movement . . . still falls short of addressing questions related to remembering in a world of things—both natural and products of cultural endeavor—where it concentrates upon memory as a product of discourse. The emphasis upon language tends to hide interesting questions which arise once we acknowledge that the sphere of material objects is ordered in ways upon which we rely for a sense of continuity and as markers of temporal change" (Radley 1990). Viewing memory as symbolic discourse, in other words, tends to downplay or ignore the impact of material culture on memory and identity formation. From the point of view of discourse analysis, objects gain meaning only when they are talked about. Radley's point is that the way things are organized, whether the objects of routine, everyday experience, like the furniture in a room or the more consciously organized objects in a museum, evokes memory and a "sense of the past," whether this is articulated through language or not. Food and household items can evoke memory, such as suggested by the examples found in the African American cookbook *Spoonbread and Strawberry Wine*. The authors (Darden and Darden 1994, xi) write, "Aunt Norma's biscuit cutter, Aunt Maude's crocheted afghan, our father's old medicine bottles (representing a medical practice of over sixty years) all evoke powerful and loving memories." The same can be said of other cultural artifacts, like music and art objects. Listening to a particular piece of music or gazing at a painting can evoke strong emotional responses connected to the past and can be formative of individual and collective memory. Memory can also be embedded in physical geography, as illustrated by Maya Angelou's vivid descriptions of her youth in a small Southern hamlet (Angelou 1974), and as discussed in Barton (2001).

There is a point to the poststructuralism argument, however, that the actual significance of this response, what it "really" means, is fashioned through language and dialogue and may change depending on the context. Thus, while the arrangement of material artifacts may evoke a sense of the past or of something else, what exactly this 'sense' is requires articulation through language.

This points further to the issue of representation. How is the past to be represented in the present, to individuals, and, more important in this context, to a collective? If we take the preceding arguments into account, the past is not only recollected, and thus represented through language, but it is also recalled through association with artifacts, some of which have been arranged and designated for that purpose. If narrative, the "power of telling," is intimately intertwined with language, with the capacity and the possibility to speak, representation can be called "the power of looking" (Hale 1998, 8) and can be associated with the capacity to see and the possibility to make visible. The questions of who can speak and to whom, as well as the issue of who can make visible, are thus central.

These are matters of great interest in the present study. How was slavery represented, in whose interests, and for what purposes? What role if any did former slaves have in this process of collective remembering through public representation? How slavery was represented in literature, music, the plastic arts, and, later, film is crucial to the formation and reworking of collective memory by the generations that followed emancipation. What social movements provide is a context in which individual biographies and thus memories can be connected with others, fashioned into a unified collective biography and thereby transformed into a political force. Social movements reconnect individuals by and through collective representations; they present the collective and represent the individual in a double sense, forging individual into collective memory and representing the individual as part of a collective.

## THE PLACE OF GENERATION IN COLLECTIVE MEMORY

If collective memory is always group based and subject to adjustment according to historically rooted needs, what are the spatial and temporal parameters that mark this process of reinterpretation? As social groups are mobile, so too are the borders of their memory and collective identity formation. The spatial parameters marking these borders vary and have attained more fluidity with the exponential development of mass media. Their basis may be political, rooted in relatively specified geographic boundaries, but still they span much space to cover exiles and expatriates. They may also be ethnic and religious, which equally can be fixed locally or widespread. While Halbwachs and Durkheim before him rooted memory in real communities, that is, those that have face-to-face contact, recent approaches expand this notion to include the "imagined" communities (Anderson 1991). This possibility and its recognition in academic literature has to do in part with the rise to significance of electronic mass media and the migration of populations, both of which fall under the umbrella term *globalization*. As Igartua and Paez (1997, 81) put it after studying the symbolic reconstruction of the Spanish civil war, "Collective memory does not only exist in the individuals, but that in fact it is located in cultural artifacts. Analyzing the contents of cultural creations, as for example films, one may see how a social group symbolically reconstructs the past in order to confront traumatic events for which it is responsible." This means that the collective memory that forms the basis for collective identity can transcend many spatial limitations when it is recorded or represented by other means. The Armenian-Canadian filmmaker Atom Egoyan records in his films traces of remembrance of the slaughter of Armenians by Turks in 1915, an event that has shaped the collective identity of Armenians ever since. This group is now spread over the globe, but its identity-forming collective memory remains apparently intact, partly due to media such as film as well as the stories passed within the community itself. Temporally the parameters of collective memory appear a bit more fixed. Research on memory has brought forth the generational basis of remembrance and forgetting as key to adjusting interpretations of the past. Survey-based research such as that carried out by Howard Schuman and Jacqueline Scott (1989) investigated whether or not there are particular events that distinguish generations and shape the actions of individuals through memory. Their study focused on Americans in the post–World War II era and found that those who came of age during the Vietnam war shared a distinctive collective memory of that period, something that distinguished this cohort from others. Other studies of "traumatic events," such as the Spanish civil war (Igartua and Paez (1997), have made similar findings. Taking their starting point in Karl Mannheim's theory of generation, these studies tend to show that "attributions of importance to national and world events of the past half century tend to be a function of having experienced an event during adolescence or early adulthood" (Schuman, Belli, and Bischoping 1997, 47).

Mannheim's original formulation proposed that those events experienced during adolescence are the ones most likely to "stick" in later life and to influence behavior. Also those passing through the life cycle at the same point in time are likely to recall the same events; thus one can speak of generational memory.

In what would generational memory consist? How would it be produced and maintained? Mannheim had a very optimistic and positive account of generational memory, at least concerning its general function, before it is filled with the historically determined specifics. The function of generational memory for Mannheim consists in offering "fresh-contact" with "the social and cultural heritage" of a social order, which "facilitates re-evaluation of our inventory and teaches us both to forget that which is no longer useful and to covet that which has yet to be won"(Mannheim 1952, 360). Here collective forgetting is as important as collective remembering for a society's self-reflection; it is in fact the role of youth or the new generation: to provide society with a fresh look at itself. Aside from this general, and generally positive, role, generational memory consists of a record of and a reaction to those "significant" events that an age cohort directly experiences. These events are those that the cohort encounters between the ages of seventeen and twenty-five, in Mannheim's calculation, that shape their worldview and set the framework that will guide their actions and responses for their entire existence. As noted, for Mannheim this means having direct experience. Later investigators have also added mediated experiences, both as formative of a generation and also in terms of retention or reproduction of that generation and others. Thus, not all those who lived through the 1960s participated in social movements, but many experienced them via television. Probably those who participated directly would have a stronger sense of belonging to "the sixties' generation," but those who experienced the events via television and are of the same age might also feel a strong sense of belonging. The question is, would those of a different age who saw the events of the 1960s on TV have any sense of belongingness, and where would the age-related boundaries fall? In any case, the role of mass media in producing and reinforcing generational identity is a much more central question in the current age than in Mannheim's.

THE CYCLE OF (GENERATIONAL) MEMORY

The notion of cultural trauma implies that direct experience is not a necessary condition for the appearance of trauma. It is in time-delayed and negotiated recollection that cultural trauma is experienced, a process that places representation in a key role. How an event is remembered is intimately entwined with how it is recollected. Here the means and media of representation are crucial, for they bridge the gaps between individuals and between occurrence and its recollection. Social psychological studies provide grounds for a theory of generational cycles in the reconstruction of collective memory and the role of media in that process.

After analyzing various examples, Pennebaker and Banasik (1997) found that approximately every twenty to thirty years individuals look back and reconstruct a "traumatic" past. In applying this theory to their study of the remembrance of the Spanish civil war, Igartua and Paez list four factors that underlie and help explain this generational cycle:

1. The existence of the necessary psychological distance that remembering a collective or individual traumatic event requires. Time may soothe and lessen the pain that remembering a traumatic event produces.

2. The necessary accumulation of social resources in order to undergo the commemoration activities. These resources can usually be obtained during one's middle age. The events are commemorated when the generation which suffered them has the money and power to commemorate them.

3. The most important events in one's life take place when one is 12–25 years old. When these people grow older they may remember the events that happened during this period.

4. The sociopolitical repression will cease to act after 20–30 years because those directly responsible for the repression, war, and so on, have either socially or physically disappeared. (1997, 83–84)

If we leave aside the assumption that an event can be traumatic in itself, this framework is useful in the analysis of collective memory and cultural trauma. Igartua and Paez emphasize the difference between a generation shaped by the direct experience of an event and those that follow, for whom memory is mediated in a different way. They also point to the issues of power and access to the means of representation, which are essential for public commemoration and thus collective memory. They also place special emphasis on the role of art and of representation generally in this process.

A discussion of representation seems appropriate here, as this is an issue that will arise throughout this chapter. Representation can be analyzed along several dimensions, as re-presenting, that is, as the presentation through words or visual images of something else where considerations of form are at least as important as content; this can be considered an aesthetic dimension. That the form may itself have a content has been pointed out by White (1987). Representation can refer to a political process concerning how a group of people can and should be represented in a political body, such as a parliament or other public arena, from the mass media to a museum. Representation has a moral dimension, which can involve both aesthetic and political aspects, when questions like "How should a people be represented?" are raised. There is a cognitive dimension, wherein representation becomes the prerogative of science and of professionals (museum curators, historians, and so on), who develop procedures and criteria of and for representation, claiming special privileges regarding the materials presented. As in representativeness, representation can refer to types and exemplars, as in Emerson's *Representative Men* (1851) or Du Bois' "talented tenth," in which individuals are said to be types that express the "best" of a race or civilization.

The complex and problematic issues of representation have been of central concern to black Americans from the earliest periods of the slave trade to the present. In what can be properly called "the struggle for representation" (Klotman and Cutler 1999), black Americans have fought for the right to be seen and heard as equals in social conditions that sought to deny it. This struggle for representation occurred in literary, visual, and more traditional political forms. It encompassed a fight to be seen as well as heard and involved who would define what was seen and heard. The first written accounts from inside the culture were the slave narratives from Briton Hammon's *Narrative* (1760) to Harriet Jacobs's *Incidents in the Life of a Slave Girl* (1861) (Klotman and Cutler 1999, xiv). The abolitionist movement and the associated free black press were important mediators and facilitators of this representation, something that affected the mode of presentation, as we will see in the following chapters.

Painting and other forms of visual representation from the inside were later to emerge. What have now come to be called the historically black colleges and universities, inaugurated during the southern "reconstruction" after the Civil War, were important in the production, conservation, and display of artifacts by black artists. These schools and their collections were central to the education of future artists, as well as other black scholars and intellectuals. Music, especially as related to work and religion, was one of the few means of cultural expression publicly available to blacks, and its importance as a means of representation as well as expression has been duly acknowledged, not least by black intellectuals such as W. E. B. Du Bois, in their attempts to find grounds for the narration of black collective identity in the trauma following the end of reconstruction. What Du Bois would call the "sorrow songs" of the slaves embodied and passed along across generations and geographical space the memories of slavery and hopes of liberation. The first film documentary by a black American appeared in 1910. Bearing the title *A Day at Tuskegee*, it offered a representation of the "new Negro" and was commissioned by Booker T. Washington. Commercial black filmmakers and music producers began to play an increasingly important role from the 1920s on, as the urban migrations and better living conditions created a sophisticated audience for "race" movies and recorded music.

Even if these representations were made from the inside, by blacks themselves, the issues of whose voice and whose image were represented was not thereby resolved. The black "community" was always diverse, even as it was unified by enforced subordination and oppression. Internal discussions concerning proper representation, as well as the means and paths of liberation, were many and divergent. This was especially so in the urban public sphere that emerged with the "great migration" in the first quarter of the twentieth century. After emancipation and the urban migrations, the possibility that a single issue could define and unite the black community and focus representation was undercut. Thus, "since there is no single, unchanging black community, the 'burden of represen-tation' involves varying viewpoints, differing degrees of objectivity and subjectivity, and competing facts and fictions" (Klotman and Cutler 1999, xxv). Here different voices and visions clamored to be seen and heard, even as representation was still intimately entwined with subordi-nation and the desire for liberation. This created a situation in which rep-resentation was a responsibility and burden; it could not easily or merely be a form of personal expression, as a black artist was always black in the eyes of the dominant culture.

Resolving cultural trauma can involve the articulation of collective identity and collective memory, as individual stories meld into collective history through forms and processes of collective representation. Collec-tive identity refers to a process of "we" formation, a process both histor-ically rooted and rooted in history. While this common history may have its origins in direct experience, its memory is mediated through narratives that are modified with the passage of time and filtered through cultural artifacts and other materializations that represent the past in the present. Whether or not they directly experienced slavery or even had ancestors who did, blacks in the United States were identified with and came to identify themselves with slavery. The historical memory of the Civil War was reconstructed in the decades that followed, and blackness came to be associated with slavery and subordination. A common history was thus ascribed and inscribed as memory, as well as indigenously passed on. In this sense, slavery is traumatic for those who share a common fate and not necessarily a common experience. Here trauma refers to an event or an experience, a primal scene, that defines one's identity because it has left scars and thus must be dealt with by later generations who have had no experience of the original event. Yet each generation, because of its distance from the event and because its social circumstances have altered with time, reinterprets and represents the collective memory around that event according to its needs and means. This process of reconstruction is limited, however, by the resources available and the constraints history places on memory.

The generational shifts noted by Pennebaker and others can be said to temporally structure the formation of collective memory, providing a link between collective (group) memory and public (collective) memory. Groups, of course, are public, but a particular group's memory may not necessary be publicly, that is officially, acknowledged or commemorated. If a collective memory is rooted in a potentially traumatic event, which by definition is both painful and also open to varying sorts of evaluation, it may take a generation to move from group memory to public memory. Sometimes it may take even longer; sometimes it may never happen at all. The case of American slavery is an example. As Ira Berlin notes in his introduction to *Remembering Slavery* (1998), slavery is remembered differently in the United States depending upon which time period and which racial group and regional location one starts from. He writes:

> Northerners who fought and won the (civil) war at great cost incorporated the abolitionists' perspective into their understanding of American nationality: slavery was evil, a great blot that had to be excised to realize the full promise of the Declaration of Independence. At first, even some white Southerners—former slave-holders among them—accepted this view, conceding that slavery had burdened the South as it had burdened the nation and declaring themselves glad to be rid of it. But during the late nineteenth century, after attempts to reconstruct the nation on the basis of equality collapsed and demands for sectional reconciliation mounted, the portrayal of slavery changed. White Northerners and white Southerners began to depict slavery as a benign and even benevolent institution, echoing themes from the planters' defense of the antebellum order . . . Such views, popularized in the stories of Joel Chandler Harris and the songs of Stephen Foster, became pervasive during the first third of the twentieth century. (Berlin 1998, xiii–xiv)

There was a long history of visual representation to draw upon as well. In his account of the "visual encoding of hierarchy and exclusion," Albert Boime (1990, 15–16), shows how "a sign system had been put into place," which supplemented written and oral justifications for slavery. Especially in the nineteenth century, white artists produced paintings that reinforced beliefs about the "happy slave," contented in his/her servitude. This was filtered through popular culture, especially through minstrelsy, wherein black-faced white actors parodied black dialect and behavior in staged performances. American culture was permeated with words, sounds, and images that took for granted that slavery was both justified and necessary, beneficial to all concerned. At the same time, there existed a countercurrent that "remembered" the opposite.

Against the attempt to reconstruct slavery to fit particular interests stood the recollections of former slaves, those passed down orally, in story and song, as well as in the written slave narratives being hailed today by many as the origins of a distinctive African American aesthetic. These voices, though significant and strong after emancipation were secondary to the optimistic hope for integration. It was this future orientation, not a reflected upon common past, that unified blacks after the Civil War. As former slaves died out, the voice of direct experience began to disappear. Already in 1867 a group of musically interested collectors could write about the songs they were about to publish, "The public had well-nigh forgotten these genuine slave songs, and with them the creative power from which they sprung" (Allen, Ware, and Garrison 1867) In the 1880s, as the dreams of full citizenship and cultural integration were quashed, the meaning of slavery would emerge as the issue of an identity conflict, articulated most clearly by the newly expanded and resourceful ranks of highly educated blacks. Through various media and forms of representation these black intellectuals reconstituted slavery as the primal scene of black identity. In this emergent identity, slavery, not as institution or experience but as a point of origin in a common past, would ground the formation of the black "community." This was not the only source of revived memories of slavery, however. In face of repressive, often violent, reactions from whites, many blacks fled the South as reconstruction ended. One of their prime motivations for migrating was the fear that slavery would be reinstated (Painter 1976). In the trauma of rejection, slavery was remembered as its memory re-membered a group. Slavery defined, in other words, group membership and a membership group (Smelser, in this volume). It was in this context that slavery was articulated as cultural trauma.

As stated previously, the idea of an African American was one result of this identity struggle. It is important to keep in mind that the notion "African American" is not itself a natural category, but rather a historically formed collective identity that first of all required articulation and then acceptance on the part of those it was meant to incorporate. It was here, in this identity formation, that the memory of slavery would be central, not so much as individual experience, but as collective memory. It was slavery, whether or not one had experienced it, that defined one's identity as an African American; it was why you, an African, were here, in America. It was within this identity that direct experience, the identification "former slave" or "daughter of slaves" became functionalized and made generally available as a collective and common memory to unite all blacks in the United States. "African American" was a self-imposed categorization, as opposed to and as meant to counter those imposed by the dominant white society. In this sense, the memory of slavery by African Americans was what Foucault would call a "counter-memory." This clearly marks a difference between black and white in social and historical understanding. While whites might have condemned slavery as an evil institution and bemoaned its effects on the body politic of American society, blacks viewed slavery as a social condition, a lived experience, producing a distinctive way of life, a culture, a community, and finally, an identity. This collective identification affected not only the past and the present, but also future possibilities, recognizing the effects of racial distinction that would reinforce the tendencies of the dominant culture to ascribe common destiny. Thus a distinct gap formed between the collective memory of a minority group and the dominant group in the society, the one that controlled the resources and had the power to fashion public memory. Even here, however, differences between regions, North and South, winners and losers of what some have called the first modern war, created conflicting modes of public commemoration and thus public memories. While both sides avoided slavery as mode of experience, except of course for the North's celebration of its role as liberator and the South's as paternalistic romanticists, to focus on the Civil War itself as a traumatic event in the nation's history, each side offered a different interpretation and developed different ceremonies and rituals to officially and publicly commemorate that event.

There were some dissenting voices, especially among liberals and radicals in the North. Kirk Savage (1994, 127), cites one very influential Northern point of view, that of William Dean Howells, America's foremost literary critic writing in the *Atlantic Monthly* in 1866, who believed that commemoration following the war should focus not on soldiers and battles, but on the ideals and ideas that the war was fought over. Howells, in what must have been a minority view, thought "ideas of warfare itself—organized violence and destruction—unfit for representation" (Savage 1994, 127). As an alternative he pointed to "The Freedman," a sculpture of a freed black slave done in 1863, as "the full expression of one idea that should be commemorated" (cited in Savage 1994, 128). Needless to say, this suggestion went unfulfilled. Instead, each side, North and South, built monuments to its soldiers and their battlefields. In his analysis of these monuments, Savage writes that "issues such as slavery were at best subsidiary in the program of local commemoration, lumped in with stories of Christian bravery and other deed of heroism"(131). With slavery out of the picture, there could be reconciliation between the opposing sides, each being allowed to mark its own heroes, thus sweeping aside one of the main contentions of the war: "Commemoration and reconciliation, two social processes that were diametrically opposed in the aftermath of the Civil War, eventually converged upon a shared, if disguised, racial politics" (132).

Without the means to influence public memory, blacks were left to form and maintain their own collective memory, with slavery as an ever shifting and reconstructed reference point. Slavery has meant different things for different generations of black Americans, but it was always there as a referent. In the 1920s, after the first wave of what has come to be called the "great migration" in the context of a newly forming black public sphere, two distinct frameworks for narrating and giving meaning to the past took form, one progressive and the other tragic. These narrative frameworks were articulated by activists in two social movements, the Harlem renaissance and Garveyism, both of which were directed primarily inward, toward the transformation of racially based collective identity. It was not until the 1950s, even the 1960s, that slavery moved outside group memory to challenge the borders, the rituals and sites, of public memory. Again it was a social movement, the civil rights movement that reopened the sore and helped transform the cultural trauma of a group into a national trauma. Since then and only since then has slavery become part of America's collective memory, not merely that of one of its constituent member's. At the end of the current century the meaning, commemoration, and representation of slavery continues to evoke emotionally charged responses.

## RE-MEMBERING AND FORGETTING

Memories of slavery disgrace the race, and race
perpetuates memories of slavery.

Tocqueville

Four million slaves were liberated at the end of the Civil War. In the first comprehensive historical account written by an American black, George

Washington Williams (1882) offered this description: "Here were four
million human beings without clothing, shelter, homes, and alas! most of
them without names. The galling harness of slavery had been cut off of
their weary bodies, and like a worn out beast of burden they stood in
their tracks scarcely able to go anywhere" (1882, 378).

This was written nearly twenty years after the event and is an act of
remembrance as much as historical writing. The author was part of a literary mobilization within the black middle class that emerged in the
decades after the Civil War. The collective aim of this semicoordinated
movement was to counter the image of blacks being put forward by
whites. As the "full and complete" integration promised by radical
reconstruction gave way to new forms of racial segregation in the South
and elsewhere, such mobilizations were of utmost importance. It was
within the context of such efforts that a new form of racial consciousness
began to take form. In addition to this monumental work, which also
appeared in a condensed "popular" version, Williams produced an
equally monumental history of black soldiers during the Civil War. Along
with these historical works were a few biographies, such as Sarah
Bradford's *Harriet, the Moses of Her People* (1886) a dramatization of
the life of Harriet Tubman, leading black Abolitionist.

While constantly growing in number, the black reading public was not
the prime audience of these and other literary efforts by the few black
authors of the time. The contemporary audience was more likely the sympathetic white reader, in need of bolstering in this reactionary period,
and, one can assume, later generations of blacks who would require alternative histories to those offered by mainstream white society. Thus, these
writers walked a narrow and rocky path between countering white stereotypes and pleasing the tastes and desires of their predominantly white
reading public. Williams's historical accounts, for example, moved
between portraying blacks as victims and depicting them as heroes in the
struggle for racial dignity and recognition. The quotation cited above
begins with the victim, in part as preparation for the heroic message of
racial uplift to follow. It was just as plausible to argue, as sympathetic
white historians later would and contemporary black novelists (who will
be discussed below) were about to, that slavery produced hidden social
networks that permitted blacks not only to survive, but also to maintain
their dignity and traditions. These networks, which some would identify
as a distinct cultural form, were an important resource after emancipation
and reconstruction. As Linda McMurry (1998, 20–21) writes, "On many
plantations and farms, the slave community functioned as an extended

family. In freedom those informal support networks became structurally organized as church groups or benevolent organizations provided aid to families in crisis." Williams painted the former slaves as victims, survivors who would triumph over their condition, proving their worthiness, only to be rejected by a white society busy painting pictures of its own.

Here lie the roots and routes of cultural trauma. For blacks this rejection after the raised hopes engendered by emancipation and reconstruction forced a rethinking of their relation to American society. This was traumatic not only because of the crushed expectations, but also because it necessitated a reevaluation of the past and its meaning regarding individual and collective identity. Many blacks and a few whites had hoped that reconstruction would, if not entirely eliminate race as the basis for identity, at least diminish its significance, as former slaves became citizens, like other Americans, and the caste system associated with servitude disappeared. This was now clearly not the case, making it necessary to reevaluate the meaning of the past and the options available in the future. Once again it would be necessary to attempt to transform tragedy into triumph with the uncovering of new strategies in the struggle for collective recognition, in the face of the threat of marginalization.

Some significant changes had occurred during reconstruction, even if the period later would be viewed as a failure. One of these concerned education and literacy. Along with presenting a military presence, the federal government organized Freedmen's Bureaus in the defeated South designed to aid former slaves, a program that included providing the grounds, if not the sufficient funds, for their formal education as well as that of their offspring. Such funding was aimed at individuals but had a collective effect in that a system of segregated schools sprung up in the South, creating the grounds for a dramatic rise in literacy rates among blacks as well as solidifying a sense of togetherness in seperatness. According to a report published by the commissioner of the bureau, Major General O. O. Howard, in 1870, five years after work had begun "there were 4,239 schools established, 9,307 teachers employed, and 247,333 pupils instructed" (cited in Williams 1882, 385). Such figures reflected only an aspect of this education revolution, as "the emancipated people sustained 1,324 schools themselves, and owned 592 school buildings" (ibid.). The federal program was thus supplemented by self-help, some of which was sponsored by organizations such as the African Methodist Episcopal (A.M.E.) and other black churches. As a result of these efforts, by 1870, "black illiteracy in the South had been reduced to 79.9%" (Christian 1995, 231).

Reconstruction had an ambiguous effect on the black church and its leaders. On the one hand, as blacks were permitted a more active role in public life, the authority of the church and its ministers, long centers of the shadow black community, was eroded. However, as ministers were among the only literate and educated blacks, the role of the black minister, if not the church, was enhanced. As will be discussed, the earliest black newspapers in the South were dominated by ministers. In addition, black churches were central in the organizing and distributing of resources during and after reconstruction. In this the church expanded its role as the center of black social as well as religious life. The two, like the sacred and the secular generally, were intimately entwined.

Along with growing literacy, an improved means of communication helped reinforce a sense of collective identity, as well as common destiny, within this first generation. Benedict Anderson (1991) has argued that it is with the assistance of mass media that "imagined" as well as "real" communities are constituted and sustained. For this generation, newspapers were the most important form of mass media. The growth in literacy, permitted by the education revolution following the end of the war, went hand in hand with the growth of black-owned and -read newspapers. The first black-owned newspaper, *Freedom's Journal,* appeared in New York City in 1827. By the 1850s most northern cities contained at least one black-owned paper, whose prime editorial concern was the abolition of slavery. Between 1865 and the end of reconstruction, 115 Southern-based, black-owned newspapers were started. According to one study (Simmons 1998, 14) the publication of black-owned newspapers in the South "signaled the first change in editorial philosophy—one from freeing slaves to one of reestablishing the racial identity of Afro-Americans and educating them so that they could survive in society." It was through this medium that self-identity could be debated and a new postslavery collective identity articulated.

The success of the failure of reconstruction was an expanding institutional base for sustaining a black community, as segregated schools and newspapers were added to the churches and other counterinstitutions like the conferences and the semisecret societies and fellowships, the Masons and Elks. Two streams existed side by side, one, the drift toward a separate black community within a dominate white society, and the other, the continuing hope that (black) community and (white) society would eventually converge. This consolidating and expanding "Negro World," as Drake and Cayton would later write in their classic study *Black Metropolis* (1945, 116), had existed since the eighteenth century.

"Through the years it had been developing into an intricate web of families, cliques, churches, and voluntary associations." It was, as they write, "the direct result of social rejection by the white society." It was just this rejection that was articulated as cultural trauma in the late nineteenth century and consolidated in the notion of the African American as a distinct "race."

## POPULAR MEMORY, POPULAR CULTURE, AND IDENTITY POLITICS

With the end of the Civil War, slavery was something that was thought by many, black as well as white, best forgotten rather than commemorated. History was not a centerpiece of the new system of education. Former slaves were, as said, more concerned with the future than with remembering slavery as anything more than a means of orienting collective agency. Alexander Crummell, an early supporter of emigration to Africa, who had lived for many years there, liked to distinguish memory from recollection in regard to slavery. On Memorial Day 1885 at Harper's Ferry, where blacks gathered to commemorate John Brown's raid, Crummell told his audience, "What I would fain have you guard against is not the memory of slavery, but the constant recollection of it" (cited in Blight 1997, 161). Popular commemoration by blacks supported this view. Since emancipation, blacks had developed their own political calendar, and where they used that of the dominant culture, as in the example above, they transformed its meaning. Thus, New Year's Day and July 4 commemorated black emancipation, rather than American independence. Slavery, or rather the emancipation from it, was taken as the symbolic starting point for hope of a new relation with American society. At the same time, the grounds of a distinct, and separate, collective consciousness was being formed through such rituals.

Other forms of popular culture carried memories of slavery into future generations. Earlier, the abolitionist movement had provided the context for the publication and spread of the so-called slave narratives, texts written by former slaves about their experiences. The aim of these texts was decidedly political, their primary purpose being to recruit supporters to the antislavery cause. Still, these narratives were the first representations of slavery from the point of view of the victim and had become central to the construction of a counter, collective memory, both in the articulation and resolution of cultural trauma. As representations, the images called forth in these narratives are framed by the circumstances of their production—they are what can be called movement texts—and their reception has varied according to time and place. Even when read as firsthand accounts of slavery, these are moral tales, which identify heroes and villains, giving voice to the pain of subordination as well as faces to the perpetrators. They help in the process of turning victims into agents and tragedy into triumph. For later generations, these narratives have functioned as exemplary texts, examples of a "black literature" and as sources of collective identity, as they recall a common heritage. Their direct political meaning thus has diminished. An exemplary slave narrative that gave voice to the aspirations of the first generation after emancipation was Booker T. Washington's *Up from Slavery* (1901), a book that moves between slave narrative and autobiography in its focus on subjectivity and agency. This tale of willful triumph over adversity is one full of hope for the future, even though it was published at a reactionary age. It would become one of the exemplary texts of what can be described as the progressive narrative, one of two competing frameworks through which black experience in the United States is remembered.

The slave narratives developed into autobiography and adventurous novels at a time when literacy rates were improving for blacks in the United States, and they played a part in the struggle over the memory of slavery. A new generation of black writers emerged out of the small black middle class, giving voice to its aspirations, as well as providing a counter-memory to that which dominated American popular culture. Examples are Paul Dunbar (1872–1906), James Weldon Johnson (1871–1938), Charles Chesnutt (1858–1932), and Frances Harper (1825–1911). What makes such writers constitute a "generation" is not their year of birth so much as their collective articulation of the aspirations of those who had experienced the raised hopes of emancipation and the crushing effects of the failure of reconstruction. Their poetry and fiction objectified, as it represented, the memory of slavery, at the same time as it articulated a generational consciousness formed in the cultural trauma that accompanied the end of reconstruction and the reestablishment of "racially" based otherness.

For this generation of black intellectuals, writers, teachers, journalists, lawyers, and others who thought of themselves as representing the collective by means of the intellect and imagination, questions of representation were intimately bound up with moral and political, as well as aesthetic, concerns. As "race" and the slave past became the prime means through which the collective was identified and more or less forced to identify itself, the issue of how the collective should be represented before and to the dominant white society became increasing central as blacks slowly attained the possibility to represent themselves through cultural means.

To understand this process as traumatic one must recall the racial stereotyping and the shifting grounds of popular memory recurrent in the dominant culture. The ending of reconstruction brought with it a resurgence of nostalgia for the "good old days" of the antebellum South. Popular culture was flooded with images of genteel whites and contented slaves, as minstrel shows and other forms of popular and serious entertainment created the so-called plantation school of literature as well as the roots of what has been called the "cult of the Confederacy" (Foster 1987). It was this conservative and reactionary cultural offensive that the black authors sought to counter with their own representations. Since for the most part whites controlled the means of representation and also made up the overwhelming majority of the reading public, this was indeed a process of delicate negotiation—one that often involved a developed sense of tongue in cheek and double entendre.

## TRAUMA'S DIALECTIC: TRANSFORMING NEGATIVE INTO POSITIVE

The term "New Negro," which in the 1920s would become the title of a groundbreaking collection of literary and artistic works, first appeared in an 1895 newspaper editorial, where it was applied to a "new class of blacks with education, class, and money" that had appeared in the thirty years since the end of the Civil War (Wintz 1988, 31). What the phrase implied was that blacks in increasing numbers had achieved social position of influence in at least some corners of American society and could more freely express feelings of racial pride in public, that is, for white eyes. If one was going to be ascribed racial status, one need not necessarily accept the ranking system of the dominant society—not, that is, if one had some means to counter it. This emerging black middle class was coming of age in a context shaped not by slavery or the hopes and expectations of emancipation, but by the failure of reconstruction and by white backlash. It was gaining a sense of itself, a generational consciousness as well as a racial one, and some cultural capital of its own. This would correspond with the schema of generational memory presented earlier, where it was noted that cultural trauma and the search for resolution would take at least a generation before the most affected groups were in a position to express their feelings publicly.

The late nineteenth century was a period of nation-building, and the notion of the grounds of collective identity for such "imagined" communities was a matter of great interest and debate. Race, by which one meant cultural heritage more than physical characteristics, was often argued as a most useful ground for collective identification. The various immigrant groups streaming into the United States were often referred to as "races." In 1896, speaking in favor of imposing limitations on immigration, U.S. senator Henry Cabot Lodge asked rhetorically what "the matter of race (was) which separates the Englishman from the Hindoo and the American from the Indian." He answered,

> It is something deeper and more fundamental than anything which concerns the intellect. We all know it instinctively, although it is so impalpable we can scarcely define it, and yet it is so deeply marked that even the physiological differences between the Negro, the Mongol, and the Caucasian are not more president or more obvious. When we speak of a race then . . . we mean the moral and intellectual characters, which in their association make the soul of a race, and which represent the product of all its past, the inheritance of all its ancestors, and the motives of all its conduct. The men of each race possess an indestructible stock of ideas, traditions, sentiments, modes of thought, an unconscious inheritance from their ancestors, upon which argument has no effect. What makes a race are their mental and, above all, their moral characteristics, the slow growth and accumulation of centuries of toil and conflict. (quoted in Stocking 1993, 4–16)

The point here is that from the end of reconstruction to the turn of the century, "race," in this very particular sense, was perhaps the most common reference point for collective identity. When the United States vigorously restated its intentions to exclude blacks from full and acknowledged participation in the construction of American society little more than a decade before Lodge was explaining the meaning of race to his colleagues in the Senate, it is not surprising that some black intellectuals seized upon the notion of race to ground the countercollective identity of this once again marginalized group. A leading spokesman for the notion of an African American race was W. E. B. Du Bois (1868–1963), a Harvard-educated sociologist, whose essay collection *The Souls of Black Folk* (1903) became the manifesto of the new Negro movement. While race may have been a pliable concept at the turn of the century, blackness was now firmly associated with subordination and difference in the minds of most white Americans. Popular and "serious" culture had been brought to bear; minstrelsy, literature, and the visual arts had cultivated the association of color with passivity, laziness, naive good humor, child-like behavior, and "primitive" sexuality. To counter these images, intellectuals like Du Bois called upon a section of the educated black middle class, a cultural avant garde he called the "talented tenth," to mount a more concerted counterattack with the means at their disposal. Toward this end, he helped form a core group of intellectuals who became known as the Niagara Movement (1905) and then the National Association for the Advancement of Colored People (NAACP) in 1909–10. Du Bois was appointed editor of the association's periodical, *Crisis,* in which he published short stories by Chesnutt and poems by Johnson alongside more directly political pieces.

As "New Negroes," black intellectuals began an earnest search for some common grounding upon which to secure a new collective identity for American blacks once again degraded by the dominant society. In the process, a long tradition of black separatism, which called for a return to Africa, was transformed into something less radical, a racially based identity that combined African and American elements into something unique, an African American (see Moses 1978). From an African American perspective, blacks in the United States were "Americans by citizenship, political ideals, language, and religion" (Rampersad 1976)—and African in terms of heritage, something that made them members of a "vast historic race" of separate origin from the rest of America. The distinctiveness of American blacks stemmed not from slavery, but rather from an African past, one filled with greatness. It was this and not the circumstances of their coming to America or the "culture" they scratched out of those circumstances that was at the heart of their racial distinctiveness.

Race functions here not only as a unifying concept, but also as one that endows purpose. Being a "sort of seventh son, born with a veil, and gifted with a second-sight in this American world" (Du Bois 1903, 3), the African American had the task to reveal to this still young and unfinished American nation a true picture of itself. Another task was to offer "civilization the full spiritual message they are capable of giving," to become a "co-worker in the kingdom of culture" (ibid.). Race involved the duty of speaking truth to power and of producing greatness. The aim here was to find the positive in the negative, the distinctiveness in the distinction. The trauma of rejection produced the need for positive identification and a plan of action, a cultural praxis as well as political and economic practice. After the hopes of full political participation faded, leaving "the half-free serf weary, wondering, but still inspired" (ibid., 5) another ideal emerged "to guide the unguided" on the path of self-knowledge. Though this, too, proved futile, "the journey at least gave leisure for reflection and self-examination; it changed the child of Emancipation to the youth with dawning self-consciousness, self-realization, self-respect." The race saw itself for the first time, "darkly as through a veil," yet "some faint revelation of [its] power, of [its] mission" emerged (ibid., 6). Du Bois' Hegelian perspective, the coming to be of racial consciousness, was one of the first steps in articulating what I will call the "progressive narrative," wherein slavery would be viewed as a stage, even a necessary one, in a path toward civilization, self-fulfillment, if not acceptance.

Elsewhere in the world, the nation-state was being held up as the ultimate measure and expression of the distinctiveness of a people, and nationalist movements were especially active in Europe. Unlike their European counterparts (the Irish, for example), American blacks "lacked an immediately accessible native language in which to center their cause" (Mishkin 1998, 48). Black speech or dialect was being parodied in popular culture and although Africa was being rediscovered as a cultural and spiritual heritage, there existed no common African language to draw upon. While writers and poets like Dunbar, Chesnutt, and Harper drew upon black dialect and character types, stories, and jokes in their attempts to locate a distinctive folk culture developed through slavery, Du Bois pointed to another sort of language, what he called "sorrow songs" and the underlying humble, good-natured character that slavery had produced and which these songs expressed. While these sorrow songs had African roots, their development was the result of a unique mixture of Africa and America. It was this that grounded the "soul" of a new race, the African American. It was this identity, born of slavery, which united all blacks in the United States, whether they lived in the North or South, in the city or the countryside, whether they were highly educated or had no schooling at all. The Massachusetts-born Du Bois wrote of his experience upon hearing the sorrow songs that expressed this commonality, "Ever since I was a child these songs have stirred me strangely. They came out of a South unknown to me, one by one, and yet at once I knew them as of me and of mine" (Du Bois 1903, 177). Here, as elsewhere in *Souls*, Du Bois spoke through his own experience to that of the "race." Like the slaves themselves, fragmented and dispersed across the continent, a new generation of blacks in America was articulating the trauma of the dashed hopes of reconstruction in a struggle to combat the solidifying national consensus concerning blacks' "otherness." They could consolidate and unify as African Americans, Du Bois reasoned, as they found solace and their common soul in the sorrow songs, as he had.

As he moved the field of struggle to cultural politics, Du Bois could contrast a soulless American culture with a soulful slave culture: "Will America be poorer if she replace her brutal dyspeptic blundering with light-hearted but determined Negro humility? Or her coarse and cruel wit with loving jovial good-humor? Or her vulgar music with the soul of the Sorrow Songs?" (ibid.). His answer was a gently put "no." While Du Bois tended to restrict the positive outcome of slave culture to sorrow songs and a distinctive character type, the next generation would expand it to include an entire way of life. This was a way of turning tragedy into triumph, uncovering a progressive route out of cultural trauma. This cognitive transformation would be articulated in the mid-1920s as a renaissance, by new "New" Negroes.

A USABLE PAST: THE PROGRESSIVE AND TRAGIC NARRATIVES

The First World War brought unforeseen changes in the material and spiritual conditions of blacks in the United States. For one, even though the American military maintained strictly segregated conditions, black soldiers volunteered for service and went into combat with equal enthusiasm as whites. Black Americans were as patriotic as their white counterparts, something that is astonishing given their treatment. Although many of those who volunteered for military service were turned away due to the racial ideas and discriminatory practices of admission boards (this was before the national draft) "more than 400,000 African Americans served in the United States armed forces during World War I, and about half of those saw duty in France" (Stovall 1996, 5). These veterans, filled with an increased sense of national and racial pride, would return to the same segregated America and all the frustrations felt by those left behind.

A year after the war's end the country suffered some of the worst race riots in its history, something that can at least in part be attributed to the perceived threats of a new, urban Negro. At the same time as the triumphant returning black veterans marched up New York's Fifth Avenue, all the way into Harlem, to the strains of an all-black orchestra directed by James Reese Europe, other, equally symbolic, events were taking place. In 1919, twenty-five race riots occurred in northern cities involving direct clashes between whites and blacks, something that would distinguish the riots from later occurrences, which were largely internal to black neighborhoods. In Chicago alone, thirty-eight persons, black and white, were killed, and five hundred were injured. In the South, there was a distinct rise in the number of lynchings, which could be attributed to the threat posed by returning veterans. Eighty-five blacks were lynched in 1919 in what was called the "Red Summer of Hate," as the KKK organized "over 200 meetings throughout the country" (Christian 1995, 316). Writing in the *Crisis,* Walter White listed the following as causes to the rioting: "racial prejudice, economic competition, political corruption and exploitation of the Negro voter, police inefficiency, newspaper lies about Negro crime, unpunished crimes against Negroes, housing, and reaction of whites and Negroes from war" (quoted in Christian 1995, 317).

In addition to the return of veterans and the raised expectations for integration and acceptance, other changes were occurring in the black population. Stimulated by the war, developments in farm production were changing the rural workforce, creating a significant decrease in the need for unskilled manual labor. The production of cotton, the mainstay of black labor, was particularly affected. These and other factors, such as the need for unskilled industrial labor in northern cities, precipitated what has come to be called the "great migration," a population shift of such magnitude that it would change the conditions of African Americans forever. In a period of sixty years (1910–70) more than six and a half million black Americans would move northward, shifting from farm to industrial work and from rural to urban living. During World War I alone, "the black population of the North increased by almost 80 percent, from 900,000 to 1.6 million. Another 350,000 African Americans joined the armed forces, and many of these soldiers resettled in the North after the war" (Barlow 1999, 16). In Chicago the black population increased 148 percent between 1910 and 1920; Columbus, Ohio, increased 74 percent; and Philadelphia, St. Louis, Kansas City, and Indianapolis all expanded their black populations by about 50 percent in the same period (Christian 1995: 319). This population shift wrought major changes in the social conditions of African Americans. For black authors, artists, and intellectuals, the shift helped produce a new audience and a new self-confidence. In 1920, New York's Harlem "contained approximately 73,000 blacks (66.9 percent of the total number of blacks in the borough of Manhattan); by 1930 black Harlem had expanded . . . and housed approximately 164,000 blacks (73.0 percent) of Manhattan's blacks" (Wintz 1988, 20).

What could be called a black public sphere emerged as urban areas expanded to accommodate the waves of migrants arriving from the southern regions of the country and soldiers home from war. Within the neighborhoods that were created or transformed, small clubs and meeting halls, restaurants, movie houses, theaters, and dance halls sprung up

in the teeming black sections of Chicago, Detroit, Cleveland, and Philadelphia. Forms of popular entertainment were created as the newly arrived refitted their ways of life to fit the urban environment. In a sense,
one could say that this new urban public sphere expanded upon and
competed with the much smaller ones created and maintained by the
educated black middle class of the previous generation. While the book
clubs, lyceums, concerts, and theater that helped constitute the previous
generation had been limited to a small elite with intimate knowledge of
each other and maintained through networks that built on face-to-face
contact, this new black public was more anonymous and open. Further,
what previously had been carried and motivated by small groups and
exemplary individuals was now borne by collective movements of a different type. There existed a tension between these social formations, one
exclusionary and personal and the other open and anonymous, that
would express itself in part as a generational struggle between an aging
new Negro and a younger offspring in the 1920s.

The development of concentrated and literate black populations facilitated the emergence of social and cultural movements that would articulate as well as signal a new social awareness and a revisioning of the collective past. The urban environment opened blacks to intellectual and
political impulses, such as the cultural radicalism of Greenwich Village
and the political radicalism associated with it: socialism and communism, as well as nationalism. These processes were interconnected
through a range of magazines, journals, and newspapers that served to
link the wide-ranging and socially diverse racial community, and through
which "race leaders" sought to influence the formation of the collective
identity. Periodicals included Marcus Garvey's *Negro World,* A. Philip
Randolph and Charles Owen's socialist *Messenger,* both of which began
publication in 1917. Randolph, who would found the all-black Brotherhood of Sleeping Car Porters Union in 1925, was the son of slaves, while
Garvey was a Jamaican immigrant.

Besides the *Crisis,* which remained under Du Bois' editorship, another
journal central to the development of the Harlem renaissance was
*Opportunity: Journal of Negro Life,* founded in 1923 as the organ of the
National Urban League. Its editor was Charles S. Johnson, a University
of Chicago–trained sociologist born in 1893 and coauthor of *The Negro
in Chicago* (1922), which followed the path opened by Du Bois' *The
Philadelphia Negro* in providing a professional, sociological, and social
work perspective on urban blacks. *Opportunity* was the organizer of literary prizes for promising young blacks. It was at the first awards dinner

in 1925 that the poet Langston Hughes met the anthropologist Zora Neale Hurston for the first time, as they were each awarded prizes, as was Countee Cullen, whose poems are discussed below. There emerged, simultaneously, a developing interest in black history, literature, and art, especially within the smaller circles of the growing urban African American middle class, and a market for a race-oriented consumer culture. Additionally, the new, urban environment opened blacks to aesthetic movements like cultural radicalism; the bohemian lifestyle and modernist ideology of Greenwich Village, with its interest in "primitivism"; and to a new mass consumer culture. More directly, political movements and ideologies such as socialism and communism also found their way into these urban black communities. Along with new forms of black nationalism, they would compete for the attention of a black population in a period of great fluctuation.

## TWO VOICES

Out of this exciting cacophony, two guiding frameworks emerged that would prove resilient in providing a cognitive map for mediating the past, present, and future orientation of the new, urban Negro. The cultural-political movement that has become known as the Harlem renaissance articulated a modernist, progressive narrative framework in which the past was interpreted as a stepping-stone toward a brighter future. And a social movement identified through the name of its leader, Marcus Garvey, gave voice to a traditionalist-romantic, tragic narrative framework, in which the past was something to be redeemed through the future. These narrative frames structured alternative ways of regarding the African and the American, as well as the meaning of slavery. These frames were articulated in a context wherein generational experience and social class were significant factors in understanding both their emergence and their acceptance.

> Someone is always at my elbow reminding me that I am a granddaughter of slaves. It fails to register depression with me. Slavery is sixty years in the past. The operation was successful and the patient is doing well, thank you. The terrible struggle that made an American out of a potential slave said "On the line!" The Reconstruction said "Get set!"; and the generation before me said "Go!" I am off to a flying start and I must not halt in the stretch to look behind and weep. Slavery is the price I paid for civilization, and the choice was not with me. It is a bully adventure and worth all that I paid through my ancestors for it. (Zora Neale Hurston, 1928, quoted in Watson 1995)

A core figure in the Harlem renaissance, Hurston (1891–1960) voices a modernist approach to the past, filtered through a narrative that is evolutionary and progressive. This is a past that points to the future. Slavery is not here forgotten, but is regarded as a usable past, an experience that can be appropriated. As heritage and tradition, the slave past can and should be collected, written down, and written about, as Hurston and others went on to do. Conceived as folk culture and compiled as source material, the past can be mined and used, a form of cultural capital to which blacks could be argued to have privileged access. From such a perspective, re-collecting the past could also be considered valuable activity, not only from the standpoint of racial pride. From an evolutionary perspective, preserving artifacts from an earlier way of life, one possibly threatened with extinction, could be viewed as socially, politically, and professionally useful. A progressive and evolutionary perspective views the past with the attitude of the outsider, though in Hurston's case, the outsider is also an insider. Raised in the small, black town of Eatonville, Florida, Hurston studied anthropology with Franz Boas at Barnard College in New York and under his direction would return to her birthplace and other areas of the South to collect this now exotic material. Together with the poet Langston Hughes (1902–1967), Hurston would return south in search of material for a play under the auspices of a wealthy white New York patron, as she would do later with the help of the W.P.A.

Here the collective past is usable in at least two senses: it is central to the maintenance of group identity, part of a collective memory, and it is source material, a cultural resource for a distinct aesthetic, explored and exploited not only by members of the group itself but by others as well. This applied equally to the visual arts. In the cultural politics of the renaissance, culture was a weapon in the struggle for racial recognition and acceptance. Many hours and pages had been spent discussing the relation between art and propaganda and "how should the Negro be represented" in aesthetic terms. Through the active intervention of Charles Johnson and Alain Locke, critic and central mediator in the representation of the Harlem renaissance, Aaron Douglas, a young, college-educated high school art teacher from Kansas, was recruited to visualize the New Negro and his/her historical coming-to-be. Following a path laid out by his mentor W. Reiss, a white, European modernist portrait artist, Douglas set out to transform internalized American ideals that identified beauty with European features and whiteness. European modernism had recently discovered Africa, and Reiss encouraged Douglas to do the same. Douglas's Africa centered on the Nile and Egyptian painting, with its flat, elongated bodies and faces drawn in profile. As one of the few black artists, Douglas not only painted but also was called upon to illustrate the novels and poetry of his fellow renaissance authors. His art deco illustrations are probably the most well known, with their lush primitive themes and flatly drawn figures.

Douglas was primarily a mural painter, and it is here that the progressive narrative behind his work is most apparent. In the murals he painted at Fisk University, black history is presented as progressive and evolutionary. While the African scenes are depicted as idyllic, they are also primitive, though in the positive sense of the term; figure and surroundings meld together in a natural, organic totality. These scenes are imagined and painted through a modernist prism, exotic and colorful, although in Douglas's work these colors tend to be muted, more like Modigliani than Gauguin. His contemporary images carried traces of this rhythmical, exotic primitivism, but he often introduced a political comment, such as the threatening noose that hangs down in the center of a cabaret in *Charleston,* an illustration that appeared in Paul Morand's *Black Magic* in 1929. Douglas's depictions of slavery, particularly in the murals *An Idyll of the Deep South* and *Slavery Through Reconstruction,* both from 1934, are done in the same style, idyllic in its depiction of the slave community, where oppression is amended by collective solidarity, expressed through work, music, and struggle. In all of these, the past is an essential link to the present/future but nothing to redeem or return to.

As it was for Douglas, Africa provided an important resource in this generation's search for identity. In the progressive narrative, Africa appears not so much as a geographical place, somewhere to actually escape to, but as metaphor for a long lost and forgotten past. This can be seen in the following poem by Countee Cullen, which appeared in the Urban League's *Survey Graphic* and then in *The New Negro,* both edited and introduced by Alain Locke in 1925.

What is Africa to me:
Copper sun and scarlet sea,
Jungle star or jungle track,
Strong bronzed men, or regal black
Women from whose loins I sprang
When the birds of Eden sang?
One three centuries removed
From the scenes his father loved,
Spicy grove, cinnamon tree,
What is Africa to me?

itle of Cullen's poem, is revealing in itself. As part of
nstitution of collective memory, the concept of her-
mension to reinterpreting the slave past by looking
ing more glorious. It places emphasis on the African
relationship between the African and the American.
As heritage, this past is still meant to be useful in the present, something
of which one sings and re-visions in order to look forward toward the
future, but it is something more than a stepping-stone. The "strong
bronzed men" and "regal black women" are "three centuries removed"
but can be called upon to orient and solidify a community facing quite
another world. It is the African, rather than the slave, culture that is the
heritage of African American. It is a different Africa that is called upon in
the tragic reconstruction of historical memory. The tragic and redemptive
narrative that guided Garveyism and other forms of black nationalism
viewed Africa as the homeland and would drop the American altogether.

## TRAGIC NARRATIVE

The same urban public sphere in which this progressive narrative was
articulated produced an alternative, tragic and redemptive, narrative
frame. This narrative took form in conjunction with the development of
an internationally based movement for Pan Africanism, a form of black
nationalism with roots in the previous generation of American blacks,
including W. E. B. Du Bois. This international movement was articulated
locally through a broad-based social movement associated with the
Jamaican-born Marcus Garvey and his United Negro Improvement Association (UNIA). The international basis of the movement was reflected
in the figure of Marcus Garvey himself, in the role of West Indians in the
reconstruction of black collective identity in this period. Like some
groups of European immigrants, some West Indians brought with them
an anticolonialist perspective, as well as an openness to ideologies like
marxism and socialism. Garvey had come to the United States looking
for support in the racial self-help philosophy of Booker T. Washington
but ended up in Harlem as the leader of what has been called the largest
black-based social movement in the history of the United States.

The grounding aim of the UNIA was "to promote the spirit of race
pride and love; to reclaim the fallen of the race; to administer to and
assist the needy; to assist in civilizing the backward tribes of Africa; to
strengthen the imperialism of independent African States; to establish
Commissionaires or Agencies in the principal countries of the world for

the protection of all Negroes, irrespective of nationality" (quoted in Moses 1978, 19).

Speaking on Emancipation Day in 1922, Garvey began:

> Fifty-nine years ago Abraham Lincoln signed the Emancipation Proclamation declaring four million Negroes in this country free. Several years prior to that Queen Victoria of England signed the Emancipation Proclamation that set at liberty hundreds of thousands of West Indian Negro slaves. West Indian Negroes celebrate their emancipation on the first day of August of every year. The American Negroes celebrate their emancipation on the first of January of every year . . . We are the descendants of the men and women who suffered in this country for two hundred and fifty years under the barbarous, the brutal institution known as slavery. You who have not lost trace of your history will recall the fact that over three hundred years ago your fore-bearers were taken from the great Continent of Africa and brought here for the purpose of using them as slaves. Without mercy, without any sympathy they worked our fore-bearers. They suffered, they bled, they died. But with their sufferings, with their blood, which they shed in their death, they had a hope that one day their posterity would be free, and we are assembled here tonight as the children of their hope. . . . each and everyone of you have a duty which is incumbent upon you; a duty that you must perform, because our fore-bearers who suffered, who bled, who died had hopes that are not yet completely realized . . . No better gift can I give in honor of the memory of the love of my fore-parents for me, and in gratitude of the sufferings they endured that I might be free; no grander gift can I bear to the sacred memory of the generation past than a free and redeemed Africa—a monument for all eternity—for all times. (Garvey in Lewis 1994, 26–27)

This is a different view of the slave past than the one offered by Zora Neal Hurston and others associated with the Harlem renaissance. In Hurston's account slavery was a stepping-off point for evolutionary development. Framed through a progressive narrative, the past was a stepping-stone to the present/future and opened up for scientific excavation, for ethnological and archeological expeditions looking for traces and remnants, which could be collected and perhaps even used by those at a new stage of development. Garveyism was neither progressive nor scientific in the sense meant here, although it did contain elements of a civilizing mission. The future will look more like the past in his account; the aim of present action is to restore and renew lost glory. Rather than catalog and trace the steps out of the past, Garvey holds the past up as a model, a vision that will regenerate the present and the future. This is not a progressive vision but one of tragedy and redemption, of loss and retrieval. While Hurston's ethnological perspective required that the past be treated with respect, as evidence and as resource, Garvey's past

demanded retribution. Slavery, which now would also include colonialism, was more than theft and the loss of freedom in forced labor; it
denied a people their dreams and stripped them of their civilization. This
lost generation now had to be redeemed by their progeny. Slavery in
other words created a duty to redeem the memory of enslaved.

These two narratives formed two opposing and often opposed ways
of relating the past to the present and future. United by the primal scene
of slavery and the previous generation's attempts to deal with the trauma
of rejection, each in its own way served as the basis for collective identity,
by linking the individual to the collective through the concept of racial
pride and the role of culture in that process. With their respective interpretations of the past they offered different paths to the future, however.
The progressive evolutionary view articulated by Hurston pointed
toward eventual integration into American society, on the basis of racial
regeneration made possible through sifting the past for present use. The
tragic-redemptive narrative pointed to a racial nation in a revitalized
Africa.

These perspectives on the slave past were fashioned by small groups of
intellectuals, in what Karl Mannheim would call "generational units,"
which were largely restricted to urban environments. In some sense, they,
especially the Harlem renaissance, could be called an avant garde of a
new generation. This was, however, a different sort of avant garde than
the "talented tenth" envisioned by Du Bois and others of the previous
generation for whom "culture" reflected and re-presented the best and
the brightest of the race. This view of black culture was rejected by
younger members of the Harlem renaissance in favor of a modernism
that was at once "primitive" and realistic, creating an idyllic past as it
represented the present, warts and all. Through incorporating folk traditions, such as jokes, folktales ("Hell: Ginny Gall way off in Ginny Gall/
where you have to eat cow cunt, skin and all," Hurston, cited in Watson
1995), and blues music into high cultural forms, such as poetry and
painting, and including sexuality, desire, and everyday life as significant
content, this avant garde younger generation blurred the borders drawn
by their elders, as they reached out to and drew inspiration from, the
surrounding mass black public. Its leadership was not exemplary in the
same way, manner, or form as the moralistic, religious, and Euro-
centered talented tenth. There were exceptions, of course—Countee
Cullen being one—and overlaps, but there were, as I discuss below, great
tensions between these two conceptions of racial representation and their
respective views and uses of the past. Africa and the slave past were

present as reference points for both, as that from which we came, but were interpreted in different ways by the different generations. The older generation found such language as Hurston's (recorded above) embarrassing and demeaning, just as they did blues lyrics and performance. For Du Bois and the generation formed by reconstruction and its failed promise of integration, the cultural trauma generated by the failures of reconstruction and the marginalization it engendered created a standpoint and a filter through which to judge present practice, which constituted a distinct generational habitus. For the new generation, the past, as Hurston expressed it, was a jumping-off point, a starting block in the race toward the future, which, because it looked black, was an open door.

Although offering another way of viewing the past, Garveyism was also optimistic about the future, but with another outcome in mind. Here Africa was a place to return to, a home in more than the spiritual sense. Rather than viewing Africa through the lens of modernism, Garveyism was traditionalist and mystical. Ethiopia was both a real place and the site of spiritual redemption: "We as a people, have a great future before us; Ethiopia shall once more see her day of glory" (cited in Moses 1978, 267). The uniforms and rituals of the Garvey movement reflected this nineteenth-century traditionalist view, as much as they did the fantasies of Garvey's predominantly working-class followers. They were part of a backward-looking movement into the future. As opposed to the progressive narrative for whom the slave past was negated by a future that transcended it, in Garvey's tragic narrative, the future realized rather than negated the past.

## CIVIL RIGHTS AND MODERNIZED BLACK NATIONALISM: THE POSTWAR GENERATION

These narrative frames developed out of the cultural trauma initiated by the failure of emancipation and then renewed in a continuous cycle of raised and crushed expectations. Transmitted as collective memory, they organized experience, providing cognitive maps that guided present actions. As such they could be transmitted from one generation to the next and, in the process, reworked and revived to fit new situations and needs. It perhaps should be repeated that "cultural trauma" is a process, one that in this case was kept in motion through the continual degradation and marginalization of American blacks. The specific content of the trauma varied, as it is articulated, given voice and image in different his-

torical circumstances. In the 1960s two social movements, civil rights
and a modernized black nationalism, provided a context for their revi-
talization. These two movements, here exemplified through two who
most visibly represented them, Martin Luther King Jr. and Malcolm X, at
once reflected the changes that American society and its black minority
had undergone since the end of the Second World War and the continued
reworking of the trauma of rejection as the basis of collective memory.
These movements were shaped in part by a new social and historical context in which the United States assumed the role of political, economic,
and, most important, moral world leader. The image of the United States
was one of a democratic nation, in which the notion of individual freedom and the right to participate in the pursuit of happiness were central
pillars in the legitimization of this role. The new role and self-image
affected domestic relations, increasing pressures to include blacks both
culturally and politically, adding leverage to the claims by blacks as marginalized second-class citizens. It was such claims, and their remedy, that
the two social movements articulated, and in this sense they expressed a
continuity with the past.

The development of electronic mass media, especially color television, added a new factor in the representation of the present and remembrance of the past. Television, which seemed to offer an authentic representation of events as they occurred, would play a central role in the
development of these social movements, including the lives of their most
visible representatives/representors. Television also helped in changing
the perception of Africa by bringing images of waves of anticolonial
movements that swept the continent in the 1960s into American homes.
These movements would have a dramatic impact on American race relations. Through this medium and the more traditional means of communication, such as the press and the public meeting, national and international movements contributed significantly in the struggle to articulate
and define "blackness" and the African American, the preferred names
and collective identities that would constitute the postwar generation. In
this struggle, the meaning and memory of slavery and the failure of
emancipation to fully integrate American blacks would remain the point
of departure of collective memory and identity formation, as the primal
scene of cultural trauma.

The great northward migration and the urbanization of blacks in both
the North and the South continued after the Second World War, leading
to an ever-greater concentration of America's black population. This
encouraged a modernization of Garveyism and other forms of black

nationalism developed by previous generations, a process that Malcolm
X both expressed and represented, but which came to fruition after his
death in 1965 in the black power community control movements in the
urban ghettos. A key factor in this modernization was the birth of a
"new" Africa, as anticolonial movements spread across the continent in
the 1960s and inspired a new generation of American blacks. As previously, these forms of black nationalism centered in the continually
expanding northern urban ghettos and were internally oriented to articulating and organizing this "community." As social movements, they
developed their own institutions and cultures, from religious temples and
self-defense to ways of dress, talk, marriage, and child rearing. Here
"blackness" came to be associated with liberating oneself from the ways
imposed by the "white devil," especially through religious teaching and
education. These movements more and more came to represent themselves through uncompromising images of moral, mental, and physical
toughness, which many, if not most, whites considered aggressive and
threatening. For Malcolm X these representations offered a role model
for oppressed and "brainwashed" urban blacks: "We Muslims regarded
ourselves as moral and mental and spiritual examples for other black
Americans" (Haley 1965, 396), making imagery and representation a
form of exemplary action. For the developing feminist consciousness,
these movements were considered to represent and be dominated by male
values and by educated, middle-class blacks as ghetto or street culture,
one that was at the same time attractive and repelling, a continued sign
of social maladjustment as well as an outcome of marginalization and
racist exclusion perpetrated by the dominant society. These images, no
matter how they were interpreted, were projected and magnified through
television and other mass media, in which the phrase "black power" and
the image of the leather-clad, bereted man with a rifle complemented the
pursed lips and tough words of Malcolm X and Amiri Baraka. This
image of blackness contrasted sharply with that promoted by the civil
rights movement, whose "good Negro" was represented either in suit or
bib overalls and cotton dress, armed with a Bible and espousing nonvio-
lent, Christian love.

What became known as the civil rights movement was by tradition
and intention rooted in interaction with whites and white society. Its
audience and its activists were multiracial and inclusionary. The black
leaders it produced could mediate between black and white worlds. The
movement exemplified Du Bois' "double consciousness," as well as the
desire for integration, a concept that nationalists like Malcolm X

ridiculed. Drawing on a tradition of protest reaching back to abolition-ism, the civil rights movement was rooted in the black church as much as in organizations like the NAACP and the Urban League. While the latter included whites as members, the black church developed its own reli-gious traditions largely separate from white institutions, especially con-cerning day-to-day activities. The civil rights movement also developed its own internal media and means of communication, but it was from the beginning directly engaged with whites. The landmark decision by the Supreme Court in 1954, which questioned the constitutionality of segre-gated schools, created a new sense of possibility. Martin Luther King Jr. explained its importance this way: "Along with the emergence of a 'New Negro,' with a new sense of dignity and destiny, came that memorable decision of May 17, 1954 . . . This decision came as a legal and socio-logical death blow to an evil that had occupied the throne of American life for several decades" (King 2003, 137–38). The movement began with protest concerning public transportation, reaching back to Ida Wells and others in the nineteenth century, and with boycotts of white stores and other services. Its demands concerned the inclusion of blacks, and its vision of America was decidedly along the lines specified in the Constitu-tion and the Bill of Rights: "one nation, indivisible, with freedom and justice for all."

The black church, as mentioned earlier, originated in response to the segregationist policies of white religious denominations and developed parallel to them. As perhaps no other institution in American society, the southern black church embodied the cultural legacy of slavery and the hope of its transcendence. Through the ritualized performance of sermon and song, the southern black church recalled the slave past as it re-membered the black community. The largest denomination and the most central in the civil rights movement was the Baptist Church, which par-ticularly retained a southern basis, as well as rural flavor. Baptist minister Martin Luther King Jr. exemplified the role of the prophet in the church's Old Testament theology, as he set out to redeem the soul of America. What became the movement's representation of "the good Negro" was southern and rural, the hard-working, former slave who now wanted the full citizenship promised with emancipation. This was an image congen-ial to many whites, especially in the North. Even northern blacks who traveled south to participate in the movement found this image appealing and took it on; Harvard-educated Bob Moses even changed his name to fit the biblical references and worldview that guided the movement.

King rose to national prominence with the Montgomery bus boycott, an event that served to catalyze what is now called the civil rights movement. In many ways this movement and Martin Luther King Jr. himself exemplified the progressive narrative. As the movement developed, its aim was to include blacks as first-class American citizens. King often expressed this demand in his sermons and speeches. King opened his first public address, a speech given at the Holt Street Baptist Church directly after Rosa Parks's arrest in December 1955, with "You are American citizens." He later continued, "This is the glory of our democracy. . . . If we are wrong, the Constitution of the United States is wrong. If we are wrong, God almighty is wrong!" In his sympathetic and incisive analysis of King's sermons and preaching techniques, Richard Lischer (1995, 148) reveals that King's sermonic material "reflects the same world-view and ethos to which white Baptists, Methodists, and Presbyterians had long been accustomed, the Brotherhood of Man and the Fatherhood of God." This view he received from his mentors within the black church and he revitalized and re-voiced to fit the needs of mobilization in the struggle to include blacks into this brotherhood on the secular plane of American society. One of the tasks King was to perform was to transform the traditions of the black church to fit the framework of the progressive narrative and to convince his fellow blacks to act according to its aims. He mobilized and motivated within the framework set by this narrative. "His goal", according to Lischer, "was the merger of black aspirations into the American dream" (142). To achieve this, King at times criticized the black church and some of his fellow ministers for passivity regarding the struggle for inclusion and civil rights; one must remember that the majority of ministers, especially in the South, were conservative and even opposed to King and *his* movement. Such publicly expressed criticism was made only before black audiences, however. Further, King had to convince those blacks who accepted the goals of inclusion and were willing to actively participate in the movement that nonviolence was the best way to achieve this end. Here it was not so much motivation that was necessary, but more a brake on the choice and use of more aggressive means.

The point is that what I've called the progressive narrative provided a framework for making action meaningful in a different way from the traditional messages of black religion, yet still within bounds set by them. As exemplified in the sermons of Martin Luther King Jr., the narrative frame enabled the mixing of the sacred and secular in ways that black religion had done since the slave era, with a message that combined sustenance here and now with hope for a better, more just future. This future was usually understood to be on earth as in heaven, that is, there was no sharp gap between the world of man and the world of God. Black preachers can be divided between the "sustainers" and the "reformers." The former was a tradition begun with the slave preachers, slave converts to Christianity and (later) free Black preachers, who "stimulate(d) hope while deferring reward" as they "projected a heavenly vision against the dark, low ceilings of slavery and segregation" (ibid., 29). This preaching strategy does not necessarily have to be cased as "otherworldly," "pie in the sky," or as the "opiate of the people." It can be seen as a strategy for sustaining human dignity for a people "not yet able to act and thereby avert(ing) the disaster of premature revolution" (Gayraud Wilmore in Lischer 1995, 29). Because of the constant threat of violence and the subordinate position of blacks generally, "sustaining" always contained a political dimension, in that the maintenance of hope in such a situation is always subversive. What the civil rights movement did was to take this hope beyond the walls of the church in a more collectively active way. This was a strategy that identified the reformer, a role that King learned from his own minister-father, Martin Luther King Sr., who, like many black ministers, combined sustaining with a more active engagement with the wider condition of blacks in American society.

The progressive narrative frame was flexible enough to contain the sustaining and reforming aspects of the black church in the move toward collective action. The movement itself took over the role that the individual minister had earlier played. Christian doctrine and nonviolence provided the sustaining, proving the moral worthiness of the movement activist. Nonviolence and a Christian worldview provided a moral high ground from which to reveal the immorality, the evilness, of segregation and the goodness of integration. Movement activists were thus doing God's work in bringing justice to the world. This strategy of inclusion thus included whites, not only as activists on the side of justice, but also those whites who currently opposed the movement, for in the end, they would inhabit a better world. This inclusion involved an underlying belief in conversion at the base of King's strategy. As opposed to the views of Malcolm X, who saw whites as "devils," enemies incapable of seeing the potential goodness in a new world that included blacks as equals, King's Christian beliefs were based on the hope not only of inclusion but also upon the conversion of enemies into brothers.

It was in this context that the new, modernizing Africa became important not so much as a root of culture and certainly not as the site of redemption, but as a symbol for freedom. This changed view of Africa, sparked by the anticolonialist movements of the early 1960s, marks a clear difference between this and the previous generation. What King found in Africa was "a throbbing desire; there seems to be an internal desire for freedom within the soul of every man" (King 2003), a universalistic notion that he found expressed in Montgomery and in the civil rights movement as a whole. This is a form of freedom based in the individual and in self-determination at the individual, rather than collective, level. The collective, the community, was a means to this end, not the end itself.

The community is one born and borne of necessity, out of segregation, and it is a source of strength and an agent of liberation, if not yet freedom. The basis of the community is the congregation, but its roots are wider, reaching back to slavery and to an ascribed racial identity, that is, to the historically reflective process of collective memory and to cultural trauma. History had created the black community, just as segregation had created the black church. It is this historical memory, accumulated over years of struggle and humiliation, that King recalls and calls upon to gather this community to collective action:

> We have . . . seen the old order in our own nation, in the form of segregation and discrimination. We know something of the long history of this old order in America. It had its beginning in the year 1619 when the first Negro slaves landed on the shores of this nation. . . . The great tragedy of physical slavery was that it led to mental slavery. So long as the Negro maintained this subservient attitude and accepted this "place" assigned to him, a sort of racial piece existed. . . . Then something happened to the Negro. Circumstances made it necessary for him to travel more. His rural plantation background was gradually being supplanted by migration to urban and industrial communities. His economic life was gradually rising to decisive proportions. His cultural life was gradually rising through the steady decline of crippling illiteracy. All of these factors conjoined to cause the Negro to take a new look at himself. Negro masses began to reevaluate themselves. The Negro came to feel he was somebody. (King 2003, 136–37)

Just as Du Bois recognized himself in the sorrow songs of slave, which gave voice to the hope of redemption as well as weariness with the present condition, King uncovers the collective in a shared history of humiliation and the desire for freedom that began with slavery. The dream that was by this time shattered was one King articulated earlier in his famous "I have a dream" speech. This too was part of a heritage rooted in the black church and colored by the memory and image of slavery.

Through his sermons and speeches, King linked the individual to the collective, just as he reinvented a black religious tradition through their performance. Through drawing upon set formulas and phrases, common points of reference and association, and couching them in familiar musical speech patterns, King linked the individual and collective, the past and the present, as he "transformed the prosaic discouragement of his audiences into the poetry of a Movement" (Lischer 1995, 104). Whether he quoted from Paul Dunbar or James Weldon Johnson or lifted phrases from the Bible or Shakespeare, King used a formulaic speech that turned the I into the We and the mundane into the historically significant. "His audiences would cheer when he *began* one of his set pieces the way fans respond to the first bars of their favorite song at a rock concert. The formulas not only verified the identity of the speaker; they also guaranteed a collaborative role for the hearer in an important moment of history" (ibid., 104).

Slavery was the first point of reference and inclusion into the American dream, the end point around which all revolved. As the dream faded, the references became more "black": "Too many Negroes are ashamed of themselves, ashamed of being black. A Negro gotta rise up and say from the bottom of his soul, 'I am somebody. I have a rich, noble, and proud heritage. However exploited and however pained my history has been, I'm black, but *I'm black and beautiful*' " (ibid., 101). Yet his narrative frame and that of the civil rights movement as a whole remained progressive and inclusionary. Toward the end of his life, as the frustrations stemming from the failures of white society and increasing violent resistance and corresponding calls for black power by a younger generation of activists, King may have more and more played the role of prophet, venting his and others' rage against American society, emphasizing its shortcomings rather than its promise, but this was done within the narrative of universal deliverance and a philosophy of Christian love. As Lischer puts it, "deliverance and love were needed by everyone in America" (217). Here he was more like Marx, who believed that the liberation of the oppressed proletariat would also entail the liberation of their oppressors.

## MALCOLM X AND MODERNIZATION
## OF AMERICAN BLACK NATIONALISM

The story of Malcolm X is well known, having been reconstructed for and by Alex Haley (1965) in a posthumously published best-selling autobiography and represented on film by Spike Lee. The white world first heard of the Nation of Islam's minister Malcolm X through the local New York broadcast of a television news program called "The Hate That Hate Produced" in 1959. Born in Omaha, Nebraska, in 1925, with the family name Little, Malcolm X was assassinated in Harlem in 1965. Like others of his generation, his life was shaped not only by skin color and gender, which conditioned his participation in the migration to the northeast, but also by the Great Depression and the Second World War. Malcolm inherited his late developing nationalism from his father, a Baptist minister and Garvey supporter, whose apparent murder at the hands of white racists represented an individual trauma for the six-year-old Malcolm. Malcolm recounts,

> I remember seeing the big, shiny photographs of Marcus Garvey that were passed from hand to hand. My father had a big envelope of them that he always took to these meetings. The pictures showed what seemed to me millions of Negroes thronged in parade behind Garvey riding in a fine car, a big black man dressed in a dazzling uniform with gold braid on it, and he was wearing a thrilling hat with tall plumes. I remember hearing that he had followers not only in the United States but all around the world, and I remember how the meetings always closed with my father saying, several times, and the people chanting after him, "Up, you mighty race, you can accomplish what you will!" (Haley 1965, 85)

As a teenager, Malcolm migrated to Boston to live with an older half-sister. Here, despite his sister's efforts to push him in the direction of middle-class inclusion, Malcolm discovered the excitement of urban ghetto life. He became a small-time hustler, for whom regular work was called a "slave" and considered something only fools or status conscious blacks would pursue. He worked as a shoe shine boy, a railroad porter, and a dish washer, only to better allow him to negotiate his hustle and "hip" lifestyle. Eventually this led him to New York and to Harlem, the center not of black art and culture, but of the hustle and the game. Imprisoned along with a friend and their two white women for robbery, Malcolm avoided direct participation in the war. In prison, he discovered Islam and the teachings of Elijah Muhammad. According to his own account this occurred through the efforts of his younger brothers and sisters, who, now living in Detroit, had become Muslim activists. He began corresponding with Elijah Muhammad, and by the time of his release had himself become a convert.

His years of correspondence with Elijah Muhammad created a bond between them and an entry into the inner circle of the religious movement. Putting his street knowledge and hustling skills to work in the movement's service, Malcolm X was soon rewarded with the title of "minister" and the role of chief organizer. He moved from city to city laying the groundwork for new temples through his recruiting talents. In part due to his efforts, the organization grew from a sect to a movement, as temples were established in most major cities with a large black population. The prime sources of recruits were the poorest sections of the ghettoes and the prisons, where blacks greatly outnumbered whites. Favorite targets were the recent migrants who peopled the storefront Christian churches. "We went 'fishing' fast and furiously when those little evangelical storefront churches let out their thirty to fifty people on the sidewalk. . . . These congregations were usually Southern migrant people, usually older, who would go anywhere to hear what they called 'good preaching'" (Haley, 318–19).

What Malcolm X offered potential recruits was "good preaching" — about how the "white devil" used Christianity to keep blacks enslaved — and an alternative religion created for and by blacks. At the core of these sermons, at least in this stage of recruitment, was what Malcolm called "the dramatization of slavery" (ibid., 312):

> I know you don't realize the enormity, the horrors, of the so-called *Christian* white man's crime. . . . Not even in the *Bible* is there such a crime! God in His wrath struck down with *fire* the perpetrators of *lesser* crimes! *One hundred million* of us black people! Your grandparents! Mine! *Murdered* by this white man. To get fifteen million of us here to make us his slaves, on the way he murdered one hundred million! I wish it was possible for me to show you the sea bottom in those days—the black bodies, the blood, the bones broken by boots and clubs! The pregnant black women who where thrown overboard if they got too sick! Thrown overboard to the sharks that had learned that following these slave ships was the way to grow fat! (ibid., 311)

Dramatic images of slavery acted as a magnet to draw new recruits to a new religion, "a special religion for the black man" (ibid., 320). "Well, there *is* such a religion. It's called Islam. Let me spell it for you, I-s-l-a-m! *Islam!*" What the new religion offered was a strict moral code, an ethos, that would circumscribe a new collective identity and an entire way of life. This identity connected the urban black to a global community of black people and to a new understanding of themselves and their place in the world. Africa, the black continent, was a source of inspiration as well as a common point of origin. This new identity was necessary, Elijah Muhammad had preached, because "You are the planet Earth's only group of people ignorant of yourself, ignorant of your own kind, ignorant of your true history, ignorant of your enemy! . . . You are members of the Asiatic nation, from the tribe of Shabazz!" (ibid., 357).

Important here is to reveal how Malcolm X modified the redemptive narrative he inherited from Marcus Garvey and Elijah Muhammad, with special reference to the meaning and recollection of slavery. Equally well known as the details of his life is the fact of Malcolm X's break with the Nation of Islam and his attempts to redirect black nationalism in a more secular direction. Just prior to his assassination in February 1965, Malcolm X completed a "Basic Unity Program" that would ground this new nationalism. It was addressed to "Afro-Americans, people who originated in Africa and now reside in America," advising them to "speak out against the slavery and oppression inflicted upon us by this racist power structure." The stated aim of the organization, which sought to unify and represent all black Americans, was to "launch a cultural revolution which will provide the means for restoring our identity that we might rejoin our brothers and sisters on the African continent, culturally, psychologically, economically, and share with them the sweet fruits of freedom from oppression and independence of racist governments" (Van Deberg 1997, 108).

One major factor influencing this revised and revitalized reference to Africa was the wave of national liberation movements that swept that continent in the 1960s, movements that inspired not only African Americans, but the political left generally. The emergence of postcolonial Africa also revitalized Pan-African ideas and moved the African continent into the political and ideological forefront. The marxist political theory motivating many of the leaders of these movements also was important in changing the modes of interpreting reality among black Americans. The marxism and socialism of the 1930s had been severely hindered by the Cold War and McCarthyism. This began to change in the 1960s as a new generation rediscovered marxist theory. The largely white "new" left developed its theoretical politics with the help of the same "Third World" national liberation movements that affected developments in black nationalism in the United States. Theories of "colonialism," "imperialism," and "underdevelopment" turned on issues of class and race, as well as self-determination. This new positive picture of Africa in Europe and America stimulated the transformation of black nationalism, from being religiously based to politically based.

Malcolm X was one of the first to articulate this transformation. One of the cornerstones of this new phase of Africanism was the idea of self-determination as a form of redemption, with the locus now moved from the individual and the group to the nation. In the Program, Malcolm X put it this way, "We assert that we Afro-Americans have the right to direct and control our lives, our history and our future rather than have our destinies determined by American racists" (ibid., 109). Central to self-determination was the control over history and its representation: "We are determined to rediscover our true African culture which was crushed and hidden for over four hundred years in order to enslave us and keep us enslaved up to today ... We, Afro-Americans, enslaved, oppressed and denied by a society that proclaims itself the citadel of democracy, are determined to rediscover our history, promote the talents that are suppressed by our racist enslavers, renew the culture that was crushed by a slave government and thereby to again become a free people" (ibid., 109).

Here slavery is not something relegated to the past; it is forever present. This slavery is economic, involving the exploitation of black labor, but it is primarily cultural, a form of slavery of the mind, which denies to the enslaved the possibility to develop their own talents. Here it would be impossible to view slavery as a past stage of development, which may have either hindered that development or promoted it. It would also be difficult to see slavery as a resource, itself the basis of a form of culture, no matter how distorted and misformed. Rather, this slavery is something lived and living; it forms a habitus that determines current behavior and thus requires a radical spiritual transformation in order to be rooted out. The rediscovery of one's true past is central to this transformation.

As developed in the Program, a central part of this rediscovery was the opening of communication channels between the new Africa and black America. This was meant in a more than symbolic sense and involved developing mass media, "independent national and international newspapers, publishing ventures, personal contacts and other available communications media" (ibid., 110). The new Africa could teach black Americans not only about their past but also their possible future. Concerning the past, Africa could teach black Americans "the truths about American slavery and the terrible effects it has on our people. We must study the modern system of slavery in order to free ourselves from it. We must search out all the bare and ugly facts without shame, for we are all victims, still slaves—still oppressed" (ibid., 111).

In this narrative, redemption will come through rejecting the legacy of slavery and, most important, the psychological burden it continues to impose on African Americans and through being reborn as blacks, no longer Negroes, hyphenated Americans or anything else than original and authentic black people. Black self-determination, whether in Africa or in separate communities or city-states on the American continent is the goal. Blacks are sojourners in the United States, a diasporic condition, an existence that can be redeemed only through rejecting the cultural heritage imposed by the white enemy. Thus the significance of renaming, either with an African-sounding name or with the even more symbolic and provocative "X." Elijah Muhammad put it this way, "Your slavemaster, he brought you over here, and your past, everything was destroyed. Today, you do not know your true language. What tribe are you from? You would not recognize your tribe's name if you heard it. You don't know nothing about your true culture. You don't even know your family's real name. You are wearing a *white man's* name! The white slavemaster, who *hates* you!" (quoted in Haley 1965, 357).

Elijah Muhammad had also preached slavery as part of a divine plan, a test of strength and thus a necessary step toward redemption. "Our slavery at the hands of John Hawkins and his fellow-slavetraders and suffered here in the Western Hemisphere for four hundred years was actually all for a Divine purpose: that Almighty Allah . . . might make himself known through us to our enemies, and let the world know the Truth that He alone is God" (quoted in Essien-Udom 1962, 132–33). Following a tradition reaching back at least to Du Bois, but with much older religious roots, this view endows not only a collective identity through creating a common past, but also a sense of purpose, a mission to tell or reveal the truth. This, combined with a strict program for changing individual behavior, a program of reform aimed at changing habits seen as stemming from slavery, provided a powerful link between individual and collective behavior and identity. Even as it could be interpreted as part of a divine plan, the memory of slavery was part and parcel of a continuing cultural trauma, one that was still very much alive. It was alive because the contemporary society and its culture were understood as an all-encompassing and oppressing Other, a totality from which one was alienated as well as excluded and against which one must struggle, so as not to be its victim or dupe. The movement and its regimen were thus a means of dealing with and resolving trauma, offering support and strength in the struggle to resist temptation and provide a path and a vehicle for redemption.

Each of the two narratives described here offers a framework for interpreting and resolving the cultural trauma that emerged at the failure of reconstruction to fully integrate blacks into American society. I have ended in the 1960s for reasons of space, but the trauma continues to this day and can be recognized in the work of Toni Morrison, Alice Walker,

Charles Johnson, and other writers, as well as in other areas of popular culture such as music and film. It also can be seen in the field of sociology in the continuing debate about the success or failure of integration, in the writings of Orlando Patterson and William Julius Wilson, for example. For this generation, which came of age in a context dominated by the struggles for civil rights, feminism, and the rise of modern black nationalism, reflections and recollections upon an imagined slave past catalyzed a burst of creative energy as well as debate. This can perhaps be understood as part of a search for collective roots by an educated, professional middle class searching for ways to link itself with other black Americans who live under entirely different conditions. The rise of black studies programs at many if not most universities was a major contributing factor here. An important outcome of the civil rights movement, and part of that movement's institutionalization, these programs provided employment opportunities and a ready audience, both face to face and mediated through books and other expressive forms. The interest in "black culture," including the history and experience of slavery, expanded greatly, encouraged and magnified by mediated events, such as the television dramatization of Alex Haley's collective biography *Roots*. These, and other factors, including legislation, made possible increasing access to the means of cultural production, providing this generation with unprecedented opportunity to articulate and represent a countermemory. That this countermemory, while collective, is not univocal, can be seen in the various interpretations of the meaning of the slave past, not only for blacks, but for American society, that abound among black intellectuals, broadly defined, today.

As proscribed by melting-pot theories and supported by empirical research, the "normal" process of assimilation, wherein "each succeeding generation becomes more 'American,'" a process in which, as Philip Roth (1999) so dramatically expresses, "immigrants flowed into America and America flowed into them," appears to have been reversed for blacks because of the cultural trauma described here. Although with apparently less cultural baggage to hinder their acculturation, succeeding generations of American blacks have rediscovered their slave past and their blackness with increasing intensity. What is specific and contextual in the contemporary reworking of cultural trauma is the rejection of the separatism and marxism that characterized the 1960s' nationalism and thus an implicit convergence through the idea of the African American as black American. This reveals the possibility of accepting the collective identification "African American" without necessarily accepting the linear form of the progressive narrative. Progress can mean something other than shedding or overcoming the past. It also gives new meaning to the idea of integration by drawing on the later Du Bois and a modernized nationalism, where a reworking of the past leads through cultural autonomy rather than assimilation. In the context of postcolonialism and the resurgence of ethnic politics generally, this permits a reconciliation not only of an internal conflict, but also of cultural trauma. This is accomplished through the coexistence of a distinctive and relatively autonomous collective history and the progressive political and economic integration into an American society that is also altered in the process.

# CHAPTER 4

# The Trauma of Perpetrators

## The Holocaust as the Traumatic Reference of German National Identity

BERNHARD GIESEN

No construction of collective identity can entirely dispense with memory. Memory supports or even creates the assumption of stability, permanence, and continuity in distinction to the incessant change of the phenomenal world and, thereby, sets up a horizon, a frame, a space of possible pasts. This space is constituted by the reference to past traumas or triumphs. There is no way to imagine a land beyond the liminal horizon of triumph and trauma. The constitutive reference to triumph or trauma can be spoken out or silenced; it is always there, enabling us to represent and present the past as our history.

Social constructions of collective identity are never unanimous, nor are our modes of remembering the past. Instead, they are prone to conflicts and subject to public debates; they vary according to the life-world of the social carrier group and are transformed by the turnover of generations. Rituals can bridge the cleavages of political conflicts and public debates, but they also sometimes cause public controversies. Although the perspectives may shift and the evaluation may differ, the institutional arenas may vary and the rituals may change, constructions of national identity cannot escape from an orientation toward the past, which does not pass away, whether traumatic or triumphant. Traumas and triumphs constitute the "mythomoteurs" of national identity (Barthes 1996). They represent liminal experiences and ultimate horizons for the self-constitution of a collective subject—like birth and death providing the ultimate horizon for the existential experience of the individual person. Only by reference to the undeniable fact of birth and the inescapable prospect of death is the individual person able to construct an encompassing identity beyond shifting encounters and experiences. Being born and being doomed to die are ultimate certainties, but no one is able to report about his or her own death to others. Thus the liminal horizon of our own existence is beyond communication and experience—what we know about birth and death is from stories about the deaths and births of others who are assumed to be like us.

Collective identity is constructed according to a similar logic. Like birth and death, which set the frame for the continuity and unity of the individual existence, referring to a past as a collective triumph or a collective trauma transcends the contingent relationships between individual persons and forges them into a collective identity. Triumphs are moments of "effervescence," in Durkheim's phrasing, or of "Charisma" and "Verzauberung" (enchantment) in Weber's and of " Erlebnis" in Dilthey's. The utmost intensity of the triumph is beyond communication in the very moment when it occurs—it is a matter of immediate experience that reaches out to the unspeakable foundations of the social order. Only in retrospection we can become fully aware of it and communicate about it. Even those members of the community who did not participate in the event itself can recall it by ritual celebrations and mythical stories. These myths represent the unique founding moment by familiar patterns and turn the unspeakable experience into a story that can be communicated. Thus the collective memory of past triumphs accounts for the emergence of communities in a similar way as the reference to the state of nature lets us understand the existence of social order. Both are categorical frames that we presuppose in order to conceive of social reality and to communicate about it.

Collective identity is, however, not only founded on past triumphs. Its reference to the past can also be traumatic. The trauma is the opposite of triumph, but it is constructed according to a similar logic. Traumas remember a moment of violent intrusion or conversion that the consciousness was not able to perceive or to grasp in its full importance when it happened (Caruth 1995). They represent the rupture of in the web of meaning, the break of order and continuity—a dark and inconceivable boundary that provides the frame for the construction of meaningful histories but has no meaning by itself. Only later on, after a period of latency, can it be remembered, worked through, and spoken out. The traumatic memory reaches back to an act of violence that breaks down and reconstructs the social bond. Thus the trauma, too, refers to a source that constitutes the social order but that has its own origin beyond and before this order. Collective identity is never exclusively triumphant or traumatic; it is never based only on an imagined homogeneity of insiders or only by the excluded otherness of outsider; it is never driven only by Eros or only by Thanatos—it is always both, but the balance may be disturbed and the levels may differ (Smelser 1998).

Because they refer retrospectively to liminal horizons of the social community, triumph and trauma have to be imagined, renarrated, and visualized in myths, pictures, and figures. Thus, the triumphant and sovereign subjectivity is embodied in the figure of the hero, who lives beyond the rules and establishes a new order. In contrast, the traumatic reference to the past is represented by the memory of victims who have been treated as objects, as cases of a category without a face, a name, a place.

Between both there is the ambivalent position of the tragic hero who defended his sovereign subjectivity but was defeated by the adversity of this world. This typology has to be completed by the figure of the perpetrator. We commonly conceive of perpetrators only in a discourse about guilt and punishment. This essay will consider the memory of the perpetrators as a collective trauma. Freud's original treatment of the trauma issue focused already on the trauma of perpetrators (Assmann 1999). Today, however, there are surprisingly few scholarly treatments of the trauma of perpetrators—in contrast to a vast range of studies investigating the individual and collective trauma of victims. Perpetrators are human subjects who, by their own decision, dehumanized other subjects and, in doing so, did not only pervert the sovereign subjectivity of the victims but challenged also their own sacredness. Every subject needs the recognition of others for its own self-consciousness, and it is exactly this recognition that is denied to the perpetrators (cp. Hegel's famous dialectics of recognition, Hegel 1927, 148ff). If a community has to recognize that its members, instead of being heroes, have been perpetrators who violated the cultural premises of their own identity, the reference to the past is indeed traumatic. The community can cope with the fundamental contradiction between identity claims and recognition only by a collective schizophrenia, by denial, by decoupling or withdrawal.

The historical paradigm case this essay deals with is the construction of German national identity after the Holocaust. Since the turn of the century, German national identity has been treated as the result of a *Sonderweg* (special path) to modernity, and this German exceptionalism, originally coined by German historians such as Meinecke, has been reaffirmed by recent publications pointing, although in a quite different way, to a primordial German national character that is seen as bound to the death camps (Goldhagen 1996; Greenfeld 1992). Like other constructions of national identity, the thesis of German exceptionalism stresses Germany's uniqueness and inimitability in distinction to other nations. The Holocaust represents this uniqueness in an exemplary way and has to be regarded as the traumatic reference for German national identity after 1945. In this essay, however, we will elaborate how it was transformed and finally gave way to a new pattern of a universalistic identity.

## THE DENIAL OF THE TRAUMA

The defeat of 1945 and the disclosure of the Holocaust resulted in the ultimate trauma of recent German history. First were the obvious and catastrophic German losses—more than ten million Germans lost their lives as soldiers on the battlefield and in prison camps, as casualties of the Allied bombing raids or as refugees on the track westward to escape the Red Army—in the bombing of Dresden more than a hundred thousand died in a single night. More than two million Germans were killed as victims of ethnic cleansing in the lost eastern provinces after the war (Naimark 1995); hundreds of thousands of women and girls were raped; twelve million refugees were displaced in the wake of Russian invasion or expelled from their homes in the eastern provinces; most German cities were turned to ruins. At the end of the war the "Grossdeutsches Reich" was in shambles, and most survivors had to face utmost atrocities just to save their bare lives. All these experiences were traumatic in their own right, but, amazingly, they did not engender a broad public movement of mourning or public rituals of collective memory (Hannah Arendt [1950] noted the remarkable absence of mourning in Germany about the devastation of the war).

As horrible as defeat and death in war may be, their atrocity would have been alleviated by the moral triumph of a collective project that could have persisted even after a defeat and could even have earned the tacit respect of the victors—a heroic war of liberation and independence, for example. But moral justification of the war was entirely and radically denied for the Germans. The aim, the form, and the circumstances of war were criminal and were so labeled by the victors. The shame connected with the German name from then on was a matter of collective identity. The trauma of 1945 did not only result from ruin and rape, death and defeat, but also from the sudden loss of self-respect and moral integrity. The utmost barbarism had happened in the nation that had previously grounded its identity on *Kultur* (culture) and that, at the beginning of the century, could claim to have furthered and supported Jewish emancipation more than its European neighbors (Diner 1988). The triumphant notion of a German *Kulturnation* (cultural nation) was replaced by the traumatizing disclosure of the Holocaust; the nation that gave birth to a prodigious *Weltliteratur* (world literature) had procreated also the unspeakable and inconceivable horror of the extermination camps. Faced with Auschwitz, there was no place left for poems, Adorno (1992) wrote.

## THE COALITION OF SILENCE

Traumas result from a sudden unmediated conversion of inside and outside, good and evil, security and destruction. In the Freudian tradition they are defined as violent events that at the time when they occurred were ignored or disregarded—the individual mind cannot perceive the possibility of its own death (Caruth 1996, 60). In a similar way, collective consciousness tends to reject perceiving the actions of its own community as barbaric in the moment when the barbaric violence occurs. Therefore collective traumas, too, require a time of latency before they can be acted out, spoken about, and worked through. Postwar Germany responded to the disclosure of the Holocaust by an "inability to mourn" (Mitscherlich and Mitscherlich 1994) or "communicative silence" (Lübbe 1981) about the unspeakable or inconceivable horror, the dark abyss into which the German nation had been precipitating. There was no way of telling a story about how it could have happened. Nobody could bear to look at the victims. All those who had devoted years of their lives to a movement whose members had to consider themselves as collaborators in a mass murder could not repair their ruined moral identity even if they had been ready to confess their guilt. There would be no second chance; life is spoilt. The trauma is insurmountable. As a moral subject the person is dead. He or she can only remain mute, look away, turn to other issues, and hope that nobody will ask the wrong questions. A tacitly assumed coalition of silence provided the first national identity after the war. Everyone assumed that the others, too, had supported the Nazi regime and would therefore agree to be silent about their common shame. No one mentioned his or her relationship to the Holocaust in informal communication—even if the involvement was only that of a bystander of history who never knew exactly what was happening. This muteness and silence contrasted to vivid informal communication about the personal involvement of the war. Even experiences like the escapes from the east-

ern *Heimat* (country), the nights in the bomb shelters, and the struggle at
the *Ostfront* (eastern front) during the last month of the Third Reich
could be addressed only by those who did not suffer personally from
traumatic shocks. But very few spoke even of their responsibility as
bystanders, collaborators, and party members with respect to the
Holocaust; those who had directly participated in the genocide, obviously, kept their silence in order to avoid imprisonment. Neither the individual trauma of rape, death, and dehumanization, nor the collective
trauma of guilt and defeat could be turned into the theme of conversation. There was a moral numbness with respect to the horror.

The postwar coalition of silence extended to two subsequent generations, both of them entangled in the Nazi regime but with different perspectives on it. The first generation consisted of those who were born
between the turn of the century and the First World War. They had experienced the economic crisis of 1929 in their most formative years, they
had voted Hitler and his party (NSDAP) into power, and they provided
the backbone of the NSDAP before its seizure of power but also during
the war. Most younger leaders of the party and most of the SS leaders
were members of this generation. For them Hitler was the political
redeemer who solved miraculously Germany's economic malaise and
wiped out the "shame of Versailles." Their family backgrounds, however, were not patterned by Nazi ideas and hence they had memories of
a different social and cultural world not dominated by Nazism. But
many of them also despised this world of their parents who were related
to the assumed decadence of the Weimar republic. Some had turned at
the end of the twenties to radical racism and antisemitism and regarded
themselves as a radical avant garde devoted to a mission of saving the
world from the "Jewish disease." In contrast to this generation that grew
up in a Germany of deeply divided camps, the generation born between
1920 and 1933 was raised in a world that provided few alternatives to
National Socialism. In a certain way it had few choices to oppose Nazi
power. This generation of *Hitlerjungen, Flakhelfer,* and young soldiers
was shaped by the war experience, educated in a radical militaristic system, and considered themselves frequently to be the charismatic carriers
of a future Nazi Germany. For them the defeat of 1945 resulted in a sudden and radical breakdown of a taken-for-granted worldview. For the
first time they were faced with a world that was not totally dominated by
the Nazi ideology.

As differently as these generations may be related to the regime and
ideology of National Socialism, they responded to the disclosure of the

Holocaust in a very similar way. The generation of 1933 remained mute because it had backed the Nazi regime although it could have known better. The *Hitlerjungen* generation, in contrast, remained silent for the very opposite reason. It could not have known better, its world had collapsed, and many felt betrayed and abused.

If the unspeakable issue could not be avoided in informal conversations among Germans, those who had been enthusiastic followers of National Socialism could sometimes cope with the trauma of total defeat and the dismantling of the horror only by simply denying obvious facts. They considered the documentary evidence to be faked by the Allied forces. Others tried to separate the program of National Socialism from its realization or insisted that "der Führer" did not know about the Holocaust. At the beginning of the fifties, a shocking figure of almost forty percent believed that the merits of National Socialism outweighed the damage it had done to the German people (Institut für Demoskopie Allensbach 1950). The vast majority maintained that they had not known anything about the mass murders or that they had been too preoccupied by mere survival to care about the monstrous rumors. "Wir wussten von nichts . . ."

Most of the horrors certainly were concealed from the German public. But even if the "final solution" was declared to be "Geheime Reichssache" (top secret), thousands of Germans participated directly in the genocide, the antisemitic rhetoric of the Nazi press increased continuously its fervor, rumors were spread, and questions could have been asked even by those who were not directly involved in the deportation and killing (Mommsen and Obst 1988). Few knew all the horrible facts, but almost everybody knew something. Most Germans deliberately or inadvertently avoided focusing their attention on the disappearance of the Jews from public life. They did not want to get involved in piercing moral questions for fear, negligence, or resentment. Thus, what, later on, became the crucial challenge for the German self-consciousness was removed to the diffuse and dim periphery of awareness and perception before.

In some respects the silencing of the past after 1945 continued the ignorance and disregard before 1945. And, to a certain degree at least, this coalition of silence included even the victorious allies (Laqueur 1980). Neither in the Soviet Union nor in the United States was the Holocaust at the center of public debates during the fifties. An increasing awareness of the immensity of the genocide started after the Eichmann trial in Jerusalem.

The coalition of silence was not limited to informal communication in intimate spheres shielded from public control, but left its traces also in the political rhetoric of Germany's public discourse (Dubiel 1999; Herf 1997). The German chancellor Adenauer, a sober and pragmatic politician, mentioned the Holocaust only rarely in official speeches. On the few occasions when he addressed the Holocaust, he referred to it in the passive mode as "the immense suffering of the Jewish people" and did not mention the perpetrators. The judeocide was, of course, not denied, but it ranged among other victims like fallen soldiers and refugees *(Vertriebenen)* who had lost their eastern *Heimat*. Instead of mentioning the crimes directly, the political rhetoric referred to the past as the "dark times of the recent past," as the "time of unfathomable barbarism," and as the "catastrophe of German history" (Dubiel 1999). And even the German movies and television series in the fifties and early sixties focused much more on the fate of prisoners of war in Siberian camps than on the Holocaust. One of the most popular series was "Soweit die Füße tragen" ("As Far as the Feet Will Carry You"), which presented the story of a German prisoner escaping from a Russian prison camp and trying to return to Germany.

Thus the crimes and their perpetrators were removed into a realm of unreal nightmares beyond conception and description. Similar to the period of latency in the case of individual traumata, here, too, the traumatizing event, the Holocaust, is removed from collective consciousness and shifted to the level of haunting dreams that occasionally found their way to cultural representations—the popular movies about Doctor Mabuse who used men like string puppets to commit horrible crimes hinted at the collective nightmare but never spoke out its direct reference.

## BLAMING THE OUTSIDE: THE DEMONIZATION OF NAZISM

Not everyone, however, consented to the coalition of silence. Some intellectuals raised their voices and posed the inconvenient question "Where have you been, Adam?" (Böll 1972). Some situations required an explanation to outside observers, to schoolchildren, to foreigners, and to those Germans who never supported the Nazi regime. Faced with those who could not be co-opted into the coalition of silence, Germans required a new exculpatory narrative. Postwar Germany constructed this narrative by primordializing the opposition between oppressors and the people. The Nazi rulers, Hitler in particular, were depicted as insane barbarians, as wild beasts, as satanic seducers who had approached the good and innocent German people from outside and deprived it of its common sense like a drug, a disease, or a diabolic obsession. The criminal domination was represented as pathological, inescapable, and fatal, whereas the people were imagined as having been seduced into blindness, unsuspicious, and completely ignorant of the atrocities of genocide. Demonization of Nazi rule removed the nation from the realm of moral responsibility and culpability. Intoxication, seduction, and blindness allowed Germans even to regard the German nation as the true victim of Nazism. This narrative of victimization was not only limited to the first postwar years. In 2000 a documentary series on German television had the title " The Refugees: Hitler's Last Victims." (This demonization of the Nazi rule was, of course, not supported by that approximately 15 percent of the German population that, even in the early fifties, considered Hitler to be one of the greatest German politicians of the century [Institut für Demoskopie Allensbach 1950].)

In this new exculpatory narrative primordialization was again used to exclude the outsider, but its direction was radically reversed. Before 1945 antisemitism rejected Jews as poisonous demons secretly invading and seducing the German nation. Now the same primordial exclusion and its rituals of purification and decoupling *(Abspaltung)* turned on the Nazis themselves. Hitler, once the charismatic redeemer and savior of Germany, was converted into a devil, a crazy epileptic, a monster, the immense misfortune of German history, an alien demon who had seduced the innocent German people. In a way the demonization of Hitler continued his previous position as a fascinating superhuman individual beyond the ordinary rules, powerful and dangerous, mad and seductive—but the hero was converted into a sorcerer, a devilish monster. The charismatic hero of Nazi Germany had turned his followers into victims who, awakening from a dream, had to recognize that his crusade had left nothing but ashes and ruins. Demonization is reversed heroification; it keeps the superhuman individual as a reference of historical meaning, but it demands radical conversion on the part of its previous followers—what has been the embodiment of charisma before is now turned into the embodiment of a haunting demon.

The pattern of radical conversion was put to the extreme by Nazis who tried to change their personal identity, assumed new names, and after several years reemerged into public life as faithful and respected democrats, supporting social democracy and taking over important public offices before their concealed identities as SS officers were disclosed (Leggewie 1998).

## DECOUPLING: EXPELLING THE PERPETRATORS

The Nazi demons were usually regarded as figures of the past, but some of them had undoubtedly survived under cover or even under their proper names as respected persons of postwar society. If their Nazi past was publicly disclosed, the German nation could not simply fall back to the narrative of demonization. They had to be expelled from civil society in order to reaffirm the boundary between the majority of decent Germans on the one side and the few surviving monsters on the other side. A new narrative was needed. It was provided by the conception of individual criminal guilt. The Nazi consociates could not be considered as alien monsters—instead they appeared as individual perpetrators who had committed horrible capital crimes and had to be treated as criminals and sentenced to life in prison according to the rules of law that were proclaimed in the name of the German people, "Im Namen des deutschen Volkes." In the narrative of individual criminal guilt, the German people are no longer in the position of victim as they were in the narrative of demonization. Instead, they take the position of the third party, defining the relationship between perpetrators and victims with respect to impartial rules of justice. In this narrative, the collective trauma was moralized, but there was no acceptance of collective guilt yet. On the contrary, the public discourse of the fifties insisted on a strict rejection of any idea of collective guilt and a strict boundary between the few unquestionably criminal perpetrators and the majority of seduced citizens and soldiers.

Of course, the position of the boundary was debatable. The opposition Social Democrats were willing to include a larger group of higher officials into the circle of perpetrators—targeting especially Globke, the previous commentator of the "Rassengesetze" and now a member of the government. In contrast, chancellor Adenauer—himself unquestionably an anti-Nazi—and his conservative coalition insisted that, although the criminal perpetrators should be punished, there also should be no distinction between two large classes of Germans—those with blemishes and those without (Dubiel 1999). Sometimes even the leading generals of the Wehrmacht who had been sentenced to prison and the young soldiers who did their military service in the *Waffen SS* were included in the community of abused people. Despite dissents and debates, most politicians of the new democracy agreed in the denial of any collective guilt of all Germans and supported the new narrative of individual criminal guilt. The parliamentary debates about denazification, about wearing military decorations in public, about paroles for mass murderers and the end of prosecution of Nazi crimes, and even about the Auschwitz trial in the early sixties, were aimed at demarcating a clear boundary between the majority of normal and "decent" Germans on the one side and the few criminal perpetrators on the other (Dubiel 1999). This demarcation did not only allow for a new construction of national identity but stressed by expulsion and oblivion the radical newness of the political system and the departure from totalitarian rule. Expelling the condemned perpetrators from civil society and ending the prosecution of newly discovered Nazi crimes simply represented different sides of the same thrust to get rid of the past.

The law court was the institutional arena in which the demarcation of individual criminal guilt was staged, ritually constructed, and reaffirmed. Although in the early fifties the imprisonment of Nazi criminals at Landsberg and the related trials were still much criticized by the conservative right, there was no way to avoid the trials if discontinuity between past and present was to be constructed. Here the roles of the accused perpetrators and the accusing public represented by the prosecutor were strictly separated, just as the rules of law on the one hand and the criminal action on the other were clearly distinguished. Both oppositions support the demarcation between an innocent nation and treacherous criminals.

Denying any collective responsibility, the ritual of trials confined the question of guilt strictly to individual acts, in particular as evidenced by formal decisions within organizations. But even if crimes were committed beyond any doubt, the perpetrators tried to relativize their guilt by referring to the inescapability of military orders: *Befehlsnotstand*. Even the commanders of Auschwitz and Treblinka presented themselves as performing strictly within their formal competencies; they emphasized that they never participated in personal cruelties (which was a lie). These, they argued, were committed by subordinate *Kapos* from Ukraine, Lithuania, and Poland; in passing the blame, they adapted their contempt for the Slavic *Untermenschen* to the new situation (Langbein 1965).

Demarcating the perpetrators and denying one's own involvement and guilt was not only the Federal Republic's way of coping with the past; the strategy was also used in the new socialist republic of East Germany. Here, the founding myth of the new state focused the idea that the repressed German people had—assisted by the glorious Red Army—succeeded in overthrowing the fascist regime. The boundary between the past and the present was declared to be radical and insurmountable; "der neue sozialistische Mensch," the new socialist human being, had nothing in common with Hitlerism and "fascism." The socialist rhetoric carefully avoided speaking of National "socialism." Any traces of continuity between past and present were shifted across the border to the "revanchist and fascist" Federal Republic of West Germany. The Federal Republic, indeed, could not deny being the legal successor of the Nazi state, because it had to provide a legal basis for the citizenship of refugees and for the claim to represent the entire Germany. The new socialist state of eastern Germany considered the Federal Republic as a fascist society in bourgeois disguise. This demarcation between good antifascist and socialist east and the fascist and capitalist west was also used to deny any responsibility for the survivors of the Holocaust—hence no restitutions and reparations were paid (Lepsius 1989). The public rituals of the GDR focused on the fascist barbarism of the past and the heroism of antifascist resistance, but the judeocide was rarely mentioned. Based on the antifascist ideology and the constitutional rupture between past and present, the politics of the GDR did occasionally even take an antisemitic turn. In socialist East Germany the Stalinist waves of purge in the early fifties centered on Jewish communists, such as Paul Merker and Leo Zuckermann, who after returning from a western exile had tried to merge antifascism and socialism in the new Germany. Like leading Jewish members of the communist parties in Hungary, Poland, and Czechoslovakia, they, too, were accused of "cosmopolitanism" and secret espionage with imperialist and bourgeois forces (Herf 1997).

In a similar and even more self-assured way, Austria tried to get rid of its Nazi past. Austria's founding myth turned the *Anschluß* (of integration into the "Third Reich") of 1938 into a military occupation by foreign forces and tried to position Austria among the liberated nations like Czechoslovakia, Holland, and Denmark as "Hitler's first victim." Here, too, responsibility and guilt for the Holocaust was simply pushed across the border, the perpetrators were defined as non-Austrian outsiders, and the Austrian people were seen as "innocent perpetrators" (Wodak 1990). And here, too, decoupling the new nation from the history of guilty perpetrators weakened its alertness with respect to new antisemitism.

But the thrust to shift the guilt across the border and to turn collaboration into victimization was not limited to German-speaking nations. Italy rapidly forgot its own fascist past and its complicity with Nazi Germany and presented itself as a nation of resistance heroism; the Flemish, Slovakian, and Croatian participation in the *Shoah* was blurred because these groups were parts of new nation-states that emerged out of anti-Nazism resistance movements.

Even within Germany the process of coping with the past by expelling the perpetrators was repeated half a century after the Holocaust: the "destasification," which took place in East Germany after the German unification in the early nineties, shows a striking similarity with the denazification of the late forties. Again the issue was to demarcate the line between the perpetrators and the majority of the decent Germans who had suffered from repressive rule, but this time it was even more difficult to turn the filthy grayish web of collaboration into a clear-cut black-and-white picture of guilt and innocence: almost a third of the entire population had been involved in *Stasi* activities, and the system of surveillance and control had expanded during four decades to reach a perfection the Gestapo never achieved. Furthermore, the Communist system in East Germany did not produce genocidal practices comparable to the *Shoah* or to the Stalinist mass murders.

The pattern established in the postwar period was to be repeated; hence the disclosure of previous *Stasi* collaboration and the public debate about it were in many respects similar to the denazification of the postwar period. Many rising political stars were ousted from office, but some of the former collaborators (such as Stolpe) were kept in prominent positions. A successor party of the old regime, the PDS (like the Deutsche Reichs Partei in the fifties) could profit from the resentment of the old elite, now deprived of their power and privilege. Rumors about clandestine networks of the old secret police spread.

And even the militant members of the 1968 revolt—who had tried to disclose the hidden "fascist" heritage of postwar Germany—could not entirely escape this pattern of decoupling and expulsion with respect to the evil of the past. In 2000 they, too, became the target of public debates and some of them—now in their fifties—had to show up in court. Coming out of age, many of them became members of the green party and some of them, like the popular German foreign minister Joseph Fischer and his colleague Trittin, even succeeded in taking important public offices. The public disclosure of photos showing the young Fischer as a street fighter battering a policeman triggered a public debate about the violence of the militants twenty years before. This time it was the generation of 1968 that had publicly to denounce and to outdistance its past. Leading members of the militant movements pointed to the spirit of the time and recalled the best intentions of the "revolutionaries," and those in public office stressed again and again in public that they had never consented to violence against human beings. Again, a strong demarcation was publicly staged between those who remembered their past as democratic revolutionaries and those who engaged in terrorism and criminal activities. Thus the attempt in 1968 to cope with the Nazi past became a paradoxical issue of contested memory.

## WITHDRAWAL: THE TIMELESS GERMAN VIRTUES

Excluding the perpetrators by legal trials continued the denazification—originally decreed by the Allied forces—as an autonomous act of the German nation, but it did not provide a positive, let alone triumphant, construction of identity. Still the collective trauma could not be addressed directly. Any prospect of a unified German nation-state seemed to be barred by the stable partition of Germany. As traumatized individuals withdraw from active engagements that presuppose a basic trust in the environment, traumatized communities can also withdraw from risky and threatening engagements to a secure realm of identity. Thus postwar Germany turned from the nation-state to timeless German virtues as the core of a new sober national identity that blended traditional and primordial elements.

These virtues varied depending on social carrier and context. The generation of *Hitlerjungen* who were raised in a militaristic life-world and who were returning from the prison camps in Siberia stressed the discipline and the spirit of sacrifice of the German soldiers and disregarded entirely the ideological context in which these virtues were used. They felt betrayed and abused and remained deeply suspicious toward the lure of ideologies. But they kept the militaristic and practical virtues that provided the backbone of their wartime experience. The petite bourgeoisie focused on honesty, reliability, and industriousness, virtues that fit the functioning of modern organizations but do not ask for a legitimization of their aims (Bauman 1989). In a weird way, the shift to discipline and work as the core of national reconstruction continued inadvertently the Nazi cult of the *Volk* as the merging of "Arbeiter der Faust und der Stirn" and hinted even at the infamous slogan "Arbeit macht frei." The culture of the "economic miracle" *(Wirtschaftswunder)* was predominantly of petite bourgeoisie origin, carried by craftsmen and clerks, holders of minor public offices and skilled workers.

These German virtues seemed to be exempted from the changing tides of history, the decay of the German nation-state, and the shame of Nazism. They were strictly decoupled from the historical context that could question and discredit them and separated from the level of state and politics. Thus the new narrative of national virtues fostered the creation of a German nation that lived below the level of politics and the state in associations, enterprises, and neighborhoods. The German mark became the cultural symbol for this prepolitical identity of the *Wirtschaftswunder*. In a certain way, this turn toward the sober virtues of working citizens could even be regarded as a belated westernization of Germany—no high-flung political romanticism anymore, no nostalgic look backward, just practical reasoning about rebuilding the cities and integrating the refugees. Based on and backed by this new self-consciousness, the Germans could even—albeit indirectly—face the survivors of the Holocaust. The Adenauer government decided relatively early to pay large sums to Israel (until 1995 almost 100 billion German marks) as restitution of Jewish property and reparations for the crimes.

But retreat from politics was not only a matter of the petite bourgeoisie, of ordinary people. It extended also to the traditional *Bildungsbürgertum* (educated bourgeoisie). The educated classes emphasized *Bildung* (education), *Innerlichkeit* (sensitivity), and *Unbestechlichkeit* (impartiality and devotion to public office) and cultivated a new *Biedermeier* (period), which did not challenge the political rule. Retreatism also marks the attitude of those intellectuals who—in the case of Nazism as well as under the communist regime—frequently sought refuge in so-called inner emigration. This inner emigration was essentially apolitical, and many of the prominent emigrants who returned from their American exile after 1945 explicitly detached themselves from politics. Thomas Mann is only one of the best-known examples of this despise for politics.

This melancholic abstention from politics continued a tradition of the German *Bildungsbürgertum*, which during its formative century was excluded from official politics and confined to the realm of culture and reason. Its intellectual leaders converted abstention into a virtue. From Kant, Schopenhauer, and Nietzsche to Ernst Jünger and Carl Schmitt, German intellectuals rarely accepted normal politics, which they found a tiresome, mundane chore. Educated and cultivated people had to detach themselves from the superficial exaltations of politics as well as from the banal calculations of money and markets. Politics could attract attention only if it appeared as an extraordinary charismatic event, challenging the heroic individual. In revolutions and wars the *Bildungsbürgertum* discovered situations in which the sublime and the sacred invaded and overwhelmed the mundane and profane field of everyday business. As soon as political decisions lost their extraordinary charismatic character and gave way to routinized craftsmanship and professional skills, they were treated as dirty business—character and identity are spoiled by politics and compromise.

In the 1950s the concept of a subpolitical associational German identity responded to the exigencies of the day as well as to the trauma of the past. Because the nation was seen as kinship and neighborhood and not as a territorial state, it was able to integrate millions of refugees from the lost eastern provinces and even an increasing stream of migrants from the second German state. Because the people considered themselves to be innocent victims betrayed and abused by the Nazi rulers, the new German identity between *Goethevereinen* (cultural association) and *Wirtschaftswunder* had to keep its distance from politics. Nobody wanted to repeat the fatal mistake of a strong ideological commitment in the political arena. The same coping strategy applied to the situation after 1989 but with different results. This time the retreat to personal networks gave way to a cleavage between east and west Germans and the construction of a particular eastern identity of common memories and lifestyles beyond politics and public discourse (Engler 1999).

## CHANGING SIDES: PUBLIC CONFLICTS AND RITUALS OF CONFESSION

### Generational Conflict and Collective Guilt

The fragile combination of a new political start and the enduring identity of decent Germans, who considered themselves to be the true victims of the catastrophe and simply wanted to be proud of their economic miracle, persisted until the 1960s, when a new generation entered the political stage. This generation was born after the war and did not have personal memories of the Nazi past. Children of this generation broke the coalition of silence and faced their parents with inconvenient questions that until then had been the mark of outsiders; they wanted to know about the guilt of their parents, and they constructed the boundary between insiders and outsiders in the midst of their own families. The trauma was now considered from an outside perspective. It became the stigma of the entire German nation. The new generation did not want to be a part of this nation that bears the stigma of perpetrators; this group shifted sides and identified with the victims. It became fashionable to give children Jewish names. Thus, the victims not only had a voice again, but also were represented by personal names within the German nation. This advocacy for the previously excluded other extended to political opposition. In contrast to the *Hitlerjungen* generation who, returning from the Russian prison camps, could effortlessly continue their hostility by focusing on Soviet totalitarianism, the new generation turned enthusiastically to socialist ideas; they not only attacked their fathers' fragile constructions of national identity but became the declared ally of the enemy. Partly because the young Germans felt the stigma of collective shame and guilt, they did not want to belong to their fathers' nation. They favored everything foreign and were afraid to be treated abroad as typical Germans.

The student rebellion of 1968, however, was not only a generational revolt or protest. Its anger and rage addressed the traumatic origin of German national identity, and it tried to reconstruct this identity. Suspicious of remainders of the old fascism and hidden signs of a new fascism in the Federal Republic, the new *außerparlamentarische* (extraparliamentary) opposition responded to the trauma by repeating furious hallucinations of the event that had caused the collective trauma and the collective fright. But it also spoke out about the trauma and crushed the carefully constructed boundaries surrounding the postwar identity of Germany. The angry young men and women attacked the myth of a democratic start, brought the issue of guilt to the fore of public debates and replaced the narratives that had presented the Germans as the victims of Nazi tyranny with a charge of tacit and overt collaboration. It was, of course, not their own guilt that required reassuring illusions, but the guilt of their fathers, from whom a moral distance must be constructed. The new narrative turned the trauma into the stigma of an entire generation. Beyond the narrow limits of individual criminal guilt, the preceding but still present generations, the voters of 1933 as well as the *Hitlerjungen*, were considered as collectively responsible for the national trauma—as voters, party members, bystanders, collaborators, and fanatic supporters, as well as contemporaries who had not prevented the horrible crime that was committed in the German name. In stigmatizing the generation of their fathers, the young Germans were not entirely impartial; they represented the victims, and in doing so they could cut the links to the nation of perpetrators that was identified with the preceding generation.

The tension between the generations produced a merciless public investigation and, for the first time, a clear public statement of a collective German guilt. More than ever before, the Holocaust entered the institutional arena of public debates in which every citizen could partake, in which secrecy and silence hinted at hidden crimes, and in which the privilege of personal experience did not count any more. From now on, the crime of the past was directly referred to. The silencing and ignoring, the covering and disguising of the crimes were replaced by a dismantling of collaboration. The circle of perpetrators was widened to include an entire generation, and the boundaries of the nation were changing.

As with other major changes of boundary construction, this shift resulted in strong political conflicts and produced deeply entrenched political camps opposing each other in public (Dubiel 1999). Whereas the conservative camp insisted on an unmasked pride of the economic miracle and tended to render the past to oblivion, the new left (which carefully avoided referring to the past as national socialism) used the term *fascist,* sometimes as a rude clop to crush the civil reputation of its opponents. Some of the most ardent followers of the 1968 rebellion became lost in the no-man's-land of violence and capital crime: at the end the *Baader-Meinhof* group and the so-called Red Army Fraction (RAF) constituted their sovereign subjectivity no longer in pursuing an enlightened vision of society but in trespassing the law. Their aim was to be persecuted as enemies of the state.

Although it was unquestionably the new left that established the Holocaust as an issue of public discourse in Germany, its radical zeal was not without ambivalence with respect to the Nazi heritage. Habermas and Marcuse, themselves intellectual leaders of the new left, accused the radical left of "Linksfaschismus" (leftist fascism) and, later on, the political center insisted that the totalitarian character of the militant left reminded them strikingly of Nazi politics. Moreover, the strong antifascist move of the new left did not prevent the leftist movement from opposing the state of Israel, which was accused of Zionist imperialism with respect to the Palestinians. Reacting to this anti-Israeli turn of the new left, some liberal Jewish intellectuals in Germany could not deny being afraid of a new antisemitism, this time from the left. Twenty years later, some of the leading actors of the militant left even changed sides and became right-wing radicals. Horst Mahler declared on German television: "The young people of the *Waffen SS* and the RAF have a lot in common" (ARD Panorama, Sept. 2, 1999); Reinhold Oberlercher, once a leader of the 1968 Hamburg student movement, advocated in 1999 the Fourth Reich, which would ban foreigners and exclude them from the labor market; Rainer Langhans, formerly a member of the *Berliner Kommune* (a leftist community), now warns against "be-devilishing" Hitler, whom he regards as a spiritual person.

This shift to a public discourse about the Holocaust was closely associated with a change in the construction of memories. The first postwar generation still had immediate experiences and strong personal memories, which persisted and were sometimes traumatic. They did not need an explicit discourse to revive and reconstruct the Nazi past. Tiny hints in the informal conversation between them were sufficient to recall the past and to signal the side they had been on with respect to Nazism. Recalling the past was not their problem—it was always lingering, haunting their memories. These personal memories were missing in the new generation; they had to rely on an elaborate public discourse to cope with the Nazi past. Hence it was not only the conflict between generations but also a shift from personal memories, silenced or reconstructed in micro conversations, to the remembrance of the past by public discourse carried by those who did not take part and could not refer to personal memories.

## Accepting the Guilt of the Nation: Rituals of Confession

The new narrative of the collective guilt of an entire generation changed the notion of guilt. It was no longer limited to the voluntary acts of individuals who decided deliberately to violate the basic moral rules of a community. Instead, it extended also to those members of a political community who, although not actively engaged in crimes, did not prevent these crimes that were committed in the name of this community. Because the new narrative decoupled the collective guilt of a political community from the active involvement of each individual member, it allowed for a ritual admittance of guilt by representatives who were innocent as individual persons. Rituals reconcile and reunite oppositions and ruptures and provide ways to overcome traumas and losses (Soeffner 1992). Public rituals of confessing the guilt for the Holocaust were performed rarely in the fifties and early sixties—and they addressed mostly a limited audience. The only exception was the speech given by German president Heuss at the memorial site in Bergen Belsen in November 1952. This ceremony was broadcast, reported in the national press, and attended by several representatives of Western nations. Here Heuss spoke the famous phrase "Diese Schande nimmt uns niemand ab" ("None will lift this shame from us"). But Heuss remained, in spite of his reputation, in the position of a respected critic, rather than being carried by a majority movement (Herf 1997, 327). Other gestures, such as the visit of ambassador Allaert to Auschwitz in March 1963, were barely noticed by the media.

More important in this respect was certainly the famous kneeling of the German chancellor Willy Brandt in Warsaw in 1970. In a spontaneous gesture, the head of the German government, visiting the monument for the victims of the ghetto uprising against German occupation, kneeled down in silence and remained so for some minutes. This representative confession of collective guilt was no longer relativized by reference to the sufferings of the Germans or to a fatal blindness and seduction. Neither could it be seen as a youngsters' untamed revolt against their parents' generation. In distinction to the generational revolt that established a cleavage between the carriers of collective guilt and the accusing generation, Brandt took the burden of the collective guilt of the nation although he was innocent as a person. Thus, he enacted a new narrative that confessed the collective guilt of the German nation, with respect to the Jewish victims, to an international public that acted as a third party.

This narrative of national guilt was not presented in a public speech but as a spontaneous and muted gesture that did not require further explication and did not allow for objections and criticism. There was no public announcement or plan to perform this gesture; even the personal staff of the chancellor did not expect it, and no large Polish audience attended it. But by its very unexpectedness, it was globally noticed and immediately reported by the major Western newspapers: the *New York Times*, as well as the *Corriere della Sera*, the *Daily Telegraph*, and other foreign newspapers, showed front-page pictures of the German chancellor kneeling at the memorial. Their comments stressed unanimously the importance of the gesture: this "touching incident" overshadowed the signing of the German-Polish treaty on the same day *(New York Times)*; it was "il momento culminante" ("the peak moment") of Brandt's visit, "un nuovo rituale" ("a new ritual") that marked a turning point in German postwar history *(Corriere della Sera)*.

Although the issue of the Holocaust had been addressed before in public by some political representatives of the federal republic (for example, by President Heuss, Mayor Reuter of Berlin, and the leader of the Social Democrats, Schumacher), it was the kneeling of Brandt in Warsaw that became an icon of recent German history—like the mass rallies of the Nuremberg *Parteitage*, the Soviet soldiers erecting the red flag on the Brandenburger Tor in 1945, and later, the fall of the Berlin wall.

This global resonance was not only due to the context of an official visit abroad. More important was the fact that it added an innovative element to a well-known ritual. Visiting the monuments of unknown soldiers who sacrificed their lives for a nation was nothing new. Originally it was performed only by the representatives of the nation to which the dead belonged. Later, it became part of the rituals performed by heads of state visiting other states and paying respect to the dead of the host nation. In this ritual the fallen soldiers, who were revered as heroes before, are regarded as victims, and the hostility of the past is blurred in a common act of mourning.

Brandt's kneeling transformed this ritual in a profound way. It added a gesture of repentance with respect to victims killed by the chancellor's own nation. Unlike the famous gestures of reconciliation performed by the French president Mitterand and the German chancellor Kohl at the cemeteries of Verdun later on, Brandt's gesture did not ignore the difference between perpetrators and victims. Although the monument of the ghetto upheaval in Warsaw depicts a heroic act of failed resistance, Brandt was not mourning the deaths of soldiers who were casualties of a war but the deaths of innocent victims. His gesture clearly differed also from a simple Canossa ritual and a voluntary humiliation of a repenting individual who is personally guilty. When guilty people repent in public, they can never avoid the suspicion of hypocrisy. Brandt's Warsaw kneeling separated the individual guilt of the ritual actor from the collective guilt of the German nation. It could be performed and was beyond suspicion of hypocrisy for the very reason that Brandt was innocent as an individual. He was believable as the representative of the German nation because he had no personal interests or past involvements to be disguised and to be masked by this gesture.

The decision to humiliate himself and take on the burden of collective guilt gained immense respect for the individual person of the German chancellor and gave way to a reconciliation between Germany, the nation of the perpetrators, and the nations of the victims. It ended the postwar period. This gesture, not the many announcements of German politicians, ended the status of moral occupation for the Federal Republic and opened the path to a new political identity recognized by its neighbors. It substituted the missing revolution and prepared the ground for a new German identity, one not imposed from outside but emerging from representative acts of the nation defining itself and accepting its guilt. Thus it is no coincidence that the chancellorship of Willy Brandt also gave way to a normalization of relations between Germany and its eastern neighbor states and that the new *Ostpolitik* (policy with the Warsaw Pact states) supported Germany's entry onto the stage of global politics. The public confession of the guilt of perpetrators even opened up a path to a triumphant rebirth of the nation. Three decades later on, remembering the thirtieth anniversary of Brandt's kneeling in Warsaw, the commentaries in the German media almost unanimously emphasized this rebirth of Germany as a consequence of the Brandt gesture. Instead of questioning it as a moment of public humiliation, it was celebrated as Germany's reentry into European politics. The trauma of perpetrators who confess their guilt was turned into a triumph that could even be regarded as a new model for public politics.

The extraordinary media response to the Brandt kneeling was not only due to the particular historical setting in which it was performed. It was also related to a deeply rooted cultural pattern of self-humiliation and self-sacrifice in the Judeo-Christian tradition. In this tradition an innocent person can, in an extraordinary public act, humiliate himself in order to relieve the burden of collective guilt from his people. Although this mythical pattern can be found also in Mesopotamian cultures, the most famous myths in this tradition are the biblical story of the original guilt and the sacrifice of Isaac and, in the new testament, the self-sacrifice of Christ. Christ is the ultimate innocent individual, the king of divine descent, the hero who is killed in order to save his people. Christian liturgical rituals remember or even repeat (see the Catholic ritual of transubstantiation) this sacrifice of the innocent. Jewish and Christian symbolism represent it by the figure of the innocent lamb that replaces the human sacrificial object; early Christian martyrs and, later on, religious virtuosi accepted suffering and death in order to do penance for the sins of others and to repeat the model set by Christ. This cultural pattern of christomimesis also underlies confession of collective guilt by political leaders, although, as with Willy Brandt, they might be raised in a largely secularized environment. Myth and ritual form and guide our actions in liminal situations even if we are not aware of the original version of the mythological or ritual pattern—as a rule of grammar that structures and directs speech acts also for those who are unable to name the rule. This holds true not only for the performing actors but also for the audience. Thus, in the German newspaper *Die Zeit,* the well-known Russian author Lew Kopelew cited an unknown survivor of the Warsaw ghetto who said: "He [Brandt] kneeled down and thereby raised his nation" (Feb. 4, 1977).

It may be revealing to compare Brandt's gesture in Warsaw with the famous ritual of remembrance performed by Reagan and Kohl in 1985 at the German war cemetery in Bitburg, where soldiers of the German *Waffen SS* also were buried. This ritual of remembrance was staged to support the postwar demarcation between the few Nazi perpetrators and the innocent German people. This time, however, not only the regular soldiers of the German *Wehrmacht*, but also members of the *Waffen SS*, were to be included in the immense group of victims. Even if some young Germans had been forced to join the *Waffen SS*, the sign of the *SS* was rightly seen as the epitome of Nazism—it marked a monstrous elite corps of most cold-blooded murderers.

Consequently the international community was outraged over the ritual at Bitburg. Beyond a vivid sensitivity toward the symbols of Nazism, this response also indicates the clash between two general tendencies: on the one hand, the construction of victims is bound to inclusion. More and more new groups are included in the mass of victims. On the other hand, this construction of victims cannot dispense with perpetrators; it is ritually staged by public acts of repentance and accepting collective guilt. The Bitburg ritual was incomplete in this respect: a repenting actor representing the group of perpetrators was missing. Noting that both representatives, Kohl as well as Reagan, were personally innocent missed the point. In contrast to the Brandt gesture in 1970, Kohl did not take on collective guilt, but tried to disperse it in the intractable space of history or to charge it to demons, thereby reviving the postwar narrative of the seduced nation. But remembrance and repentance cannot be separated if the collective identity of perpetrators is involved. Representing the nation in a ritual of repentance in a believable way is fostered by the innocence of the representative as a person. Kohl failed to see the opportunity in what he presented as an excuse.

But the heritage of the Brandt ritual of atonement and repentance prevailed. Shortly after the visit at Bitburg, the German president Weizäcker gave one of his most impressive memorial addresses on the occasion of the fortieth commemoration of May 1945; solemnly, he recalled the different groups of victims, most prominently among them the Jewish citizens. Ten years later, at the fiftieth commemoration, thousands of Germans attended observances at the memorial sites at the concentration camps, and January 27, the day when the camp Auschwitz/Birkenau was liberated, was officially instituted as a German memorial day for the victims of Nazism.

## THE OBJECTIFICATION OF THE TRAUMA: SCHOLARLY DEBATES AND MUSEUMS

In the first postwar period the trauma was embodied in haunting personal memories. The *Unfähigkeit zu trauern* ("the inability to mourn,"

Mitscherlich) resulted in public silence and the social expulsion of the perpetrators. The institutional arena where the Holocaust was spoken about was the law court. In contrast, the second period was patterned by political conflicts and public debates carried by a generation who had no personal memories anymore, and by public confessions of guilt. Its arena was the political space of civil society. Every citizen could participate, engage in ardent debates, be a passionate partisan on the public issue, and join political camps. It was national identity that was at stake, and even if the participants try to surpass each other in laying claims on the issue, there are no a priori privileges in defining collective identity in public discourse. But claims to be close to the moral core of collective identity will be raised and contested. Stigmas are attached to those who are regarded as the outsiders of the moral order and who, in their turn, are trying to defend themselves against the stigma of perpetrators. The trauma, unspeakable in the years after 1945, had been turned into the stigma of collective guilt, publicly contested, and debated between generations. In the next stage, the stigma will become the theme of stories and histories that can be narrated and represented to an audience that is no longer haunted by personal memories or stigmatized by collective guilt.

## The Professional Historians Take Over

During the eighties the memory of the Holocaust was increasingly transferred to a new institutional arena, that is, scholarly debate and historical research. When the number of eyewitnesses is shrinking and personal memories are fading, when new generations can no longer listen and respond to their fathers' stories, then historians and other professional custodians of the past have to preserve relics, reports, and remainders. Scholarly reconstructions extend the range of memory and submit it to seemingly impersonal methods of investigation and evaluation.

Historians can investigate their objects, even if they are not studying the history of their own group. In principle at least, the memory produced by historical research is disembodied, abstract, and detached from the identity of the scholar. If the past is rendered to the professional experts, it becomes an object of comparisons, explained by particular conditions and understood by imagining a special context. In distinction to the narrative of national guilt, the past is turned into a field of objective causes and conditions that move history and result in historical events. Questions of guilt and responsibility are shifted into the background, and moral commitments are to be separated from the professional investigation of the case and the impartial assessment of truth. The professional expert acts on behalf of the general community, and this community extends to include all reasonable subjects in the case of the scientist and scholar.

As soon as the experts take over the reconstruction of the past, debates about these reconstructions tend not only to be decoupled from issues of personal identity, but also to be institutionalized and tempered by the sober rituals of scholarly methods. Therefore, the shift from general public debate to the field of professional specialists, who replace or supplement the judges and politicians as representatives of the nation and as the impartial third party, is commonly expected to produce a more detached and less passionate perspective.

However, this expectation holds true only if the debate about the Holocaust is confined within the shielded fields of scholarly debates. But the general interest in the national trauma could not be banned from the exclusive halls of historical science. The historians (many of them members of the *Hitlerjungen* generation, but also leading liberal intellectuals of postwar Germany) were eager to present their findings to a larger public audience, and the national audience showed a strong and sensitive resonance. As soon as the issue was turned again into a matter of general concern, the very attempt to deal with the Holocaust as a matter of normal historical research provoked violent public objections and triggered intense debates.

The first important controversy about the Holocaust, however, still remained largely within the scholarly community. It was the debate between so-called functionalist and intentionalist explanations of the judeocide. Intentionalists focused the original antisemitism of Hitler and the Nazi leaders. They explained the Nazi organizations and even the entire war at the *Ostfront* as a deliberate and controlled attempt to exterminate the Jewish people. According to them, all parts of the Nazi mythology could be suspended, revoked, or mocked in internal communication among the Nazi leaders—but not antisemitism. Antisemitism was the mythomoteur of Nazism. In contrast, functionalists like Mommsen analyzed the Holocaust as a result of a highly developed differentiation of tasks on the one hand and a complex field of internal rivalries and tensions between different offices and Nazi organizations on the other (Mommsen 1983). Far from being a centrally planned and meticulously executed campaign, the Holocaust appears here as the result of an organizational chaos wherein even the high-ranking participants did not specifically know about the genocidal activities of other parts. Nobody—not even Hitler himself—was in full control, and nobody had exhaustive and reliable information about the complete reality of the genocide. If the Holocaust is explained as the—at least partly—unintended consequence of internal rivalries and conflicts between Nazis or as a function of an organizational system, then, indeed, the question of guilt and responsibility is suspended and the ties that link the Holocaust to the national identity are weakened.

As hefty as the controversy between intentionalists and functionalists has been, it was too complex to enter the general public sphere, and it never questioned the monstrosity of the Holocaust itself, whatever its core conditions may have been. In contrast, the famous German *Historikerstreit* of the 1980s got tremendous public attention because it addressed directly the question of German national identity and brought out the lingering ambivalence with respect to the trauma.

The *Historikerstreit* confronted the protagonists of German exceptionalism, who insisted on the uniqueness of the Holocaust and its absolute importance for German identity on the one side with a new rightwing revisionism on the other (Nolte 1987; Hillgruber 1987; Diner 1987; Habermas 1987a, 1987b; LaCapra 1994; Maier 1997). Pointing to some new historical evidence, the conservative revisionists tried to normalize the German war crimes and to position them in the context of a European civil war in which Stalin, not Hitler, had set the model of exterminatory crusades. This strategy obviously lightened the burden of moral responsibility and questioned the uniqueness of the Holocaust; it did not exonerate the Germans, and it did not shift the guilt across the border, but it dissolved and suspended the question of guilt in a broad display of genocidal practices of the "European civil war" triggered by Soviet communism. It blurred the boundaries. Not surprisingly the reaction of the liberal public audience led by Habermas was strong. Historicizing the Holocaust and embedding it in a historical context was considered an act of alienation and misappropriation of the very idea of German identity that the new generation had adopted.

In a different way, but with comparable results, the issue was again brought to the fore of public attention due to a debate negotiating the book *Hitler's Willing Executioners* (Goldhagen 1996). The debate revived the generational revolt of the sixties and, again, expanded the group of perpetrators to include almost all Germans in the Nazi Reich. Even the professional historians who questioned the scholarly merits of the book were accused of masking the past and hence of ex post facto collaboration. But both camps in this debate contributed—certainly without intending it—to a blurring of boundaries that constitute a moral discourse. The historians around Mommsen did so in insisting on the impartial treatment of a national trauma in the public sphere and on scholarly investigation even if it deals with matters of identity. Goldhagen's supporters did so because Goldhagen primordialized German antisemitism and thus removed it from the range of moral decisions. Furthermore, including everyone in the group of perpetrators risks eroding the distinction between guilt and innocence that is at the core of moral discourse.

To a lesser degree, this erosion of the moral distinction by widening the group of perpetrators could be found in the *Wehrmachtsausstellung* (an exhibition of documents about the Wehrmacht) of the nineties (Heer and Naumann 1995). It presented almost a thousand documents to prove the many connections between the regular German army at the *Ostfront* and the judeocide, the readiness of officers and common soldiers to cooperate with the *Einsatzgruppen* (special squadrons), and in particular the undeniable fact that many of them did know about the Holocaust. Again the circle of perpetrators was widened, and one of the seemingly safe havens of "inner emigration," the *Wehrmacht,* was discovered to be deeply entangled in the crimes. And again, the large public resonance and clamor that the exhibition received did not result from scholarly debates but from its implications for the new German identity as the nation of perpetrators. A cleavage divided Germany's reaction to crimes documented by the exhibition—the majority of the public audience was deeply moved and concerned by the atrocities, and prominent politicians and public intellectuals gave the introductory speeches for the exhibitions. A strong minority of conservatives, in contrast, refused to admit to the guilt and the entanglement of the German *Wehrmacht.* Finally, even the German parliament dealt with the issue in a memorable and impressive debate. At stake was again the fundamental demarcation between the majority of decent Germans on the one side and the minority of criminal Nazi monsters on the other.

In the case of the *Wehrmachtsausstellung,* this new German identity was supported by a scholarly attempt to revise the traditional master narratives of the decent German soldier and, at first, it was only the defenders of this traditional identity who rallied against it. But scholarly discourse was by no means unanimously supporting the revisionist cause; at the end of the nineties an increasing number of historians challenged the scholarly basis of the exhibition. They pointed to a small number of the photo-documents that were mistaken as proofs for the *Wehrmacht's* murderous actions but that, in fact, showed the victims of the Russian NKWD or the German SS. Finally, the organizers closed the exhibition in response to scholarly criticism. Obviously the trauma was still disturbing and dividing the German public. The diagnosis of the experts was accepted only if it could soothe the pain or relieve the trauma; most Germans resisted turning their national identity into just another object of impartial scholarly investigation.

Of course, this was not a general ban on historical research about the Holocaust, and not all attempts to submit the Holocaust to historical research provoked passionate public controversy. On the contrary, with the number of witnesses fading away, there was an increasing demand for the collection of memories and remainders. The turn toward oral history, autobiographical narration, and history of *mentalités* was a response to this demand (Niethammer 1983). It extended the perspective to include everyday life and seemingly banal details that reflected the penetration of Nazism into the life of ordinary Germans.

But here, again, the once clearly demarcated boundary between the few criminal perpetrators and the majority of innocent and abused Germans was blurred. It dissolved in a history of complex contexts and entanglement; finally it depicted the manifold ways of ignoring and tacit consenting, of cowardice and fascination. It described the subtle ramifications on the way to the Holocaust, but—in contrast to the trials of the postwar period—it refused to proclaim a final verdict of guilty or not guilty: indissoluble and entangled, all Germans had been guilty and not guilty at the same time.

Of course, the professional administration and scholarly investigation of the past is not an invention of the late twentieth century; instead, it dates back to the establishment of history as an academic discipline and the institutional conservation of past objects in the nineteenth century (Nora 1992; Giesen 1999). The general civil concern with the past as organized in historical associations, and the idea that the past can be appropriated by every citizen according to his or her own taste, receded in the second half of the nineteenth century and was gradually replaced by an exclusive professional handling of historical matters that turned the nonprofessionals to a lay audience consuming the past for curiosity and education. Obviously the historians' narrative of the national trauma established a strong perspective of a third party, but it merged the positions of perpetrators and victims. Finally there were even German victims and Jewish collaborators. The once clear-cut distinction between victims and perpetrators is blurred.

*Museums and Memorial Sites:*
*From Lay Associations to Official Committees*

This transformation of voluntary movements that want to preserve the remainders of the past as a matter of general civic concern into professional organizations was repeated in the case of the Holocaust. Although most of the concentration camps, in particular Auschwitz, Dachau, Bergen Belsen, and Ravensbrück, had been turned into memorial sites shortly after the war, it was in the eighties that the Holocaust was a focus for local movements of citizens who tried to collect local knowledge and to discover the traces of the national trauma within their own local community. Frequently organized by teachers of the 1968 generation, these lay associations dug out the remainders, established local memorial sites, and reconstructed the maps of the cities with respect to a past that their parents had shifted to a distant demon in Berlin. But the traces of Gestapo and of pogrom, of vanished Jewish citizens and Nazi rituals, could be found in every city—the Holocaust was not just a matter of Hitler and Auschwitz; it happened everywhere in Germany. Thus the lay memorial movements and associations appropriated the national trauma on a local level. In the nineties, however, these laic movements were increasingly superseded and replaced by professional museology and by official national policies to construct memorial monuments (Schafft and Zeidler 1996; Puvogel 1989). This turn toward professionalism is not limited to the German collective memory. Holocaust museums were founded in Washington, Los Angeles, and more than a hundred other cities, and Holocaust archives were sponsored by American movie directors. In Germany the professional care for the national trauma reached its peak in the planning of a large Holocaust memorial as the national monument of the new united Germany in the center of Berlin. A huge committee was assembled to decide about the different suggestions provided by internationally known artists and architects, and each of these suggestions had its ardent followers and opponents in the committee as well as in the public debate about the issue.

On the German as well on the Jewish side, this shift toward museology and monumentalization hints at the thrust to preserve and to appropriate a memory that is endangered by the passing away of the generation of witnesses. This longing for roots can lead to individual investigation of the fate of ancestors, but it results mostly in a collective construction of a past, first by voluntary associations of citizens, then by official organizations and committees chaired by experts who act on behalf of the nation. At the end, the differentiation between past and present is no longer an achievement of the individual consciousness but a spatial distinction between *les lieux de memoire* that are exclusively devoted to memory and the regular and mundane spheres of action that are discharged from the burden of the past; between the professional specialists of the past and the laic audience that faces the past only on special occasions and otherwise indulges in oblivion. They know the past is stored and in good hands.

### The Mythologization of Trauma: The Holocaust as an Icon of Evil

Most important in this respect is certainly the television series *Holocaust,* which attracted unusual attention in the German public sphere. Presenting the Holocaust and the Nazi heritage in the context of a non-documentary movie was not entirely new: Wolfgang Staudte's movie *Rosen für den Staatsanwalt* had addressed the issue of Nazism as early as the 1950s, but this as well as most other movies dealing with the dark legacy of Nazism did not dare to present the judeocide directly. In contrast the most popular TV series dealt with the fate of German POWs in Russian camps and their attempts to return home *(Soweit die Füße tragen)*. In distinction to the many attempts to describe the horrors of the war or the persistence of secret Nazi networks, the *Holocaust* series told the story of two German families—one Jewish, the other Nazi—in a convincing, detailed, and moving way. Mediated through the movie, the process of remembering was shifted again to the German families, to children who refused to accept the narrative of the seduced nation, and to parents who still defended themselves occasionally by maintaining that only the participants could understand, but who mostly felt estranged by their own almost-forgotten past.

Far from resuscitating the political debates of the sixties or exacerbating the scholarly debates, the presentation of the past in German movies like *Heimat* and *Die Blechtrommel* and U.S. movies like *Schindler's List* (Loshitzky 1997) and *Holocaust* transferred the issue to a new institutional arena that tends to overcome opposition and conflicts by the ritual construction of communality. Nobody in the audience could disagree with the fundamental evaluation of the Holocaust, because the movies presented a story and not an argument.

In contrast to scholarly research, reconstructions of the past in the mass media have to abstain from referring to abstract figures and arguments; instead they must narrate a story about good and bad people.

They have to create suspense and emotions and offer clear-cut anchors for identification (Rosenthal 1995). Entanglement and indifference, gradual shifts and uncertainties of evaluation can be presented only at the beginning of the story and only to a very limited degree; sheer coincidence and structural constraints are hardly accepted as moving forces of a story. Instead, there must be action and responsibility, heroes and villains, suspense and—at the end of the story—an absolutely clear distinction between perpetrators and victims, guilt and innocence. In this way the media staging of the Holocaust succeeds also in the representation of the victims as subjects with a face, a name, and a voice. Those who have been reduced to mere objects are remembered as "co-humans," as suffering subjects, as members of the national community.

Thus, the media staging of the Holocaust not only creates unanimity and the unification of oppositions, but also constructs an identification with the past, even if personal memories are no longer at hand, and it fosters this identification because it is based on voluntary decision instead of traumatic intrusion. It creates a collective memory that would not have existed without it. In this respect it represents the past in the way museums do, as the utmost otherness and without personal memories. The vividness and liveliness of the narrated story blurs the fact that it is not the audience's own personal story that they tell or listen to. They can produce and consume this disconnected past as exotic alterity and even as sentimental entertainment. In the extreme, the Holocaust is converted into "funny" entertainment and presented as a souvenir in the shops of museums: in St. Petersburg, Florida, a visit to the local Holocaust museum ranges among the "40 fun things to do" in a flyer for tourists; the museum shop offers, for $39.95, a scale relic of a Polish boxcar used to transport Jews to the death camps. In Los Angeles the famous Simon Wiesenthal Museum of Tolerance is promoted like a Disneyworld of horror: "Make the Museum of Tolerance part of an exciting and informative itinerary for your group. Check us out for group discounts, special bonuses." The show itself is praised as " high tech, hands-on, experiential, unique interactive exhibits" (*New York Times*, March 18, 1999). The utmost horror is abused for selling kitsch (Young and Baigell 1994).

Today, the Holocaust has acquired the position of a free-floating myth or a cultural icon of horror and inhumanity—similar to Genghis Khan's raids, to witch hunting, or to slave trade. It is not a particularly German problem anymore; every person can refer to it regardless of his or her origin, history and descent, and it is understood by every member of a worldwide audience. This mythological use of the Holocaust contrasts markedly to the traumatic postwar period when the ultimate horror was beyond explanation and description—an abyss of total inconceivability. Myths turn violence and unspeakably shocking experiences into a story that can be narrated and listened to. They transform the unbearable and absurd as a meaningful sequence of action—not necessarily presented as everyday banalities but as a process that will not offend the audience. Today the mythological use of the holocaust has turned what once was inconceivable and traumatic into an almost trivial and well-known background knowledge in which new stories are embedded and which is evoked to explain, to interpret, and to evaluate. Independent of individual memories and recollections, of collective trauma and personal guilt, the Holocaust has ascended to the status of an undisputed master narrative. In a strange turn, the hell has been sanctified. It is not only staged in the media, but also referred to by various political camps, and is used to raise money for various campaigns and movements; it disguises strategic action in moral terms, and it ends by creating conflicts about the right to claim it as one's own cause. It was this instrumentalization of the Holocaust for daily purposes and its trivialization in the media against which the German writer Martin Walser raised his voice in his provocative public confession that he is switching off the TV if it is showing a movie about the Holocaust. But he also attempted to re-individualize German guilt by stating that everybody has to face his own bad conscience privately, thus criticizing "the incessant presentation of our disgrace" ("Dauerpräsentation unserer Schande"). Ignaz Bubis, the head of the German Jewish community, responded strongly to this by calling this statement "mental arson." In 1999 the controversy between Walser and Bubis divided Germany again into two moral camps; more than half a century after it happened, the Holocaust is at the core of the serious public discourse about Germany's national identity.

Therefore, focusing on the dissolution of collective trauma into global entertainment does not tell the complete story. Certainly, the transformation of the repressed trauma into a national discursive universe is a story of disembodiment and externalization, of decoupling collective memory and identity from personal memory and individual responsibility, of turning internal ambivalence into external presentations of common values staged by professional specialists and appealed to by almost every political actor in the pursuit of a democratic majority. It may even be described as the transformation of a collective nightmare into a myth of commercial entertainment.

But the extraordinary resonance of these media events in Germany cannot be explained by the sheer weirdness and awe-inspiring alterity of their content. It rather hints at a collective memory that exists, is reproduced, and can be appealed to, even if personal memories fade away. Beyond the manifold ways to exploit the trauma of the past for present-day interests remains a deeply rooted collective sensitivity to racism and xenophobia. In response to xenophobic outbursts in the mid-nineties, more than two million Germans came together in the "Lichterkettenbewegung" (public rallies involving lighted candles). This cannot be reduced to individual interests or to the shifting tides of mass entertainment. It is a matter of collective memory and identity. It transferred the spontaneous gesture of Brandt into the ritual of a huge popular movement.

Any attempt to construct a new Germany after 1989 has to take this into account. The soil in Berlin on which the new center of German government is to be erected is soaked with memories of persecution and Nazi rule. The construction workers in Berlin discover remainders and relics buried by a thin layer of sand and shambles repeatedly. Attempts to get rid of the past and attempts to remember it coalesce in the debate about the Holocaust memorial; appeals to respect the past and to leave the ruins untouched collide with the urge to turn them into a new construction manifesting the new democratic identity after the Holocaust. In all these debates the reference to the Holocaust itself is never challenged; instead, the arguments are moved and twisted by the quest for the right, the most authentic, the most adequate, and the most dignified way to refer to the trauma of the nation.

## THE GLOBALIZATION OF THE TRAUMA:
## A NEW MODE OF UNIVERSALISTIC IDENTITY

In Karl Jaspers's famous distinction between different notions of guilt with respect to the Holocaust ranges the so-called metaphysical guilt. The metaphysical guilt refers not to the collective guilt of a political community, but it extends to all human beings. After the Holocaust people have to give up their original trust in the irresistible progress of civilization and in the victorious endeavor of humankind to overcome barbarism. Faced with the Holocaust we have to consider the optimistic anthropology of the enlightenment as a possibly fatal illusion. If this could happen in the heartland of modern European culture, then there is no safe haven where a relapse into barbarism can be excluded. Instead, the human condition has to be rewritten to include a deeply rooted and original tendency toward barbaric violence. Viewed from this perspective, the Holocaust is turned from a particular German trauma into a global trauma of humankind. This negative anthropology of the Holocaust hints at religious roots in the narrative of the original sin of all human beings and the hope for salvation and redemption. It was Germany that committed the original sin of modern history, that had to give up the paradise of the enlightenment's modernism, and that had to respond to the question "Where have you been, Adam?" But the consequences of this exodus extend to all members of the human species; it could also have happened elsewhere.

This extension of the trauma beyond the national identity of Germany to humankind is not only a subject of secular theological debates among intellectuals. It can be found also on the level of rituals constructing national identity.

The public confession of German guilt shows an entirely new pattern of constructing national identity. It is no longer a ritual remembrance of past triumphs or a remembrance of its own victims as represented by the columns of victory and the monuments of fallen soldiers in the nineteenth century. It is no longer recalling the paradise of a mythical past set up as an ideal for the present. And certainly it is no longer a revival of an endangered tradition or an appeal to national virtues that resist the changing tides of history. Memory aims at an axiological reversal of history, at a radical rupture in the stream of events: we recall the past to prevent it from ever being repeated.

In this insistence on a radical discontinuity between past and future, the new pattern of national identity shows signs of modernism and universalism. Modernity commonly sees the attractiveness of the future as the main motive of historical action and as the Archimedeal point of temporal order. In contrast to classical modernity and the universalistic patterns of identity associated with it, the new pattern of identity is based not on the attractiveness of the future but on the horror of the past. At the turn of the century, the great social and technological utopias have lost a lot of their alluring fascination, the designs of the future are patterned more by scenarios of catastrophe than by salvation-promising accounts of an ideal society, progress has lost its powerful appeal as the prime motive of acceleration in historical action, and the moral discourse of Western societies is focusing more on the demarcation of evil than the definition of the common good.

The one great "Progress of History" has been dissolved again into many little progresses, the side effects and risks of which can be deliberated and debated. The small steps of progress in technology and medicine, in social reform and ecology, can hardly be tightened and condensed into a great project of identity that sets history in global motion and inspires everyone to aspire to the emancipation of humankind. Progressive politics is especially impeded by everyday problems; it has lost its charismatic appeal and complains that the voters are bored and even disgusted by politics. The temporal horizon of history has been reversed. Today, the horror of the past and the remembrance of the victims replace the attraction of utopias that once produced the victims. It is only remembrance, and not the utopia, that is able to provide the unquestionable basis of a universalistic collective identity (Habermas 1985, 1987c).

The new pattern of constructing collective identity by public confessions of guilt got its first and most impressive contour in the German remembrance of the Holocaust, but later on it was not limited to the German case. In many Western nations, political representatives have solemnly admitted the guilt of the past. The French president has deplored the extensive voluntary French collaboration in the deportation of French Jews in the war, Norwegian president Bruntland has noted that—contrary to the national master narrative of resistance—more Norwegians died in the ranks of the *Waffen SS* than as victims of the German occupation, the Pope apologized solemnly for the Catholic Church's failure to intervene in the persecution of the European Jews, Poland—itself a nation of victims—debates its own genocidal crimes committed on Polish Jews under the German occupation in Jedwabne (Gross 2001), and the Italian postfascist leader Fini laid flowers in a cemetery of the victims of the German occupation (the "fossi adriatici" executions) even though his own party is considered to be a successor to the fascist collaborators in Italy.

The new pattern of public confessions of guilt extends even beyond the case of the Holocaust of the European Jews. The American president Clinton intended to confess the guilt of white Americans for racism and slavery as well as for the genocide committed on Native Americans; the Dutch government asked for apologies to the victims of colonial exploitation; the Australian government did the same for the genocide of the Australian aborigines; and French public debate, in spite of the pompous celebrations of its bicentenary, paid increasing attention to the victims of *la terreur* in the French Revolution. The French president apologizes to the descendants of Alfred Dreyfus; the Pope apologizes solemnly for the inquisition, the crusades, and the persecution of the Jews; the Queen of England apologizes for the wrongs done to the aborigines of New Zealand. Sometimes these apologies are reluctantly given in response to public pressure, and sometimes the act of confessing guilt or asking for apologies is still lacking, but a strong public movement is pressing for it; the massacre of Amritsar in 1919 and the Irish famine in the 1840 are cases in point for the British public debate. The Pope's plea for apology extended even to the victims of the crusades and the persecution of heretics in the middle ages.

The global spread of these rituals of confessing guilt results even in amazing and questionable acts of taking responsibility. When President Clinton visited Africa in 1998 he asked the African people to forgive the Americans with respect to the Rwanda genocide: because the American government disregarded some reports, it did not prevent the genocide by military intervention. In a similar way, the military intervention in Bosnia and Kosovo by European and American troops was justified by the moral obligation to prevent a genocide—we would have been guilty if we had not invaded the territory of a foreign nation.

This "politics of apology" (Cunningham 1999), the widespread readiness to see responsibility and to ask for forgiveness, does not presuppose a direct and personal involvement in the crime—it occurs not in spite of a lack of involvement, but because of it. The political representatives can take responsibility and admit a collective guilt for the very reason that they are not responsible as persons. It is not individual moral or criminal guilt that is at stake but a ritual confession of a collective guilt, and the presuppositions of this representative confession differ from those of a confession of a personal wrongdoing. Again Willy Brandt is the paradigm. He who was a political refugee from the Nazi terror and never a citizen of the Third Reich confessed the guilt of his fellow Germans, whom he represented as a politician (Weiss 1998). This representation of a moral community—and in this ritual the nation is imagined as a moral community—presupposes that the representative is beyond any suspicion of masking his personal interests and history behind his public office. Otherwise the—always fragile and precarious—claim to represent the nation is eroded by one of the most critical risks of moral communities: the suspicion of hypocrisy.

Contrary to common assumptions about authenticity, the representation of the nation succeeds here, not because the representative is presented as "one of us," sharing the same memories with the other members of the community; instead, individual identity and memory on the one hand and collective identity and memory on the other hand are no longer tightly coupled. As in other universalistic constructions of identity, the particular identity of the individuals, their biographies, and their life-worlds are set apart from the public constructions of identity. It is because of this very separation that individuality can aspire to autonomy and public discourse can focus on its own dynamics, on the common good in distinction to the sum of individual happiness.

The separation of individual crime and collective guilt shows some striking parallels to the postaxial-age distinction between the impersonal conception of the sacred and the embodiment of the sacred in the person of the hero. The charismatic center of society has to be clearly separated from its representation in particular individuals—and the triumphant hero who merges the public and the private is bound to tragic defeat. In a similar way but with reversed perspective, the public memory of victims has to be separated from the private guilt of individual perpetrators.

As in the German case, rituals revoking the old national myth are frequently prepared and supported by intellectual debates and scholarly revisions of traditional narratives. The new historiography of the French Revolution attacked the sacralizing view of the Annales school and disclosed the totalitarian character of the Jacobinian rule and the exterminatory goals of the revolutionary crusades against royalist resistance in the Vendée and other provinces (Furet 1989; Eisenstadt 1998). New French historians scrutinized the history of communism and exposed the mass murders resulting from the attempt to establish a radically new society (Courtois 1997). The widespread support of the Germans by collaborators in France, in the Netherlands, and in Belgium is no longer ignored and hidden behind a triumphant history of resistance movements; the refusal to accept and rescue Jewish refugees by Swiss authorities as well as the almost complete disregard of reports about the extermination camps in the British and American press during the Second World War are no longer denied.

Although spreading rapidly in Western democracies, these revisions are rarely accepted unanimously by all participants in public discourse. Revisions of national narratives cannot avoid objections, and the wide public acceptance of a new ritual of remembrance may even provoke a counteracting revisionist attack against the new orthodoxy. The carrier groups of the old master narrative cannot deny the event that resulted in the trauma of collective identity, but they mostly try to remove it from the core of national identity and to normalize it as a deplorable side effect of historical turmoil. The piercing challenge to the traditionally triumphant constructions of national identity is reflected in accusations of shamelessness, dishonesty, and scholarly incorrectness.

In the debates about revisionism and antirevisionism, the new or the classical historiography of the nation, the rise of the state or the story of its victims, criticism of the dominant narrative is no longer a privileged domain of left-wing intellectuals. The French debate about resistance and collaboration, the French origins of fascism, and even some publicly presented denials of the Holocaust, show that the general public as well as intellectuals, liberals as well as conservatives, are involved in the revisionism. Slowly, deconstructivist criticism has invaded the camp even of its most ardent opponents.

As widespread as the revisionism of national master narratives may be, it is also hard to deny that cultures and political communities differ strongly in their acceptance of rituals of repentance and mourning for past victims. The readiness of the German public to accept the Holocaust legacy contrasts strikingly with the long-lasting refusal of the Austrian public to admit collaboration and to expel the perpetrators. Evidently the national identity of Austria was mainly based on its demarcation from Germany, to which all the guilt of the Holocaust was shifted. Austria did not consider itself to be the legal and moral successor of the Third Reich (Lepsius 1993). For different reasons, but also in a striking way, the political representatives of postwar Japan tried for a long time to avoid mentioning the issue of Japanese war crimes in China and Korea during the Second World War. The Nanking massacres are among the most brutal episodes of genocide in this century but were never included in official speeches by political representatives of postwar Japan. Only recently, as a result of long negotiations, has the Japanese government conceded to war crimes committed by individual Japanese soldiers and signed a document that contained an official apology for the war crimes in Korea.

The Turkish government has never admitted even the existence of the Armenian genocide of 1915 and recently declared itself to be offended by an official French statement about it. This refusal to admit the guilt of the past is remarkable, as the contemporary Turkish nation was born entirely after the event, and the old Ottoman Empire broke down after 1918. The repercussions of today's Kurdish separatism and the threat of possible Armenian claims on Turkish territory may support this refusal, but only uncompromising strategic thinking would accept this as a satisfying explanation. The Turkish government did not deny the deaths of Armenian victims, but it refused to accept this as the collective guilt or responsibility of the Turkish nation. Instead, the deaths of the Armenians are attributed to individual perpetrators and considered an accidental collateral damage of war.

Occasionally officials not only refuse to admit to the guilt of collaboration but also continue the master narrative of resistance. Here, the claim to rank among the victims becomes crucial. It is accepted only in nations that can reconstruct their history convincingly as victimization and cut out any political triumph. The public conflicts between the international Jewish community on one side and the Polish government and the Catholic Church on the other provide an example. Should the victims of Auschwitz be labeled as Jewish or Polish, as Jewish by descent or Catholic by confession? Both the Jews and the Poles can claim the status of victims, but the Jews have suffered from antisemitic pogroms in Poland before and after the German occupation, and not vice versa. Hence the Jewish claims and not the Polish are approved and recognized by Western nations.

Other genocides are still too recent to be addressed by political representatives. Sometimes the politically responsible individuals are still in power, as in Iraq and Serbia. Serbia, Croatia, and Bosnia have all completely denied involvement in war crimes, but each has accused its adversary of mass murder by displaying the naked bodies of unidentifiable victims to the international press. The evidence of Srebenica cannot be disregarded, but the involvement of the Serbian nation and its government is still an issue for public debate and revision. In Serbia the genocidal practices of the Bosnian war have evidently not even begun to be addressed as a cultural trauma.

Contrasting cases are Cambodia and Rwanda, where half of the population participated in slaughtering the other half. Here, the mass murder was certainly not a terrible secret planned by a government and executed by specialized military units but, indeed, the voluntary and passionate deed of ordinary men, women, and youngsters. Nobody can deny the evidence of genocide. Although the perpetrators were defeated and driven across the borders for a time, the trauma is omnipresent, and its public remembrance risks disrupting the fragile coexistence of the opposing camps or ethnic groups. Almost every family is concerned and was involved in the killing as perpetrators or victims and sometimes as both.

But even if there is resistance to accepting the new master narrative of national identity, even if many cases have not passed their time of latency, even if strategic reasoning may oppose it and the guardians of traditional master narratives are attacking it, the new pattern of collective identity is adopted by ever more contemporary societies. It is no longer limited to official declarations of political representatives or leaders but extends also to the level of individual citizens and organizations. Church organizations apologize for the abuse of children, South Africans apologize to fellow citizens for apartheid, Australians apologize to Aborigines for the assimilative policy of separating Aboriginal children from their parents, and so on.

We may ask for the structural conditions fostering and supporting this diffusion in particular among the Western nations. Certainly many of them can refer to the Judeo-Christian mythology of sacrifice, repentance, and redemption. We have already outlined the importance of the idea of original collective guilt and redemption by the self-sacrifice of the innocent individual. This cultural pattern dates back to the Augustinian idea of the original sin, of the sacrifice of Isaac by Abraham and, in particular, of the self-sacrifice of Christ, the ultimately innocent hero, who by his death saved his people from a collective guilt. Western politicians confessing the guilt of the nation are hence relying—mostly without being aware of it—on a pattern of christomimesis that is deeply rooted in occidental mythology. In contrast to this connection between collective guilt and individual innocence, the Confucian tradition can hardly conceive of a collective guilt or responsibility. From a Confucian perspective, the attribution of guilt to individual and community is reversed. While war crimes committed by individual Japanese perpetrators can be easily admitted, the nation has to remain without blemishes. This cultural difference accounts for the reluctance, even refusal, of the Japanese government to admit to a national responsibility for the Nanking massacres. In a similar way, although for different reasons, the Turkish government rejects any international pressure to apologize for or even to recognize a national responsibility for the Armenian genocide. While not denying the massacre and the number of victims, the official Turkish response blames individual perpetrators. The truth about the motivations of the perpetrators might disturb and destroy the official founding myth of modern Turkey. It was not for religious hatred but for reasons of ethnic cleansing in the pursuit of a modern nation-state that the so-called Young Turks, now revered as the founding fathers of modern Turkey, expelled millions of Armenians and let them starve on death marches.

As convincing as they might be, cultural patterns, such as the common culture of sacrifice or the collapse of the great utopias, cannot—each taken alone—completely explain the rise of the new pattern of collective identity in the Western world. The Judeo-Christian heritage is an ancient one and cannot—taken alone—explain the new phenomenon; the collapse of the great utopias and the turn toward memory extends to different nations in different degrees. Therefore, we have to look for an additional contemporary condition fostering the acceptance of the new rituals of confession, and we may find this in the changing conditions of international communication and observation. A triumphant celebration of past victories or a ritual construction of ethnic purity not only excludes outsiders but also offends them if they are present and attending the ritual as observers.

This situation could be ignored in premodern societies. The excluded others had neither voice to object to the offense nor eyes to observe it. They were slaves, exotic visitors, or simply absent. Even in the nineteenth century the presence of excluded others could be widely disregarded, given the state of media communication. Celebrating the victory over France by the elaborate rituals of the *Sedantag* in Germany was hardly reported in the French press. International public attention was focused on political decisions and economic tendencies; letters and written reports arrived with some delay, and telegraphic messages had to be condensed to the bare essentials. Symbolic politics was not limited to gestures of military threat or the movements of warships and armies; in order to reach the international level it had to be directly addressed to the head of state. Popular feelings and triumphant celebrations were of internal affairs. The *demos* was not an international actor yet.

Given the omnipresence of today's international media reporting, however, the presence of third parties and excluded communities can no longer be ignored; they are part of the audience that the performance of a national ritual has to account for. The potential inclusion of outsiders as unoffended bystanders is indispensable for the construction of national identity in a tight network of international cooperation. Even if the international audience is not directly offended, as in the case of the famous processions of Northern Irish Protestants through Catholic neighborhoods, the celebration of the collective's past victory has to account for its reaction. Rituals of collective identity are no longer a matter of just two parties, the insiders and the excluded and offended outsiders. Instead, they are constantly monitored and morally evaluated by a large third party, that is, the international public.

The celebration of victorious traditions, therefore, can survive only if the focus is shifted from the level of serious and solemn national ritual to the level of harmless folklore, which does not offend outsiders but attracts even tourists' attention. Insisting on a positive construction of collective identity is accepted by outsiders—and that means by the vast majority of others in a globalized world—only if the alleged identity is constructed as a nonpolitical one that can be aestheticized by outside observers or as the identity of a victimized group. Victims can rightfully claim compensation and recognition by others. Ignoring or downplaying triumphant periods in one's own history and even fighting for the public recognition as victims becomes, therefore, a prominent strategy of staging postmodern identities in political arenas. The traumas of the past are here converted into the power of the present day.

If the offensive exclusion of outsiders is challenged by a large third party monitoring the construction of collective identity, so is the missionary inclusion of outsiders that is the hallmark of universalism. Certainly inclusive missionary movements do continue to exist, but in Western societies their mobilizing power is confined mainly to levels of action below or above the nation-state. Some of them appear as short-lived tides that replace the sense of temporal stability, on which identity used to be based, by simultaneous coordination on a global scale. Others have been transformed into fundamentalist movements trying to reestablish a pure and just society but failing to attract a nationwide audience in Western societies. There are, certainly, many sectarian communities of true believers even in these societies, but opportunities to mobilize an entire nation on this basis are limited.

If missionary inclusion fails along with triumphant national master narratives, the quest is for a new conception of collective identity that accounts for the presence of outsiders and can be recognized by them. Rituals of remembrance provide a path to this new idea of collective identity. They abandon the traditional modes of constructing collective identity in manifold ways. They focus on victims instead of victors, on the past instead of the future, on the similar fate of the outsiders instead of the homogeneity of the insiders, on the discontinuity between past and present instead of its continuity, on common history instead of a sum of individual identities. Thus, they hint at a new way of alleviating the tension between the universal and the particular, which always has been a core problem of national identity in an international world.

But even this new turn of reconciling the universal and the particular in the construction of collective identity cannot escape entirely of dark unintended side effects. If the memory of genocide is passed over to institutionalized public rituals of remembering and accepted as a national cultural code, it risks being turned into a decanted and lighthearted routine that discharges the individual members of the community from the burden of the past. Sensitive observers may be concerned if haunting and traumatic memories are transformed into cheap public gestures of routinized respect, if the immensity of horror is replaced by the omnipresent reference to a past that never passes away but has lost its traumatic impact. Thus, the construction of official memorials of the Holocaust and the firm establishment of a pedagogic of the Holocaust may even produce the tragic opposite of its original moral intention, that is, dissolving the trauma on the individual level by externalizing it in official memorials and museums. But despite these paradoxical effects, the manifestation of remembering and reconciliation in memorials prevails.

Such a reconciliation between the descendants of perpetrators and of victims does not result from the simple fact that the generation of the direct and indirect perpetrators is fading away and that their offspring can point to their individual innocence. Collective identity is at stake, and only collective rituals can mark the opposition between past and future and heal the fundamental breakdown of commonality between perpetrators and victims. Just as traditions that attempt to continue the past require rituals of commemoration, so ruptures between past and present, too, require rituals of repentance and cultures of memory. Neither can persist if we recall the events only occasionally, incidentally, and individually. Cultivating memories by rituals and memorials creates a collective identity that is protected against doubts and objections. Therefore, rituals of confession of guilt are not a harassing duty of political rhetoric in postutopian democracies. On the contrary, they provide the only way of getting the recognition of national identity beyond the reclaiming of artificial primordialities and questionable utopias.

# CHAPTER 5

# The Trauma
# of Social Change

*A Case of Postcommunist Societies*

PIOTR SZTOMPKA

## THE STUDY OF CHANGE AT THE CORE OF SOCIOLOGY

Change is a universal and pervasive factor of social life. There is no society without change. Seemingly stable, unchanging phenomena are just cognitively frozen phases in the constant flow of social events, snapshots of the world, which, as such, never stops in its tracks. Ontologically, society is nothing else but change, movement and transformation, action and interaction, construction and reconstruction, constant *becoming* rather than stable *being*. The very metaphor of social life carries this message quite cogently. Life is there as long as it is lived. Society is there as long as it is changing. The dynamic perspective is the only ontologically warranted approach in sociology.

This has been recognized from the beginning of the discipline. In fact classical sociology was born as a science of social change at the macro level, an epochal, massive change from traditional to modern society. Its proper domain was a "first great transition" (Polanyi 1944) epitomized by industrialization, urbanization, mass education, and mass culture. Later it focused on the "second great transition" brought about by automatization, robotization, computerization, spreading of leisure and travel. Presently it is concerned with the "third great transition," primarily the revolution in communication and information, leading toward the "global age" (Albrow 1996) and the "knowledge society." Thus at its core sociology has always remained, to our days, the study of rising, developing, maturing, and decaying modernity.

The all-embracing change has not omitted the reflexive awareness of change, expressed both by the common people and by the social sciences. The perspectives on social change have themselves been undergoing remarkable change. The classical epoch of sociology, the nineteenth century, was pervaded with the idea of *progress*. The mood was triumphalist and optimistic: change was taken to be synonymous with betterment, improvement, and amelioration of the human condition. It was grasped by the concepts of evolution, growth, and development: inevitable and irreversible unraveling of inherent potentialities of society. Change was raised to the level of autotelic value; it was seen as always good, sought and cherished for its own sake.

But already in the nineteenth century first doubts appear, and they become even more pronounced in the twentieth century (Alexander and Sztompka 1990). The discourse of progress is slowly undermined by another perspective: the discourse of *crisis*. Several authors notice that major social change, developmental or progressive in some respects, may yet incur grave social costs. First, it is observed that otherwise progressive processes do not run in a smooth, linear fashion, but rather—to put it metaphorically—through "blood, sweat, and tears," temporary breakdowns, backlashes, even lasting reversals. Hegelian and Marxian dialectics are the prime examples of this view. Second, as the changes expand and deepen, we see ever more clearly that progress does not realize itself in a uniform manner in all domains, areas, or spheres of social life. Processes that can be judged as progressive in some domains are found to produce various adverse side effects, unintended consequences, "spill-offs" in other domains.

This selective focus on crisis in some fields as a price for the triumphs of modernity can be illustrated by six well-known themes initiated in the nineteenth century but pervading sociological thought to our time. There is the theme of *lost community*, or destroyed Gemeinschaft, raised by Ferdinand Tönnies. There is the theme of *anomie*, or moral chaos, empasized by Emile Durkheim. There is the theme of iron cage of *bureaucracy*, or extreme instrumental, manipulative rationality, dwelled upon by Max Weber. There is the theme of decaying *mass culture* and the dangers of massification raised by Ortega Y Gasset. More recently, there is the theme of *ecological destruction*, degradation of nature, the depletion of resources, and "limits to growth." Finally, the critical focus embraces the industrialization of war, *genocide,* and the spreading of terrorism and violence.

The third line of criticism undermining the idealization of progress and fetishization of change shows that progress is not uniformly and unequivocally good for all members of society: what is good for some may be bad for others. The question "Progress for whom?" or "Who pays for progress?" is put on the agenda by Karl Marx with the theme of *alienation* and class oppression and is taken up—not necessarily from a marxist perspective—by numerous later authors focusing on injustice, inequality, and exploitation.

In the second half of the nineteenth century, this selective critique of change as producing crisis in specific domains, or crisis for some groups, takes an interesting turn: crisis is no longer treated as temporary, at least potentially to be healed, but as a chronic, permanent, and endemic feature of modern society, putting a question mark under a whole project of modernity (Holton 1990). The very notion of progress is considered as obsolete, and the optimistic progressivists as utterly naive. The extreme manifestation of the discourse of crisis is the mood of catastrophism. From the pole of triumph to the pole of catastrophe, the pendulum swings all the way.

This opens the way to the emergence of a third, more balanced, perspective, a third type of discourse about social change, which recognizes the perennial *ambivalence* of its effects. This new discourse first manifests itself at the level of common thinking, then through the media, literature, and eventually through sociological debate. I label it the discourse of *trauma,* as it revolves around this central notion, borrowed as a metaphor from medicine and psychiatry and slowly acquiring new social and cultural meaning.

The career of the concept of trauma as applied to society begins with the realization that change itself, irrespective of the domain it touches, the groups it affects, and even irrespective of its content, may have adverse effects, bring shocks and wounds to the social and cultural tissue. The focus shifts from the critique of particular types of change to the disturbing, destructive, shocking effects of change per se. The classical assumption that change is an autotelic value is finally lifted; the fetish of change is undermined. It is countered with the hypothesis that people put value on security, predictability, continuity, routines, and rituals of their lifeworld. The most paradoxical and challenging observation is that even the changes that are truly beneficial, welcome by the people, dreamed about and fought for—may turn out to be painful. The forerunner of this idea was Emile Durkheim with his well-known notion of "anomie of success."

## TRAUMATOGENIC SOCIAL CHANGE

Saying simply that social change produces trauma is a gross simplification. We took as a starting point of the argument the assumption that social life is synonymous with incessant change. If any change were to produce trauma, it would mean that all societies were permanently and irreparably traumatized. The theory of trauma would lose any empirical meaning and would become purely tautological. It would also carry a pessimistic message running counter to our intuitions, which indicate that traumas occur only in *some* societies, at *some* moments, that they are weaker or stronger, and that they are not eternal; they appear and go. The sensible approach is to propose that only some types of changes bring about traumas, and therefore that only some societies in some periods of their history become traumatized. The notion of trauma turns into a *variable* and acquires empirical usefulness. The crucial question is: Which types of change are traumatogenic?

The traumatogenic change seems to exhibit four traits. First, it is characterized by specific speed. The obvious case is the change that is *sudden* and *rapid*, occurring within a span of time relatively short for a given kind of process. For example: revolution is rapid relative to historical time (even when it takes weeks or months), collapse of the market is sudden relative to long-range economic waves, death in an accident is sudden relative to biographical time. The less obvious case, which nevertheless also falls under the same rubric of sudden and rapid change is the process that is prolonged and cumulative but eventually reaches a *threshold of saturation* beyond which it turns out to be fundamentally, qualitatively new. It suddenly appears to be unbearable, produces a shock of realization about something that was ignored before. Such rapid awakening to threats is typical for the processes of ecological decay, depletion of resources, pollution, traffic congestion, cultural imperialism, and growing poverty, to take some examples from the social domain; or progressing illness, aging, alcoholism, drug addiction, and advancing incapacity, if we look at the personal level. In the first case, there is a shock of sudden events, and in the second case there is a shock of sudden awareness of otherwise prolonged processes. Suddenness, or rapidity, is a common denominator in both cases.

The second trait of traumatogenic change has to do with its scope. It is usually *wide, comprehensive, either in the sense that it touches* many aspects of life—be it *social life or personal life*—or that it affects many actors and many actions. Revolution is a good example of traumatogenic social change because it usually embraces not only the political domain, but also law, economy, morality, culture, art, sometimes even language, and it also affects the fate of many groups, if not all the population. Retirement is a good example of traumatogenic personal change because it transforms most life patterns, time and budgets, routines of leisure, networks of social relations, memberships in groups, life standards, and the everyday conduct of the retired individual.

Third, traumatogenic change is marked by specific content, particular substance, either in the sense that it is *radical, deep, fundamental*—that is, it touches the core aspects of social life or personal fate—or in that it affects universal experiences, whether public or private. For example, the shift in dominant values, transfer of power, or overturning of prestige hierarchies changes the very constitution of society, whereas the rise of crime, corruption, and pollution degrades the context of everyday life, threatening the immediate life-world of every societal member.

The fourth feature of traumatogenic change has to do with the specific mental frame with which it is encountered by people. It is faced with an *unbelieving mood;* it is at least to some extent unexpected, surprising, precisely "shocking" in the literal sense of this term. The devaluation of currency (at the societal level) and the diagnosis of cancer (at the personal level) provide good examples.

To summarize: we define as potentially traumatogenic only such changes as are sudden, comprehensive, fundamental, and unexpected. This narrows our focus but not yet sufficiently. The changes meeting this description still make up a very wide and heterogenous category. For example, it would include such cases as:

death in the family

divorce

loss of property in natural disaster

car accident

bankruptcy of the firm

restructuring of the enterprise

fight among friends

collapse of the stock exchange

terrorist attack

foreign conquest

breakdown of the political and economic regime

revolution

Some order is needed in this mixed bag of events, and our next step must be an attempt at classification. One criterion was implicitly suggested when we separated societal and personal changes. At the individual level of biography we experience such events as marriage, childbirth, divorce, death in the family, purchase of a new house, losing a job, retirement, and so on. The traumas these events bring about are *personal,* mostly psychological. They fall beyond the purview of sociology. We come a bit closer but not yet entirely to a sociological perspective if we consider mass events, occurring to a number of people simultanously. Take some examples: a hurricane leaving thousands homeless, an epidemic of a grave disease affecting large segments of a population, an economic crisis resulting in massive unemployment. When such disasters hit, the victims are at first facing them alone, experiencing them individually, as a multitude of private disasters. The trauma is their own and not yet shared, suffered side by side, but not yet together with others.

Truly *collective* traumas, as distinct from massive traumas, appear only when people start to be aware of the common plight, perceive the similarity of their situation with that of others, define it as shared. They start to talk about it, exchange observations and experiences, gossip and rumors, formulate diagnoses and myths, identify causes or villains, look for conspiracies, decide to do something about it, envisage coping methods. They debate, even quarel and fight among themselves about all this. Those debates reach the public arena, are taken by the media, expressed in literature, art, movies. The whole "meaning industry" full of rich narratives focuses on giving sense to the common and shared occurrences. Then the expression of trauma may go beyond the subjective, symbolic, or ideal level and acquire more tangible social forms: intense interaction, outbursts of protest, forming of groups, collective mobilization, creating social movements, associations, organizations, political parties. Only when we observe such phenomena we are in the proper domain of sociology. Traumatogenic changes become "societal facts sui generis" in the sense given to this term by Emile Durkheim. For the sake of sociological analysis we can leave out individual traumas, as well as massive traumas, and devote the remaining discussion exclusively to the level of collective traumas.

Another way to approach this classificatory task is to distinguish domains touched by traumatogenic changes. One is the biological substratum of a society, the *population*. The extreme consequence of a traumatogenic change may be the extermination of societal members. Wars, famines, and epidemics provide tragic examples. A bit less extreme is the decay of biological fitness of the population, marked by such indicators as the rate of deaths at childbirth, life expectancy, suicide rates, frequency of diseases, mental disorders, and so on. A forerunner of such a perspective on trauma was Pitirim Sorokin, who in *Sociology of Revolution* (1967 [1928]) analyzed in detail the disastrous impact of the Bolshevik revolution on the biological capacity of the Russian people. A contemporary example of parallel focus is to be found in the studies of suicide rates in Estonia, Hungary, and Poland after the collapse of the communist system and major systemic changes known as postcommunist transformation. Looking for traumatic effects at the biological level is close to a medical or epidemiological perspective. However important, it falls beyond the scope of sociological analysis proper.

We reach a truly sociological level of analysis when we turn to structural traumas, affecting *social organization*: the social networks, matrixes of groups, associations, formal organizations, hierarchies of stratification, class divisions, and so on. A forerunner of such a perspective was Ferdinand Tönnies with his studies of decaying "Gemeinschaft" (1955 [1877]), followed by rich research on the collapse of communities under the impact of industrialization and urbanization. Another line of research focused on atomization and individualization of social life, exemplified best by David Riesman's *The Lonely Crowd* (1961). There is a rich tradition of studies that show the impact of technological inventions on the organization of labor. Recently much attention has been paid to the destructive effects of autocratic regimes on the organization of civil society. These are only few examples from a wide domain of sociological concerns.

But there is one more domain that can be affected by traumatogenic changes. This is *culture*: axio-normative and symbolic belief systems of a society. The shocks of change may reverberate in the area of affirmed values and norms, patterns and rules, expectations and roles, accepted ideas and beliefs, narrative forms and symbolic meanings, definitions of situations and frames of discourse. One forerunner of this perspective on trauma was Emile Durkheim, with his influential notion of "anomie," or normative chaos, rephrased so fruitfully by Robert Merton (1996 [1938]), and the whole research tradition in the sociology of deviance.

Another early formulation comes from William I. Thomas and Florian Znaniecki, who in their monumental *The Polish Peasant in Europe and America* (1927) documented the plight of emigrants finding themselves in a cultural environment entirely at odds with their earlier life-world, the deeply ingrained, accustomed habits of thinking and doing.

The rest of our discussion will focus on this cultural level of trauma. The phenomenon of *cultural trauma* is particularly interesting for two reasons. First, the cultural tissue is most sensitive to the impact of traumatogenic changes, precisely because culture is a depository of continuity, heritage, tradition, identity of human communities. Change, by definition, undermines or destroys all these. Second, wounds inflicted to culture are most difficult to heal. Culture obtains a particular inertia, and once the cultural equilibrium is broken, it is most dificult to restore it. Cultural traumas are enduring, lingering; they may last over several generations.

## CULTURAL TRAUMAS IN THE AGE OF CHANGE

The twentieth century is sometimes described as the "age of change." The speed, scope, depth, and wonder of changes—driven by scientific and technological innovations, challenges of competition, emancipatory aspirations of the masses, progressivist ideologies, universal education, and so on—are perhaps unparalleled in any period of earlier history. Therefore particularly large pools of changes become potentially traumatogenic, that is, sudden, comprehesive, fundamental, and unexpected. Their impact on the cultural fabric of societies is strong and varied.

One source of cultural traumas is the intensifying *intercultural contact,* or confrontation of diverse cultures, often resulting in tension, clash, and conflict. The most traumatizing situations occur when the imposition and domination of one culture are secured by force. Imperial conquest, colonialism, and religious proselityzing provide prime examples. But even when the spreading of alien culture is more peaceful, by virtue of economic strength, technological superiority, or the psychological attractiveness of cultural products flowing from the core toward the periphery, the result is often the break of cultural stability, continuity, and identity of indigenous groups, a milder and yet resented form of cultural trauma. Even the labels given in the literature to such processes of cultural *globalization*—cultural imperialism, cultural aggression, McDonaldization, Americanization—typically indicate resentment and a defensive mood.

Another source of cultural traumas is the intensifying *spatial mobility* of people, who as emigrants and refugees, but also as business travelers and tourists, find themselves in the milieu of the alien culture. Whereas in the earlier case it was the culture that was spreading out to embrace unprepared people, here it is the people who voluntarily put themselves under the jurisdiction of cultures other than their own. The relative ease of such movement is another aspect of the process of globalization.

The third source of cultural traumas is the *change of fundamental institutions* or regimes, for example, basic political and economic reforms carried out in societies lacking the requisite cultural background, the ingrained competence to deal with new institutions, or, even more grave, when new cultural imperatives fitting the reformed institutions run counter to established cultural habits and traditions. Similar effect may be produced by new technological inventions that require specific skills, care, and discipline from users, if all these are missing. Another case is the transformation of the accustomed life milieu from rural to urban and lack of preparedness for the new life-world. In all these cases cultural traumas result from the processes of modernization or its components: industralization, democratization, technological progress, urbanization, and so on. The traumatizing effect is strongest when modernization is imposed, rather than originating from within, as an indigenous development. The true laboratory for observing the dramatic traumas of *forced modernization* is sub-Saharan Africa. But even when change of regime is originating from below, realizing aspirations of the people, it inevitably engenders some forms of cultural trauma, as it clashes with deeply embedded, thoroughly internalized, earlier "habits of the heart" (Tocqueville 1945 [1835]; Bellah et al. 1985), which create, at least temporarily, the "learned incapacity" to follow cultural imperatives of the new system. This is clearly visible in most postcommunist societies, which, finding themselves in the orbit of democracy, free market, and open culture, have for some time remained trapped in the "civilizational incompetence" (Sztompka 1993b) inherited from the system of real socialism.

The fourth source of traumatogenic change is located at the level of beliefs, creeds, doctrines, ideologies. The *changes of ideas* may take various forms. One is the acquisition of new knowledge, which may shatter established convictions and stereotypes. For example the news about the Holocaust, revealed at the end of World War II, produced a traumatic shock accompanied by guilt feelings among the antisemitic groups in the United States and France (discussed elsewhere in this volume). Another case is the revision of established historical accounts destroying cherished myths about the past. For example, new perspectives on the French

Revolution (Furet 1981), show it to be much less heroic, and much more bloody, than previously believed; the "discovery" of America is simultaneously seen as a tragedy for the American Indians; the whole history of the USSR is rewritten, showing terror and extermination rather than a workers' paradise. Still another case is the appearance of new ideas that may raise sensitiveness and modify perceptions of otherwise well-known facts. For example, the birth of ecological awareness, feminist consciousness, or the concept of universal human rights makes everybody see the conquest of nature, gender oppression, and other inequalities and injustices in a completely new light. In all these cases the clash of old and new beliefs produces at the cultural level the phenomena akin to the well-known psychological effects of "cognitive dissonance."

PRECIPITATING FACTORS:
TRAUMATIZING CONDITIONS AND SITUATIONS

The cultural disorganization and accompanying disorientation are necessary but not sufficient conditions for a full-fledged trauma to emerge. At most they create a ripe soil, a facilitating climate of anxiety and uncertainty. Against this background there must appear a set of conditions or situations, perceived as pernicious, dangerous, or threatening. It is only these that serve as *triggering, precipitating factors* for the emergence of trauma. Most often these conditions or situations are brought about by the same major change that caused cultural disorganization. They may be a direct result of certain policies or reforms undertaken by the government in the aftermath of revolutionary upheaval. Or they may derive from some more general, global tendencies in the wider environment of a society. But they are not directly related to culture; rather they affect the social life of the members of the changing society or the social structure of their society. Traumatizing events or situations may produce dislocations in the routine, accustomed ways of acting or thinking, changing the life-world of the people in often dramatic ways, reshaping their patterns of acting and thinking. What is potentially traumatizing differs among various societies. For example, in the case of postcommunist transformation the list of such triggering factors would include: unemployment, inflation, waves of crime, poverty, stretched economic conditions, overturned hierarchies of prestige, inefficiency of political elites, and so on.

Some of these are more universal, affecting everybody (e.g., inflation or crime); others are more particular, affecting only some segments of the population (unemployment, status degradation). Falling against the background of cultural disorientation, a condition that makes the people more sensitive and anxious, events or situations such as these may engender the traumatic syndrome. But before they do, there is a stage of *cultural labeling*, framing, and redefining.

Trauma, like many other social conditions is at the same time *objective and subjective*: it is usually based in actual occurences or phenomena, but it does not exist as long as those do not become visible and defined in a particular way. The defining, framing, interpretative efforts do not occur in a vacuum. There is always a preexisting pool of available meanings encoded in the shared culture of a given community or society. Individual people do not invent meanings, but rather draw selectively from their surrounding culture and apply existing meanings to the potentially traumatizing events. Hence, the traumatizing conditions or situations are always *cultural constructions*. A limiting case, always possible in the human world is grasped by the famous Thomas Theorem: "If people define situations as real, they are real in their consequences" (Merton 1996). There may be traumas that are not rooted in any real traumatizing conditions or situations, but only in the widespread imaginations of such events. For instance, if enough people believe in the imminent collapse of the bank (otherwise entirely healthy), widespread panic will result. If enough people are convinced that the charismatic leader has committed treason (even if he is in fact innocent), a legitimation crisis will ensue. But the opposite is also possible: the events or situations with objectively strong traumatizing potential may not lead to actual trauma, because they are explained away, rationalized, reinterpreted in ways that make them invisible, innocuous, or even benign or beneficial.

A paradoxical fact is that the cultural templates applied in defining and interpreting new, disturbing conditions or situations are most often drawn from the established, traditional cultural pool, representing the obsolete culture, already being replaced, as an effect of major change, by a new cultural syndrome. Therefore conditions or situations that would be fully congruent with a new culture are defined as unacceptable. For example, the privatization of health services, the reform of pensions, the demand for tuition at the universities—three new policies of the post-communist governments—are interpreted in terms of old socialist cultural expectations, as violating the paternalistic obligations of the state, and are experienced as highly traumatic. The same reforms are clearly meeting the expectations of the new, capitalist, market culture.

The cultural traumas generated by major social changes, and triggered by traumatizing conditions and situations interpreted as threatening, unjust, and improper, are expressed as complex *social moods,* characterized by a number of collective emotions, orientations, and attitudes. First, there is a general climate of anxiety, insecurity, and uncertainty (Wilkinson 1999), which sometimes manifests itself in the phenomenon of "moral panics" (Thompson 1998). Second, there is a prevailing syndrome of distrust, both toward people and institutions (Sztompka 1999). Third, there is a disorientation concerning collective identity. Fourth, there is widespread apathy, passivism, and helplessness. Fifth, there is pessimism concerning the future, matched with nostalgic images of the past. Of course, not all these symptoms accompany every case of trauma, and not all these symptoms are equally manifested by various groups or subgroups within a society.

### SENSITIVENESS TO CULTURAL TRAUMAS

Perhaps for each traumatogenic change there are some *core groups* that experience and perceive it strongly, and *peripheral groups* for whom it is irrelevant or marginal. Some groups, due to their structural and cultural location, are more insulated and some are more susceptible to the impact of traumatogenic change. The question "Trauma for whom?" opens an important area of contingency.

We may indulge in some speculation about the factors responsible for the differences among various groups in their susceptibility to trauma. It seems that the crucial variable may be the access to resources—to cultural, social, as well as economic and political capital—helpful in perceiving, defining, and actively facing traumas. Culturally, the central factor seems to be education. On the one hand, the higher people's level of education, the more perceptive and more sensitive to cultural traumas they become. But at the same time, they are better equipped to express and fight trauma. No wonder that some of the more subtle and hidden traumas have been first perceived, diagnosed, and opposed by intellectuals, philosophers, and social scientists, who have provided ready-made definitions and symbolic frames for other people to pick up. Usually more educated groups also have better skills for actively coping with cultural traumas. A general, diversified, broad education may be more important here than narrow specialization, because cultural traumas often demand relearning, reskilling, and resocializing. And such flexibility is much better served by a multidirectional, rounded education. But other kinds of cultural capital, apart from education, may also play a part. For those kinds of trauma that originate in a cultural clash, or multiculturalism, a tolerant, relativistic, cosmopolitan orientation—as opposed to ethnocentrism or dogmatism—will allow people to cope with trauma better.

In the realm of social capital, one may indicate a factor known as "social rootedness," or wide personal contacts. For example, in studies of postcommunist societies, it was observed that those who have rich social networks of acquaintances, numerous friends, and strong family support will be much better prepared to cope with the traumatic reorientation to capitalist entrepreneurship, free markets, and individualistic responsibility.

And finally, for many kinds of trauma the capital in the literal sense— economic or political, that is, *wealth or power*—may provide important cushioning resources, insulating against trauma or providing efficient means to deal with trauma.

## COPING WITH CULTURAL TRAUMA

Cultural traumas evoke various reactions from the affected society. People respond in different ways as they attempt to cope with trauma. To sort out the strategies they apply, I will use a typology developed with reference to kindred phenomena that clearly falls, as an exemplification, under the rubric of cultural trauma. I have in mind the classical treatment of *anomie,* and social adaptations to anomic conditions, proposed by Robert K. Merton in a seminal article of 1938.

Merton describes four typical adaptations to anomie: innovation, rebellion, ritualism, and retreatism. The first pair are active, constructive adaptations, and the second pair are passive adaptations. Let us generalize this typology and apply it, mutatis mutandis, to cultural traumas. Innovation may take various forms. It may target culture directly and through socialization, indoctrination, or educational measures make an effort either to redefine a cultural dissonance as less grave or only temporary, or by the opposite strategy may articulate the cultural dualism as radical and irreconcilable, idealizing new cultural ways and totally denouncing the old. Such "cultural propaganda," which may be spontaneous or purposefully directed, aims toward alleviating the incongruence within a culture brought about by traumatogenic change. Another form of innovation targets the resources needed to insulate the people against cultural trauma. The efforts toward enriching cultural capital, for example by obtaining education; or social capital, by entering the network of voluntary associations; or financial capital by entrepreneurial activities—

allow people to locate themselves more securely in a new cultural reality. *Rebellion* would indicate a more radical effort aimed at the total transformation of culture in order to replace the traumatic condition with a completely new cultural setup. Countercultural movements, anarchic political groups, and some religious sects provide the best illustrations of this adaptation. A passive, ritualistic reaction would mean turning (or rather returning) to established traditions and routines, and cultivating them as safe hideouts to deflect cultural trauma. And finally, *retreatism* in this connection would mean ignoring trauma, repressing it, striving to forget, and acting as if trauma did not exist. This can provide a kind of subjective insulation against the traumatic condition.

## TRAUMATIC SEQUENCE

When the concept of trauma is borrowed from medicine and psychiatry, one must notice a certain duality of meaning that occurs in these fields. Sometimes the term *trauma* is referring to an event that produces damage, for example, being hit by a car. If this usage were retained for our purposes, trauma would be synonymous with the traumatogenic change. But on other occasions trauma means a shock to the organism resulting from a damaging event, for example, a broken spine. In our context it would mean the traumatic condition of a society resulting from the traumatogenic change.

I propose to combine the two usages. Trauma thus is neither a cause nor a result, but a process, a dynamic sequence of typical stages, having its beginning, but also—at least potentially—its resolution. Let us call it a *traumatic sequence*. The process resembles one identified by Neil Smelser in the emergence of social movements and called "the value-added dynamics" (Smelser 1962). I will apply it mutatis mutandis, with some modifications, for the description of a traumatic sequence. And thus, in my reconstruction the sequence can be analytically dissected into six stages:

1.  Traumatogenic change (sudden, comprehensive, deep, and unexpected)

2.  Disorganization of culture and accompanying cultural disorientation of actors ("structural conduciveness" is the term Smelser uses in his theory for analogous phenomena)

3.  Traumatizing situations or events, appearing as a result of traumatogenic change in areas other than culture and affecting the

life-world of the people ("structural strain" and "precipitating events" in Smelser's terminology)

4. Traumatic condition, expressed by a set of traumatic symptoms, mental or behavioral (new shared ways of conduct or "generalized beliefs" in Smelser's language)

5. Posttraumatic adaptations employing various strategies of coping with trauma ("social control" in Smelser's theory)

6. Overcoming trauma, by consolidation of a new cultural complex (the closing phase of the sequence)

The traumatic sequence does not hang in a vacuum, but runs in the wider context of other processes that occur at the same time but have nothing to do with trauma. From the perspective of the traumatic sequence they may be treated as *parametric*. One set of parametric processes consists of everything of importance that happens in the wider world, outside of a given society, but in the global era has repercussions within a society, for example, market fluctuations, military conflicts, policies of superpowers, and so on. Sometimes these events facilitate traumas, but sometimes they may help to alleviate traumas. Another set of parametric changes is intrasocietal and initiated by the traumatogenic change in the law, politics, economics, and everyday life of the society. For example, revolution, as a traumatogenic change, is usually followed by the turnover of political elites, major reforms, building of new institutions, and creating of new infrastructures of everyday life. Again, some of these processes may aggravate trauma, while others may have a healing effect. The third type of parametric process has a completely different nature. It is the universal and inevitable process of *generational turnover*. The carriers of cultural legacies and traditions that clash with new cultural imperatives imposed by traumatogenic change are generations who were socialized, indoctrinated, or habituated in an earlier cultural milieu. This means that the powerful impact of a culture derived from earlier history, and internalized by the generations whose lives were spent during its prevailing grip, may become much weaker as the new generations emerge, raised under different conditions, in the changed, reformed society. This process running parallel to the traumatic sequence becomes very helpful at the stage of overcoming trauma and achieving final reconsolidation of a culture.

The traumatic sequence may be represented in a diagram, as shown on page 170.

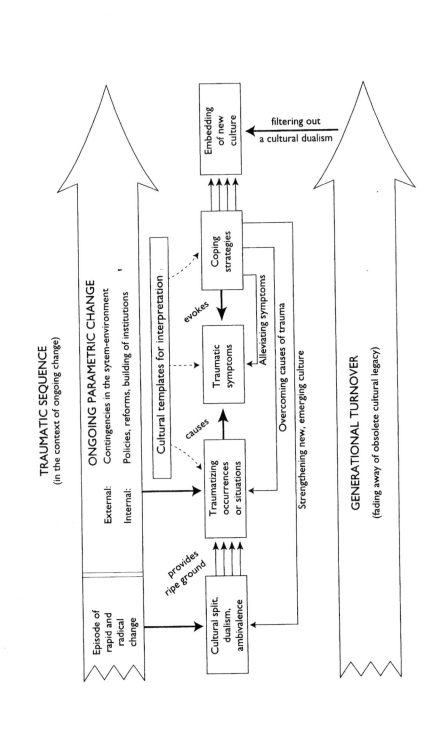

## POSTCOMMUNIST "TRAUMA OF VICTORY": AN ILLUSTRATION

Let us now follow in more detail the stages in the sequence, using for the purpose of illustration the case of the "Revolution of 1989," that is, the collapse of the communist system in East-Central Europe. I will refer mostly to evidence from Poland, but the general observations seem relevant for other countries of the region.

### Traumatogenic Change

There cannot be any doubt that the collapse of communism was a traumatogenic change par excellence. First, it was sudden and rapid. Of course it was preceded by a long and complex historical process, but in that "miraculous autumn," the process acquired tremendous acceleration. Second, the change was truly systemic, multidimensional, embracing politics, economics, culture, everyday life. It was also experienced by the whole population of former communist societies; nobody was exempt from its impact. Third, it was hitting the foundations of the earlier system. It signified a complete reversal of deep premises of social life: from autocracy to democracy in the domain of politics; from central planning to the market in the domain of economics; from censorship to open, pluralistic thought in the domain of culture; and from the "society of shortages" (Kornai 1992) to the society of rampant consumerism. Fourth, the revolution was certainly unexpected—at least at this scale and at this time—not only by the common people but also by professional Sovietologists. What makes the collapse of communism a particularly interesting example of traumatogenic change is also that it was a "trauma of victory" (to paraphrase Durkheim's "anomie of success"). The change was almost universally judged as beneficial and progressive, often welcome with enthusiasm, and yet it has turned out to produce trauma, at least for some segments of postcommunist societies. Finally, the traumatic sequence is in this case still uncompleted, the transformation with all that it implies still in the making, the revolution unfinished—providing an actual laboratory for studying the theory of cultural trauma.

### Cultural Disorganization and Disorientation

As a first, rough approximation, we may say that the cultural landscape in the period immediately following the break looked somewhat like the following. On one side, there was a pervasive, historically inherited repertoire of cultural rules, shaped under the influence of the old communist regime and its characteristic "habitus." This was created either as an effect of prolonged indoctrination or through defensive reactions against indoctrination and autocratic control. An example of an effect of the former type is the support of egalitarianism and "disinterested envy" (Marody 1987) of the more affluent or successful, an acceptance of state paternalism, anti-elitism, anti-intellectualism; an example of the effect of the latter type is the opportunistic double standards, camouflage in mediocrity, and common or even institutionalized practice of evading rules imposed by the regime, with insubordination treated as a virtue. The combined effects of those two mechanisms were embodied in a particular mental constellation described by some authors as "Homo Sovieticus" (Zaslavsky 1994; Tischner 1991).

On the other side there were the seeds of a completely different culture, functionally demanded by the new democratic and capitalist institutions, with relatively few people already culturally prepared for and fully capable of operating in the new organizational context (possessing "civilizational competence" (Sztompka 1993b) required by Western civilization). The clash of those two incompatible cultures meant for most people that their internalized, trained ways of life lost effectiveness and even became counterproductive or negatively sanctioned in the new system, while the new cultural rules appeared to them as alien, imposed, and coercive. And those few who were ready to embrace the cultural rules of the new system and were rewarded by the effectiveness and success of their actions in the new environment (i.e., who commanded "civilizational competence"), paid the price of constant frustrations in encounters with obsolete yet binding bureaucratic principles and pervasive red tape, as well as suspicion, envy, or outright rejection by others persisting in their old, accustomed mental habits.

To paraphrase a concept introduced by Jeffrey Alexander (Alexander 1992; Alexander and Smith 1993) one may say that the cultural "discourse of real socialism" is radically opposed to the "discourse of emerging capitalism." There are several dimensions along which both discourses differ; they constitute the "binary opposites" (to use Alexander's language): a) collectivism vs. individualism, b) solidarity in poverty vs. competition, c) egalitarianism vs. meritocratic justice, d) camouflage in mediocricity vs. conspicuous success, e) security vs. risk, f) reliance on fate vs. emphasis on agency, g) counting on social support vs. self-reliance, h) blaming failures on a system vs. personal responsibility and self-blame, i) passivism and escape to the private sphere vs. participation and activism in public sphere, and j) dwelling on the remembrances of the glorious past vs. actively anticipating and constructing the future.

The incompatibility of those inherited cultural rules of "bloc culture," typical for the autocratic, centrally planned societies of real socialism, and the opposite principles of Western culture, functionally demanded by the new sociopolitical system of capitalism and democracy, engendered a true *cultural shock*. Disorganization at the level of cultural precepts and the *disorientation* at the level of internalized personal habits were the first results of traumatogenic change. But these were only a phase in the traumatic sequence, not yet a trauma in the full sense; they merely established a background of conducive conditions for the emergence of post-communist trauma.

The polarized image presented above is a simplified first approximation, common to all postcommunist societies. But in fact long before the break of 1989, in varying degrees and to varying extents, in each of those societies there also existed alternative cultural complexes: both national cultural traditions and the inroads of the globalized Western culture. The differing strengths of those alternative cultural influences were responsible for great variety among the countries politically enclosed within the same communist bloc, with the common, imposed "bloc culture"; Poland was not the same as GDR, Hungary not the same as Romania, Czechoslovakia not the same as Russia.

Some of the local cultures were better prepared for democracy, more congruent with democratic and market institutions (e.g., the Czechs), while some were fundamentally at odds with democratic institutions (e.g., Russia). Some countries cultivated a strong nationalist spirit, attempting to keep a certain, even if limited, measure of national sovereignty and autonomy (e.g., Poland) while others were more reconciled with imperial Soviet domination (e.g., Bulgaria). Some countries were able to preserve strong religious commitments and find in the Church an alternative center of authority and a powerful ally in the resistance against the autocratic regime (e.g., Poland), whereas others were highly secularized (e.g., DDR and Czechoslovakia).

There were also pronounced differences among the societies of the region in the impact of so-called Western culture, originating in the most developed, industrialized, urbanized mass societies of Western Europe and America. To some degree that culture was smuggled in unwittingly with the institutions of modernity: industrial production, urban settlements, mass education. Of course "socialist" modernity was strangely

incomplete, missing some of its crucial political and economic components (it was a "fake modernity" [Sztompka 1991b]), and yet it had
important culture-generating impact: "Changes sometimes dubbed as
'modernization' produce fundamental shifts in people's values and
behaviours. . . . Industrialization of the economy, collectivization of agri-
culture, the resulting migration to the cities, as well as increased literacy
and access to higher education all changed Soviet societies, making them
more 'modern' and therefore more open to democratic and market reforms" (Reisinger et al. 1994, 200–201). This may be labeled as a "convergence theory" mechanism of building the third alternative cultural
complex—a kind of Trojan horse—while still in the period of communist rule.

Apart from that, some components of Western culture penetrated
directly from the West into various societies of the region (through family links with a diaspora of emigrants in Western societies and through
mass media, personal exchanges, tourism, etc.), though with varying
intensity depending on the rigidity of cultural gates raised by local
authorities (again Poland differed favorably from Bulgaria, Yugoslavia
from DDR, etc.). This may be labeled as a "globalization theory" mechanism, through which Western, democratic, and capitalist culture penetrated communist societies long before the breakdown of the system.

To the extent that those two alternative cultural complexes were
developed alongside the bloc culture, they exerted a salutary, mitigating
influence against the cultural shock brought about by the collapse of
communism and the resulting obsolescence of its accustomed meanings,
symbols, and rules.

### Traumatizing Conditions and Situations

Parallel with this impact on culture, the collapse of communism started a
rapid process of structural and organizational reforms of the political
and economic sort, the building of new infrastructures of institutions,
reshaping of the environment of everyday life. Reforms of that scale
could not be faultless and smooth. Some were outright mistaken; others,
even when successful, incurred various social costs. There were also some
parametric processes in the external, international environment and particularly in the economic domain, which added to the burdens of change,
for example, the breakdown of the Russian market and the necessity to
reorient exports toward the West, and the rise of gasoline prices on world
markets, contributing to inflation.

As a result of all these influences, a number of adverse conditions and situations emerged soon after the revolution. They may be listed in four categories. The first category includes new forms of risks and threats. Perhaps most painful of these was growing unemployment and the pervasive threat of unemployment. Then comes inflation, threatening household budgets and savings. There was a sudden crime wave, including new forms of organized crime, and widespread perception of inefficient law enforcement. The flow of immigrants from the poorer countries of the disintegrating bloc produced encounters with aliens and their idiosyncratic cultural patterns. And there appeared the pervasive theme of competition, necessitating efforts, decisions, and choices, experienced as a burden by unprepared people. The second category includes the deterioration of life standards. There appeared relatively large and visible enclaves of poverty. The established status hierarchies were overturned and social distances stretched. The more pressing needs of reform, as well as the state budget shortages, led to the further decay of already obsolete infrastructure of roads, train lines, and public transportation, adding to the discomforts of everyday life. The fourth category includes more acute perceptions of old, inherited problems. This refers to the switch in social awareness, with new ideas, concepts, and doctrines instilled by the systemic change. People pay much more attention to ecological destruction; complain about low health and fitness standards; demand full restitution of private property nationalized under communist regime; see more clearly factionalism, nepotism and corruption; despair about inefficiency and amoralism of politicians and administrators. All these issues were present before, but sometimes they become more acute and in all cases are perceived as more acute. Finally, the fourth category includes dilemmas and discontents born by the necessity to account for the past. The very controversial public debates concerning the "decommunization" and "lustration" of the earlier collaborators with the communist regime, the unraveling of crimes and oppression committed by former regimes, the raising of doubts about the compromise of the "round table talks" preceding the abdication of communists from power—all this adds to the climate of uncertainty and suspicion.

## Variety of Cultural Interpretations

All events, occurrences, or situations described above—unemployment, inflation, crime, and so on—become traumatizing only if they are defined as such by considerable groups of people, if those definitions are mutually reinforced through communication, expressed in generalized form through public debates, or crystallized in the ideologies of parties or movements. Whether traumatizing events are defined as such or not depends on the assumed *frame of reference*. An event or situation acquires a quality of full-fledged trauma, that is, something disruptive, shocking, and painful, only relative to some standard of normal, orderly expectations. The bare facts are filtered through the symbolic, collectively shared, that is, cultural, lenses.

Polish culture provided rich resources, which allowed the aftermath of the collapse of communism to be interpreted in a positive light and helped to explain away, rationalize, or diminish the importance of adverse, potentially traumatizing events and situations as inevitable but temporary "pains of transition," a necessary price for major victory. The strong legacy of nationalism provided a ready-made frame of "regained sovereignty," and the intepretation of change in such terms, as expressed in the slogan "We are now in our own house," which ignored or deemphasized all inconveniences and discomforts encountered within its walls. Another traditional Polish orientation—the strong pro-Western attitude and even fetishization of the West as the domain of political freedom and economic abundance, as expressed in the notion of "joining" or "returning to Europe," allowed people to forget about obstacles encountered on this road. The third core element of Polish cultural heritage—Roman Catholicism—allowed an emphasis on the return to the core of Western christendom and the discounting of other cultural and ideological losses related to the influx of consumerism or hedonism. The elation linked with the realization of these three aspirations, deeply embedded in the Polish tradition, provided a kind of insulation against the "pains of transition." These three strong cultural themes provided the resources needed to interpret the postrevolutionary changes within "the progressivist narrative"—to use the concept introduced by Jeffrey Alexander (see chapter 1).

But, as we said, in spite of the relative insulation of some groups, the majority of the society was still in the grip of inherited "bloc culture." As long as the old bloc culture prevailed, the potentially traumatizing events and situations (unemployment, insecurity, rise of crime, etc.) were easily defined as traumatic, as they violated the learned cultural expectations of the bloc culture. The bloc culture was also devoid of relevant recipes for effectively dealing with them. No wonder that those still immersed in a bloc culture showed considerable frustration and helplessness. One particularly pernicious component of the bloc culture aggravating the perception of changes as painful or even unbearable was the set of taken-for-granted expectations and claims concerning such provisions as job security, minimum social services (health, education, leisure), child care, and retirement pensions. At the same time there was the belief that those provisions should be distributed equally. People were indoctrinated and habituated to believe that they have a justified claim to them, independent of the contributions they provide themselves to the wider society, that they make up their unconditional rights. When the new capitalist, market regime introduced competitive, individualistic principles, acknowledging differences of achievement, and when the new democratic, liberal state withdrew from various domains of life, leaving them to private efforts—wide groups perceived this as a breach of obligations by the state. They looked at unemployment, lowering of life standards, inflation, and weak protection against rising crime as unforgivable violations of a social contract. The tradition of egalitarian paternalism and social security provided the symbolic cultural resources for framing the postrevolutionary change as "the tragic narrative," to refer again to Alexander's concept (see chapter 1).

Only as the culture itself is transformed do the other definitions of the same events—as the inevitable costs or sacrifices on the progressive road toward democratic and capitalist society of the Western type—have a chance to emerge, and with them a new repertoire of coping strategies as well as the willingness to resort to them.

It is interesting to note that the more groups or social categories that are objectively affected by the "pains of transition" and the more they are immersed in the vestiges of bloc culture (e.g., the workers in the state-owned enterprises), the more they emphasize three symbolic and ethically infused cultural themes: security, equality, and justice; whereas those groups that are more successful, that adapt better to new conditions and are already embraced by the new democratic and capitalist culture (e.g., the new entrepreneurial class), refer rather to the idea of individual freedom and the pragmatic themes of efficiency and prosperity (Marody 1996, 15). These differences were crucial for the diversification of meaning attached to the very process of postcommunist transition. Several authors indicate a clear polarization: those who succeed in the new conditions, who are ready and able to use the new opportunities, construe the process as "modernization," or "joining Europe," or "civilizational advancement"; whereas those who lose, whose status deteriorates and for whom opportunities seem unaccessible, give to the process a completely different meaning—it is a "sellout of the country" to foreign corporations, the "conspiracy of former communists," the "cultural imperialism of the United States," or the dilution of national and Catholic values in cosmopolitan, globalized culture. This spectrum of meaning becomes spontaneously transferred to the domain of political programs and ideologies or is skillfully tapped by party organizers and political entrepreneurs, resulting in the emergence of excessive numbers of political parties, from the extreme right to the extreme left.

Thus the attitude toward transition determines new paramount social divisions. In the research carried out in 1991 in the industrial city of Lodz, Anita Miszalska found the following distribution: 12.4 percent of the respondents express the "syndrome of anxiety in face of social degradation," and they are nostalgically craving for the return of a communist regime; 11.5 percent express the "syndrome of frustrated hopes"; 12.1 percent represent the "syndrome of disorientation and threat"; 20 percent seem "undecided and waiting"; 33 percent demand "acceleration of reforms and a complete break with the communist past"; and only 7.9 percent are "fully satisfied with change and expect only continuation of policies" (Miszalska 1996, 93–106). We could say that only the last group does not experience the postcommunist trauma, either because it is insulated from the "pains of transition," for example, by economic power, or because it has access to the new cultural definitions of the pains as temporary and healable.

### Traumatic Condition: The Symptoms of Trauma

The various factors of existential uncertainty, operating against the background of cultural dislocation and ambivalence, and interpreted and defined with the help of inherited symbolic frames of reference, result in variously distributed cultural trauma. One may spot five symptoms of trauma in the years immediately following the break of 1989, pervading large segments of Polish society.

*Distrust Syndrome*   After the elation and enthusiasm of the anticommunist revolution, the postrevolutionary malaise, or "the morning-after syndrome," sets in, and with it comes a profound collapse of trust. As I extensively discuss it in other places (Sztompka 1999), I wish to point out only some main dimensions of the phenomenon.

From the peaks of trust enjoyed by the first democratic government of Tadeusz Mazowiecki, trust in governmental institutions is consistently falling. The case of Lech Walesa is particularly telling, as we observe the dramatic fall of his popularity once he took presidential office. Evaluating their earlier charismatic and heroic leader, 24 percent of the people declared that he brought shame on Poland by the way he handled his presidential job (*Polityka*, June 25, 1994). Other politicians were also treated with great suspicion: 87 percent of a nationwide sample claimed that politicians take care only of their own interests and careers and neglect the public good (*Gazeta Wyborcza [GW]*, July 11, 1994), 77 percent believed that they use their offices for private profit (*CBOS Bulletin*, October 1995, 1), and 87 percent that they take care of their own careers exclusively (*GW* no.159, 1994). If anything goes wrong in society, 93 percent of the people declared, "the politicians and bureaucrats are guilty" (Koralewicz and Ziolkowski 1990, 62). The veracity of people in high office is also doubted: 49 percent of citizens did not believe information given by the ministers (*GW*, March 25, 1994); 60 percent were convinced that even the innocuous data on levels of inflation or GNP growth, released by the state statistical office, were entirely false (*CBOS Bulletin*, January 1994). Not much trust was attached to fiduciary responsibility of the government or the administration: 70 percent believed that the public bureaucracy is completely insensitive to human suffering and grievances (Giza-Poleszczuk 1991, 76). The institutions of public accountability did not fare any better: 52 percent disapproved of the verdicts of the courts (*CBOS Bulletin* no. 7, 1994, 72), and 79 percent claimed that verdicts will not be the same for persons of different social status (Giza-Poleszczuk 1991, 88); the tax collecting offices are believed to be helpless against tax fraud by 62 percent of the respondents, and only 14 percent considered them effective in their job (*CBOS Bulletin* no. 8, 1993, 26); 72 percent disapproved of the operations of the police (*CBOS Bulletin* no. 7, 1994, 72). The only exception is the army, which consistently preserves its relatively high level of trustworthiness (with 75 to 80 percent expressing consistent approval, a striking Polish phenomenon, accounted for only by some historically rooted sentiments going back to the time of heroic fights against foreign invaders).

The mass media, even though much more independent and not linked directly to the state, do not fare much better. Apparently they have not yet regained people's trust because of their instrumental role under socialism. Three years after the break, 48 percent of the people still did not believe what they heard on television, and 40 percent distrusted the newspapers (*Eurobarometer*, February 1993).

Even the Catholic Church, traditionally one of the most trusted institutions (with declared trust of 82.7 percent in a nationwide sample in

1990; see Marody 1996, 252) seems to be affected by the climate of distrust, especially when it usurps a more political role; 54 percent disapproved of such an extension of the Church's functions, and 70 percent-
would like the Church to limit its activities to the religious sphere (GW,
May 10, 1994).

Finally, if we look at interpersonal trust in everyday life, people also
perceive its decay. In one of the surveys, 56 percent estimated that mutual
sympathy and help have markedly deteriorated (OBOP Bulletin,
October 1996, 2). According to the Polish General Social Survey, the tendency of falling interpersonal trust persisted up to 1994. The belief that
"most people can be trusted" was expressed by 10.1 percent of the
nationwide sample in 1992, 8.9 percent in 1993, and 8.3 percent in
1994. And the opposite view that "one is never careful enough in dealing
with other people" was supported by 87.8 percent in 1992, 89.5 percent
in 1993, and 90.3 percent in 1994 (Marody 1996, 224).

*Bleak Picture of the Future*   The second symptom of cultural trauma is
a pessimistic view of the future. In 1991 only 13.6 percent of the respondents in the working class city of Lodz considered the direction of
changes to be right and proper (Miszalska 1997, 50). In the same year
nationwide polls showed that 59 percent of the people predicted the
worsening of their personal economic situation (CBOS Bulletin no. 1,
1992, 9). Two years later, in another poll 58 percent of the respondents
appraised the current political and economic situation as deteriorating
(GW, February 22, 1994). Only 29 percent believed that privatization
brings "changes for the better" (GW, April 17, 1994). When asked about
the fate of their society in the future, only 20 percent trusted that the situation will improve, 32 percent expected a turn for the worse, and 36
percent hoped that it will at least remain stable (GW, April 17, 1994).
Another poll showed as many as 64 percent pessimists, against just 20
percent optimists (CBOS Bulletin no. 1, 1994, 5). More concretely, referring to the overall economic situation, 62 percent believed that it will not
improve (Eurobarometer, February 1993) and 55 percent expected costs
of living to rise (CBOS Bulletin, January 1994). A confirmation of the
dismaying picture is found in the list of problems that people worry
about: 73 percent indicate a lack of opportunity for their children as
something that worries them most (CBOS Bulletin, January 1993).

*Nostalgic Image of the Past*   Another indicator of trauma is the com-
parison of the present socioeconomic situation with the past. Asked

about their personal conditions, 53 percent felt that they were living worse than before (GW, June 17, 1994). In the industrial city of Lodz the percentage was even higher—75 percent (Miszalska 1996, 68). During the whole year of 1993, only around 12 to 13 percent defined their living conditions as good (CBOS Bulletin no. 1, 1994, 7). Appraising the situation of others three years after the break, around half of the respondents believed that people were generally more satisfied under socialism. This surprising result was confirmed by three independent polls, estimating the percentages at 52 percent, 48 percent, and 54 percent (GW, June 28, 1994).

*Political Apathy*   In spite of the more open political opportunities, the use of them by common people is very limited. Electoral absenteeism is high. In the first democratic presidential elections in Poland, almost 50 percent of citizens chose to abstain, and in later municipal elections overall participation was around 34 percent, falling down to 20 percent in the cities. In the parliamentary elections of 1991 only 43 percent participated, and 57 percent abstained (Miszalska 1996, 172–88). Enrollment in the rich spectrum of newly formed political parties is very low. Most of them remain political clubs frequented only by professional politicians, with the idiom "sofa parties" devised to ridicule their overblown aspirations. Citizens' initiatives at the grassroots level are still rare, and local self-government is still undeveloped and preempted by bureaucratic administration.

*Postcommunist Hangovers: Traumas of Collective Memory*   The final symptom of trauma is the reevaluation of the communist past and the role played in that period by the people variously implicated in its support. The magnanimity of the victors allowed the first democratic government of Tadeusz Mazowiecki to declare a policy of a "broad line" cutting off the past and evaluating people only on the merit of their contributions to the new, free, democratic order. But soon the issue of responsibility, retribution, or revenge was raised, especially by the groups negatively affected by the changes. The slogans "decommunization" and "lustration" were raised by the populist-oriented parties of the right. "Militant decommunizers would have spread the nets widely and were never deterred by such obstacles as burden of proof, reasonable doubt, due process, or any other concept subsumed under the 'rule of law'" (Brown 1997, 29).

The controversial and sometimes highly emotional public debate that has ensued (see *Transitions,* February 1997 and September 1998), allowed the introduction of certain distinctions. First, most participants agree that outright criminal acts committed by the communist authorities or party apparatchiks should be brought to the courts of law. Two periods are selected for particular attention: the Stalinist time up to 1956, and the martial law crushing the Solidarnosc movement in 1981–82. But even here, except for cases of particular personal viciousness or abuses of office, it can be argued that the authorities acted according to the laws of the day. A counterargument must invoke some parallel to the Nuremberg trials and the notion of basic lawlessness of some antihuman laws. Anyway, a number of court trials have been started and linger to the present day.

The second category contains high-ranking communist politicians, who—with the benefit of hindsight—may be seen as collaborators of the foreign, Soviet regime and traitors to their nation. Some would forbid any political roles for them in the present democratic system. But again controversy arises when their past moral responsibility is matched with their present potential usefulness for the country. They happen to be very well trained and skilled professionals of politics—qualifications that are not in abundance among oppositional activists, who have no earlier experience of rule. The present policy leans to pragmatic arguments about using the "cadres," and in fact the conduct of former communists who have gained political offices in a new system (e.g., the highly popular President Aleksander Kwasniewski) provides evidence that this attitude is correct and fruitful (Brown 1997, 33). But of course the opponents from the extreme right do not desist in their personal attacks under the banner of anticommunist purge.

The third category includes the unknown echelons of those who have been implicated in some form of collaboration with the secret police. It has been accepted that such a role would disqualify a politician, and therefore all candidates for high office are now required to file a statement denying collaboration. A special independent court was established to check those statements at random. It also took almost ten years of debates to force through the parliament a law allowing citizens harmed by the secret police to look at their files in the secret archives, to discover who was spying on them or denouncing them. The opponents of the law raised doubts about the veracity of the archives, which could have been purged of some evidence over the years or could even contain evidence faked for political purposes.

The proponents of "decommunization" have their weakest case when it is applied to the fourth category of villains: the rank-and-file members of the communist party, of whom there were more than two million, and whose political role or influence on political events was absolutely minimal. Some of them, a narrow minority, came to the party because of their leftist ideological convictions. But for most of them it was an opportunistic choice, allowing fuller participation in occupational and public life, proceeding with normal careers, and often contributing considerably to the life of society, when the communist system seemed to be strongly entrenched and destined to persist for centuries. Should they now be punished for leftist beliefs or for innocuous opportunism? How can one measure their guilt compared to their professional contributions? This is another contested problem.

The very scope and intensity of the debate surrounding these issues indicates that there is a trauma of collective memory, with strong sentiments of guilt or shame, self-righteousness or forgiveness, concerning the communist past. "Some see it as a rigorous pursuit of justice, others as the perpetuation of injustice; some maintain it is essential for a new beginning, others that it vitiates democracy right from the start; some see it as a breakthrough, others as a massive diversion" (Brown 1997).

There are three more specific "traumas of memory" that in the postcommunist period are the subject of lively public debate and strongly contested, opposite points of view. The first concerns the episode of martial law and crushing of the Solidarnosc movement in December 1981, and particularly the role of the communist leader of that time General Wojciech Jaruzelski. The public opinion is polarized: some believe that it was a necessary "lesser evil" in the face of inevitable Soviet invasion and therefore a patriotic deed, while some construe it as national treason in the service of Soviet masters. The second and related controversy relates to the decision of President Reagan's administration to stand by idly and not to warn Solidarnosc leadership of the coming martial law, even though the administration was fully aware of the plans brought to the United States by the high-ranking colonel in the Polish Army Ryszard Kuklinski. Was the American decision a prudent attempt to prevent bloodshed or rather another Yalta-like sellout of Poland in the name of American geopolitical interest? And should colonel Kuklinski be treated as a traitor and a spy at the service of foreign government or as a national hero fighting in disguise for national liberation (Michnik 1998). The third "postcommunist hangover" concerns the agreement reached between the communist regime and the opposition during the round table talks of 1989, and particularly the supposed secret clauses added at the behind-the-scene talks at the village of Magdalenka outside of Warsaw, concerning the immunity and certain political and economic privileges for communist leadership. Was it the inevitable price for the peaceful and bloodless abdication of power or rather treason, or at least political incompetence of the Solidarnosc negotiators? And what was the role of the opposition's charismatic leader Lech Walesa in the "Magdalenka sellout"? All three traumas linger on, occasionally reappearing in heated public debates, often cynically manipulated for political benefits by various political parties.

## Coping with Trauma

Faced with traumas, people resort to various strategies to cope with them. I shall present these strategies applying the already discussed typology of adaptive reactions to anomie developed by Robert K. Merton (Merton 1996 [1938]).

First, there are *innovative strategies*. Here the people take the systemic change as given, not to be reversed, and make attempts at creative reshaping of their personal situation within the system, in order to alleviate trauma. They try to strengthen their position in the new circumstances by raising or mobilizing resources: either economic capital (monetary resources) or social capital (interpersonal resources).

Almost immediately after the break of 1989 we could observe on a large scale three methods of *accumulating economic capital*. There was an outburst of small-scale trading and peddling in the streets, state enterprises were sending trucks of merchandise to the cities and selling directly from them to save on wholesale and retail overhead, spontaneous bazaars were opening at sport stadiums and street corners, and crossborder traffic was immensely intensified by speculators and traders profiting from price differences. Another method was taking extra jobs or supplying other paid services outside of a job. This was typical for professionals: lawyers taking consulting practices in enterprises, medical doctors opening private offices apart from jobs held at state hospitals, academics getting involved in teaching or training outside of the universities. Temporary employment abroad—legal or illegal—and intensive saving on considerably higher foreign wages or salaries was another strategy that had been used to some extent under communism but became much more common after the full opening of the borders.

Even more interesting strategies are aimed at *raising the social capital,* interpersonal resources that become a kind of background support or springboard for launching a career or raising living standards. One of those, used quite extensively, was pooling the savings of extended families to support one delegated family member in starting an enterprise, specialized farm, or other business venture. Another, typical for the members of the earlier political or managerial elite (communist "nomenklatura"), was to use their networks of acquaintance, influence, and privileged information for profitable market deals (e.g., purchasing at below-market prices the whole enterprises they had formerly managed, which were undergoing privatization). This practice has a label in the sociological literature: the "conversion of social capital into economic capital" or the "endowment of the nomenklatura." Another characteristic process was the eruption of voluntary associations, foundations, clubs, and community organizations. People were seeking collective support in their fight with traumas and were pooling individual resources for more efficient efforts.

Finally, we can observe a true educational boom. Education has become perceived as a crucial asset, transferrable into occupational or professional positions, higher living standards, or raised prestige. The numbers of students at the university level have more than doubled from 403,824 in 1990 to 927,480 in 1997, accompanied by similar expansion of the schools providing higher education, from 112 in 1990 to 213 in 1997 (*Rocznik Statystyczny* 1997, 240). Apart from state-run schools, where education is in principle free, new private institutions of higher education are cropping up, and in spite of high tuition they draw great numbers of students. There were 18 such schools in 1992 and 114 in 1997 (*Rocznik Statystyczny* 1997, 244). Equally significant is the strikingly changing profile of educational choices. They become clearly oriented toward future occupational opportunities, which was not at all true under communism. Hence the most popular departments at the universities now are law, business administration, management and finance, medicine, computer science, sociology, political science, and European studies. Under communism, students were choosing history of art, archaeology, musicology, philosophy, and other esoteric subjects, just for the fun of studying and enjoying a kind of temporal leave from their mundane, dreary existence, as their academic credentials were irrelevant for their future occupational success. Among private schools the most successful are those offering practice-oriented instruction in management, economics, and public policy. All those fields are obviously related to the emerging employment opportunities in a market-based economy and democratic polity.

The strategies described above are legitimate, falling within the scope of normatively prescribed conduct, even if they sometimes stretch the letter of the law and operate at the border of legality. But of course there are also *illegitimate adaptations* to new conditions, attempts to raise economic or social capital by illicit means, running against moral or legal rules. People are clearly aware of spreading corruption, nepotism, and favoritism. In the nationwide poll carried out in 1992, 86 percent of the respondents defined corruption as a very grave social problem, and 54 percent claimed that giving bribes is the only effective way to deal with the administration, even in simple and uncontroversial cases (*CBOS Bulletin,* April 1992, 40–42). In another poll, 48 percent saw public administration as the seat of corruption (*GW,* March 19, 1994). As the domains of life where corruption is most pervasive, the respondents indicated the public and governmental sphere: public institutions (44 percent), courts and judiciary (41 percent), police (39 percent) (*CBOS Bulletin* no. 5, 1994, 113). Even more disturbing is the spread of common crime, with burglaries, robberies, and car thefts becoming incomparably more common than before. Finally, the emergence of gangs, mafias, and other criminal organizations is a vicious parallel, at the level of the underworld, of the flourishing associational life in the wider society.

So much for innovative responses. Irrespective of their moral or legal qualifications, they are all activist and future oriented, revealing originality and resourcefulness. But—following Merton—we may also find the opposite, *retreatist adaptations,* an escape from trauma toward passivism, resignation, and marginalization. Faced with sudden changes and uncertainty in their life-world, many people turn to the discourse of fate, adopting providentialism or a "wait-and-see" orientation. In 1994 68.3 percent of the respondents from the city of Warsaw believed that "planning for the future is impossible because too much depends on chance," 74.2 percent complained that "most people do not realize how their lives are guided by chance," and 62.8 percent claimed that "most of us are victims of forces that we can neither understand nor control" (Marody 1996, 216). Other people turn their hopes toward benevolent help from the state or an autocratic strongman or a savior-to-come. The craving for paternalistic care, a strong ruler, and simple solutions to economic problems opens the door for all kinds of populists and demagogues. There is still a persistent expectation, typical of the old regime, "that the state is responsible for all aspects of economic and social life and, therefore, should solve all problems" (Ekiert and Kubik 1997, 26). This attitude perhaps explains why 65 percent of the people would still choose a state-owned enterprise as a preferred workplace, and only 15 percent a private one (*CBOS Bulletin* no. 4, 1995, 98). The case of Stanislaw Tyminski, the businessman from Canada who was able to draw almost one-fifth of the votes in the presidential elections by empty promises of immediate prosperity, seems a telling indicator of that populist-claimant orientation.

Another retreatist reaction may be called *ghettoization*. We observe the revival of all sorts of primordial social bonds of an exclusive sort, building barriers around ethnic, regional, or occupational communities, and attempting to gain some privileges irrespective of or even against the interests of wider society. Once such special interests obtain their representation in the political arena, we observe displays of group egoism or factionalism (e.g., by the peasants or coal miners fighting for monopolistic privileges or the inhabitants of some cities or regions violently defending their autonomy or former status as independent cities in the face of major reform of local government). Finally, a retreatist strategy resorted to quite widely is system-blame, or in other words complaining about external conditions and shunning any responsibility for problems. It takes various forms. One is to blame the past and seek the sources of present troubles in the days of communism, and the villains of present traumas among former communists. The calls for "decommunization" (i.e., purging those formerly involved in any political roles, including mere membership in the communist party) are a typical manifestation of this strategy. A more restrained version is the policy of "lustration," eliminating from public office those who had any links with former secret services. But system-blame may also be directed differently. Some people blame capitalism and democracy for their current predicament and exhibit nostalgic cravings for the past. They would condone slowing down or braking the development of capitalism (e.g., of privatization and marketization) and call for state intervention and control close to the "central planning" of the past. Finally, there are also widely circulating conspiracy theories blaming the international corporations, global financial markets, George Soros, or the bureaucrats of the European Union for all perceived problems and troubles.

The third type of adaptive responses falls under the Mertonian label of "ritualism." These are cases when people find some measure of security in following traditional, accustomed patterns of action, even if under changed circumstances they lead nowhere. A particularly paradoxical example of such misplaced strategies is turning to the "repertoires of contention" developed during the period of democratic opposition, and particularly during the eighteen months of the Solidarnosc movement in

1980–81, against new, democratically elected power. One of the unfortunate legacies of that period is a reluctance to resort to routine political processes of democracy in order to resolve grievances, and the tendency instead to continue the strategies and tactics of the "movement society," once instrumental as the subinstitutional alternative to official politics but no longer necessary under new political conditions. It is a bit paradoxical, for example, to see industrial strikes, sit-ins, protest marches, rallies, and prolonged fasts, organized in the nineties by the trade-union Solidarnosc, used against the activists and veterans of the Solidarnosc movement now serving in the parliament or the government. Other actions of a similar sort are directed at misplaced targets, as for example the march on the Polish Parliament of the aggrieved and striking workers of a metallurgical plant in Warsaw owned now by the Italian conglomerate Lucchini.

As Ekiert and Kubik claim on the basis of thorough analysis, "Poland of the early 1990s would rank among the most contentious nations in the world" (Ekiert and Kubik 1997, 17). Their count of "protest events" shows 306 for the year 1990, 292 for 1991, 314 for 1992, and 250 for 1993 (ibid., 19). The number of workers on strike doubled between 1990 and 1991, from 115,687, to 221,547 (ibid., 21). During the year from 1992 to 1993, the number of those who believed that nothing could be attained without strikes rose from 20 percent to 40 percent (*CBOS Bulletin* no. 5, 1993, 115).

All three types of adaptive strategies discussed above—innovation, retreatism, and ritualism—took the existence of the new system for granted and aimed only at carving out some better niche for oneself or one's group within the system. The fourth strategy differs from them in being truly radical. It attempts to alleviate traumas by attacking the foundations of the system, either under the banner of reversal to communist or socialist institutions, or in the name of some not too clearly specified "third way" or "middle of the road" system combining the effectiveness of capitalism with the social security of socialism. After Merton, we shall call this adaptive response "rebellion." In Poland the most radical forms of the contesting orientation are to be found among considerable segments of the peasantry, who resort to forced blockades of the roads and even of the state borders, destroy transports of imported grain and other foodstuffs, and organize violent demonstrations in the nation's capital to force their demands of protectionism, curbing competition, closure from the developed Western Europe, stopping the bid to join the European

Union, and returning to some traditionalist, provincial, secure enclave of folk economy and folk culture at the margins of modern Europe. There are also some groups of youth united in the "Republican League," who proclaim anarchic ideas and organize various street events, rallies, and happenings to carry their message.

## TOWARD THE OVERCOMING OF TRAUMA

Contrary to many pessimistic expectations, postcommunist trauma seems to enter the healing phase relatively quickly. In the Polish case, already in the middle of the nineties most negative trends are reversing and several traumatic symptoms seem to be disappearing.

How could one explain the reversal of those trends and visible healing of traumatic symptoms? If my theoretical account of the etiology of postcommunist trauma makes any sense, there are three directions the answer must take. First, it must be shown that the *traumatizing situations* seen as immediate, precipitating factors of trauma are disappearing or are at least redefined, losing their salience. Second, it must be shown that the *coping strategies* adopted against trauma, or at least some of them, have real healing effects. And third, it must be shown that the *cultural ambivalence,* or split between the legacy of the bloc culture and the emerging democratic and capitalist culture, is no longer acute, and therefore the cultural definitions of various "pains of transition" as traumatic are less probable to arise. Let us follow these three explanatory avenues in turn.

It seems that the most important factor for eliminating postrevolutionary malaise, uncertainty, and anomie is a widespread perception of *continuity and success of democratic and market reforms.* In the political realm, a very important achievement was the enactment in 1997 of a new constitution, patterned on classical Western constitutionalism. Another was the successful multiple turnover of power through elections (Juan Linz's "test of democracy" [Linz in Przeworski et al. 1995]), proving that the fundamental mechanism of parliamentary democracy actually operates. The new democratic institutions have confirmed their resilience: the Constitutional Tribunal has been involved in several cases correcting faulty legislation and its head has become one of the most respected public officials, the ombudsman office has been highly active in defending citizens' rights, and the free, independent media have been providing visibility of political life and have unraveled abuses of power. Functioning democracy enhances the feelings of stability, security, accountability, and transparency—all fundamentally important for alleviating anxiety, distrust, pessimism, and apathy.

The second important factor confirming the success of transition was the *vigorous take-off of economic growth*. The enactment of a constitution and a series of specific laws dealing with the economic sphere have built a legal foundation under the new capitalist economy. The principle of private ownership has been reaffirmed, and the continuing privatization of state-owned enterprises, as well as the consistent reinstating of property confiscated during the communist period, proves that the policy is stable and irreversible. At the same time a new capitalist infrastructure—banks, stock exchange, brokers, insurance companies, credit associations, mutual funds, and so on—has rapidly emerged. All this has provided a framework conducive to a true explosion of entrepreneurship, which over some years has evolved from street peddling and illicit financial speculations to large-scale industrial ventures. Stability and certainty of the terms of trade, as well as a secure business environment, contribute in important measure to the climate of economic vitality. The delayed results of early "shock therapy" applied in 1990 according to the Balcerowicz plan, plus a period of reasonable and professional management of reforms by the former communists in power from 1994 to 1998, finally started to assert themselves. Poland came to the fore of the postcommunist societies. GDP growth reached 6.1 percent in 1996, 6.0 percent in 1997, and almost the same in 1998. At the same time inflation fell from 20.1 percent in 1996 to 16 percent in 1997, 12 percent in 1998, and 8 percent in 1999.

Macro success has been reflected at the micro level. The personal costs of reforms began to be outweighed by benefits. Large segments of the population started to experience rising wages, growing prosperity, comfort, and sometimes true wealth. The new quality of everyday life—an easier, more attractive, and "colorful" life-world—is now perceived by large segments of the population. After the drabness and grayness of socialist city landscapes, the misery of the "queuing society," the deprivations of the economy of shortage, and the tyranny of a producer's market, most people enjoy the opportunities of the consumer society to a much greater extent than do their blasé Western counterparts. Shopping, dining out, driving fast cars, taking trips to other countries, entertaining lavishly, and enjoying increased leisure are newly discovered pleasures that raise the general mood of satisfaction and optimism.

The next set of factors conducive to the alleviation of trauma has to do with the *expansion of personal and social capital, the* growth of resourcefulness, at least of some considerable segments of the population. A sizable, relatively affluent middle class, which feels more secure and rooted, has emerged in Poland (Mokrzycki 1995). With the powerful rush for higher education, the level of scholarship has been significantly raised, and with that an overall feeling of competence in the new conditions. With the proliferation of voluntary associations, clubs, and organizations, spontaneous social participation rises and personal networks expand. Again, this social process gives people the feeling of security, roots, and support.

Apart from the new forms of personal and social capital, there are old, traditional resources successfully tapped under the new conditions. Strong personal networks of friendships, acquaintanceships, and partnerships were inherited from the communist period, when internal exile, privatization of life, and "amoral familism," to apply Eugene Banfield's phrase (Banfield 1967), were typical adaptive measures. When asked about the secret of their business successes, top Polish entrepreneurs almost unanimously indicated their rich personal networks, even before their actual capital assets. In the Polish General Social Survey, 60.43 percent indicated "good connections" as a decisive or very important factor of life chances (Marody 1996, 63). Another traditional resource available in Polish conditions is strong and extended families. They provide insurance in case of life calamities; support in raising children, therefore allowing the pursuit of educational aspirations or professional careers for the parents; and pooled capital for new business enterprises. The third less tangible but perhaps also important resource is religious community. In Poland, one of the most religious countries of Europe, with more than 90 percent Catholics and some 60 percent churchgoers, the support and security provided by the Church may be important in alleviating the trauma of transition.

Factors of another type, *external contingencies* that happen to be advantageous, are helpful in alleviating trauma. One of these is the political will of NATO countries to extend the alliance to the East, and particularly the strong American support for the Polish bid to NATO, resulting in the formal inclusion of Poland in March 1999. The prospect of lasting military security and a guarantee of political sovereignty seem to be assured. This is not a trifling matter in a country so badly mauled by history: invaded innumerable times from the east, south, north, and west; partitioned among imperial European powers for the whole of the nineteenth century up to World War I; and suffering Nazi occupation and

Soviet domination for a large part of the twentieth century. It is no wonder that the bid for NATO is a matter on which Poles came closer to unanimity than on any other political issue. It is supported by about 80 percent of the citizens, with 10 percent against it and 10 percent undecided (*CBOS Bulletin*, no.90, 1997, 1). The motivations for support indicated by the respondents mention most often national security (68 percent) and full sovereignty (56 percent) (*CBOS Bulletin* no.27, 1997, 6–8). The negotiations with the European Union have a slightly different meaning. In spite of some doubts and anxieties that it raises in segments of the population more vulnerable to foreign competition (for example, among the farmers, 75 percent of whom express worries and only 16 percent hopes; *CBOS Bulletin* no.66, 1998, 2), there is one widely understood asset: the unification of the Polish legal system—and hence the political and economic regime—with well-established market democracies of the West provides a strong, external guarantee that new institutions will be lasting and firm. With incorporation into the EU a new kind of accountability appears: of the whole polity, economy, and legal system before the authorities of the union. The reversal of reforms seems even less probable. Thus external security and external accountability allow for more predictability and trust. This seems to be recognized by 71 percent of the Poles, who in 1998 supported joining the EU (*CBOS Bulletin* no.66, 1998, 4).

Another contingent development that is helpful in alleviating trauma is the prolonged economic boom in the West, and particularly the United States (which seems to continue in spite of some recent market turbulence). It implies the availability of free resources and the interest of foreign investors in new emerging markets. Poland got ahead of all countries of the region in cumulative foreign direct investment. It reached 20.3 billion US dollars as of December 1997 (*International Herald Tribune,* June 24, 1998, 12). For some years it was a crucial factor invigorating the Warsaw stock exchange, and the sale of goverment bonds to foreign banks has helped to reduce the deficit.

Now let us note that some significant contributions to those healthy developments come from the *coping strategies* used by the people in order to counter trauma. Of course not all strategies work in this direction. Innovative strategies of the legitimate sort help to transform the traumatizing situations, whereas illicit innovativeness (corruption, crime, mafias) only adds to uncertainty and anomie. The same negative, counterproductive impact is effected by rebellious strategies, whereas retreatist and ritualistic adaptations are more neutral in this respect, lacking any immediate effectiveness vis-à-vis traumatizing situations. Thus the overall importance of coping strategies depends on the relative proportion of the various reactions to trauma. It seems that in the Polish case, the innovative strategies aimed at raising the economic and social capital have been applied quite widely, providing a part of the explanation for the diminishing salience of traumatizing situations.

Still, the background, namely, *cultural ambivalence or split* between the heritage of the "bloc culture" and the democratic and market culture must be somehow accounted for. Only if this legacy fades away or disappears may we expect lasting healing of the postcommunist trauma. And here the most significant effect is exerted by the universal and inevitable process of generational turnover. The carriers of cultural legacies are generations that were socialized, indoctrinated, or habituated in a particular cultural milieu. This means that the powerful legacies of bloc culture derived from earlier history, and internalized by the generations whose lives were spent during the rule of communism, may lose their grip as the new generations emerge, raised under different conditions, in a democratic, market society. And this is precisely what is happening in postcommunist societies. The young people graduating from universities and starting careers today have been practically insulated from the destructive cultural impact of the communist system. For them it is history long past. They were raised when the system was already falling apart and educated in a free, democratic society. Thus they have not fallen prey to all those "trained incapacities," "civilizational incompetences," "cultures of cynicism," and "deficiences of trust" haunting the generation of their fathers. They have also been saved from the anxieties and uncertainties of oppositional combat, the elation of revolution and the early disappointments of transition. Their world is relatively stable, established, secure, and predictable. And their culture is no longer ambivalent, internally split. They are the children of a new epoch, the carriers of a new culture inoculated against postcommunist trauma.

## CULTURAL TRAUMA AS THE MEANS OF SOCIAL BECOMING

Within the incessant flow of social change, the cultural trauma may appear in a double capacity: as the consequence of some other changes (traumatogenic in character), but also as an instigator of another stream of changes effected by coping actions. This scenario is optimistic. Trauma appears as a stimulating and mobilizing factor for human agency, which through coping with and overcoming of trauma contributes to the "morphogenesis of culture" (Archer 1986). Here cultural trauma, in spite of its immediate negative, painful consequences, shows its positive, functional potential as a force of *social becoming* (Sztompka 1991a, 1993b). In spite of the disruption and disarray of cultural order that trauma brings about, in a different time scale it may be seen as the seed of a new cultural system. But trauma is not necessarily creative.

The alternative scenario indicates that mobilization against trauma may be too small, and coping strategies ineffective. Then trauma initiates a self-amplifying vicious spiral of *cultural destruction:* traumatic symptoms become more grave; cultural incompetence and disorientation deepens; social activism is paralyzed; and widespread distrust, apathy, pessimism, and resignation lead to the loss of cultural identity. In the long run this is a sure prescription for the collapse of culture and dispersal of a society. Perhaps the story of the collapse of great empires, or the degradation of aboriginal communities, could be rephrased along the lines of this scenario.

Why is trauma itself so ambivalent, sometimes constructive and sometimes destructive? Hypothetically, one may suggest that there exists some threshold beyond which trauma is too deep or too pervasive to be healed. The *resistance potential* against trauma manifested by a society seems to depends on the following factors. First is the strength of initiating traumatogenic change. The change of great scope and depth that hits the institutional core rather than periphery of the old culture may give it a deadly blow and paralyze efforts to resist. Second, it depends on the gap between old and new cultural syndrome. If new culture is radically new, that is, does not have any common or overlapping components with the old one, or in other words, did not have any inroads into the old cultural universe, the dissonance may apppear overpowering. Third, an important factor is the relative size of traumatized groups. If trauma affects all or most groups, rather than being selective, it may be more difficult to fight. Finally, the chance to overcome trauma depends on the scope of individual resources, such as education, connections, rootedness, financial capital, and so on, that can be mobilized in defense against trauma and insulate against its impact. It depends as well on the openness of the channels of mobility, which allow individuals to escape the traumatized groups or social positions and liberate themselves from trauma. If these safety valves are missing, trauma may become unmanageable.

## CODA

In this chapter I have outlined a perspective on social change recognizing the intrinsic *ambivalence of social change*. Change is behind all triumphs of humankind, but it is also a source of trauma. Perhaps this reflects a perennial predicament of a human condition.

The proposed theory of cultural trauma, which was illustrated by selected evidence from postcommunist societies of East-Central Europe, and particularly from Poland, is mostly tentative and hypothetical. In many places it merely indicates the areas of "defined ignorance" (Merton 1996). It is up to the future research and analysis to provide more adequate understanding.

# CHAPTER 6

# On the Social Construction of Moral Universals

*The "Holocaust" from War Crime to Trauma Drama*

JEFFREY C. ALEXANDER

If we bear this suffering, and if there are still Jews left, when it is over, then Jews, instead of being doomed, will be held up as an example. Who knows, it might even be our religion from which the world and all peoples learn good, and for that reason and for that alone do we have to suffer now.

Anne Frank, 1944

"Holocaust" has become so universal a reference point that even contemporary Chinese writers, who live thousands of miles from the place of Nazi brutality and possess only scanty knowledge of the details of the Holocaust, came to call their horrendous experiences during the Cultural Revolution "the ten-year holocaust."

Sheng Mei Ma, 1987

The term history unites the objective and the subjective side, and denotes . . . not less what happened than the narration of what happened. This union of the two meanings we must regard as of a higher order than mere outward accident; we must suppose historical narrations to have appeared contemporaneously with historical deeds and events.

G. W. F. Hegel, *The Philosophy of History*

How did a specific and situated historical event, an event marked by ethnic and racial hatred, violence, and war, become transformed into a generalized symbol of human suffering and moral evil, a universalized symbol whose very existence has created historically unprecedented opportunities for ethnic, racial, and religious justice, for mutual recognition, and for global conflicts to become regulated in a more civil way? This cultural transformation has been achieved because the originating historical event, traumatic in the extreme for a delimited particular group, has come over the last fifty years to be redefined as a traumatic event for all of humankind. Now free floating rather than situated—universal rather than particular—this traumatic event vividly "lives" in the memories of contemporaries whose parents and grandparents never felt themselves even remotely related to it.

In what follows, I explore the social creation of a cultural fact, and the effects of this cultural fact upon social and moral life.

MASS MURDER UNDER THE PROGRESSIVE NARRATIVE

In the beginning, in April 1945, the Holocaust was not the "Holocaust." In the torrent of newspaper, radio, and magazine stories reporting the discovery by American infantrymen of the Nazi concentration camps, the empirical remains of what had transpired were typified as "atrocities." Their obvious awfulness, and indeed their strangeness, placed them for contemporary observers at the borderline of that unfortunately abused category of behavior known as "man's inhumanity to man." Nonetheless, qua atrocity, the discoveries were placed side by side—metonymically and semantically—with a whole series of other brutalities that were considered to be the natural results of the ill wind of this second, very unnatural, and most inhuman world war.

The first American reports on "atrocities" during that Second World War had not, in fact, even referred to actions by German Nazis, let alone to their Jewish victims, but to the Japanese army's brutal treatment of American and other allied prisoners of war after the loss of Corregidor in 1943. On January 27, 1944, the United States released sworn statements by military officers who had escaped the so-called Bataan Death March. In the words of contemporary journals and magazines, these officers had related "atrocity stories" revealing "the inhuman treatment and murder of American and Filipino soldiers who were taken prisoner when Bataan and Corregidor fell." In response to these accounts, the U.S. State Department had lodged protests to the Japanese government about its failure to live up to the provisions of the Geneva Prisoners of War Convention *(Current History,* March 1944, 6, 249). Atrocities, in other words, were a signifier specifically connected to war. They referred to war-generated events that transgressed the rules circumscribing how national killing could normally be carried out. Responding to the same incident, *Newsweek,* in a section entitled "The Enemy" and under the headline "Nation Replies in Grim Fury to Jap Brutality to Prisoners," reported that "with the first impact of the news, people had shuddered at the story of savage *atrocity* upon Allied prisoners of war by the Japanese" (February 7, 1944, 19, italics added).

It is hardly surprising, then, that it was this nationally specific and particular war-related term that was employed to represent the grisly Jewish mass murders discovered by American GIs when they liberated the Nazi camps. Through April 1945, as one camp after another was discovered, this collective representation was applied time after time. When toward the end of that month, a well-known Protestant minister explored the moral implications of the discoveries, he declared that, no matter how horrifying and repulsive, "it is important that the full truth be made known so that a clear indication may be had of the nature of the enemy we have been dealing with, as well of as a realization *of the sheer brutalities that have become the accompaniment of war."* The *New York Times* reported this sermon under the headline "Bonnell Denounces German Atrocities" (April 23, 1945, 23, italics added). When alarmed American congressmen visited Buchenwald, the *Times* headlined that they had witnessed firsthand the "*War Camp Horror*" (April 26, 1945, 12, italics added). When a few days later the U.S. Army released a report on the extent of the killings in Buchenwald, the *Times* headlined it an "Atrocity Report" (April 29, 1945, 20). A few days after that, under the headline "Enemy Atrocities in France Bared," the *Times* wrote that a just released report had shown that "in France, German brutality was not limited to the French underground or even to the thousands of hostages whom the Germans killed for disorders they had nothing to do with, but was practiced almost systematically against entirely innocent French people" (May 4, 1945, 6).

The Nazis' anti-Jewish mass murders had once been only putative atrocities. From the late thirties on, reports about them had been greeted with widespread public doubt about their authenticity. Analogizing to the allegations about German atrocities during World War I that later had been thoroughly discredited, they were dismissed as a kind of Jewish moral panic. Only three months before the GIs' "discovery" of the

camps, in introducing a firsthand report on Nazi mass murder from a
Soviet liberated camp in Poland, *Collier's* magazine acknowledged: "A
lot of Americans simply do not believe the stories of Nazi mass executions of Jews and anti-Nazi Gentiles in eastern Europe by means of gas
chambers, freight cars partly loaded with lime and other horrifying
devices. These stories are so foreign to most Americans' experience of life
in this country that they seem incredible. Then, too, some of the atrocity
stories of World War I were later proved false" (January 6, 1945, 62).
From April 3, 1945, however, the date when the GIs first liberated the
concentration camps, all such earlier reports were retrospectively
accepted as facts, as the realistic signifiers of Peirce rather than the "arbitrary" symbols of Saussure. That systematic efforts at Jewish mass murder had occurred, and that the numerous victims and the few survivors
had been severely traumatized, the American and worldwide audience
now had little doubt. Their particular and unique fate, however, even
while it was widely recognized as representing the grossest of injustices,
did not itself become a traumatic experience for the audience to which
the mass media's collective representations were transmitted, that is, for
those looking on, either from near or from far. Why this was not so
defines my initial explanatory effort here.

## Symbolic Extension and Psychological Identification

For an audience to be traumatized by an experience that they themselves
do not directly share, symbolic extension and psychological identification are required. This did not occur. For the American infantrymen who
first made contact, for the general officers who supervised the rehabilita-
tion, for the reporters who broadcast the descriptions, for the commissions of congressmen and influentials who quickly traveled to Germany
to conduct on-site investigations, the starving, depleted, often weird-
looking and sometimes weird-acting Jewish camp survivors seemed like a
foreign race. They could just as well have been from Mars, or from Hell.
The identities and characters of these Jewish survivors rarely were personalized through interviews or individualized through biographical
sketches; rather, they were presented as a mass, and often as a mess, a
petrified, degrading, and smelly one, not only by newspaper reporters
but by some of the most powerful general officers in the Allied high
command. This depersonalization made it more difficult for the survivors' trauma to generate compelling identification.
     Possibilities for universalizing the trauma were blocked not only by

the depersonalization of its victims but by their historical and sociological specification. As I have indicated, the mass murders semantically were immediately linked to other "horrors" in the bloody history of the century's second great war and to the historically specific national and ethnic conflicts that underlay it. Above all, it was never forgotten that these victims were Jews. In retrospect, it is bitterly ironic, but it is also sociologically understandable, that the American audience's sympathy and feelings of identity flowed much more easily to the non-Jewish survivors, whether German or Polish, who had been kept in better conditions and looked more normal, more composed, more human. Jewish survivors were kept for weeks and sometimes even for months in the worst areas and under the worst conditions of what had become, temporarily, displaced persons camps. American and British administrators felt impatient with many Jewish survivors, even personal repugnance for them, sometimes resorting to threats and even to punishing them. The depth of this initial failure of identification can be seen in the fact that, when American citizens and their leaders expressed opinions and made decisions about national quotas for emergency postwar immigration, displaced German citizens ranked first, Jewish survivors last.

How could this have happened? Was it not obvious to any human observer that this mass murder was fundamentally different from the other traumatic and bloody events in a modern history already dripping in blood, that it represented not simply evil but "radical evil," in Kant's remarkable phrase (Kant, 1960), that it was unique? To understand why none of this was obvious, to understand how and why these initial understandings and behaviors were radically changed, and how this transformation had vast repercussions for establishing, not only new moral standards for social and political behavior, but unprecedented, if still embryonic, regulatory controls, it is important to see the inadequacy of commonsense understandings of traumatic events.

## Lay Trauma Theory

There are two kinds of commonsense thinking about trauma, forms of thinking that comprise what I call "lay trauma theory." These commonsensical forms of reasoning have deeply informed thinking about the effects of the Holocaust. They are expressed in the following, strikingly different conceptualizations of what happened after the revelations of the mass killings of Jews.

The Enlightenment version: The "horror" of onlookers provoked the postwar end of antisemitism in the United States. The common-sense assumption here is that, because people have a fundamentally "moral" nature—as a result of their rootedness in Enlightenment and religious traditions—they will perceive atrocities for what they are, and react to them by attacking the belief systems that provided legitimation.

The psychoanalytic version: When faced with the horror, Jews and non-Jews alike reacted, not with criticism and decisive action, but with silence and bewilderment. Only after two or even three decades of repression and denial were people finally able to begin talking about what happened and to take actions in response to this knowledge.

Enlightenment and psychoanalytic forms of lay trauma thinking have permeated academic efforts at understanding what happened after the death camp revelations. One or the other version has informed not only every major discussion of the Holocaust, but virtually every contemporary effort to investigate trauma more generally, efforts that are, in fact, largely inspired by Holocaust debates.

*An Alternative: The Theory of Cultural Trauma*

What is wrong with this lay trauma theory is that it is "naturalistic," either in the naively moral or the naively psychological sense. Lay trauma theory fails to see that there is an interpretive grid through which all "facts" about trauma are mediated, emotionally, cognitively, and morally. This grid has a supra-individual, cultural status; it is symbolically structured and sociologically determined. No trauma interprets itself; before trauma can be experienced at the collective (not individual) level, there are essential questions that must be answered, and answers to these questions change over time. In the introduction to this book, I made a systematic presentation of the alternative model collectively developed by the authors of this book. This model, which emphasizes the cultural rather than simply the social structural or individual elements of trauma, has not only been empirically illustrated but theoretically elaborated in the intervening chapters. In the present chapter, I will contribute further to this theoretical discussion, and relate it to a different but obviously still related empirical case.

THE CULTURAL CONSTRUCTION OF TRAUMA:
CODING, WEIGHTING, NARRATING

Elie Wiesel, in a moving and influential statement in the late 1970s, asserted that the Holocaust represents an "ontological evil." From a sociological perspective, however, evil is epistemological, not ontological. For a traumatic event to have the status of evil is a matter of its *becoming* evil. It is a matter of how the trauma is known, how it is coded. "At first glance it may appear a paradox," Diner has noted—and certainly it does—but, considered only in and of itself, "Auschwitz *has* no appropriate narrative, only a set of statistics" (Diner 2000, 178). Becoming evil is a matter, first and foremost, of representation. Depending on the nature of representation, a traumatic event may be regarded as ontologically evil, or its badness, its "evility," may be conceived as contingent and relative, as something that can be ameliorated and overcome. This distinction is theoretical, but it is also practical. In fact, decisions about the ontological versus contingent status of the Holocaust were of overriding importance in its changing representation.

If we can deconstruct this ontological assertion even further, I would like to suggest that the very existence of the category "evil" must be seen not as something that naturally exists but as an arbitrary construction, the product of cultural and sociological work. This contrived binary, which simplifies empirical complexity to two antagonistic forms and reduces every shade of gray between, has been an essential feature of all human societies, but especially important in those Eisenstadt (1982) has called the Axial Age civilizations. This rigid opposition between the sacred and profane, which in Western philosophy has typically been constructed as a conflict between normativity and instrumentality, not only defines what people care about but establishes vital safeguards around the shared normative "good." At the same time, it places powerful, often aggressive barriers against anything that is construed as threatening the good, forces defined not merely as things to be avoided but as sources of horror and pollution that must be contained at all costs.

*The Material "Base": Controlling the Means of Symbolic Production*

Yet, if this grid is a kind of functional necessity, how it is applied very much depends on who is telling the story and how. This is first of all a matter of cultural power in the most mundane, materialist sense: Who controls the means of symbolic production? It was certainly not incidental to the public understanding of the Nazis' policies of mass murder, for example, that for an extended period of time it was the Nazis themselves who were in control of the physical and cultural terrain of their enactment. This fact of brute power made it much more difficult to frame the mass killings in a distinctive way. Nor is it incidental that, once the extermination of the Jews was physically interrupted by Allied armies in 1945, it was America's "imperial republic"—the perspective of the triumphant, forward-looking, militantly and militarily democratic new world warrior—that directed the organizational and cultural responses to the mass murders and their survivors. The contingency of this knowledge is so powerful that it might well be said that, if the Allies had not won the war, the "Holocaust" would never have been discovered. Moreover, if it had been the Soviets and not the Allies who "liberated" most of the camps, and not just those in the Eastern sector, what was discovered in those camps might never have been portrayed in a remotely similar way. It was, in other words, precisely and only because the means of symbolic production were not controlled by a victorious postwar Nazi regime, or even by a triumphant communist one, that the mass killings could be called the Holocaust and coded as evil.

### Creating the Culture Structure

Still, even when the means of symbolic production came to be controlled by "our side," even when the association between evil and what would become known as the Holocaust trauma was assured, this was only the beginning, not the end. After a phenomenon is coded as evil, the question that immediately follows is, How evil is it? In theorizing evil, this refers to the problem, not of coding, but of weighting. For there are degrees of evil, and these degrees have great implications in terms of responsibility, punishment, remedial action, and future behavior. Normal evil and radical evil cannot be the same.

Finally, alongside these problems of coding and weighting, the meaning of a trauma cannot be defined unless we determine exactly what the "it" is. This is a question of narrative: What were the evil and traumatizing actions in question? Who was responsible? Who were the victims? What were the immediate and long-term results of the traumatizing actions? What can be done by way of remediation or prevention?

What these theoretical considerations suggest is that even after the physical force of the Allied triumph and the physical discovery of the Nazi concentration camps, the nature of what was seen and discovered had to be coded, weighted, and narrated. This complex cultural construction, moreover, had to be achieved immediately. History does not wait; it demands that representations be made, and they will be. Whether or not some newly reported event is startling, strange, terrible, or inexpressibly weird, it must be "typified," in the sense of Husserl and Schutz, that is, it must be explained as a typical and even anticipated example of some thing or category that was known about before. Even the vastly unfamiliar must somehow be made familiar. To the cultural process of coding, weighting, and narrating, in other words, what comes before is all-important. Historical background is critical, both for the first "view" of the traumatic event and, as "history" changes, for later views as well. Once again, these shifting cultural constructions are fatefully affected by the power and identity of the agents in charge, by the competition for symbolic control, and the structures of power and distribution of resources that condition it.

## Nazism as the Representation of Absolute Evil

What was the historical structure of "good and evil" within which, on April 3, 1945, the "news" of the Nazi concentration camps was first confirmed to the American audience? To answer this question, it is first necessary to describe what came before. In what follows, I will venture some observations, which can hardly be considered definitive, about how social evil was coded, weighted, and narrated during the interwar period in Europe and the United States.

In the deeply disturbing wake of World War I, there was a pervasive sense of disillusionment and cynicism among mass and elite members of the Western "audience," a distancing from protagonists and antagonists that, as Paul Fussell has shown, made irony the master trope of that first postwar era. This trope transformed "demonology"—the very act of coding and weighting evil—into what many intellectuals and lay persons alike considered to be an act of bad faith. Once the coding and weighting of evil were delegitimated, however, good and evil became less distinct from one another, and relativism became the dominant motif of the time. In such conditions, coherent narration of contemporary events becomes difficult if not impossible. Thus it was that, not only for many intellectuals and artists of this period but for many ordinary people as well, the startling upheavals of these interwar years could not easily be sorted out in a conclusive and satisfying way.

In this context of the breakdown of representation, racism and revolution, whether fascist or communist, emerged as compelling frames, not only in Europe but also in the United States. Against a revolutionary narrative of dogmatic and authoritarian modernism on the Left, there arose the narrative of reactionary modernism, equally revolutionary but fervently opposed to rationality and cosmopolitanism. In this context, many democrats in Western Europe and the United States withdrew from the field of representation itself, becoming confused and equivocating advocates of disarmament, nonviolence, and peace "at any price." This formed the cultural frame for isolationist political policy in both Britain and the United States.

Eventually, the aggressive military ambition of Nazism made such equivocation impossible to sustain. While racialism, relativism, and narrative confusion continued in the United States and Britain until the very beginning of the Second World War, and even well into it, these constructions were countered by increasingly forceful and confident representations of good and evil that coded liberal democracy and universalism as unalloyed goods, and Nazism, racism, and prejudice as deeply corrosive representations of the polluting and profane.

From the late 1930s on, there emerged a strong, and eventually dominant, antifascist narrative in Western societies. Nazism was coded, weighted, and narrated in apocalyptic, Old Testament terms as "the dominant evil of our time." Because this radical evil aligned itself with violence and massive death, it not merely justified but compelled the risking of life in opposing it, a compulsion that motivated and justified massive human sacrifice in what came later to be known as the last "good war." That Nazism was an absolute, unmitigated evil, a radical evil that threatened the very future of human civilization, formed the presupposition of America's four-year prosecution of the world war.

The representation of Nazism as an absolute evil emphasized not only its association with sustained coercion and violence, but also, and perhaps even especially, the manner in which Nazism linked violence with ethnic, racial, and religious hatred. In this way, the most conspicuous example of the practice of Nazi evil—its policy of systematic discrimination, coercion, and, eventually, mass violence against the Jews—was initially interpreted as "simply" another horrifying example of the subhumanism of Nazi action.

### Interpreting "Kristallnacht": Nazi Evil as Antisemitism

The American public's reaction to *Kristallnacht* demonstrates how important the Nazis' anti-Jewish activities were in crystallizing the polluted

status of Nazism in American eyes. It also provides a prototypical example of how such representations of the evils of antisemitism were folded
into the broader and more encompassing symbolism of Nazism.
*Kristallnacht* refers, of course, to the rhetorically virulent and physically
violent expansion of the Nazi repression of Jews that unfolded throughout German towns and cities on November 9 and 10, 1938. These activities were widely recorded. "The morning editions of most American
newspapers reported the *Kristallnacht* in banner headlines," according to
one historian of that fateful event, "and the broadcasts of H. V.
Kaltenborn and Raymond Gram Swing kept the radio public informed of
Germany's latest adventure" (Diamond 1969, 198). Exactly why these
events assumed such critical importance in the American public's continuing effort to understand "what Hitlerism stood for" (ibid., 201) goes
beyond the simple fact that violent and repressive activities were, perhaps
for the first time, openly, even brazenly displayed in direct view of the
world public sphere. Equally important was the altered cultural framework within which these activities were observed. For *Kristallnacht*
occurred just six weeks after the now infamous Munich agreements, acts
of appeasement to Hitler's expansion, which at that time were understood, not only by isolationists but by many opponents of Nazism, indeed by the vast majority of the American people, as possibly reasonable
accessions to a possibly reasonable man (ibid., 197). What occurred, in
other words, was a process of understanding fueled by symbolic contrast,
not simply observation.

What was interpretively constructed was the cultural difference
between Germany's previously apparent cooperativeness and reason-
ableness—representations of the good in the discourse of American civil
society—and its subsequent demonstration of violence and irrationality,
which were taken to be representations of anti-civic evil. Central to the
ability to draw this contrast was the ethnic and religious hatred Germans
demonstrated in their violence against Jews. If one examines the American public's reactions, it is clearly this anti-Jewish violence that is taken
to represent Nazism's evil. Thus, it was with references to this violence
that the news stories of the *New York Times* employed the rhetoric of
pollution to further code and weight Nazi evil: "No foreign propagandist
bent upon blackening the name of Germany before the world could
outdo the tale of beating, of blackguardly assaults upon defenseless and
innocent people, which degraded that country yesterday" (quoted in
Diamond 1969, 198). The *Times'* controversial columnist Anne O'Hare
McCormick wrote that "the suffering [the Germans] inflict on others,

now that they are on top, passes all understanding and mocks all sympathy," and she went on to label *Kristallnacht* "the darkest day Germany experienced in the whole postwar period" (quoted in Diamond 1969, 199). The *Washington Post* identified the Nazi activities as "one of the worst setbacks for mankind since the Massacre of St. Bartholomew" (quoted in Diamond 1969, 198–99).

This broadening identification of Nazism with evil, simultaneously triggered and reinforced by *Kristallnacht*'s anti-Jewish violence, stimulated influential political figures to make more definitive judgments about the antipathy between American democracy and German Nazism than they had up until that point. Speaking on NBC radio, Al Smith, the former New York governor and democratic presidential candidate, observed that the events confirmed that the German people were "incapable of living under a democratic government" (quoted in Diamond 1969, 200). Following Smith on the same program, Thomas E. Dewey, soon to be New York governor and a future presidential candidate, expressed the opinion that "the civilized world stands revolted by the bloody pogrom against a defenseless people . . . by a nation run by madmen" (quoted in Diamond 1969, 201). Having initially underplayed America's official reaction to the events, four days later President Franklin Roosevelt took advantage of the public outrage by emphasizing the purity of the American nation and its distance from this emerging representation of violence and ethnic hatred: "The news of the past few days from Germany deeply shocked public opinion in the United States . . . I myself could scarcely believe that such things could occur in a twentieth-century civilization" (quoted in Diamond 1969, 205).

Judging from these reactions to the Nazi violence of *Kristallnacht*, it seems only logical that, as one historian has put it, "most American newspapers or journals" could "no longer . . . view Hitler as a pliable and reasonable man, but as an aggressive and contemptible dictator [who] would have to be restrained" (quoted in Diamond 1969, 207). What is equally striking, however, is that in almost none of the American public's statements of horror is there explicit reference to the identity of *Kristallnacht*'s victims as Jews. Instead, they are referred to as a "defenseless and innocent people," as "others," and as a "defenseless people" (quoted in Diamond 1969, 198, 199, 201). In fact, in the public statement quoted above, President Roosevelt goes well out of his way to present his polluting judgment of the events as reflecting a typically American standard, strenuously removing his moral outrage from any link to a specific concern for the fate of the Jews. "Such news from *any part* of the world," the president insists, "would inevitably produce a similar profound reaction among Americans *in any part* of the nation" (ibid., 205, italics added). In other words, despite the centrality of the Nazis' anti-Jewish violence to the emerging American symbolization of Nazism as evil, there existed—at that point in historical and cultural time—a reluctance for non-Jewish Americans to identify with Jewish people as such. Jews were highlighted as vital representations of the evils of Nazism: their fate would be understood only in relation to the German horror that threatened democratic civilization in America and Europe. This failure of identification would be reflected seven years later in the distantiation of the American soldiers and domestic audience from the traumatized Jewish camp survivors and their even less fortunate Jewish compatriots whom the Nazis had killed.

## Anti-Antisemitism: Fighting Nazi Evil by Fighting for the Jews

It was also during the 1930s, in the context of the Nazi persecution of German Jews, that there emerged in the United States a historically unprecedented attack on antisemitism. It was not that Christians suddenly felt genuine affection for, or identification with, those whom they had vilified for countless centuries as the killers of Christ. It was that the logic of symbolic association had dramatically and fatefully changed. Nazism was increasingly viewed as the vile enemy of universalism, and the most hated enemies of Nazism were the Jews. The laws of symbolic antinomy and association thus were applied. If Nazism singled out the Jews, then the Jews must be singled out by democrats and anti-Nazis. Antisemitism, tolerated and condoned for centuries in every Western nation, and for the preceding fifty years embraced fervently by proponents of American "nativism," suddenly became distinctly unpopular in progressive circles throughout the United States (Gleason 1981; Higham 1984).

What I will call "anti-antisemitism" became particularly intense after the United States declared war on Nazi Germany. The nature of this concern is framed in a particular clear manner by one leading historian of American Jewry: "The war saw the merging of Jewish and American fates. Nazi Germany was the greatest enemy of both Jewry and the United States" (Shapiro 1992, 16). For the first time, overly positive representations of Jewish people proliferated in popular and high culture alike. It was during this period that the phrase "Judeo-Christian tradition" was born. It appeared as Americans tried to fend off the Nazi enemy that threatened to destroy the sacred foundations of Western democratic life (Silk 1986).

## Constructing the Progressive Narrative in the War against Nazism

Nazism marked a traumatic epoch in modern history. Yet, while coded as evil and weighted in the most fundamental, *weltgesichte* (world-historical) terms, it was narrated inside a framework that offered the promise of salvation and triggered actions that generated confidence and hope. What I will call the "progressive narrative" proclaimed that the trauma created by social evil would be overcome, that Nazism would be defeated and eliminated from the world, that it would eventually be relegated to a traumatic past whose darkness would be obliterated by a new and powerful social light. The progressivity of this narrative depended on keeping Nazism situated and historical, which prevented this representation of absolute evil from being universalized and its cultural power from being equated, in any way, shape, or form with the power possessed by the good. In narrative terms, this asymmetry, this insistence on Nazism's anomalous historical status, assured its ultimate defeat. In the popular consciousness and in the dramas created by cultural specialists, the origins of Nazism were linked to specific events in the interwar period and to particular organizations and actors within it, to a political party, to a crazy and inhuman leader, to an anomalous nation that had demonstrated militaristic and violent tendencies over the previous one hundred years.

Yes, Nazism had initiated a trauma in modern history, but it was a liminal trauma presenting "time out of time" in Victor Turner's sense. The trauma was dark and threatening, but it was, at the same time, anomalous and, in principle at least, temporary. As such, the trauma could and would be removed, via a just war and a wise and forgiving peace. The vast human sacrifices demanded by the winds of war were measured and judged in terms of this progressive narrative and the salvation it promised. The blood spilled in the war sanctified the future peace and obliterated the past. The sacrifice of millions could be redeemed, the social salvation of their sacred souls achieved, not by dwelling in a lachrymose manner on their deaths, but by eliminating Nazism, the force that had caused their deaths, and by planning the future, which would establish a world in which there could never be Nazism again.

*Inside the Progressive Narrative:*
*Framing Revelations about the Jewish Mass Murder*

While initially received with surprise, and always conceived with loathing, the gradual, halting but eventually definitive revelations of Nazi plans for displacing, and quite possibly murdering, the entirety of European Jewry actually confirmed the categorizing of evil already in place: the coding, weighting, and narrating of Nazism as an inhuman, absolutely evil force. What had been experienced as an extraordinary trauma by the Jewish victims was experienced by the audience of others as a kind of categorical vindication. In this way, and for this reason, the democratic audience for the reports on the mass murders experienced distance from, rather than identification with, the trauma's victims. The revelations had the effect, in some perverse sense, of normalizing the abnormal.

The empirical existence of Nazi plans for the "Final Solution," as well as extensive documentation of their ongoing extermination activities, had been publicly documented by June 1942 (Dawidowicz 1982; Laqueur 1980; Norich 1998–99). In July of that year more than twenty thousand persons rallied in Madison Square Garden to protest the Nazis' war against the Jews. Though he did not attend in person, President Franklin Roosevelt sent a special message that what he called "these crimes" would be redeemed by the "final accounting" following the Allied victory over Nazism. In March 1943, the American Jewish Congress announced that two million Jews had already been massacred and that millions more were slated for death. Its detailed descriptions of the "extermination" were widely reported in the American press. By March 1944, when the Germans occupied Hungary and their intention to liquidate its entire Jewish population became known, Dawidowicz shows that "Auschwitz was no longer an unfamiliar name" (Dawidowicz 1982).

Yet, it was this very familiarity that seemed to undermine the sense of astonishment that might have stimulated immediate action. For Auschwitz was typified in terms of the progressive narrative of war, a narrative that made it impossible to denormalize the mass killings, to make the Holocaust into the "Holocaust." As I indicated in my earlier reconstruction of the discourse about atrocity, what eventually came to be called the Holocaust was reported to contemporaries as a war story, nothing less but nothing more. In private conferences with the American president, Jewish leaders demanded that Allied forces make special efforts to target and destroy the death camps. In describing these failed efforts to trigger intervention, a leading historian explains that the leaders "couldn't convince a preoccupied American President and the American public of the significance of Auschwitz for their time in history" (Feingold 1974, 250). In other words, while Auschwitz was coded as evil, it simply was not weighted in a sufficiently dire way.

In these symbolically mediated confrontations, attention was not focused on the mass killings in and of themselves. What was definitely not illuminated or asserted was the discovery of an evil unique in human history. The evil of that time had already been discovered, and it was Nazism, not the massive killing of European Jews. The trauma this evil had created was a second world war. The trauma that the Jews experienced in the midst of their liquidation was represented as one among a series of effects of Nazi evil. When the *London Times* reported Adolph Hitler's death, on May 2, 1945—in the month following the death camp revelations—its obituary described the German dictator as "the incarnation of absolute evil," and only briefly mentioned Hitler's "fanatical aversion to Jews" (quoted in Benn 1995, 102). As one historian has put it, "The processed mass murders became merely another atrocity in a particularly cruel war" (quoted in Benn 1995, 102). The mass murders were explained, and they would be redeemed, within the framework of the progressive struggle against Nazism.

To fully understand the initial, frame-establishing encounter between Americans and the Jewish mass murder, it is vital to remember that narratives, no matter how progressive and future oriented, are composed of both antagonists and protagonists. The antagonists and their crimes were well established: the German Nazis had murdered the Jews in a gigantic, heinous atrocity of war. The protagonists were the American GIs, and their entrance into the concentration camps was portrayed, not only as a discovery of such horrendous atrocities, but as another, culminating stage in a long and equally well known sequence of "liberation," with all the ameliorating expectations that utopian term implies. "When the press entered the camps of the western front," the cultural historian Barbie Zelizer writes, "it found that the most effective way to tell the atrocity story was as a chronicle of liberation" (Zelizer 1998, 63). In fact, Zelizer titles her own detailed reconstruction of these journalist encounters "Chronicles of Liberation" (Zelizer 1998, 63–85). When readers of the *New York Times* and *Los Angeles Times* were confronted on April 16 with the photo from Buchenwald of bunk beds stuffed to overflowing with haunted, pathetically undernourished male prisoners, they were informed that they were looking at "freed slave laborers" (Zelizer 1998,

183). On May 5, the *Picture Post* published a six-page spread of atrocity photos. Framing the heart-wrenching visual images, the theme of forward progress was palpable. One collective caption read: "These Were Inmates of Prison Camps Set Free in the Allied Advance: For Many We Came Too Late" (Zelizer 1998, 129).

Photos of dead or tattered and starving victims were often juxtaposed with pictures of well-dressed, well-fed German citizens from the surrounding towns, pointedly linking the crime to the particular nature of the German people themselves. In a sidebar story titled "The Problem That Makes All Europe Wonder," the *Picture Post* described "the horror that took place within the sight and sound of hundreds of thousands of seemingly normal, decent German people. How was it possible? What has happened to the minds of a whole nation that such things should have been tolerated for a day?" (quoted in Zelizer 1998, 128). These same photos often included a representative GI standing guard, passing judgment, looking on the scene. The text alongside another widely circulated photo in the *Picture Post* made the progressive answer to such questions perfectly plain: "It is not enough to be mad with rage. It is no help to shout about 'exterminating' Germany. Only one thing helps: the attempt to understand how men have sunk so far, and the firm resolve to face the trouble, the inconvenience and cost of seeing no nation gets the chance to befoul the world like this again" (quoted in Zelizer 1998, 129).

It was within this highly particularized progressive narrative that the first steps toward universalization actually took place. Because the Jewish mass killings came at the chronological conclusion of the war, and because they without doubt represented the most gruesome illustration of Nazi atrocities, they came very quickly to be viewed not merely as symptoms but as emblems and iconic representations of the evil that the progressive narrative promised to leave behind. As the novelist and war correspondent Meyer Levin wrote of his visit to Ohrdruf, the first camp American soldiers liberated, "It was as though we had penetrated at last to the center of the black heart, to the very crawling inside of the vicious heart" (quoted in Abzug 1985, 19). On the one hand, the trauma was localized and particularized—it occurred in this war, in this place, with these persons. On the other hand, the mass murder was universalized. Within months of the initial revelations, indeed, the murders frequently were framed by a new term, "genocide," a crime defined as the effort to destroy an entire people, which, while introduced earlier, during the war period itself, became publicly available and widely employed only after the discovery of the Nazi atrocities.

In response to this new representation, the scope of the Nuremburg War Crimes Tribunal was enlarged. Conceived as a principal vehicle for linking the postwar Allied cause to progressive redemption, the trials were now to go beyond prosecuting the Nazi leaders for crimes of war to considering their role in the mass murder against the Jewish people. Justice Robert Jackson, the chief American prosecutor, promised that the trial would not only prosecute those responsible for the war but would present "undeniable proofs of incredible events"—the Nazi crimes (quoted in Benn 1995, 102). The first three counts of the twenty-thousand-word indictment against the twenty-three high-ranking Nazi officials concerned the prosecution of the war itself. They charged conspiracy, conducting a war of aggression, and violating the rules of war. The fourth count, added only in the months immediately preceding the October trial in Nuremburg, accused the Nazi leaders of something new, namely of "crimes against humanity." This was the first step toward universalizing the public representation of the Jewish mass murder. From the perspective of the present day, however, it appears as a relatively limited one, for it functioned to confirm the innocent virtue and national ambitions of one particular side. In its first report on the indictments, for example, the *New York Times* linked the Jewish mass murder directly to the war itself, and placed its punishment within the effort to prevent any future "war of aggression." Under the headline, "The Coming War Trials," the paper noted that "the authority of this tribunal to inflict punishment is directly from victory in war" and that its goal was "to establish the principle that no nation shall ever again go to war, except when directly attacked or under the sanction of a world organization" (October 9, 1945, 20). The Nuremburg trial was not, in other words, perceived as preventing genocide or crimes against humanity as such. At that time, the commission of such crimes could not be conceived apart from the Nazis and the recently concluded aggressive war.

The force of the progressive narrative meant that, while the 1945 revelations confirmed the Jewish mass murder, they did not create a trauma for the postwar audience. Victory and the Nuremburg war trials would put an end to Nazism and alleviate its evil effects. Postwar redemption depended on putting mass murder "behind us," moving on, and getting on with the construction of the new world.

> From the end of the war until the early 1960s, a "can-do," optimistic spirit pervaded America. Those who had returned from the war were concerned with building a family and a career, not with dwelling on the horrors of the past . . . It did not seem to be an appropriate time to focus on a painful past, particularly a past which seemed to be of no direct concern to this country.

This event had transpired on another continent. It had been committed by
another country against "an-other" people. What relevance did it have for
Americans? (Lipstadt 1996, 195–214)

[As for] the terms in which Americans of the mid-1950s were prepared to
confront the Holocaust: a terrible event, yes, but ultimately not tragic or depressing; an experience shadowed by the specter of a cruel death, but at the
same time not without the ability to inspire, console, uplift. . . . Throughout
the late 1940s and well into the 50s, a prevalent attitude was to put all of
"that" behind one and get on with life. (Rosenfield 1995, 37–38)

After the War, American Jewry turned—with great energy and generos-
ity—to liquidating the legacy of the Holocaust by caring for the survivors
[who] were urged to put the ghastly past behind them, to build new lives in
their adopted homes . . . When a proposal for a Holocaust memorial in New
York City came before representatives of the leading Jewish organizations in
the late 1940s, they unanimously rejected the idea: it would, they said, give
currency to the image of Jews as "helpless victims," an idea they wished to
repudiate. (Novick 1994, 160)

It was neither emotional repression nor good moral sense that created
the early responses to the mass murder of the Jews. It was, rather, a system
of collective representations that focused its beam of narrative light on the
triumphant expulsion of evil. Most Americans did not identify with the
victims of the Jewish trauma. Far from being implicated in it, Americans
had defeated those responsible for the mass murders and righteously
engaged in restructuring the social and political arrangements that had
facilitated them. This did not mean that the mass murder of Jews was
viewed with relativism or equanimity. According to the progressive narrative, it was America's solemn task to redeem the sacrifice of this largest of
all categories of Nazi victims. In postwar America, the public redeemed the
sacrifices of war by demanding the thorough de-Nazification, not only of
Germany but of American society. As Sumner Welles eloquently framed
the issue a month after the GIs had entered the Nazi death camps, "The
crimes committed by the Nazis and by their accomplices against the Jewish
people are indelible stains upon the whole of our modern civilization."

They are stains which will shame our generation in the eyes of generations
still unborn. For we and our governments, to which we have entrusted power
during these years between the Great Wars, cannot shake off the responsibility
for having permitted the growth of world conditions which made such horrors possible. The democracies cannot lightly attempt to shirk their responsibility. No recompense can be offered the dead . . . But such measure of
recompense as can be offered surely constitutes the moral obligation of the
free peoples of the earth as soon as their victory is won. (Welles 1945, 511)

### Making Progress: Purifying America
### and Redeeming the Murder of the Jews

Propelled by the logic of this progressive understanding of redemption, the public legitimation of antisemitism in America's immediate postwar years was repeatedly attacked and some of its central institutional manifestations destroyed. The long-standing anti-antisemitism framing the progressive narrative, and crystallized during the interwar years by leading figures in the American intellectual and cultural elite, culminated in the immediate postwar period in a massive shift of American public opinion on the Jewish question (Stember 1966). Only days after the hostilities ceased, in response to an appeal from the National Council of Christians and Jews, the three candidates for mayor of New York city pledged to "refrain from appeals to racial and religious divisiveness during the campaign." One of them made explicit the connection of this public anti-antisemitism to the effort to remain connected to, and enlarge upon, the meaning of America's triumph in the anti-Nazi war.

> This election will be the first held in the City of New York since our victory
> over nazism and Japanese fascism. It will therefore be an occasion for a
> practical demonstration of democracy in action—a democracy in which
> all are equal citizens, in which there is not and never must be a second class
> citizenship and in which . . . the religion of a candidate must play no part in
> the campaign. (*New York Times*, October 1, 1945, 32)

In an influential article, Leonard Dinnerstein has documented the vastly heightened political activism of Jewish groups in the immediate postwar period from 1945 to 1948 (Dinnerstein 1981–82). He records how these newly surfaced, and often newly formed groups held conferences, wrote editorials, and issued specific proposals for legal and institutional changes. By 1950, these activities had successfully exposed and often defeated anti-Jewish quotas and, more generally, created an extraordinary shift in the practical and cultural position of American Jews. During the same month that New York's mayoral candidates announced their anti-antisemitism, the *American Mercury* published an article, "Discrimination in Medical Colleges," replete with graphs and copious documentation, detailing the existence of anti-Jewish quotas in some of America's most prestigious professional institutions. While the specific focus was anti-Jewish discrimination, these facts were narrated in terms of the overarching promise of America and democracy. The story began with a vignette about "Leo, a bright and personable American lad," who "dreamed of becoming a great physician."

[He]made an excellent scholastic record [but] upon graduation . . . his first application for admission to a medical school . . . was mysteriously turned down. He filed another and another—at eighty-seven schools—always with the same heartbreaking result . . . Not one of the schools had the courage to inform Leo frankly that he was being excluded because he was a Jew . . . The excuse for imposing a quota system usually advanced is that there ought to be some correlation between the number of physicians of any racial or religious strain and the proportion of that race or religion in the general population [but] the surface logic of this arithmetic collapses as soon as one subjects it to *democratic or sheerly human,* let alone scientific, tests. [It is] spurious and *un-American* arithmetic. (vol. 61, no. 262, [October 1945], 391–99, italics added)

Earlier that year, an "Independent Citizens Committee" had asked three hundred educators to speak out against restricting Jewish enrollment in the nation's schools. Dartmouth president Ernest Hopkins refused, openly defending Dartmouth's Jewish quota on the grounds that German Nazism had been spurred because a large proportion of the German professions had become Jewish. A storm of public aprobrium followed Hopkins' remarks. The *New York Post* headlined, "Dartmouth Bars Jews 'To end anti-semitism,' Says Prexy." The next day, the rival tabloid, *PM*, placed Hopkins's picture side by side with Nazi ideologue Alfred Rosenberg and accused the Dartmouth president of "spouting the Hitler-Rosenberg line" (quoted in "Sense or Nonsense?" *Time*, no. 46 [August 20, 1945], 92, italics added). In an article entitled "Anti-Semitism at Dartmouth," the *New Republic* brought a progressive perspective to the controversy by suggesting that it could bring "us a step nearer to amelioration of one of the outstanding blots on American civilization *today.*" Antisemitism belonged to the outmoded past that had been shattered by the anti-Nazi war: "We can *no longer* afford the luxury of these *obsolete* myths of racial differentiation, Mr. Hopkins; if you don't believe it, ask Hitler" (no. 113 [August 20, 1945], 208–9, italics added).

In the years that followed, the fight against quotas continued to be informed by similar themes. In 1946, an educational sociologist wrote in the *American Scholar* that such restrictions were "in contradistinction to the *growing* realization which has come as a result of the war." Quotas must be abolished if postwar progress were to be made.

*Today,* our society as a whole sees the relationship between social welfare and prejudices which thwart the development of the capacities of individuals. This threat to the basic concepts of democracy is so plain that almost all of us, except the vested interests, have seen it. The question is whether or not the colleges and universities have seen it and are willing to bring their practices into line with *present day* insights, even though some of their most precious traditions be jeopardized. (Dodson 1946, 268, italics added)

Similar connections between the anti-Nazi war, anti-quotas, and the progress of anti-antisemitism informed another popular magazine article the following year: "It is extremely regrettable that *in 1946*, the children of [parents] who are returning from all parts of the world where they have been engaged in mortal combat to preserve democracy, are confronted with the same closed doors that greeted their 'alien' fathers" (Hart 1947, 61). In 1949, *Collier's* published an article describing the "scores of college men to whom fraternities for 'full-blooded Aryans' are a little nauseating *in this day*." Quoting the finding of an Amherst College alumni committee that exclusive fraternities gave young men "a false and undemocratic sense of superiority," the article claimed that "the anti-discrimination movement is hopping from campus to campus" (Whitman 1949, 34–35).

While Jewish voluntary organizations had begun to organize in 1943–45, they entered the American public sphere as aggressive political advocates only from 1945, an intervention that marked the first time Jews had forcefully entered the civil sphere as advocates for their own rather than others' causes. In the prewar period, and even less in earlier times, such an explicit and aggressively Jewish public intervention would certainly have been repelled; in fact, it would only have made antisemitism worse. In the postwar period, however, despite its failure to identify with the Jewish victims of Nazism, the American non-Jewish audience was determined to redeem them. If, as Dinnerstein writes, Jewish groups intended to "mobilize public opinion against intolerance, and [thus to] utilize the courts and legislative bodies" in their antisemitic fight, they were able to carry on these political activities only because postwar public opinion had already been defined as committed to "tolerance" (Dinnerstein 1981–82, 137).

Progress toward establishing civil relations between religious and ethnic groups was woven into the patriotic postwar narratives of the nation's mass circulation magazines. *Better Homes and Gardens* ran such stories as "Do You Want Your Children to Be Tolerant?": "The old indifference and local absorption cannot continue. If we relapse into our *before-the-war* attitudes and limitations, war will burst upon us as suddenly and as unexpectedly as the atomic bomb fell upon the people of Hiroshima—and we shall be as helpless" (Buck 1947, 135, italics added). In another piece in *Better Homes and Gardens* that same year, "How to Stop the Hate Mongers in Your Home Town," a writer observed: "I suspect that many a decent German burgher, hearing tales of Nazi gangs, likewise shrugged off the implications of uncurbed racial and religious persecution" (Carter 1947, 180). The following year, the *Saturday Evening Post* profiled "the story of the Jewish family of Jacob Golomb." The lengthy article concluded with the by now widely expected forward-looking line.

> As a family, the Golombs are more than just nice folks who lead busy, fruitful, decent lives; a family whose sons have sprung, in time of national emergency, with promptness to the defense of their country. As members of a race with a long history of persecution, they have kept the faith, since Abraham Golomb's time, that the United States really was, or *would soon be,* the land of the genuinely free. They are still convinced. (Perry 1948, 96, italics added)

Four years later, America's most popular photo magazine published "*Life* Goes to a Bar Mitzvah: A Boy Becomes Man" (no. 33 [October 13, 1952], 170ff).

The anti-antisemitism theme also entered popular culture through the movies. In the 1945 box office hit *Pride of the Marines*, the Jewish protagonist Larry Diamond chided a friend for pessimism about the possibility of eliminating prejudice in the postwar years. He did so by connecting their present situation to the progressive ideals that had sustained their the anti-Nazi war: "Ah, come on, climb out of your foxholes, what's a matter you guys, don't you think anybody learned anything since 1930? Think everybody's had their eyes shut and brains in cold storage?" (Short 1981, 161). Diamond goes on to remark that, if and when prejudice and repression dare to show their ugly heads in the postwar United States, he will fight to defeat them, just as he has learned to fight in the war: "I fought for me, for the right to live in the USA. And when I get back into civilian life, if I don't like the way things are going, O.K. it's my country; I'll stand on my own two legs and holler! If there's enough of us hollering we'll go places—Check?" (ibid.) The narrative of progress is forcefully extended from the anti-Nazi war into the post-Nazi peace. Diamond had been "the pride of the marines," and the war's progressive narrative is fundamentally tied to assertions about the utopian telos of the United States. As the movie's closing music turns into "America the Beautiful," Diamond wraps it up this way: "One happy afternoon when God was feeling good, he sat down and thought of a rich beautiful country and he named it the USA. All of it, Al, the hills, the rivers, the lands, the whole works. Don't tell me we can't make it work in peace like we do in war. Don't tell me we can't pull together. Don't you see it guys, can't you see it?" (ibid., 161–62).

Two years later, a movie promoting anti-antisemitism, *Gentleman's Agreement,* won the Academy Award for best motion picture and another, *Crossfire,* had been nominated as well. Both are conspicuously progressive, forward-looking narratives. In the final dialogue of *Gentlemen's Agreement,* the film's future-oriented, utopian theme could not be more clear. "Wouldn't it be wonderful," Mrs. Green asks Phil, "if it turned out to be everybody's century, when people all over the world, free people, found a way to live together? I'd like to be around to see some of that, even a beginning" (quoted in Short 1981, 180).

As they had immediately before and during the war, "Jews" held symbolic pride of place in these popular culture narratives because their persecution had been preeminently associated with the Nazi evil. In fact, it was not tolerance as such that the progressive narrative demanded, but tolerance of the Jews. Thus, despite their feelings of solidarity with their foreign coreligionists, Jewish leaders carefully refrained from publicly endorsing the wholesale lifting of anti-immigration quotas after 1945. They realized that the idea of immigration remained so polluted by association with stigmatized others that it might have the power to counteract the ongoing purification of Jewishness. In the preceding half century, anti-immigration and antisemitism had been closely linked, and Jews did not want to pollute "Jewishness" with this identity again. While demonstrating their support in private, Jewish leaders resolutely refused to make any public pronouncements against lifting the immigration quotas (Dinnerstein 1981–82, 140).

## Conclusion

What Dinnerstein has called the "turnabout in anti-Semitic feelings" represented the triumph over Nazism, not recognition of the Holocaust trauma. News about the mass murder, and any ruminations about it, disappeared from newspapers and magazines rather quickly after the initial reports about the camps' liberation, and the Nazis' Jewish victims became represented as displaced persons, potential immigrants, and potential settlers in Palestine, where a majority of Americans wanted to see a new, and redemptive, Jewish state. This interpretation suggests that it was by no means simply real politik that led President Truman to champion, against his former French and British allies, the postwar creation of Israel, the new Jewish state. The progressive narrative demanded a future-oriented renewal. Zionists argued that the Jewish trauma could be redeemed, that Jews could both sanctify the victims and put the trauma behind them, only if they returned to Jerusalem. According to the Zionist worldview, if Israel were allowed to exist, it would create a new race of confident and powerful Jewish farmer-warriors, who would redeem the anti-Jewish atrocities by developing such an imposing military power that the massive murdering of the Jews would never, anywhere in the world, be allowed to happen again. In important respects, it was this convergence of progressive narratives in relation to the war and the Jewish mass killings that led the postwar paths of the United States and the state of Israel to become so fundamentally intertwined. Israel would have to prosper and survive for the redemptive telos of America's progressive narrative to be maintained.

These cultural-sociological considerations do not suggest that the postwar American fight against antisemitism was in any way morally inauthentic. It was triggered by grassroots feelings as deep as those that had motivated the earlier anti-Nazi fight. When one looks at these powerful new arguments against antisemitism, it is only retrospectively surprising to realize that the "atrocities" revealed in 1945—the events and experiences that defined the trauma for European Jews—figure hardly at all. This absence is explained by the powerful symbolic logic of the progressive narrative, which already had been established in the prewar period. With the victory in 1945, the United States got down to the work of establishing the new world order. In creating a Nazi-free future, Jewishness came for the first time to be analogically connected with core American symbols of "democracy" and "nation."

In the course of this postwar transformation, American Jews also became identified with democracy in a more primordial and less universalistic way, namely as newly minted, patriotic representations of the nation. "After 1945," a leading historian of that period remarks, "other Americans no longer viewed the Jews as merely another of the many exotic groups within America's ethnic and religious mosaic. Instead, they were now seen as comprising one of the country's three major religions" (Shapiro 1992, 28). This patriotic-national definition was expressed by the Jewish theologian Will Herberg's insistence on the "Judeo-Christian" rather than "Christian" identity of the religious heritage of the United States (Shapiro 1992, 53). As I have indicated, what motivated this intense identification of anti-antisemitism with the American nation was neither simple emotional revulsion for the horrors of the Jewish mass killings nor commonsense morality. It was, rather, the progressive narrative frame. To end antisemitism, in President Truman's words, was to place America alongside "the moral forces of the world" (quoted in Shapiro 1992, 143). It was to redeem those who had sacrificed themselves for the American nation, and, according to the teleology of the progressive narrative, this emphatically included the masses of murdered European Jews.

The critical point is this: what was a trauma for the victims was not a trauma for the audience. In documenting this for the American case, I have examined the principal carrier group for the progressive narrative, the nation that in the immediate postwar world most conspicuously took the lead in "building the new world upon the ashes of the old." I have shown that the social agents, both Jewish and non-Jewish Americans, who took the lead in reconstructing a new moral order, dedicated themselves to redeeming those who had been sacrificed to the anti-Nazi struggle, and most especially to the Jewish victims, by putting an end to antisemitism in the United States. The goal was focused, not on the Holocaust, but on the need to purge postwar society of Nazilike pollution.

## TOWARD THE "HOLOCAUST":
### JEWISH MASS MURDER UNDER THE TRAGIC NARRATIVE

In the second part of this chapter, I will show how a different kind of narrative developed in relation to the Nazis' mass murder of the Jews, one that gave the evil it represented significantly greater symbolic weight. I will treat this new culture structure both as cause and effect. After reconstructing its internal contours, I will examine the kind of "symbolic action" it caused, and how these new meanings compelled the trauma of the mass murders to be seen in a radically different way, with significant consequences for social and political action that continue to ramify to the present day. After completing this analytic reconstruction of the new cultural configuration, I will proceed to a concrete examination of how it was constructed in real historical time, looking at changes in carrier groups, moral contexts, and social structural forces. Finally, I will examine some of the long-term ramifications of the highly general, decontextualized, and universal status that the trauma of the Holocaust came to assume.

### The New Culture Structure

Ever since Dilthey defined the method specific to the *Geisteswissenschaften*—literally "sciences of the spirit," but typically translated as "human sciences"—it has been clear that what distinguishes the hermeneutic from the natural scientific method is the challenge of penetrating beyond the external form to inner meaning of actions, events, and institutions. Yet to enter into this thicket of subjectivity is not to embrace impressionism and relativism. As Dilthey emphasized, meanings are governed by structures just as surely as economic and political processes; they are just governed in different ways. Every effort at interpretive social science must begin with the reconstruction of this culture structure.

## Deepening Evil

In the formation of this new culture structure, the coding of the Jewish mass killings as evil remained, but its weighting substantially changed. It became burdened with extraordinary gravitas. The symbolization of the Jewish mass killings became generalized and reified, and, in the process, the evil done to the Jews became separated from the profanation of Nazism per se. Rather than seeming to "typify" Nazism, or even the nefarious machinations of any particular social movement, political formation, or historical time, the mass killings came to be seen as not being typical of anything at all. They came to be understood as a unique, historically unprecedented event, as evil on a scale that had never occurred before. The mass killings entered into universal history, becoming a "world historical" event in Hegel's original sense, an event whose emergence onto the world stage threatened, or promised, to change the fundamental course of the world. In the introduction to an English collection of his essays on Nazi history and the Holocaust, the German-Israeli historian Dan Diner observes that "well into the 1970s, wide-ranging portraits of the epoch would grant the Holocaust a modest (if any) mention." By contrast, "it now tends to fill the entire picture." He continues, "The growing centrality of the Holocaust has altered the entire warp and woof of our sense of the passing century . . . The incriminated event has thus become the epoch's marker, its final and inescapable wellspring" (Diner 2000, 1).

The Jewish mass killings became what we might identify, in Durkheimian terms, as a sacred-evil, an evil that recalled a trauma of such enormity and horror that it had to be radically set apart from the world and all of its other traumatizing events, and which became inexplicable in ordinary, rational terms. As part of the Nazi scheme of world domination, the Jewish mass killing was heinous, but at least it had been understandable. As a sacred-evil, set apart from ordinary evil things, it had become mysterious and inexplicable. One of the first to comment upon, and thus to characterize, this postprogressive inexplicability was the Marxist historian Isaac Deutscher. This great biographer of Trotsky, who had already faced the consequences of Stalinism for the myth of communist progress, was no doubt already conditioned to see the tragic dimensions of the Holocaust. In 1968, in "The Jewish Tragedy and the Historian," Deutscher suggested that comprehending the Holocaust "will not be just a matter of time," that is, that there would not be progress in this regard.

> I doubt whether even in a thousand years people will understand Hitler, Auschwitz, Majdanek, and Treblinka better than we do now. Will they have a better historical perspective? On the contrary, posterity may even understand it all even less than we do.
> Who can analyze the motives and the interests behind the enormities of Auschwitz . . . We are confronted here by a huge and ominous mystery of the generation of the human character that will forever baffle and terrify mankind. (Deutcher 1968, 163)

For Deutscher, such a huge and mysterious evil, so resistant to the normal progress of human rationality, suggested tragedy and art, not scientific fact-gathering. "Perhaps a modern Aeschylus and Sophocles could cope with this theme," he suggested, "but they would do so on a level different from that of historical interpretation and explanation" (Deutcher 1968, 164).

Geoffrey Hartman, the literary theorist who has directed Yale University's Video Archive for the Holocaust since 1981 and has been a major participant in post-sixties' discussions of the trauma, points to the enigma that, while no historical event has ever "been so thoroughly documented and studied," social and moral "understanding comes and goes; it has not been progressive." By way of explaining this lack of progress, Hartman acknowledges that

> The scholars most deeply involved often admit an "excess" that remains dark and frightful . . . Something in the . . . Shoah remains dark at the heart of the event . . . A comparison with the French Revolution is useful. The sequence *French Revolution: Enlightenment* cannot be matched by *Holocaust: Enlightenment*. What should be placed after the colon? "Eclipse of Enlightenment" or "Eclipse of God"? (Hartman 1996, 3–4)

To this day, the Holocaust is almost never referred to without asserting its inexplicability. In the spring of 1999, a *New York Times* theater reviewer began his remarks on "The Gathering," a newly opened drama, by asserting that "the profound, agonizing mystery of the Holocaust echoes through the generations and across international borders," presenting "an awesome human and theological enigma as an old century prepares to give way to a new millennium."

This separateness of sacred-evil demanded that the trauma be renamed, for the concept of "mass murder," and even the notion of "genocide," now appeared unacceptably to normalize the trauma, to place it too closely in proximity to the banal and mundane. In contrast, despite the fact that the word "Holocaust" did have a formally established English meaning—according to the *Oxford English Dictionary,* "something wholly burnt up" (Garber and Zuckerman 1989, 199)—it no longer performed this sign function in everyday speech. Rather, the term entered into ordinary English usage, in the early 1960s, as a proper rather than a common noun. Only several years after the Nazis' mass murder did Israelis begin to employ the Hebrew word *shoah,* the term by which the Torah evoked the kind of extraordinary sufferings God had periodically consigned to the Jews. In the official English translation of the phrase "Nazi *shoah*" in the preamble to the 1948 Israeli Declaration of Independence, one can already find the reference to "Nazi holocaust" (Novick 1999, 132). With the decline of the progressive narrative, in other words, as "Holocaust" became the dominant representation for the trauma, it implied the sacral mystery, the "awe-fullness," of the transcendental tradition. "Holocaust" became part of contemporary language as an English symbol that stood for that thing that could not be named. As David Roskies once wrote, "It was precisely the nonreferential quality of 'Holocaust' that made it so appealing" (quoted in Garber and Zuckerman 1989, 201).

This new linguistic identity allowed the mass killings of the Jews to become what might be called a bridge metaphor: it provided the symbolic extension so necessary if the trauma of the Jewish people were to become a trauma for all humankind. The other necessary ingredient, psychological identification, was not far behind. It depended on configuring this newly weighted symbolization of evil in a different narrative frame.

## Suffering, Catharsis, and Identification

The darkness of this new postwar symbolization of evil cast a shadow over the progressive story that had thus far narrated its course. The story of redeeming Nazism's victims by creating a progressive and democratic world order could be called an ascending narrative, for it pointed to the future and suggested confidence that things would be better over time. Insofar as the mass killings were defined as a Holocaust, and insofar as it was the very emergence of this sacred-evil, not its eventual defeat, that threatened to become emblematic of "our time," the progressive narrative was blocked, and in some manner overwhelmed, by a sense of historical descent, by a falling away from the good. Recent Holocaust commentators have drawn this conclusion time and again. According to the progressive narrative, the Nazis' mass murder of the Jews would provide a lesson for all humankind, a decisive learning process on the way to a better world. Reflecting on the continuing fact of genocidal mass murders in the post-Holocaust world, Hartman revealingly suggests that "these developments raise questions about our species, our preconceptions that we are the human, the 'family of man.' Or less dramatically, we wonder about the veneer of progress, culture, and educability."

In dramaturgical terms, the issue concerns the position occupied by evil in the historical narrative. When Aristotle first defined tragedy in the *Poetics,* he linked what I have here called the weight of the representation of suffering to temporal location of an event in plot:

> Tragedy is the representation of a complete, i.e., whole action *which has some magnitude* (for there can be a whole action without magnitude). A whole is that which has a beginning, a middle and a conclusion. A beginning is that which itself does not of necessity follow something else, but after which there naturally is, or comes into being, something else. A conclusion, conversely, is that which itself naturally follows something else, either of necessity or for the most part, but has nothing else after it. A middle is that which itself naturally follows something else, and has something else after it. Well-constructed plots, then, should neither begin from a random point nor conclude at a random point, but should use the elements we have mentioned [i.e., beginning, middle, and conclusion]. (Aristotle 1987, 3.2.1, italics added)

In the progressive narrative frame, the Jewish mass killings were not an end but a beginning. They were part of the massive trauma of World War II, but in the postwar period they and related incidents of Nazi horror were regarded as a birth trauma, a crossroads in a chronology that would eventually be set right. By contrast, the newly emerging world-historical status of the mass murders suggested that they represented an end point, not a new beginning, a death trauma rather than a trauma of birth, a cause for despair, not the beginning of hope. In place of the progressive story, then, there began to emerge the narrative of tragedy. The endpoint of a narrative defines its telos. In the new tragic understanding of the Jewish mass murder, suffering, not progress, became the telos toward which the narrative was aimed.

In this tragic narrative of sacred-evil, the Jewish mass killings become not an event in history but an archetype, an event out-of-time. As archetype, the evil evoked an experience of trauma greater than anything that could be defined by religion, race, class, region—indeed, by any conceivable sociological configuration or historical conjuncture. This transcendental status, this separation from the specifics of any particular time or space, provided the basis for psychological identification on an unprecedented scale. The contemporary audience cares little about the second and third installments of Sophocles' archetypal story of Oedipus, the tragic hero. What we are obsessed with is Oedipus' awful, unrecognized, and irredeemable mistake, how he finally comes to recognize his responsibility for it, and how he blinds himself from guilt when he understands its full meaning. Tragic narratives focus attention not on some future effort at reversal or amelioration—"progress," in the terms I have employed here—but on the nature of the crime, its immediate aftermath, and on the motives and relationships that led up to it.

A tragic narrative offers no redemption in the traditionally religious, Judeo-Christian sense. There is no happy ending, no sense that something else could have been done, and no belief that the future could, or can, necessarily be changed. Indeed, protagonists are tragic precisely because they have failed to exert control over events. They are in the grip of forces larger than themselves, impersonal, even inhuman forces that often are not only beyond control but, during the tragic action itself, beyond comprehension. This sense of being overwhelmed by unjust force or fate explains the abjection and helplessness that permeates the genre of tragedy, and the experience of pity it arouses.

Instead of redemption through progress, the tragic narrative offers what Nietzsche called the drama of the eternal return. As it now came to be understood, there was no "getting beyond" the story of the Holocaust. There was only the possibility of returning to it: not transcendence but catharsis. Hartman resists "the call for closure" on just these grounds: "Wherever we look, the events of 1933–1945 cannot be relegated to the past. They are not over; anyone who comes in contact with them is gripped, and finds detachment difficult." Quoting from Lawrence Langer's *Admitting the Holocaust*, Hartman suggests that "those who study it must "reverse history and progress and find a way of restoring to the imagination of coming generations the depth of the catastrophe" (Hartman 1996, 2, 5).

As Aristotle explained, catharsis clarifies feeling and emotion. It does so not by allowing the audience to separate itself from the story's characters, a separation, according to Frye, that defines the very essence of comedy (Frye 1971). Rather, catharsis clarifies feeling and emotion by forcing the audience to identify with the story's characters, compelling them to experience their suffering with them and to learn, as often they did not, the true causes of their death. That we survive and they do not, that we can get up and leave the theater while they remain forever prostrate—this allows the possibility of catharsis, that strange combination of cleansing and relief, that humbling feeling of having been exposed to the dark and sinister forces that lay just beneath the surface of human life, and of having survived. We seek catharsis because our identification with the tragic narrative compels us to experience dark and sinister forces that are also inside of ourselves, not only inside others. We "redeem" tragedy by experiencing it, but, despite this redemption, we do not get over it. Rather, to achieve redemption we are compelled to dramatize and redramatize, experience and reexperience the archetypal trauma. We pity the victims of the trauma, identifying and sympathizing with their horrible fate. Aristotle argued the tragic genre could be utilized only for the "sorts of occurrence [that] arouse dread, or compassion in us" (Aristotle 1987, 4.1.2). The blackness of tragedy can be achieved only if, "first and foremost, the [suffering] characters should be good," for "the plot should be constructed in such a way that, even without seeing it, someone who hears about the incidents will shudder and feel pity at the outcome, as someone may feel upon hearing the plot of the Oedipus" (Aristotle 1987, 4.2.1, 4.1.1.3). It is not only the fact of identification, however, but its complexity that makes the experience of trauma as tragedy so central to the assumption of moral responsibility, for we identify not only with the victims but with the perpetrators as well. The creation of this cultural form allows the psychological activity of internalization rather than projection, acceptance rather than displacement.

### The Trauma Drama: Eternal Return and the Problem of Progress

In the tragic narration of the Holocaust, the primal event became a "trauma drama" that the "audience" returned to time and time again. This became, paradoxically, the only way to ensure that such an event would happen "never again." This quality of compulsively returning to the trauma drama gave the story of the Holocaust a mythical status that transformed it into the archetypical sacred-evil of our time. Insofar as it achieved this status as a dominant myth, the tragedy of the Holocaust challenged the ethical self-identification, the self-esteem, of modernity—indeed, the very self-confidence that such a thing as "modern progress" could continue to exist. For to return to the trauma drama of the Holocaust, to identify over and over again with the suffering and helplessness of its victims, was in some sense to give that confidence-shattering event a continuing existence in contemporary life. It was, in effect, to acknowledge that it *could* happen again.

In this way, the tragic framing of the Holocaust fundamentally contributed to postmodern relativism and disquiet. Because the tragic replaced the progressive narrative of the Nazi mass murder, the ethical standards protecting good from evil seemed not nearly as powerful as modernity's confident pronouncements had promised they would be. When the progressive narrative had organized understanding, the Nazi crimes had been temporalized as "medieval," in order to contrast them with the supposedly civilizing standards of modernity. With the emergence of the more tragic perspective, the barbarism was lodged within the essential nature of modernity itself. This is the radical and corrosive theme of Bauman's provocative *Modernity and the Holocaust*. While Bauman himself professes to eschew any broader universalizing aims, the ethical message of such a perspective seems clear all the same. Instead of maintaining and perfecting modernity, as the postwar progressive narrative would have it, the path to a more just and peaceful society seems to lead to postmodern life (Bauman 1989).

It would be wrong, however, to imagine that because a trauma drama lies at the center of the Holocaust's tragic narration, with all the ambition of exciting pity and emotional catharsis that this implies, this lachrymose narrative and symbol actually became disconnected from the ethical and the good. While it is undeniable that the Jewish mass killings came to assume a dramaturgical form, their significance hardly became aestheticized, that is, turned into a free-floating, amoral symbol whose function was to entertain rather than to instruct. The events of the Holocaust were not dramatized for the sake of drama itself, but rather to provide what Martha Nussbaum once described as "the social benefits of pity" (Nussbaum 1992). The project of renaming, dramatizing, reifying, and ritualizing the Holocaust contributed to a moral remaking of the (post)modern (Western) world. The Holocaust story has been told and retold in response not only to an emotional need but a moral ambition. Its characters, its plot, and its pitiable denouement have been transformed into a less nationally bound, less temporally specific, and more universal drama. This dramatic universalization has deepened contemporary sensitivity to social evil. The trauma drama's message, as every tragedy's, is that evil is inside all of us, and in every society. If we are all the victims, and all the perpetrators, then there is no audience that can legitimately distance itself from collective suffering, either from its victims or its perpetrators.

This psychological identification with the Jewish mass killings and the symbolic extension of its moral implications beyond the immediate parties involved has stimulated an unprecedented universalization of political and moral responsibility. To have created this symbol of sacred-evil in contemporary time, then, is to have so enlarged the human imagination that it is capable, for the first time in human history, of identifying, understanding, and judging the kinds of genocidal mass killings in which national, ethnic, and ideological groupings continue to engage today. This enlargement has made it possible to comprehend that heinous prejudice with the intent to commit mass murder is not something from an earlier, more "primitive" time or a different, "foreign" place, committed by people with values we do not share. The implication of the tragic narrative is not that progress has become impossible. It has had the salutary effect, rather, of demonstrating that progress is much more difficult to achieve than moderns once believed. If progress is to be made, morality must be universalized beyond any particular time and place.

## The New Social Processes

Most Western people today would readily agree with the proposition that the Holocaust was a tragic, devastating event in human history. Surely it was, and is. One implication of my discussion thus far, however, is that this perception of its moral status is not a natural reflection of the event itself. The Jewish mass killings first had to be dramatized—as a tragedy. Some of the most eloquent and influential Holocaust survivors and interpreters have disagreed sharply, and moralistically, with this perspective, insisting on that fictional representations must not be allowed to influence the perception of historical reality. In 1978, Elie Wiesel excoriated NBC for producing the *Holocaust* miniseries, complaining that "it transforms an ontological event into soap-opera" and that "it is all make-believe." Because "the Holocaust transcends history," Wiesel argued, "it cannot be explained nor can it be visualized" (Wiesel 1978, 1). In response to *Schindler's List,* Claude Lanzman said much the same thing. Writing that the Holocaust "is above all unique in that it erects a ring of fire around itself," he claimed that "fiction is a transgression" and that "there are some things that cannot and should not be represented" (quoted in Hartman 1996, 84).

I am obviously taking a very different perspective here. Thus far, I have reconstructed the internal patterning of the culture structure that allowed the new, tragic dramatization to take place. I would like now to turn to the historically specific social processes, both symbolic and social structural, that made this new patterning attractive and, eventually, compelling. While my reference here is primarily to the United States, I believe some version of this analysis also applies to those other Western societies that attempted to reconstruct liberal democracies after the Second World War.

We have earlier seen how the struggle against antisemitism became one of the primary vehicles by which the progressive narrative redeemed those who had been sacrificed in the war against Nazi evil. Fighting antisemitism was not the only path to redemption, of course; for America and its victorious allies, there was a whole new world to make. At the same time, the struggle against antisemitism had a special importance. The understanding of Nazism as an absolute evil stemmed not only from its general commitment to anti-civil domination, but also from its effort to legitimate such violence according to the principles of prejudice and primordiality. Because the Jewish people were by far the most conspicuous primordial target, symbolic logic dictated that to be anti-Nazi was to be anti-antisemitic.

As I have suggested earlier, the rhetorics and policies of this anti-antisemitism did not require that non-Jewish Americans positively identify with Jews, any more than the role that the Holocaust played in the postwar progressive narrative depended on a sense of identification with the weary and bedraggled survivors in the concentration camps themselves. To narrate the Holocaust in a tragic manner, however, did depend on just such an identification being made. This identification was a long time in coming, and it depended on a number of factors unrelated to public opinion and cultural change. Nonetheless, it certainly depended, in addition to such social structural factors, on the fact that the cultural idiom and the organizational apparatus of antisemitism had, indeed, been attacked and destroyed in the early "progressive" postwar years, and that, for the first time in American history, Jews seemed, to a majority of Christian Americans, not that much different from anybody else.

As this tragic narrative crystallized, the Holocaust drama became, for an increasing number of Americans, and for significant proportions of Europeans as well, the most widely understood and emotionally compelling trauma of the twentieth century. These bathetic events, once experienced as traumatic only by its Jewish victims, became generalized and universalized. Their representation no longer referred to events that took place at a particular time and place but to a trauma that had became emblematic, and iconic, of human suffering as such. The horrific trauma of the Jews became the trauma of all humankind.

## The Production of New Social Dramas

How was this more generalized and universalized status achieved? Social narratives are not composed by some hidden hand of history. Nor do they appear all at once. The new trauma drama emerged in bits and pieces. It was a matter of this story and that, this scene and that scene from this movie and that book, this television episode and that theater performance, this photographic capturing of a moment of torture and suffering. Each of these glimpses into what Meyer Levin had called, in April 1945, "the very crawling inside of the vicious heart" contributed some element to the construction of this new sensibility, which highlighted suffering, helplessness, and dark inevitability, and which, taken together and over time, reformulated the mass killing of the Jews as the most tragic event in Western history. It is not the purpose of the present discussion to provide anything approaching a thick description of this process of symbolic reconstruction, but only to identify the signposts along this new route and the changing "countryside" that surrounded it.

## Personalizing the Trauma and Its Victims

In the course of constructing and broadcasting the tragic narrative of the Holocaust, a handful of actual dramatizations—in books, movies, plays, and television shows—played critically important roles. Initially formulated for an American audience, these works were distributed worldwide, seen by tens and possibly hundreds of millions of persons, and talked about incessantly by high-, middle-, and low-brow audiences alike. In the present context, what is most important about these dramas is that they achieved their effect by personalizing the trauma and its characters. This personalization brought the trauma drama "back home." Rather than depicting the events on a vast historical scale; rather than focusing on larger-than-life-leaders, mass movements, organizations, crowds, and ideologies; these dramas portrayed the events in terms of small groups, families and friends, parents and children, brothers and sisters. In this way, the victims of trauma became everyman and every-woman, every child and every parent.

The prototype of this personalizing genre was Anne Frank's famous *Diary*. First published in Holland in 1947, the edited journals appeared in English in 1952. They became the basis for a Pulitzer-Prize-winning Broadway play in 1955 and in 1959 a highly acclaimed and equally pop-ular but more widely influential Hollywood movie. This collective repre-sentation began in Europe, as the journal recorded by a young Dutch girl in hiding from the Nazis, and evolved, via a phase of Americanization, into a universal symbol of suffering and transcendence. This transmogri-fication was possible, in the first place, precisely because Anne's daily jot-tings focused less on the external events of war and Holocaust—from which she was very much shut off—than on her inner psychological tur-moil and the human relationships of those who shared her confinement. Anne's father, Otto Frank, the only family member to survive the camps, supervised the publications and dramatizations of his daughter's jour-nals, and he perceived very clearly the relationship between Anne's per-sonal focus and the *Diary*'s potentially universalizing appeal. Writing to Meyer Shapiro, a dramatist who insisted, by contrast, on the specifically Jewish quality of the reminiscence, Otto Frank replied that "as to the Jewish side you are right that I do not feel the same you do."

> I always said, that Anne's book is not a war book. War is the background. It is not a Jewish book either, though [a] Jewish sphere, sentiment and sur-rounding is the background . . . It is read and understood more by gentiles than in Jewish circles. So do not make a Jewish play out of it. (quoted in Doneson 1987, 152)

When dramatists for the *Diary* were finally chosen—Francis Goodrich and Albert Hackett—Frank criticized their initial drafts on similar grounds.

> Having read thousands of reviews and hundreds of personal letters about Anne's book from different countries in the world, I know what creates the impression of it on people and their impressions ought to be conveyed by the play to the public. Young people identify themselves very frequently with Anne in their struggle during puberty and the problems of the relations [between] mother-daughter are existing all over the world. These and the love affair with Peter attract young people, whereas parents, teachers, and psychologists learn about the inner feelings of the young generation. When I talked to Mrs. [Eleanor] Roosevelt about the book, she urged me to give permission for [the] play and film as only then we could reach the masses and influence them by the mission of the book which she saw in Anne's wish

to work for mankind, to achieve something valuable still after her death, her horror against war and discrimination. (quoted in Doneson 1987, 153)

This impulse to facilitate identification and moral extension prompted the dramatists to translate into English the *Diary*'s pivotal Hanukkah song, which was sung and printed in the original Hebrew in the earlier book version. The Hacketts explained their reasoning in a letter to Frank. To have left the song in its original Hebrew, they wrote,

> would set the characters in the play apart from the people watching them ... for the majority of our audience is not Jewish. And the thing that we have striven for, toiled for, fought for throughout the whole play is to make the audience understand and identify themselves ... to make them one with them ... that will make them feel "that, but for the grace of God, might have been I." (quoted in Doneson 1987, 154)

Frank agreed, affirming that it "was my point of view to try to bring Anne's message to as many people as possible even if there are some who think it a sacrilege" from a religious point of view (quoted in Doneson 1987, 154). Years later, after the unprecedented success of both the theater and screen plays, the Hacketts continued to justify their decision to abandon Hebrew in the dramaturgic terms of facilitating psychological identification and symbolic extension.

> What we all of us hoped, and prayed for, and what we are devoutly thankful to have achieved, is an identification of the audience with the people in hiding. They are seen, not as some strange people, but persons like themselves, thrown into this horrible situation. With them they suffer the deprivations, the terrors, the moments of tenderness, of exaltation and courage beyond belief. (quoted in Doneson 1987, 155)

In the course of the 1960s, Anne Frank's tragic story laid the basis for psychological identification and symbolic extension on a mass scale. In 1995, the director of Jewish Studies at Indiana University reported that

> *The Diary of a Young Girl* is ... widely read in American schools, and American youngsters regularly see the stage and film versions as well. Their teachers encourage them to identify with Anne Frank and to write stories, essays, and poems about her. Some even see her as a kind of saint and pray to her. During their early adolescent years, many American girls view her story as their story, her fate as somehow bound up with their fate. (Rosenfeld 1995, 37)

The symbolic transformation effected by Anne Frank's *Diary* established the dramatic parameters and the stage for the rush of books, television shows, and movies that in the decades following crystallized the mass murder of the Jews as the central episode in a tragic rather than progressive social narrative. As this new genre became institutionalized, representation of Nazism and World War II focused less and less on the historical actors who had once been considered central. In 1953, the acclaimed Billy Wilder movie *Stalag 17* had portrayed the grueling plight of U.S. soldiers in a German prison of war camp. It never mentioned the Jews (Shapiro 1992, 4). In the early 1960s, a widely popular evening television show, *Hogan's Heroes,* also portrayed American soldiers in a Nazi prison. It didn't mention "Jews" either. Indeed, the prison camp functioned as a site for comedy, lampooning the misadventures arising from the casual intermixing of Americans with Nazi camp guards and often portraying the latter as bemusing, well-intended buffoons. By the late 1960s, neither comedy nor romance was a genre that audiences felt comfortable applying to that earlier historical time. Nor was it possible to leave out of any dramatization what by then were acknowledged to be the period's central historical actors, the concentration camp Jews.

This transition was solidified in Western popular culture by the miniseries *Holocaust,* the stark family drama that unfolded over successive evening nights to a massive American audience in April 1978. The four-part, nine-and-a-half-hour drama, watched by nearly 100 million Americans, personalized the grisly and famous landmarks of the Third Reich, following ten years in the lives of two fictional families, one assimilated Jews, the other of a high-ranking SS official.

This extraordinary public attention was repeated, to even greater cathartic effect, when the bathetic drama was later broadcast to record-breaking television audiences in Germany. German critics, commentators, and large sections of the pubic at large were transfixed by what German commentators described as "the most controversial series of all times" and as "the series that moved the world." During and after this German broadcast, which was preceded by careful public preparation and accompanied by extensive private and public discussion, German social scientists conducted polls and interviews to trace its remarkable effects. They discovered that the resulting shift in public opinion had put a stop to a burgeoning "Hitler revival" and quelled long-standing partisan demands for "balance" in the presentation of the Jewish mass murder. In the wake of the drama, neutralizing terms like "the final solution" gave way in German popular and academic discussion to the English term *Holocaust,* and the German Reichstag removed the statute of limitations on Nazis who had participated in what were now defined, not as war crimes, but as crimes against humanity. The trauma drama thus continued to work its universalizing effects.

### Enlarging the Circle of Perpetrators

Corresponding to the personalization that expanded identification with the victims of the tragedy, there developed a new understanding of the perpetrators of the Holocaust that removed them from their historically specific particularities and made them into universal figures with whom members of widely diverse groups felt capable, not of sympathizing, but of identifying. The critical event initiating this reconsideration was undoubtedly the 1961 trial of Adolph Eichmann in Jerusalem. Here was a personal and singular representation of the Nazis' murders brought back into the present from the abstract mists of historical time, compelled to "face the music" after being captured by Israeli security forces in a daring extralegal mission right out of a spy novel or science fiction book. The trial received extraordinary press coverage in the United States. That summer, Gallup conducted a series of in-depth interviews with five hundred randomly selected residents of Oakland, California, and found that 84 percent of those sampled met the minimum criterion for awareness of this faraway event, a striking statistic given American indifference to foreign affairs (Lipstadt 1996, 212, n. 54). At least seven books were published about Eichmann and his trial in the following year (ibid., 196).

The first legal confrontation with the Holocaust since Nuremburg, the trial was staged by Israel, not to generalize away from the originating events, but to get back to them. As Prime Minister Ben-Gurion put it, the trial would give "the generation that was born and educated after the Holocaust in Israel . . . an opportunity to get acquainted with the details of this tragedy about which they knew so little" (Braun 1994, 183). The lessons were to be drawn from, and directed to, particular places and particular peoples, to Germany, the Nazis, Israel, and the Jews—in Ben-Gurion's words, to "the dimensions of the tragedy which *our people* experienced" (ibid., 213, italics added). By the time it was over, however, the Eichmann trial paradoxically had initiated a massive universalization of Nazi evil, best captured by Hannah Arendt's enormously controversial insistence that the trial compelled recognition of the "banality of evil." This framing of Nazi guilt became highly influential, even as it was sharply and bitterly disputed by Jews and non-Jews alike. For as a banally evil person, Eichmann could be "everyman." Arendt herself had always wanted to make just such a point. In her earliest reaction to the Nazi murders, the philosopher had expressed horror and astonishment at the Nazis' absolute inhumanity. For this she was rebuked by her mentor and friend Karl Jaspers, who cautioned against making the Nazis into "monsters" and "supermen." To do so, Jaspers warned, would merely confirm the Nazis in their grandiose Nietzchean fantasies and relieve others of responsibility as well. Because of Arendt's singular influence, the antagonists in the trauma began to seem not so different from anybody else. The trial and its aftermath eventually became framed in a manner that narrowed the once great distance between postwar democratic audience and evil Nazis, connecting them rather than isolating them from one another. This connection between audience and antagonist intensified the trauma's tragic dramaturgy.

During this same period, other forces also had the effect of widening the circle of "perpetrators." Most spectacularly, there was Stanley Milgram's experiment demonstrating that ordinary, well-educated college students would "just follow the orders" of professional authority, even to the point of gravely endangering the lives of innocent people. These findings raised profoundly troubling questions about the "good nature" of all human beings and the democratic capacity of any human society. Milgram appeared on the cover of *Time* magazine, and "the Milgram experiment" became part of the folklore of the 1960s. It generalized the capacity for radical evil, first demonstrated by the Nazis, to the American population at large, synergistically interacting with the symbolic reconstruction of perpetrators that Arendt on Eichmann had begun. In one interview Milgram conducted with a volunteer after he had revealed to him the true nature of the experiment, the volunteer remarked: "As my wife said: 'You can call yourself Eichmann'" (quoted in Novick 1999, 137).

In the decades that followed, other powerful cultural reconstructions of the perpetrators followed in this wake. In 1992, Christopher Browning published a widely discussed historical ethnography called *Ordinary Men: Reserve Police Battalion 101 and the Final Solution in Poland* (Browning 1992), which focused on the everyday actions and motives of Germans who were neither members of the professional military nor particularly ideological, but who, nonetheless, carried out systematic and murderous cleansings of the Jews. When four years later Daniel Goldhagen published *Hitler's Willing Executioners: Ordinary Germans and the Holocaust* (Goldhagen 1996), his aim was to shift blame back to what he described as the unprecedented and particular kind of antisemitism, what he called "eliminationist," of the Germans themselves. Browning's critical response to Goldhagen was based on historical evidence, but it also decried the moral particularity that Goldhagen's argument seemed to entail. Indeed, Browning connected his empirical findings about the "ordinariness" of perpetrators to the necessity for universalizing the moral implications of Nazi crimes, and in doing so he pointed all the way back to Milgram's earlier findings.

> What allowed the Nazis to mobilize and harness the rest of society to the mass murder of European Jewry? Here I think that we historians need to turn to the insights of social psychology—the study of psychological reactions to social situations . . . We must ask, what really is a human being? We must give up the comforting and distancing notions that the perpetrators of the Holocaust were fundamentally a different kind of people because they were products of a radically different culture. (Browning 1992, A72)

In the realm of popular culture, Steven Spielberg's blockbuster movie *Schindler's List* must also be considered in this light. In a subtle but unmistakable manner, the movie departicularizes the perpetrators by showing the possibilities that "even Germans" could be good.

## Losing Control of the Means of Symbolic Production: Deposing the Agents of the Progressive Narrative

It was in this context of tragic transformation—as personalization of the drama increased identification beyond the Jewish victims themselves, and as the sense of moral culpability became fundamentally widened beyond the Nazis themselves—that the United States government, and the nation's authoritative interlocutors, lost control over the telling of the Holocaust story. When the American government and its allies defeated Nazi Germany in 1945 and seized control over strategic evidence from the death camps, they had taken control over the representation process away from the Nazis and assured that the Jewish mass murder would be presented in an anti-Nazi way. In this telling of the story, naturally enough, the former Allies—America most powerfully, but Britain and France as well—presented themselves as the moral protagonists, purifying themselves as heroic carriers of the good. As the 1960s unfolded, the Western democracies were forced to concede this dominant narrative position. This time around, however, control over the means of symbolic production changed hands as much for cultural reasons as by the force of arms.

In the "critical years" from the mid-1960s to the end of the 1970s, the United States experienced a sharp decline in its political, military, and moral prestige. It was during this period that, in the eyes of tens of millions of Americans and others, the domestic and international opposition to America's prosecution of the Vietnam war transformed the nation, and especially its government and armed forces, into a symbol, not of salvationary good, but of apocalyptic evil. This transformation was intensified by other outcroppings of "the sixties," particularly the revolutionary impulses that emerged out of the student and black power movements inside the United States and guerilla movements outside it. These "real world" problems caused the United States to be identified in terms that had, up until that time, been reserved exclusively for the Nazi perpetrators of the Holocaust. According to the progressive narrative, it could only be the Allies' World War II enemy who represented radical evil. As America became "Amerika," however, napalm bombs were analogized with gas pellets and the flaming jungles of Vietnam with the gas chambers. The powerful American army that claimed to be prosecuting a "good war" against Vietnamese communists—in analogy with the lessons that Western democracies had learned in their earlier struggle against Nazism—came to be identified, by influential intellectuals and a wide swath of the educated Western public, as perpetrating genocide against the helpless and pathetic inhabits of Vietnam. Bertrand Russell and Jean-Paul Sartre established a kind of counter-"War Crimes Tribunal" to apply the logic of Nuremberg to the United States. Indefensible incidents of civilian killing, like the My Lai Massacre of 1968, were represented, not as anomalous incidents, but as typifications of this new American-made tragedy.

This process of material deconstruction and symbolic inversion further contributed to the universalization of the Holocaust: it allowed the moral criteria generated by its earlier interpretation to be applied in a less nationally specific and thus less particularistic way. This inversion undermined still further the progressive narrative under which the mass killings of the Jews had early been framed. For the ability to leave the trauma drama behind, and to press ahead toward the future, depended on the material and symbolic existence of an unsullied protagonist who could provide salvation for survivors by leading them into the promised land. "Vietnam" and "the sixties" undercut the main agent of this progressive narrative. The result was a dramatic decline in the confidence that a new world order could be constructed in opposition to violence and coercion; if the United States itself committed war crimes, what chance could there be for modern and democratic societies ever to leave mass murder safely behind?

As a result of these material and symbolic events, the contemporary representatives of the historic enemies of Nazism lost control over the means of symbolic production. The power to present itself as the purified protagonist in the worldwide struggle against evil slipped out of the hands of the American government and patriotic representatives more generally, even as the framing of the drama's triggering trauma shifted from progress to tragedy. The ability to cast and produce the trauma drama, to compel identification and channel catharsis, spread to other nations and to antigovernment groups, and even to historic enemies of the Jewish people. The archetypical trauma drama of the twentieth century became ever more generalized and more accessible, and the criteria for moral responsibility in social relations, once closely tied to American perspectives and interests, came to be defined in a more evenhanded, more egalitarian, more self-critical—in short, a more universalistic—way.

Perhaps the most visible and paradoxical effect of this loss of the American government's control over the means of symbolic production was that the morality of American leadership in World War II came to be questioned in a manner that established polluting analogies with Nazism. One issue that now became "troubling," for example, was the justification for the Allied fire bombings of Dresden and Tokyo. The growing climate of relativism and reconfiguration threatened to undermine the coding, weighting, and narrating that once had provided a compelling rationale for those earlier events that were, in themselves, so massively destructive of civilian life. In a similar manner, but with much more significant repercussions, the symbolic implications of the atomic bombings of Hiroshima and Nagasaki began to be fundamentally reconfigured. From being conceived as stages in the unfolding of the progressive narrative, the atomic bombings came to be understood by influential groups of Westerners as vast human tragedies. Younger generations of Americans, in fact, were increasingly responsive to the view of these events that had once been promoted exclusively by Japan, the fascist Axis power against which their elders had waged war. The interpretation of the suffering caused by the atomic bombings became separated from the historical specifics of time and place. With this generalization, the very events that had once appeared as high points of the progressive narrative came to be constructed as unjustifiable, as human tragedies, as slaughters of hundreds of thousands of innocent and pathetic human beings—in short, as typifications of the "Holocaust."

Perhaps the most pointed example of what could happen after America lost control over the Holocaust story was the manner in which its redemptive role in the narrative was challenged. Rather than being portrayed as the chief prosecutors of Nazi perpetrators—as chief prosecutors, the narrative's protagonists along with the victims themselves—the American and the British wartime governments were accused of having at least indirect responsibility for allowing the Nazis to carry out their brutal work. A steady stream of revisionist historical scholarship emerged, beginning in the 1970s, suggesting that the antisemitism of Roosevelt and Churchill, and of their American and British citizens, had prevented them from acting to block the mass killings. For they had received authenticated information about German plans and activities as early as June 1942.

This analogical linkage between the Allies and the perpetrators quickly became widely accepted as historical fact. On September 27, 1979, when the President's Commission on the Victims of the Holocaust issued a report recommending the American establishment of a Holocaust Museum, it listed as one of its primary justifications that such a public construction would give the American nation an opportunity to compensate for its early, "disastrous" indifference to the plight of the Jews (quoted in Linenthal 1995, 37). When the museum was eventually constructed, it enshrined this inversion of the progressive narrative in the exhibitions themselves. The third floor of the museum is filled with powerfully negative images of the death camps and is attached by an internal bridge to a tower whose rooms display actual artifacts from the camps. As visitors approach this bridge, in the midst of the iconic representations of evil, they confront a photomural of a U.S. Air Force intelligence photograph of Auschwitz-Birkenau, taken on May 31, 1944. The text attached to the mural informs visitors: "Two freight trains with Hungarian Jews arrived in Birkenau that day; the large-scale gassing of these Jews was beginning. The four Birkenau crematoria are visible at the top of the photograph" (quoted in Linenthal 1995, 217). Placed next to the photomural is what the principal ethnographer of the museum project, Edward Linenthal, has called "an artifactual indictment of American indifference." It is a letter, dated August 14, 1944, from Assistant Secretary of War John J. McCloy. According to the text, McCoy "rejected a request by the World Jewish Congress to bomb the Auschwitz concentration camp." This rejection is framed in the context not of physical impossibility, nor in terms of the vicissitudes of a world war, but as the result of moral diminution. Visitors are informed that the U.S. Air Force "could have bombed Auschwitz as early as May 1944," since U.S. bombers had "struck Buna, a synthetic-rubber works relying on slave labor, located less than five miles east of Auschwitz-Birkenau." But, despite this physical possibility, the text goes on to note, the death camp "remained untouched." The effective alignment of Allied armies with Nazi perpetrators is more than implicit: "Although bombing Auschwitz would have killed many prisoners, it would also have halted the operation of the gas chambers and, ultimately, saved the lives of many more" (quoted in Linenthal 1995, 217–18). This authoritative reconstruction, it is important to emphasize, is not a brute empirical fact, any more than the framework that had previous sway. In fact, within the discipline of American history, the issue of Allied indifference remains subject to intense debate (Linenthal 1995, 219–24). At every point in the construction of a public discourse, however, factual chronicles must be encased in symbolically coded and narrated frames.

Eventually, this revision of the progressive narrative about exclusively Nazi perpetrators extended, with perhaps even more profound consequences, to other Allied powers and to the neutrals in that earlier conflict as well. As the charismatic symbol of French resistance to German occupation, Charles de Gaulle had woven a narrative, during and after the war, that purified his nation by describing his nation as first the victim, and later the courageous opponent, of Nazi domination and the "foreign" collaborators in Vichy. By the late 1970s and 1980s, however, a younger generation of French and non-French historians challenged this definition, seriously polluting the earlier Republican government, and even some of its postwar socialist successors, by documenting massive French collaboration with the antidemocratic, antisemitic regime.

In the wake of these reversals, it seemed only a matter of time until the nations who had been "neutral" during the earlier conflict would also be forced to relinquish symbolic control over the telling of their own stories, at least in the theater of Western opinion if not on their own national stage. Austria, for example, had long depicted itself as a helpless victim of Nazi Germany. When Kurt Waldheim ascended to secretary general of the United Nations, however, his hidden association with the Hitler regime was revealed, and the symbolic status of the Austrian nation, which rallied behind their ex-president, began to be publicly polluted as a result. Less than a decade later, Switzerland became subject to similar inversion of its symbolic fortunes. The tiny republic had prided itself on its long history of decentralized canton democracy and the kind of benevolent, universalizing neutrality of its Red Cross. In the mid-nineties, journalists and historians documented that the wartime Swiss government had laundered, that is, "purified," Nazi gold. In return for gold that had been plundered from the bodies of condemned and already dead Jews,

Swiss bankers gave to Nazi authorities acceptable, unmarked currency that could much more readily be used to finance the war.

This discussion of how the non-Jewish agents of the progressive narrative were undercut by "real world" developments would be incomplete without some mention of how the Israeli government, which represented the other principal agent of the early, progressive Holocaust story, also came to be threatened with symbolic reconfiguration. The rise of Palestinian liberation movements inverted the Jewish nation's progressive myth of origin, for it suggested, at least to more liberally inclined groups, an equation between Nazi and Israeli treatment of subordinate ethnic and religious groups. The battle for cultural position was not, of course, given up without a fight. When West German chancellor Helmut Schmidt spoke of Palestinian rights, Israeli prime minister Menachem Begin retorted that Schmidt, a Wehrmact officer in World War II, had "remained faithful to Hitler until the last moment," insisting that the Palestine Liberation Organization was a "neo-Nazi organization" (quoted in Novick 1994, 161). This symbolic inversion vis-à-vis the newly generalized and reconfigured Holocaust symbol was deepened by the not unrelated complicity of Israel in the massacres that followed the Lebanon invasion and by the documented reports of Palestinian torture and occasional death in Israeli prisons.

## THE HOLOCAUST AS BRIDGING METAPHOR:
## THE ENGORGEMENT OF EVIL
## AND ITS ETHICAL MANIFESTATION

Each of the cultural transformations and social processes I have described has had the effect of universalizing the moral questions provoked by the mass killings of the Jews, of detaching the issues surrounding the systematic exercise of violence against ethnic groups from any particular ethnicity, religion, nationality, time, or place. These processes of detachment and deepening emotional identification are thoroughly intertwined. If the Holocaust were not conceived as a tragedy, it would not attract such continuous, even obsessive attention; this attention would not be rewarded, in turn, if the Holocaust were not understood in a detached and universalizing way. Symbolic extension and emotional identification both are necessary if the audience for a trauma, and its social relevance, is to be dramatically enlarged. I will call the effects of this enlargement the "engorgement of evil."

Norms provide standards for moral judgment. What is defined as evil in any historical period provides the most transcendental content for such judgments. What Kant called radical evil, and what I have called here, drawing on Durkheim, sacred-evil, refers to something considered absolutely essential to defining the good "in our time." Insofar as the "Holocaust" came to define inhumanity in our time, then, it served a fundamental moral function. "Post-Holocaust morality" could perform this role, however, only in a sociological way: it became a bridging metaphor that social groups of uneven power and legitimacy applied to parse ongoing events as good and evil in real historical time. What the "Holocaust" named as the most fundamental evil was the intentional, systematic, and organized employment of violence against members of a stigmatized collective group, whether defined in a primordial or an ideological way. Not only did this representation identify as radical evil the perpetrators and their actions but it polluted as evil nonactors as well. According to the standards of post-Holocaust morality, one became normatively required to make an effort to intervene against any Holocaust, regardless of personal consequences and cost. For as a crime against humanity, a "Holocaust" is taken to be a threat to the continuing existence of humanity itself. It is impossible, in this sense, to imagine a sacrifice that would be too great when humanity itself is at stake.

Despite the moral content of the Holocaust symbol, then, the primary, first-order effects of this sacred-evil do not work in a ratiocinative way. Radical evil is a philosophical term, and it suggests that evil's moral content can be defined and discussed rationally. Sacred-evil, by contrast, is a sociological term, and it suggests that defining radical evil, and applying it, involves motives and relationships, and institutions, that work more like those associated with religious institutions than with ethical doctrine. In order for a prohibited social action to be powerfully moralized, the symbol of this evil must become engorged. An engorged evil overflows with badness. Evil becomes labile and liquid; it drips and seeps, ruining everything it touches. Under the sign of the tragic narrative, the Holocaust became engorged, and its seepage polluted everything with which it came into contact.

## METONYMY

This contact pollution established the basis for what might be called metonymic guilt. Under the progressive narrative, guilt for the genocidal mass killings depended on being directly and narrowly responsible in the legal sense worked out and applied at the Nuremburg trials. It wasn't simply a matter of being "associated" with mass murders. In this legal framework, any notion of collective responsibility—the guilt of the Nazi party, the German government, much less the German nation—was ruled as unfair, as out of bounds. But as the Holocaust became engorged with evil, and as post-Holocaust morality developed, guilt could no longer be so narrowly confined. Guilt now came from simple propinquity, in semiotic terms from metonymic association.

To be guilty of sacred-evil did not mean, anymore, that one had committed a legal crime. It was about the imputation of a moral one. One cannot defend oneself against an imputed moral crime by pointing to exculpating circumstances or lack of direct involvement. The issue is one of pollution, guilt by actual association. The solution is not the rational demonstration of innocence but ritual cleansing: purification. In the face of metonymic association with evil, one must engage in performative actions, not only in ratiocinative, cognitive arguments. As the "moral conscience of Germany," the philosopher Jurgen Habermas, put it during the now famous *Historichstreich* among German historians during the 1980s, the point is to "attempt to expel shame," not to engage in "empty phrases" (quoted in Kampe 1987, 63). One must *do* justice and *be* righteousness. This performative purification is achieved by returning to the past, entering symbolically into the tragedy, and developing a new relation to the archetypal characters and crimes. Habermas wrote that it was "only after and through Auschwitz" that postwar Germany could once again attach itself "to the political culture of the West" (ibid.). Retrospection is an effective path toward purification because it provides for catharsis, although of course it doesn't guarantee it. The evidence for having achieved catharsis is confession. If there is neither the acknowledgment of guilt nor sincere apology, punishment in the legal sense may be prevented, but the symbolic and moral taint will always remain.

Once the trauma had been dramatized as a tragic event in human history, the engorgement of evil compelled contemporaries to return to the originating trauma drama and to re-judge every individual or collective entity who was, or might have been, even remotely involved. Many individual reputations became sullied in this way. The list of once admired figures who were "outed" as apologists for, or participants in, the anti-Jewish mass murders stretched from such philosophers as Martin Heidegger to such literary figures as Paul de Man and such political leaders as Kurt Waldheim. In the defenses mounted by these tarnished figures or their supporters, the suggestion was never advanced that the Holocaust does not incarnate evil—a self-restraint that implicitly reveals the trauma's engorged, sacred quality. The only possible defense was that the accused had, in fact, never been associated with the trauma in any way.

More than two decades ago, the U.S. Justice Department established an "Office of Special Investigation," the sole purpose of which was to track down and expel not only major but minor figures who had been associated in some manner with Holocaust crimes. Since then, the bitter denunciations of deportation hearings have echoed throughout virtually every Western country. In such proceedings, the emotional-cum-normative imperative is to assert the moral requirements for humanity. Media stories revolve around questions of the "normal," as in how could somebody who seems like a human being, who since World War II has been an upstanding member of the (French, American, Argentinean) community, ever have been involved in what now is universally regarded as an antihuman event? Issues of legality are often overlooked, for the issue is purification of the community through expulsion of a polluted object. Frequently those who are so polluted give up without a fight. In the spate of recent disclosures about Jewish art appropriated by Nazis and currently belonging to Western museums, directors have responded simply by asking for time to catalog the marked holdings to make them available to be retrieved.

## ANALOGY

The direct, metonymic association with Nazi crimes is the most overt effect of the way in which evil seeps from the engorged Holocaust symbol, but it is not the cultural process most often employed. The bridging metaphor works much more typically, and profoundly, through the device of analogy.

In the 1960s and 1970s, such analogical bridging powerfully contributed to a fundamental revision in moral understandings of the historical treatment of minorities inside the United States. Critics of earlier American policy, and representatives of minority groups themselves, began to suggest analogies between various minority "victims" of white American expansion and the Jewish victims of the Holocaust. This was particularly true of Native Americans, who argued that genocide had been committed against them, an idea that gained wide currency and that eventually generated massive efforts at legal repair and monetary payments. Another striking example of this domestic inversion was the dramatic reconfiguration, in the 1970s and 1980s, of the American government's internment of Japanese-American citizens during World War II.

Parallels between this action and Nazi prejudice and exclusion became widespread, and the internment camps became reconfigured as concentration camps. What followed from this symbolic transformation were not only formal governmental "apologies" to the Japanese-American people but actual monetary "reparations."

In the 1980s, the engorged, free-floating Holocaust symbol became analogically associated with the movement against nuclear power and nuclear testing and, more generally, with the ecological movements that emerged during that time. Politicians and intellectuals gained influence in their campaigns against the testing and deployment of nuclear weapons by telling stories about the "nuclear holocaust" that would be unleashed if their own democratic governments continued their nuclear policies. By invoking this Holocaust-inspired narrative, they were imagining a disaster that would have such generalized, supranational effects that the historical particularities of ideological rightness and wrongness, winners and losers, would no longer matter. In a similar manner, the activists' evocative depictions of the "nuclear winter" that would result from the nuclear holocaust gained striking support from the images of "Auschwitz," the iconic representations of which were rapidly becoming a universal medium for expressing demented violence, abject human suffering, and "meaningless" death. In the environmental movement, claims were advanced that the industrial societies were committing ecological genocide against species of plant and animal life, and that there was a danger that earth itself would be exterminated.

In the 1990s, the evil that seeped from the engorged metaphor provided the most compelling analogical framework for framing the Balkan events. While there certainly was dispute over which historical signifier of violence would provide the "correct" analogical reference—dictatorial purge, ethnic rampage, civil war, ethnic cleansing, or genocide—it was the engorged Holocaust symbol that propelled first American diplomatic and then American-European military intervention against Serbian ethnic violence. The part played by this symbolic analogy was demonstrated during the early U.S. Senate debate in 1992. Citing "atrocities" attributed to Serbian forces, Senator Joseph Lieberman told reporters that "we hear echoes of conflicts in Europe little more than fifty years ago." During this same period, the Democratic presidential nominee, Bill Clinton, asserted that "history has shown us that you can't allow the mass extermination of people and just sit by and watch it happen." The candidate promised, if elected, to "begin with air power against the Serbs to try to restore the basic conditions of humanity," employing antipathy to distance himself from the polluting passivity that had retrospectively been attributed to the Allies during the initial trauma drama itself (quoted in *Congressional Quarterly,* August 8, 1992, 2374). While President Bush initially proved more reluctant than candidate Clinton to put this metaphorical linkage into material form—with the resulting deaths of tens of thousands of innocents—it was the threat of just such military deployment that eventually forced Serbia to sign the Dayton Accords and to stop what were widely represented, in the American and European media, as its genocidal activities in Bosnia and Herzegovina.

When the Serbians threatened to enter Kosovo, the allied bombing campaign was initiated and justified by evoking the same symbolic analogies and the antipathies they implied. The military attacks were represented as responding to the widely experienced horror that the trauma drama of the Holocaust was being reenacted "before our very eyes." Speaking to a veterans' group at the height of the bombing campaign, President Clinton engaged in analogical bridging to explain why the current Balkan confrontation should not be understood, and thus tolerated, as "the inevitable result . . . of centuries-old animosities." He insisted that these murderous events were unprecedented because they were a "systematic slaughter," carried out by "people with organized political and military power," under the exclusive control of a ruthless dictator, Slobodan Milosevic. "You think the Germans would have perpetrated the Holocaust on their own without Hitler? Was there something in the history of the German race that made them do this? No. We've got to get straight about this. This is something political leaders do" (*New York Times,* May 14, 1999, A12).

The same day in Germany, Joschka Fischer, foreign minister in the coalition "Red-Green" government, appeared before a special congress of his Green Party to defend the allied air campaign. He, too, insisted that the uniqueness of Serbian evil made it possible to draw analogies with the Holocaust. Fischer's deputy foreign minister and party ally, Ludger Volmer, drew rousing applause when, in describing President Milosevic's systematic cleansing policy, he declared "my friends, there is only one word for this, and that word is *fascism.*" A leading opponent of the military intervention tried to block the bridging process by symbolic antipathy. "We are against drawing comparisons between the murderous Milosevic regime and the Holocaust," he proclaimed, because "doing so would mean an unacceptable diminishment of the horror of Nazi fascism and the genocide against European Jews" (*San Francisco Chronicle,* May 14, 1999, A1). Arguing that the Kosovars were not the Jews and

Milosevic not Hitler protected the sacred-evil of the Holocaust, but the attempted antipathy was ultimately unconvincing. About 60 percent of the Green Party delegates believed the analogies were valid and voted to support Fischer's position.

Two weeks later, when the allied bombing campaign had not yet succeeded in bringing Milosevic to heel, President Clinton asked Elie Wiesel to make a three-day tour of the Kosovar Albanians' refugee camps. A spokesperson for the U.S. embassy in Macedonia explained that "people have lost focus on why we are doing what we are doing" in the bombing campaign. The proper analogy, in other words, was not being consistently made. The solution was to create direct, metonymic association. "You need a person like Wiesel," the spokesperson continued, "to keep your moral philosophy on track." In the lead sentence of its report on the tour, the *New York Times* described Wiesel as "the Holocaust survivor and Nobel Peace Prize winner." Despite Wiesel's own assertion that "I don't believe in drawing analogies," after visiting the camps analogizing was precisely the rhetoric in which he engaged. Wiesel declared that "I've learned something from my experiences as a contemporary of so many events." What he had learned was to apply the post-Holocaust morality derived from the originating trauma drama: "When evil shows its face, you don't wait, you don't let it gain strength. You must intervene" (Rolde 1999, 1).

During that tour of a camp in Macedonia, Elie Wiesel had insisted that "the world had changed fifty years after the Holocaust" and that "Washington's response in Kosovo was far better than the ambivalence it showed during the Holocaust." When, two weeks later, the air war, and the growing threat of a ground invasion, finally succeeded in expelling the Serbian forces from Kosovo, the *New York Times* "Week in Review" reiterated the famous survivor's confidence that the Holocaust trauma had not been in vain, that the drama erected upon its ashes had fundamentally changed the world, or at least the West. The Kosovo war had demonstrated that analogies were valid and that the lessons of post-Holocaust morality could be carried out in the most utterly practical way.

> It was a signal week for the West, no doubt about it. Fifty-four years after the Holocaust revelations, America and Europe had finally said "enough," and struck a blow against a revival of genocide. Serbian ethnic cleansers were now routed; ethnic Albanians would be spared further murders and rapes. Germany was exorcising a few of its Nazi ghosts. Human rights had been elevated to a military priority and a pre-eminent Western value. (Wines 1999, 1)

Twenty-two months later, after Western support has facilitated the electoral defeat of Milosevic and the accession to the Yugoslav presidency of the reformer Vojilslav Kostunica, the former president and accused war criminal was arrested and forcedly taken to jail. While President Kostunica did not personally subscribe to the authority of the war crimes tribunal in the Hague, there was little doubt that he had authorized Milosevic's imprisonment under intensive American pressure. Though the pressure to arrest was initiated by the U.S. Congress rather than the U.S. President, George W. Bush responded to the arrest by Holocaust typification. He spoke of the "chilling images of terrified women and children herded into trains, emaciated prisoners interned behind barbed wire and mass graves unearthed by United Nations investigators," all traceable to Milosevic's "brutal dictatorship" (quoted in Perlez 2001, 6). Even those Serbian intellectuals like Aleksa Djilas who criticized the Hague tribunal as essentially a political, and thus particularistic, court, there was recognition that the events took place within a symbolic framework that would inevitably universalize them and contribute to the possibility of a new moral order on a less particularist scale. "There will be a blessing in disguise through his trial," Djilas told a reporter on the day after Milosevic's arrest.

> Some kind of new international order is being constructed, intentionally or not . . . Something will crystallize: what kinds of nationalism are justified or not, what kinds of intervention are justified or not, how much are great powers entitled to respond, and how. It will not be a sterile exercise. (Erlanger 2001, 8)

In the 1940s, the mass murder of the Jews had been viewed as a typification of the Nazi war machine, an identification that had limited its moral implications. Fifty years later, the Holocaust itself had displaced its historical context. It had itself become the master symbol of evil in relation to which new instances of grievous mass injury would be typified.

## LEGALITY

As the rhetoric of this triumphant declaration indicates, the generalization of the Holocaust trauma drama has found expression in the new vocabulary of "universal human rights." In some part, this trope has simply degendered the Enlightenment commitment to "the universal rights of man," first formulated in the French Revolution. In some other part, it blurs the issue of genocide with social demands for health and basic economic subsistence. Yet from the beginning of its systematic employment in the postwar period, the phrase has also referred specifically to a new legal standard for international behavior that would simultaneously generalize and make more precise and binding what came to be regarded as the "lessons" of the Holocaust events. Representatives of various organizations, both governmental and nongovernmental, have made sporadic but persistent efforts to formulate specific, morally binding codes, and eventually international laws, to institutionalize the moral judgments triggered by metonymic and analogic association with the engorged symbol of evil. This possibility has inspired the noted legal theorist Martha Minow to suggest an unorthodox answer to the familiar question: "Will the twentieth century be most remembered for its mass atrocities?" She notes, "A century marked by human slaughter and torture, sadly, is not a unique century in human history. Perhaps more unusual than the facts of genocides and regimes of torture marking this era is the invention of new and distinctive legal forms of response" (Minow 1998, 1).

This generalizing process began at Nuremberg in 1945, when the long-planned trial of Nazi war leaders was expanded to include the moral principle that certain heinous acts are "crimes against humanity" and must be recognized as such by everyone (Drinan 1987, 334). In its first report on those indictments, the *New York Times* insisted that, while "the authority of this tribunal to inflict punishment is directly derived from victory in war," it derived "indirectly from an intangible but nevertheless very real factor which might be called the dawn of a world conscience" (October 9, 1945, 20). This universalizing process continued the following year, when the United Nations General Assembly adopted Resolution 95, committing the international body to "the principles of international law recognized by the charter of the Nuremberg Tribunal and the judgment of the Tribunal" (quoted in Drinan 1987, 334). Two years later, the United Nations issued the *Universal Declaration of Human Rights,* whose opening preamble evoked the memory of "barbarous acts which have outraged the conscience of mankind." In 1950, the International Law Commission of the United Nations adopted a statement spelling out the principles that the *Declaration* implied.

> The core of these principles states that leaders and nations can be punished for their violations of international law and for their crimes against humanity. In addition, it is not a defense for a person to state that he or she was required to do what was done because of an order from a military or civilian superior. (quoted in Drinan 1987, 334)

In the years since, despite President Truman's recommendation that the United States draft a code of international criminal law around these principles, despite the "human rights" foreign policy of a later Democratic president, Jimmy Carter, and despite the nineteen U.N. treaties and covenants condemning genocide and exalting the new mandate for human rights, new international legal codes were never drafted (Drinan 1987, 334). Still, over this same period, an increasingly thick body of "customary law" was developed that militated *against* nonintervention in the affairs of sovereign states when they engage in systematic human rights violations.

> The long-term historical significance of the rights revolution of the last fifty years is that it has begun to erode the sanctity of state sovereignty and to justify effective political and military intervention. Would there have been American intervention in Bosnia without nearly fifty years of accumulated international opinion to the effect that there are crimes against humanity and violations of human rights which must be punished wherever they arise? Would there be a safe haven for the Kurds in northern Iraq? Would we be in Kosovo? (Ignatieff 1999, 62)

When the former Chilean dictator Augusto Pinochet was arrested in Britain and detained for more than a year in response to an extradition request by a judge in Spain, the reach of this customary law, and its possible enforcement by national police first became crystallized in the global public sphere. It was at about the same time that the first internationally sanctioned War Crimes Tribunal since Nuremberg began meeting in the Hague to prosecute those who had violated human rights from any and all sides of the decade's Balkan wars.

## THE DILEMMA OF UNIQUENESS

As the engorged symbol bridging the distance between radical evil and what at some earlier point was considered normal or normally criminal behavior, the reconstructed Holocaust trauma became enmeshed in what might be called the dilemma of uniqueness. The trauma could not function as a metaphor of archetypal tragedy unless it was regarded as radically different from any other evil act in modern times. Yet it was this very status—as a unique event—that eventually compelled it to become generalized and departicularized. For as a metaphor for radical evil, the Holocaust provided a standard of evaluation for judging the evility of other threatening acts. By providing such a standard for comparative judgment, the Holocaust became a norm, initiating a succession of metonymic, analogic, and legal evaluations that deprived it of "uniqueness" by establishing its degrees of likeness or unlikeness to other possible manifestations of evility.

In this regard, it is certainly ironic that this bridging process, so central to universalizing critical moral judgment in the post-Holocaust world, has time after time been attacked as depriving the Holocaust of its very significance. Yet these very attacks often revealed, despite themselves, the trauma drama's new centrality in ordinary thought and action. One historically oriented critic, for example, mocked the new "Holocaust consciousness" in the United States, citing the fact that the Holocaust "is invoked as reference point in discussions of everything from AIDS to abortion" (Novick 1994, 159). A literature professor complained about the fact that "the language of 'Holocaust'" is now "regularly invoked by people who want to draw public attention to human-rights abuses, social inequalities suffered by racial and ethnic minorities and women, environmental disasters, AIDS, and a whole host of other things" (Rosenfeld 1995, 35). Another scholar decried the fact that "any evil that befalls anyone anywhere becomes a Holocaust" (quoted in Rosenfeld 1995, 35).

While no doubt well-intentioned in a moral sense, such complaints miss the sociological complexities that underlie the kind of cultural-moral process we are exploring here. Evoking the Holocaust to measure the evil of a non-Holocaust event is nothing more, and nothing less, than to employ a powerful bridging metaphor to make sense of social life. The effort to qualify as the referent of this metaphor is bound to entail sharp social conflict, and in this sense social relativization, for successful metaphorical embodiment brings to a party legitimacy and resources. The premise of these relativizing social conflicts is that the Holocaust provides an absolute and nonrelative measure of evil. But the effects of the conflict are to relativize the application of this standard to any particular social event. The Holocaust is unique and not-unique at the same time. This insoluble dilemma marks the life history of the Holocaust since it became a tragic archetype and a central component of moral judgment in our time. Inga Clendinnen has recently described this dilemma in a particularly acute way, and her observations exemplify the metaphorical bridging process I have tried to describe here.

> There have been too many recent horrors, in Rwanda, in Burundi, in one-time Yugoslavia, with victims equally innocent, killers and torturers equally devoted, to ascribe uniqueness to any one set of atrocities on the grounds of their exemplary cruelty. I find the near-random terror practiced by the Argentinean military, especially their penchant for torturing children before

their parents, to be as horrible, as "unimaginable," as the horrible and unimaginable things done by Germans to their Jewish compatriots. Certainly
the scale is different—but how much does scale matter to the individual
perpetrator or the individual victim? Again, the willful obliteration of
long-enduring communities is surely a vast offence, but for three years
we watched the carpet-bombings of Cambodia, when the bombs fell on
villagers who could not have had the least understanding of the nature of
their offence. *When we think of innocence afflicted, we see those unforget-
table children of the Holocaust staring wide-eyed into the camera of their
killers, but we also see the image of the little Vietnamese girl, naked, screaming, running down a dusty road, her back aflame with American napalm.*
If we grant that "holocaust," the total consumption of offerings by fire,
is sinisterly appropriate for the murder of those millions who found their
only graves in the air, it is equally appropriate for the victims of Hiroshima,
Nagasaki and Dresden [and for] Picasso's horses and humans screaming [in
*Guernica]* under attack from untouchable murderers in the sky. (Clendinnen
1999, 14, italics added)

## FORGETTING OR REMEMBERING?
## ROUTINIZATION AND INSTITUTIONALIZATION

As the sense that the Holocaust was a unique event in human history
crystallized, and its moral implications became paradoxically generalized, the tragic trauma drama became increasingly subject to memorialization. Special research centers were funded to investigate its most
minute details and to sponsor debates about its wider applications. College courses were devoted to it, and everything from university chairs to
streets and parks were named for it. Monuments were constructed to
honor the tragedy's victims. Major urban centers in the United States, and
many outside it as well, constructed vastly expensive, and vastly ex-
pansive, museums to make permanent its moral lessons. The U.S. military
distributed instructions for conducting "Days of Remembrance," and
commemorative ceremonies were held annually in the Capitol rotunda.

Because of the dilemma of uniqueness, all of these generalizing processes were controversial; they suggested to many observers that the
Holocaust was being instrumentalized and commodified, that its morality and affect were being displaced by specialists in profit making, on the
one hand, and specialists in merely cognitive expertise, on the other. In
recent years, indeed, the idea has grown that the charisma of the original
trauma drama is being routinized in a regrettably, but predictably,
Weberian way.

The moral learning process that I have described in the preceding pages does not necessarily deny the possibility that instrumentalization develops *after* a trauma drama has been created and *after* its moral lessons have been externalized and internalized. In American history, for example, even the most sacred of the founding national traumas, the Revolution and the Civil War, have faded as objects of communal affect and collective remembering, and the dramas associated with them have become commodified as well. Still, the implications of what I have presented here suggest that such routinization, even when it takes a monetized and commodified form, does not necessarily indicate meaninglessness. Metaphorical bridging shifts symbolic significance, and audience attention, from the originating trauma to the traumas that follow in a sequence of analogical associations. But it does not, for that, inevitably erase or invert the meanings associated with the trauma that was first in the associational line. Nor does the effort to concretize the cultural meanings of the trauma in monumental forms have this effect. The American Revolution and the Civil War both remain resources for triumphant and tragic narration, in popular and high culture venues. It is only very infrequently, and very controversially, that these trauma dramas are subjected to the kind of comic framing that would invert their still sacred place in American collective identity. As I have mentioned earlier, it is not commodification, but "comedization"—a change in the cultural framing, not a change in economic status—that indicates trivialization and forgetting.

## MEMORIALS AND MUSEUMS: CRYSTALLIZING COLLECTIVE SENTIMENT

A less Weberian, more Durkheimian understanding of routinization is needed. When they are first created, sacred-good and sacred-evil are labile and liquid. Objectification can point to the sturdier embodiment of the values they have created, and even of the experiences they imply. In the present period, the intensifying momentum to memorialize the Holocaust indicates a deepening institutionalization of its moral lessons and the continued recalling of its dramatic experiences rather than a routinization and forgetting of the events. When, after years of conflict, the German parliament approved a plan for erecting a vast memorial of two thousand stone pillars to the victims of the Holocaust at the heart of Berlin, a leading politician proclaimed: "We are not building this monument solely for the Jews. We are building it for ourselves. It will help us confront a chapter in our history" (quoted in Cohen 1999, 3).

In the Holocaust museums that are sprouting up throughout the

Western world, the design is not to distance the viewer from the object in a dry, deracinated, or "purely factual" way. To the contrary, as a recent researcher into this phenomenon has remarked, "Holocaust museums favor strategies designed to arouse strong emotions and particular immersion of the visitor into the past" (Baer unpublished). The informational brochure to the Simon Wiesenthal Museum of Tolerance in Los Angeles, which houses the West Coast's largest Holocaust exhibition, promotes itself as a "high tech, hands-on experiential museum that focuses on . . . themes through interactive exhibits" (ibid.).

From its very inception in 1979, the Holocaust Museum in Washington, D.C., metonymically connected to the engorged symbolism of evil. According to the official *Report,* submitted to President Jimmy Carter by the President's Commission on the Victims of the Holocaust, the purpose of the museum was to "protect against future evil" (quoted in Linenthal 1995, 37). The goal was to create a building through which visitors would reexperience the original tragedy, to find "a means," as some central staff members had once put it, "to convey both dramatically and soberly the enormity of the human tragedy in the death camps" (quoted in Linenthal 1995, 212). Rather than instrumentalizing or commodifying, in other words, the construction was conceived as a critical means for deepening psychological identification and broadening symbolic extension. According to the ethnographer of the fifteen-year planning and construction process, the design team insisted that the museum's interior mood should be so "visceral" that museum visitors "would gain no respite from the narrative."

> The feel and rhythm of space and the setting of mood were important. [The designers] identified different qualities of space that helped to mediate the narrative: constructive space on the third floor, for example, where as visitors enter the world of the death camps, the space becomes tight and mean, with a feeling of heavy darkness. Indeed, walls were not painted, pipes were left exposed, and, except for fire exits and hidden elevators on the fourth and third floors for people who, for one reason or another, had to leave, there is no escape. (Linenthal 1995, 169)

According to the museum's head designer:

> The exhibition was intended to take visitors on a journey . . . We realized that if we followed those people under all that pressure as they moved from their normal lives into ghettos, out of ghettos onto trains, from trains to camps, within the pathways of the camps, until finally to the end . . . If visitors cold take that same journey, they would understand the story because they will have experienced the story. (quoted in Linenthal 1995, 174)

The dramatization of the tragic journey was in many respects quite literal, and this fosters identification. The visitor receives a photo passport/
identity card representing a victim of the Holocaust, and the museum's
permanent exhibition is divided into chronological sections. The fourth
floor is "The Assault: 1933–39," the third floor "The Holocaust: 1940–
44," and the second floor "Bearing Witness: 1945." At the end of each
floor, visitors are asked to insert their passports to find out what happened to their identity-card "alter egos" during that particular phase of
the Holocaust tragedy. By the time visitors have passed through the entire
exhibit, they will know whether or not the person with whom they have
been symbolically identified survived the horror or perished (Linenthal
1995, 169).

The identification process is deepened by the dramatic technique of
personalization. The key, in the words of the project director, was connecting museum visitors to "real faces of real people" (quoted in Linenthal 1995, 181).

> Faces of Holocaust victims in the exhibition are shattering in their power . . .
> Polish school teachers, moments before their execution, look at visitors in
> agony, sullen anger, and despair . . . Two brothers, dressed alike in matching
> coats and caps, fear etched on their faces, gaze at the camera, into the eyes
> of the visitors . . . The Faces . . . assault, challenge, accuse, and profoundly
> sadden visitors throughout the exhibition. (Linenthal 1995, 174)

At every point, design decisions about dramatization were made with the
narrative of tragedy firmly in mind. In deciding against displays that
might portray what some Holocaust writers have called the prisoners'
"passive resistance," designers were afraid of triggering progressive narratives of heroism and romance. As a historian associated with such decisions remarked, the fear was that such displays might contribute to an
"epic" Holocaust narrative in which resistance would gain "equal time"
with the narrative of destruction (quoted in Linenthal 1995, 192). This
dark dramatization, however, could not descend into a mere series of
grossly displayed horrors, for this would undermine the identification
upon which the very communication of the tragic lessons of the
Holocaust would depend.

> The design team faced a difficult decision regarding the presentation of hor-
> ror. Why put so much effort into constructing an exhibition that was so hor-
> rible that people would not visit? They worried about word-of-mouth evalu-
> ation after opening, and feared that the first visitors would tell family and
> friends, "Don't go, it's too horrible" . . . The museum's mission was to teach

people about the Holocaust and bring about civic transformation; yet . . .
the public had to *desire* to visit. (Linenthal 1995, 198, italics in original)

It seems clear that such memorializations aim to create structures that
dramatize the tragedy of the Holocaust and provide opportunities for
contemporaries, now so far removed from the original scene, powerfully
to reexperience it. In these efforts, personalization remains an immensely
important dramatic vehicle, and it continues to provide the opportunity
for identification so crucial to the project of universalization. In each
Holocaust Museum, the fate of the Jews functions as a metaphorical
bridge to the treatment of other ethnic, religious, and racial minorities.
The aim is manifestly not to "promote" the Holocaust as an important
event in earlier historical time, but to contribute to the possibilities of
pluralism and justice in the world of today.

## FROM LIBERATORS TO SURVIVORS: WITNESS TESTIMONIES

Routinization of charisma is certainly an inevitable fact of social life, and
memorialization a much-preferred way to understand that it can institutionalize, not only undermine, the labile collective sentiments that once
circulated in a liquid form. It is important, nonetheless, not to view the
outcome of such processes in a naturalistic, noncultural way. It is not
"meaning" that is crystallized, but particular meanings. In terms of
Holocaust memorialization and routinization, it is the objectification of
a narrative about tragedy that has been memorialized over the last
decade, not a narrative about progress.

The postwar memorials to World War II were, and are, about heroism
and liberation. They centered on American GIs and the victims they
helped. If the Holocaust had continued to be narrated within the progressive framework of the anti-Nazi war, it would no doubt have been
memorialized in much the same way. Of course, the very effect of the
progressive narrative was to make the Holocaust less visible and central,
with the result that, as long as the representation of contemporary history remained within the progressive framework, few efforts to memorialize the Holocaust were made. For that very reason, the few that were
attempted are highly revealing. In Liberty State Park, in New Jersey,
within visual sight of the proud and patriotic Statue of Liberty, there
stands a statue called *Liberation*. The metal sculpture portrays two figures. The larger, a solemn American GI, walks deliberately forward, his

eyes on the ground. He cradles a smaller figure, a concentration camp
victim, whose skeletal chest, shredded prison garb, outstretched arms,
and vacantly staring eyes exemplify his helplessness (Young 1993, 320–
32). Commissioned not only by the State of New Jersey but also by a
coalition of American Legion and other veterans' organizations, the
monument was dedicated only in 1985. During the ceremony, the state's
governor made a speech seeking to reconnect the progressive narrative
still embodied by the "last good war" to the growing centrality of the
Holocaust narrative, whose symbolic and moral importance had by then
already begun to far outstrip it. The defense and patriotic tone of the
speech indicates that, via this symbolic linkage, the state official sought
to resist the skepticism about America's place in the world, the very critical attitude that had helped frame the Holocaust in a narrative of
tragedy.

> To me, this monument is an affirmation of my American heritage. It causes
> me to feel deep pride in my American values. The monument says that
> we, as a collective people, stand for freedom. We, as Americans, are not
> oppressors, and we, as Americans, do not engage in military conflict for
> the purpose of conquest. Our role in the world is to preserve and promote
> that precious, precious thing that we consider to be a free democracy.
> Today we will remember those who gave their lives for freedom. (Young
> 1993, 321)

The *Liberation* monument, and the particularist and progressive sentiments it crystallized, could not be further removed from the memorial
processes that have crystallized in the years since. Propelled by the tragic
transformation of the Jewish mass murder, the actions and beliefs of
Americans are often implicitly analogized in these memorials with those
of the perpetrators, and the U.S. Army's liberation of the camps plays
only a minimal role, if any at all. In these more universalized settings, the
focus is on the broader, world-historical causes and moral implications of
the tragic event, on creating symbolic extension by providing opportunities for contemporaries to experience emotional identification with the
suffering of the victims.

It is in the context of this transformation that there has emerged a new
genre of Holocaust writing and memorializing, one that focuses on a new
kind of historical evidence, direct "testimony," and a new kind of historical actor, the "survivor." Defined as persons who lived through the camp
experiences, survivors provide a tactile link with the tragic event. As
their social and personal role was defined, they began to write books,
give speeches to local and national communities, and record their mem-

ories of camp experiences on tape and video. These testimonies have become sacralized repositories of the core tragic experience, with all the moral implications that this suffering has come to entail. They have been the object of two amply funded recording enterprises. One, organized by the Yale University Video Archive of the Holocaust, was already begun in 1981. The other, the Shoah Visual History Foundation, was organized by the film director Steven Spielberg in 1994, in the wake of the worldwide effects of his movie *Schindler's List.*

Despite the publicity these enterprises have aroused, and the celebrity that has accrued to the new survivor identity, what is important to see is that this new genre of memorialization has inverted the language of liberation that was so fundamental to the earlier, progressive form. It has created not heroes, but antiheroes. Indeed, those who have created and shaped this new genre are decidedly critical of what they see as the "style of revisionism that crept into Holocaust writing after the liberation of the camps." They describe this style as a "natural but misguided impulse to romanticize staying alive and to interpret painful endurance as a form of defiance or resistance" (Langer 2000, xiv). Arguing that survivor testimony reveals tragedy, not triumph, they suggest that it demands the rejection of any progressive frame.

> No one speaks of having survived through bravery or courage. These are hard assessments for us to accept. We want to believe in a universe that rewards good character and exemplary behavior. We want to believe in the power of the human spirit to overcome adversity. It is difficult to live with the thought that human nature may not be noble or heroic and that under extreme conditions we, too, might turn brutal, selfish, "too inhuman." (Greene and Kumar 2000, xxv–xxvi)

In reacting against the heroic, progressive frame, some of these commentators go so far as to insist on the inherent "meaninglessness" of the Holocaust, suggesting that the testimonies reveal "uncompensated and unredeemable suffering" (Langer 2000, xv). Yet it seems clear that the very effort to create survivor testimony is an effort to maintain the vitality of the experience by objectifying and, in effect, depersonalizing it. As such, it helps to sustain the tragic trauma drama, which allows an ever-wider audience redemption through suffering. It does so by suggesting the survival, not of a few scattered and particular victims, but of humanity as a whole.

> The power of testimony is that it requires little commentary, for witnesses are the experts and they tell their own stories in their own words. The perpe-

trators work diligently to silence their victims by taking away their names, homes, families, friends, possessions, and lives. The intent was to deny their victims any sense of humanness, to erase their individuality and rob them of all personal voice. Testimony reestablishes the individuality of the victims who survived—and in some instances of those who were killed—and demonstrates the power of their voices. (Greene and Kumar 2000, xxiv)

Those involved directly in this memorializing process see their own work in exactly the same way. Geoffrey Hartman, the director of the Yale Video Archive, speaks about a new "narrative that emerges through the alliance of witness and interviewer" (Hartman 1996, 153), a narrative based on the reconstruction of a human community.

However many times the interviewer may have heard similar accounts, they are received as though for the first time. This is possible because, while the facts are known, while historians have labored—and are still laboring—to establish every detail, each of these histories is animated by something in addition to historical knowledge: there is a quest to recover or reconstruct a recipient, an "affective community" . . . and [thus] the renewal of compassionate feelings. (ibid., 153–154)

However "grim its contents," Hartman insists, testimonies do not represent an "impersonal historical digest," but rather "that most natural and flexible of human communications, a story—a story, moreover, that, even if it describes a universe of death, is communicated by a living person who answers, recalls, thinks, cries, carries on" (ibid., 154). The president of the Survivors of the Shoah Visual History Foundation, Michael Berenbaum, suggesting that the goal of the Spielberg group is "to catalogue and to disseminate the testimonies to as many remote sites as technology and budget will permit, [a]ll in the service of education," ties the contemporary moral meaning of the historical events to the opportunity for immediate emotional identification that testimonies provide: "In classrooms throughout the world, the encounter between survivors and children [has] become electrifying, the transmission of memory, a discussion of values, a warning against prejudice, antisemitism, racism, and indifference" (Berenbaum and Peck 1998, ix).

## IS THE HOLOCAUST WESTERN?

While the rhetoric of Holocaust generalization refers to its *weltgeschichte* relevance—its *world*-historical relevance—throughout this essay I have tried to be careful in noting that this universalization has primarily been confined to the West. Universalization, as I have described it, depends on symbolically generated, emotionally vicarious participation in the trauma drama of the mass murder of the Jews. The degree to which this participation is differentially distributed throughout the West is itself a question that further research will have to pursue. This "remembering" is much more pronounced in Western Europe and North America than in Latin America. Mexicans, preoccupied with their national traumas dating back to the European Conquest, are much less attached to the "Holocaust" than are their northern neighbors—against whose very mythologies Mexicans often define themselves. The result may be that Mexican political culture is informed to a significantly lesser degree by "post-Holocaust morality." On the other hand, it is also possible that Mexicans translate certain aspects of post-Holocaust morality into local terms, that is, being willing to limit claims to national sovereignty in the face of demands by indigenous groups who legitimate themselves in terms of broadly human rights.

Such variation is that much more intense when we expand our assessment to non-Western areas. What are the degrees of attachment to, vicarious participation in, and lessons drawn from the "Holocaust" trauma in non-Western civilizations? In Hindu, Buddhist, Confusion, Islamic, African, and still Communist regions and regimes, reference to the "Holocaust," when made at all, is by literary and intellectual elites with markedly atypical levels of participation in the global discourse dominated by the United States and Western Europe. Of course, non-Western regions and nations, as I have indicated in the introduction to this book, have their own identity-defining trauma dramas. What is unclear is the degree to which the cultural work that constructs these traumas, and responds to them, reaches beyond issues of national identity and sovereignty to the universalizing, supranational ethical imperatives increasingly associated with the "lessons of post-Holocaust morality" in the West.

The authorized spokespersons for Japan, for example, have never acknowledged the empirical reality of the horrific mass murder their soldiers inflicted on native Chinese in Nanking, China, during the run up to World War II—the "Rape of Nanking." Much less have they apologized for it or made any effort to share in the suffering of the Chinese people in a manner that would point to a universalizing ethic by which members of different Asian national and ethnic groupings could be commonly judged. Instead, the atomic bombings of Hiroshima have become an originating trauma for postwar Japanese identity. While producing an extraordinary commitment to pacifism, the dramatization of this trauma, which was inflicted upon Japan by its wartime enemy, the United States, has had the effect of confirming rather than dislodging Japan in its role as narrative agent. The trauma has functioned, in other words, to steadfastly oppose any effort to widen the circle of perpetrators, which makes it that much less likely that the national history of Japan will be submitted to some kind of supranational standard of judgment.

Such submission is very difficult, of course, in any strongly national context, in the West as well as in the East. Nonetheless, the analysis presented in this article compels us to ask this question: Can countries or civilizations that do not acknowledge the Holocaust develop universalistic political moralities? Obviously, non-Western nations cannot "remember" the Holocaust, but, in the context of cultural globalization, they certainly have become gradually aware of its symbolic meaning and social significance. It might also be the case that non-Western nations could develop trauma dramas that are functional equivalents to the Holocaust. It has been the thesis of this essay that moral universalism rests upon social processes that construct and channel cultural trauma. If this is indeed the case, then globalization will have to involve a very different kind of social process than the ones that students of this supranational development have talked about so far: East and West, North and South must learn to share the experiences of one another's traumas and to take vicarious responsibility for the other's afflictions.

Geoffrey Hartman has recently likened the pervasive status of the Holocaust in contemporary society to a barely articulated but nonetheless powerful and pervasive legend.

> In Greek tragedy . . . with its moments of highly condensed dialogue, the framing legend is so well known that it does not have to be emphasized. A powerful abstraction, or simplification, takes over. In this sense, and in this sense only, the Holocaust is on the way to becoming a legendary event. (Hartman 1996, 16)

Human beings are storytelling animals. We tell stories about our triumphs. We tell stories about tragedies. We like to believe in the verisimilitude of our accounts, but it is the moral frameworks themselves that are real and constant, not the factual material that we employ them to describe. In the history of human societies, it has often been the case that narrative accounts of the same event compete with one another and that they eventually displace one another over historical time. In the case of the Nazis' mass murder of the Jews, what was once described as a prelude and incitement to moral and social progress has come to be reconstructed as a decisive demonstration that not even the most "modern" improvements in the condition of humanity can ensure advancement in anything other than a purely technical sense. It is paradoxical that a decided increase in moral and social justice may eventually be the unintended result.

# September 11, 2001, as Cultural Trauma

NEIL J. SMELSER

If the screen industry's most talented scriptwriter had been asked to draft a scenario for a quintessential cultural trauma, that script could not have surpassed the actual drama that occurred on September 11, 2001. Nineteen terrorists—none detected, none apprehended—boarded four commercial airliners at different airports, hijacked them, and turned them toward a mission of destruction and death. They crashed two aircraft into the towers of the World Trade Center in lower Manhattan, causing the collapse of both and the loss of several thousand lives. Another smashed into the Pentagon building in Washington, D.C., destroying one portion of it and killing more people. The mission of the fourth plane was aborted, probably by passenger heroism, and the airliner crashed on a rural site in western Pennsylvania, killing passengers, crew, and terrorists but inflicting no damage to any targets. Occurring early in the day, the events were seen on national television or heard about by virtually the entire American population on that day and seen worldwide as well.

Our imaginary scriptwriter could not have created two more symbolically perfect targets—the single most salient symbol of American-dominated global capitalism and the single most visible symbol of American military domination. These were simultaneously the perfect symbols—of anathema—for the Al Qaeda terrorist groups that masterminded the attacks, as well as their sympathetic audiences. The profound symbolic significance was lost on no one. Immediately elevated to near-sacred status, those symbols themselves were an integral part of what made the events so traumatic.

Also in conformity with the perfect script, the events were appreciated almost immediately by the American population as perhaps the greatest trauma in the nation's history. Comparisons were made with the most immediately available historical event—the Japanese attack on Pearl Harbor almost exactly sixty years earlier—but most people refused to compare September 11 with anything, uniquely shocking and horrible as its immediate effects were. In the months following the attacks, statesmen, historians, politicians, and people in the street uttered variations of the sentiment that the country will never be the same, and that both the reverberation of tragic events and the aggressive "war on terrorism"—as it has come to be called—would be without end. In a word, September 11 seemed designed to fit Alexander's initial definition of cultural trauma: "When members of a collectivity feel they have been subjected to a horrendous event that leaves indelible marks upon their group consciousness, marking their memories forever, and changing their future identity in fundamental and irrevocable ways" (ch. 1, this volume). It also possessed all the ingredients enunciated by Sztompka: a trauma is "sudden, comprehensive, fundamental, and unexpected" (ch. 5, this volume).

So much for an initial acknowledgment that the events of September 11 are a genuine cultural trauma. I will elaborate on the specific traumatic elements presently. The main purpose of this essay—written about four months after the date of the attack and therefore necessarily myopic in many respects—is to trace out the consequences and meanings of those events in various directions. Because this epilogue is appended to a general book on cultural trauma, two larger questions lie at the background of my efforts:

What insights about the events of September 11 can be generated in light of what we know about cultural traumata in general?

What implications do the national reactions to September 11 have for our theoretical and empirical understandings of the notion of cultural trauma?

## THE TRAUMATIC INGREDIENTS OF SEPTEMBER 11

At the outset it is worth reminding ourselves of all the ingredients of a cultural trauma—identified many times in the pages of this volume—which became evident in the few short months after the date of the attack. These can be enumerated:

An initial reaction of shock, disbelief, and emotional numbing, not unlike responses to other significant disasters except in their intensity. This intensity was a product of the suddenness, scope, and drama of the attacks—an intrusion on the American nation that, despite the earlier bombing of the World Trade Center in 1993, was experienced as an incredible violation of the nation.

Many other affective and collective-behavior reactions, also evident in major disasters: fear, anxiety, terror, and some evidence of mental disturbances in a small number of affected people—some of whom may have been predisposed because of histories of impaired mental health (Wolfenstein 1957).

Widespread collective mourning, both spontaneous and officially scheduled, with a level of emotionality perhaps unprecedented in a nation not especially known for its affective openness. The mourning focused on the innocent people killed in the World Trade Center and the Pentagon, but even more on the policemen and firemen who lost their lives while carrying out rescue activities. This mourning was accompanied by a profound idolization of the latter, especially the New York Fire Department personnel, whose status as heroes soon became as firmly fixed as other military heroes in the nation's history. This idolization provides us with our first clue that this cultural trauma was not exclusively or even predominantly negative in its impact, and indeed was a trauma of a different type from almost all others considered in this volume.

An immediate sense of the indelibility of the trauma, a feature underscored by several authors in this volume (Eyerman; Giesen; Sztompka; and Smelser). There were widespread feelings expressed that the year 2001 was a scarred or ruined year, that the world must be regarded as having a pre-September 11 and post-September 11 reality, that the events would not only never be forgotten but also that we would never be *able* to forget them. However tempered these reactions may become over time, it is difficult to believe that this social psychology will not endure in significant ways over centuries of future history.

Closely related to unforgettability, a sense of national brooding over the events, akin to a repetition-compulsion that generates something like a feeling of illegitimate neglect, if not guilt, if we do not attend to the memories and their meanings. In this case, too, however, the brooding is not entirely of a morbid sort but has many positive effects to be noted later.

A collective endowment of the events with a sacred character, not in any specifically religious sense of the term, but a general recognition that they stand as a monumental instant in the history of the nation. The people who visit "ground zero" in downtown Manhattan have come to resemble pilgrims hoping to catch a glimpse of something-they-know-not-what that will give more concreteness and vividness to things. The hundreds of letters of support, hats, T-shirts, and other paraphernalia hanging on the construction fences are like so many relics, reminiscent of symbolic objects and graffiti on and near the Berlin wall when it was standing.

The emergence of deliberate efforts to remember the events collectively, through commemorative ceremonies, public observation of anniversaries, and the erection of monuments (Giesen).

Sustained public interest in the remembering process, including, down the line, some contestation among politically interested groups over *how* the remembering should take place. A few argued for a complete rebuilding of the Word Trade Center towers—a combination of forgetting and defiant remembering. The mayoral transition from Mayor Rudolph Guilani to Mayor Michael Bloomberg was marked by a call by Guiliani for a great monument on the site (e.g., gigantic beams of light rising skyward) and a countercall by Bloomberg for a more modest monument alongside the reconstruction of business and income-generating facilities. As time goes on the contestations over the proper rememberings of the events will invariably become more complex and symbolically elaborated.

A culminating sense that American identity had been altered fundamentally—wounded, perhaps sobered and strengthened ("America is a better place to live after September 11"), but in all events, marked permanently (see Alexander; Giesen; Smelser).

So much for a recitation of the textbook features of cultural trauma as we have come to understand them. But as already hinted, this recitation tells only half the story. The country responded in a great variety of other ways that were superimposed on the trauma and put it in a historically

and culturally different context. We turn to those additional ingredients
and their explanation in the remainder of this epilogue.

## SOLIDARITY, NATIONAL MOBILIZATION, REVENGE, AND GLORY

A welling-up of community solidarity has been recorded in the wake of
many community disasters, as people pull together collectively to rescue
victims, to comfort the survivors of victims, and to rebuild what has
been lost. September 11 was no exception; the response was extraordinary. The burst of solidarity was not confined to the sites of the attacks
(New York and Washington), but was a national response. There was
an outpouring of sympathy to the cities affected ("We are all New
Yorkers"). It included a sense that every citizen was affected and thus
equal to all other citizens under adversity and threat. It included feelings
of well-being toward other fellow citizens ("New Yorkers are nicer than
they used to be"), a temporary upward blip in people's trust in other
groups (Muslim Americans excepted), and their trust in political authorities and community leaders.

Like most wartime situations, the attacks also occasioned a setting
aside of routine conflicts and sore points in the polity. Both major political parties proclaimed the need for bipartisanship in the response to
national threat, and early measures put forward to deal with the crisis
and to avenge it received strong support from both democrats and repub-
licans. This support included extreme measures, such as establishing military tribunals for trying terrorists and sustained detention of migrants
under suspicion. There was a temporary "forgetting" of such deep conflicts as the controversial "Florida" election, which left the Bush presidency under a shadow of quasi legitimacy. The general support of the cit-
izenry of President Bush ran between 80 and 90 percent for months after
the attacks. Black Americans, who had given President Bush only 10
percent of their votes less than a year earlier, responded in public opinion
polls that 75 percent were now supportive of him. What opposition there
was included apprehension against overreactions in the interest of vigilance and security at the expense of civil liberties. There was an expression among some Muslim Americans and other voices that America
would not have been attacked in this way if it had not supported Israel so
strongly over the years and inflamed Muslims and Arab nations. And
finally there were voices from a tiny few from the extreme political left
that blamed American imperialist practices for the attacks and from the

extreme fundamentalist right that America had brought this on itself by its moral laxness and corruption.

Strong patriotic sentiments were a part of the picture of community solidarity. The American flag was displayed universally—a baffling and alarming scene to some foreign witnesses who imagined the negative side of what such displays might mean in their own countries. More than one observer remarked that Halloween in October, Thanksgiving in November, and Christmas in December of 2001 resembled the Fourth of July in their symbolism and national spirit.

The deification of heroes fallen in rescue efforts was noted above. Corresponding to this was a process of demonization of the suspected perpetrators of the attack. The Bush administration identified Osama bin Laden and the Al Qaeda network early, and the accusation stuck. It was subsequently cemented even more solidly by the showing of televised film footage of bin Laden and his associates talking about and celebrating the attack. The identification of a hated out-group only served to strengthen the general feelings of collective solidarity in familiar ways.

An impulse to mobilize to avenge the attacks and to strengthen "homeland" security was another expected part of the surge of solidarity. This included public support for the immediate military mobilization and subsequent attack first to bring down the Taliban regime in Afghanistan and then to cripple the Al Qaeda organization by killing and capturing its members. Many citizens felt the urge to be supportive of the national effort and many responded in real and symbolic ways, such as children's mailing of dollars of relief for families of those killed. The scientific community, through its academies, and many philanthropic foundations and universities responded by pledging their expertise and resources to the homeland security effort and initiating programs of inquiry and research designed to understand and cope with the ongoing threat of terrorism.

In sum, the September 11 catastrophe unfolded as a fully ambivalent event—simultaneously shocking and fascinating, depressing and exhilarating, grotesque and beautiful, sullying and cleansing—and leaving the country feeling both bad and good about itself. It was a trauma to be sure, but a trauma with a rare historical twist.

## THE EMERGENCE OF PRIMORDIAL CULTURAL THEMES

In my chapter on psychological trauma and cultural trauma in this volume, I put forth the principle that it is not possible to derive the nature of a traumatic response from the "external" characteristics of the traumatizing event (see ch. 2). The character of the traumatic response must also be found in the *context*—psychological or cultural, as the case may be—into which it comes to be embedded. This principle seems to apply in every case study of cultural trauma analyzed in this volume.

One might be tempted to modify this principle in light of the September 11 bombings. Because of their scope, intensity, timing, and symbolism, it would be difficult to conceive that they would *not* be traumatic in nature. Nevertheless, the principle holds. The events occurred in the context of American society and American culture at the beginning of the twenty-first century, and the shape of the national reaction was intimately conditioned by that context. The reactions to similar events in other national contexts would have unfolded differently. It remains in this essay to reflect on the most important elements of that context.

Looking at the American reaction to September 11 in its entirety, one is compelled to notice a certain old-fashioned quality to it: a reassertion of the virtues of nation and community; unashamed flag-waving patriotism; a feeling that we, as Americans, under attack, were one again; and a feeling of pride in the American way of life, its values, its culture, and its democracy. For the moment—how long a moment cannot be estimated—the themes of the 1980s and 1990s that had preoccupied the intellectual press, spokespersons for minority groups and identity movements, and some academics seemed to recede into the background as so many cultural luxuries. These were the themes of multiculturalism, the politics of identity, primordial group conflicts, and the relativism of postmodernism—all asserting in their respective ways a *lack* of common values and national and cultural unity. The eclipse of these divisive elements was not and cannot be considered permanent; they will return in one form or another as part of the tendency to return to the "normalcy" of political partisanship and group conflict.

On reflection, this effect should not be surprising. It was the nation that was attacked, and those national values and themes, often latent except for expression on ritual occasions, that rose appropriately to salience under conditions of crisis. To say this is to make no judgments about the healthiness of the response, but rather to record it. Furthermore, it should not be put out of mind that episodes of extreme national fear and unity have always had their darker potential—for the muting of political opposition, sometimes self-imposed; for scapegoating of internal minority groups thought to be dangerous or somehow linked to the danger, and for the compromise of civil liberties in the name of vigilance and security. All that being noted, it remains now to identify those primordial cultural themes that received expression and, in part, explain the distinctiveness of the American response to the contemporary trauma.

## Cultural Guilt and Its Resolution

The thread of guilt in the American cultural tradition is found in Max Weber's famous work on Protestantism and capitalism (Weber 1958 [1904]), in which he portrayed the ascetic Protestantism found in colonial New England and in the new nation as a joyless religion, with a stern rejection of sexual pleasures, expressive arts, and self-indulgence in general. That thread has been one with which American culture has struggled continuously. Another thread, scarcely mentioned by Weber but forcefully brought into focus in the later works of Sigmund Freud (for example, Freud 1961 [1930]) has do with the phenomenon of aggression, about which, like sensual pleasures, no society has been able to assume a neutral attitude. Because the central topic of this essay is violence and war, it would repay us to look into what is perhaps a typical American resolution of conflicts surrounding aggressive behavior.

In 1942 Margaret Mead, at the height of her career, wrote a small book titled *And Keep Your Powder Dry* (Mead 1965 [1942]). As the title suggests, the book was about war, and in particular World War II, which had just begun. Mead's self-assigned aim was to bring insights about American "national character"—an acceptable social science term then if not subsequently—to the wartime situation.

One chapter in Mead's book was titled "The Chip on the Shoulder," meant to capture Americans' cultural attitudes toward aggression. The backdrop of that imagery is a general prohibition of fighting, but an enjoinment to fight if one is picked on, pushed around, or taken advantage of:

> In many parts of America small boys deliberately put chips on their shoulders and walk about daring anyone to knock the chip off. By putting a chip on his shoulder and then waiting to have it knocked off, a boy can epitomize all the contradictory orders which have been given. He isn't being aggressive, going about knocking nice little boys down . . . He doesn't hit anybody. But he has to get some practice in fighting; he must have a few fights to his credit just to be sure he can fight. And he has to reassure himself that he is tough enough to take it. So he sets the chip on his shoulder, which defines the situation: here is a boy who knows he shouldn't start a fight, who wants to prove he is game, who defines the boy who knocks off the chip as strong enough to be a legitimate opponent, for it is always right to fight back. (Mead 1965 [1942], 151)

The issue of "who started it" is a constant theme in situations of sibling rivalry and schoolyard fighting, as if determining that settles the matter of innocence and culpability. The codes of honor and feuding, traditionally identified as core ingredients in the Southern and mountain cultures (Nisbett and Cohen 1996), carry the same ingredients of legitimate revenge for a wrong committed.

Mead did not use the language of responsibility and guilt, but the sense is clear. Aggression and destructiveness are things to be guilty about, but, *if provoked, aggression is justified*, responsibility for it diminished, and guilt absolved. Mead made specific reference to Pearl Harbor in this connection: "The Pearl Harbor which woke America up was just the fact that Japan came along and pushed the chip off our shoulder and left us free to fight where our hands had been tied before." America "fights best when other people start pushing us around" (Mead 1965 [1942], 157).

Read sixty years later, Mead's observations may seem crudely oversimplified. Yet as a formula that yields one ingredient in the understanding of the American reaction to the events of September 11, her points cannot be left out of account. The nature of those attacks was such that it was very easy to read them as a savage, unprovoked attack on an innocent people and nation. Within days a ready attacker was identified in Osama bin Laden and the Al Qaeda terrorists—more or less fully believed immediately by the American public, and then given final credence by the airing of the film footage. According to the accepted meaning, the great innocent giant was under assault, and full, legitimate revenge—without guilt or responsibility—was justified. Mead mentioned that it was not the defeat at Pearl Harbor that woke Americans up but rather the aggression. The same observation can be ventured about September 11.

The evident victimization of the United States by the attacks came to serve—in an unplanned way—as a considerable asset for the United States in mobilizing the support and cooperation of other countries. Our already established allies (NATO nations, mainly) rallied quickly to the American side, partly out of a sense of identification; some had been the targets of terrorism themselves, and imagined the same happening to them. A former enemy, Russia, somewhat unexpectedly joined in, partly for geopolitical reasons and partly to gain legitimacy in fighting its own internal war (Russian leadership gains by labeling the Chechnya situation "terrorism"). Many Muslim countries were shocked as well, proclaiming the attack as not in keeping with the teachings of Allah and giving often ambivalent support in ferreting out the Afghan-based Al Qaeda terrorists.

Joining with a "guiltless" United States, however, set up an extremely delicate equilibrium. Eliminating Osama bin Laden and his organization is one thing. But seeking out terrorists elsewhere—Iraq, Iran, Pakistan, Indonesia, and Somalia, for instance—which was the United States' firm political and military resolve, is another. It immediately sets up the prospect that this country will again lose its newfound innocence, be branded as an international aggressor on account of its avidity, and experience isolation and opposition of other countries not so convinced of the necessity of aggressive unilateral pursuit. The political and international capital gained by undertaking aggression on the basis of being a blameless victim of trauma has a certain fickleness about it, and is in constant danger of evaporating.

It is instructive to look at other wars and violent moments in American history in relation to the evident responses to and meanings of September 11 as they have been reviewed—and in the context of the "importance of being innocent." As suggested, Pearl Harbor was a comparable "natural" for the United States, as evidently unprovoked and perfidious as it was when it occurred—no matter how complexly historians ultimately will assess it and its background. The "culture" created by the attack—as well as the venom felt toward Hitler's Germany—facilitated one of the great wartime mobilizations in history. Yet the "delicate equilibrium" showed up in two contexts during World War II, and left the country with two corresponding national traumas for which it now carries burdens of guilt. The first is the incarceration of Japanese Americans in camps in the context of the national (especially West Coast) hysteria about a Japanese invasion and the loyalty of Japanese Americans. The second was the dropping of atomic bombs on the cities of Hiroshima and Nagasaki in 1945. Both these lines of action were generally felt to be fully justified at the time—in the context of a fully justified war. Yet over time the country has paid a great price in compensation, regret and guilt over the former, and a strong ambivalence and division over the latter. Both sets of events stand out as national scars incurred in the context of an otherwise heroic and blameless national mission.

Other wars have not been regarded as so glorious. World War I was generally regarded as one into which the nation was dragged, but as it moved along it gained a crusade-like status of a war to make the world safe for democracy, a status much compromised by the country's failure to follow through in the establishment of a postwar peace. The Korean War was from the beginning a thoroughly ambivalent war, thought to be justified by many in the light of suspected aggression by mainland

Chinese and Soviet communism, but criticized as a reckless adventure in a remote part of the world by others, despite the involvement of the United Nations. Only in the decades following the Korean War has its heroic status in the context of the Cold War come to be established.

The Vietnamese war is a very different story. Legitimized by its advocates and perpetrators as necessary to stem the tide of international communism (the "domino theory"), that justification never really stuck, even in the partial way it did for the Korean War. That fact, accompanied by stalemates and failures in the war itself and by revelations of American cruelties to the civilian population established that war as one in which the country was illegitimately involved and therefore blameworthy. For that reason, it has been something of a national shame ever since. In the Gulf War of 1992, the United States experienced an extraordinary burst of patriotism against Iraq and Saddam Hussein, labeled as an unprovoked aggressor against Kuwait and our Middle Eastern interests and a person regarded as evil. At the time I observed that the mighty if temporary surge of patriotic enthusiasm had to be explained in part by reference to the dark shadow of Vietnam: the Gulf War was a welcome, "clean" war, provoked from outside, about which it was possible to experience both relief and fervor.

Other wars and warlike adventures have left the country with a sense of national shame as well. The partial eradication of the American Indian population during the westward expansion has come to be commonly regarded as an episode of genocide, and the territorial wars against Mexico do not stand as episodes of particular national pride, symbols such as the Alamo notwithstanding. The American Civil War is an anomaly among these comparisons. It was a different kind of moral crusade for each side—it still is to some historically muted extent today—that was divisive rather than uniting (despite its political outcome), and, in all events, has come to be set aside from all other wars because of its irrevocable entwining with perhaps the greatest of the country's internal traumas—the institution of slavery (see Eyerman).

The common threads that run through all these comparisons are those of responsibility and blame for national aggression. The purposes of the brief comparisons are to demonstrate that the "war" begun by the assaults of September 11 stands at one extreme of the continuum, and for that reason accounts for the relatively unified and total response of the country to those events.

There is one other line of reasoning worth bringing to mind as an expression of American ambivalence toward outright political aggression and domination. That has to do with the special pattern of American domination in the second half of the twentieth century that has been referred to as "the American hegemony."

The contemporary pattern of American world dominance is an *economic* dominance, realized through greater economic productivity (and its concomitant, wealth) based on a superior, science-based technology. This dominance is realized and exercised by the mechanisms of trade among nations, capital and financial investment, influence in an international monetary system, and the periodic exercise of economic sanctions. There is also an aspect of military domination, but this is *not* realized primarily through military conquest and administration of occupied territory, but through a technologically superior arsenal of weaponry, occasional wars and "peacekeeping" interventions, and, above all else, military intimidation. American hegemony also has a less tangible ideological ingredient, namely a conviction of the moral superiority of a particular (American) version of democracy, and its accompanying characteristics of personal liberty, constitutional rights of citizens, and mass political participation. This ideological dimension affects American foreign policies toward other nations, generally favoring nations like itself politically and distancing itself from or applying pressures on nations unlike itself. It should be underscored that while the military and ideological dimensions are always present, they are secondary to economic domination in the American system of hegemony.

The contrasts between this form of world domination and two contrasting cases of imperialism and colonialism emerge from these defining characteristics. Imperialism is, above all, a system based on military conquest, territorial occupation, and direct governmental/military control by the dominant imperial power. This characterization clearly applies to the classical Roman and Ottoman empires, and is also evident but not so unequivocal in other cases, such as the Austro-Hungarian empire and the Soviet empire. The political sovereignty of occupied regions is not an issue; the notion simply does not apply to militarily occupied and controlled territories. Imperial powers are also dominant economically, but the mechanisms are extraction and exploitation of resources through the mechanisms of expropriation, direct control of economic activities, and coercion (including slavery in some cases).

If we regard the eighteenth-, nineteenth-, and twentieth-century European cases as the major referents, colonialism overlaps with but is distinguishable in important ways from imperialism. Military conquest, territorial opposition, and administrative rule—sometimes military, sometimes civil—is the essence, but in practice the administrative rule varied from direct rule resembling imperialism to indirect rule involving a symbiotic relationship between colonial rulers and indigenous authorities. Nineteenth- and twentieth-century colonialism also involved more striking economic contrasts between the technological and industrial superiority of the (developed) colonial powers and the (undeveloped) colonial countries. The resultant pattern was the extraction of primary products necessary as resources for industrial production (e.g., cotton from India and Egypt) or for consumption in the colonial countries (e.g., tea, sugar, coffee, spices).

The conclusion from the observations made in this section is that the United States is a country that, while it has engaged in many wars and warlike adventures, has done so in the context of a deep ambivalence toward international aggression. As demonstrated, it is most comfortable with forms of domination other than those involving territorial conquest and occupation. It is uncomfortable if it regards itself as the political aggressor, but comfortable—and very aggressive—in striking out against aggressors against itself.

There are several other features of American national culture that dovetail with its deeply rooted posture toward international aggression and yield some additional defining characteristics. Three of these further characteristics—dualistic morality, nationalism-patriotism, and instrumentalism—come to mind.

*Dualistic Morality*

In his classic book on American society, published first in 1951, Robin Williams listed "moral orientation" as one of the core values in American culture (Williams 1970 [1951]). He pointed out that this had been consistently noticed as a major thread in American society by foreign visitors from Tocqueville on. The moral thread has also been central in literature as well as popular entertainment, notably the western film. More recently, national political crises such as Watergate and the effort to impeach President Clinton have drawn both benign and cynical amusement from people abroad, who wonder why Americans take morality in politics so seriously. The roots of this moral orientation are historically complex, but they are no doubt closely linked to the theme of cultural guilt just stressed.

It is not surprising that the national reaction to the threats of terrorism should have taken on not only a moral but also a *dualistic* cast. In his early responses President Bush took up the language of evil, personalizing the latter in Osama bin Laden, and continued to repeat the theme. His public utterances were also sprinkled with cowboy, posse, "dead-or-alive" talk, all consistent with the good vs. evil symbolism, and framing the national response as a moral crusade against a "sacred evil" (see ch. 4, this volume). Some critics ridiculed the president for the immaturity and mischief they saw in this rhetoric, but it has to be acknowledged that he was resonating with a core cultural theme, and one that had come to the fore in the minds of many citizens in their reactions to the attacks. What the moralism "adds" to the noted feelings of victimization is a certain uncritical sense of sacredness, sometimes bordering on martyrdom. When freedom from guilt and an absolute sense of right go together, they provide perhaps the most powerful motivating and legitimizing force for exacting revenge.

No attempt is made in this essay to assess the motive or cultural psychology of those who launched the attack of September 11. One point, however, must be noted. In the ideology that was evoked by the leaders and in the ranks of the Al Qaeda organization—and by those in the Muslim world who applauded the events—one telling theme emerged. These and other attacks were justified by referring to the cultural trauma that the Muslim and Arab worlds had *themselves* suffered through centuries of Western, and recently American, economic, military, and cultural penetration and through the Western establishment and support of the state of Israel. Without entering into the rights and wrongs of that history, it can be pointed out that when two antagonists confront one another, each armed with the sure conviction that it has been traumatized by the other, we have an unfailing recipe for a polarization of the pious, rigidity of ideological positions, and violence perpetrated in the name of the holy.

### Nationalism-Patriotism

This feature also found its way into Williams's list of core American values (Williams, 489–92). In a way this inclusion seems odd, because all modern nations, if not all nations, have experienced some variety of nationalism in their histories. It is the *type* of nationalism and patriotism that should be the point of reference as context for response to crisis. The American variation includes the notion that Americans and American society are "chosen" in some special sense that involves a sense of moral superiority among nations and peoples (Bellah 1975). It also includes

deep pride in American institutions, especially its version of political
democracy, its attendant freedoms and constitutional guarantees, and its
sense of equality of its citizens before the law and in their opportunities
to succeed in life. Interestingly, however, this pride in the national polity
is mingled with a distrust of the managing agent of that polity, government. It has been remarked with both truth and exaggeration that
Americans as a people love their nation but hate their state. Finally,
Americans have developed an often vague but very strong sense of what
it is to be "American" and what it is to be "un-American"—an outlook
baffling to other nations who do not conceive of their national traditions
in that way. The idea of "un-American," moreover, has sometimes
proved to be the paradoxical legitimizing rationale for savage attacks on
Americans and abrogation of the civil liberties that are otherwise
regarded as a treasured ingredient in the society's political tradition.

This special national-patriotic sense, like American moralism in general, was another ingredient that endowed the American response to the
attacks of September 11 with its special righteous character. The nation,
believed to be a model for the world in the eyes of most of its citizens,
had been wrongfully assaulted, and it was only natural that it should
respond assertively and aggressively against those who had violated it.

### Instrumentalism

As part of his list of values, Williams included "efficiency and practical-
ity" (464–69) and "science and secular rationality" (487–89). These
emphases are a complex product of the values of individualism, activism,
and mastery of the environment, as well as the evolved mythology of the
conquest of frontiers. They include a certain pragmatism, combined, as
noted by Tocqueville, with an antitheoretical and antireflective emphasis.
Instrumentalism connotes, finally, a sense that if there is a problem or
task to be done, the thing to do is to attack it directly and without ceremony. The high value placed on science and technology dovetails com-
fortably with instrumentalism, and much of the high valuation of these in
American society—despite recent periods of disillusionment and criticism—traces to their evident contributions to the advancement of the
society's standard of living, and the level of health in its population.

America's success in twentieth-century wars has also been attributed
by many to its superior science and technology. Citing the Manhattan
project and the successful invasion of Normandy as prototypical, many
claim that it was superior American science and technological know-

how that tipped the scales in World War II. A related claim was that it was American scientific and technological superiority that overcame the superiority in numbers of the communist bloc in the Cold War. And in the wake of the September 11 attacks, not only did the United States start and quickly win a technological war against Afghan-based terrorists, but scientists and others have argued that the best long-term defense against terrorism itself is the scientifically based technology of weaponry as well as detection and other preventive systems. What this complex of instrumentalism "added" to the character of the national response to September 11 was the sense that eradicating terrorists was a "job to be done" and we ought to proceed with that job efficiently and with the most advanced technological means available. To say this is not to assess the *actual* efficiency of the conduct of the Afghan and other wars, but rather to comment on both the spirit and methods that inspired the American execution of them.

My objective in making explicit these several cultural elements in the American context is to throw light on the fact that, with only apparent paradox, September 11 constituted simultaneously a serious cultural trauma, a burst of national unity, a reaffirmation of Americanism, a substantial national mobilization, a righteous mission, and a cause for celebration.

## SOME THEORETICAL OBSERVATIONS

It remains, in conclusion, to amplify the implications of the September 11 trauma by relating them to some of the theoretical themes found in this volume.

### September 11: A "Simple" Trauma?

One overall emphasis found in the work of all the authors in this volume is a constructionist one, namely that cultural traumas are a complex process of selective remembering and unremembering, social interaction and influence, symbolic contestation, and successful assertions of power. Alexander asserts that "no structure interprets itself" (ch. 4) and that "events are not inherently traumatic. Trauma is a socially mediated phenomenon" (ch. 1). My own version of this principle is that "cultural traumas are, for the most part historically made, not born" (ch. 2). Sztompka posits a "traumatic sequence" through which trauma work proceeds (ch. 5). In every empirical analysis of historical traumas contained in this volume, this axiom is confirmed.

As the preceding section indicates, September 11 was no exception. It was given shape by several special features of American culture and American character. At the same time, it must be acknowledged that the story of every cultural trauma is unique. Moreover, even though it is obviously too early to make grand historical judgments, this particular trauma has been marked by a certain simplicity; its traumatic ingredients were *fused, telescoped,* and *undifferentiated.* The following reflections give concreteness to this assessment:

With respect to the dimension of time alone, the traumatic process was truncated. The moment of the attacks to the recognition that they constituted a national trauma was a matter of short days, if not hours. They were quickly identified as attacks by specific groups of Muslim terrorists. This trauma thus contrasts with the other cases presented in this volume, namely, the emergence of black identity and the trauma of slavery within it among African Americans (Eyerman, ch. 3) and the German coming to terms with the Nazi slaughter of Jews (Giesen, ch. 4). Both processes involved decades of "trauma work" and are still evolving.

The scope of the trauma and the identity of the victims were established immediately. In answer to Sztompka's query "Trauma for whom?" there was an instant consensus that it was a trauma for everybody, for the nation. Another striking instance of lack of differentiation was that there was no significant divergence in the reactions of government and community leaders, the media, and the public in assigning meaning to the events as a national tragedy and outrage. This wave engulfed the small expressions of difference and dissent from the extreme right and extreme left. The response contrasts notably with the reactions to the Vietnam War, which were divergent and bitterly conflicting almost from the beginning.

Because of this relative unanimity, there was little evidence of social division around the trauma. All relevant groups rallied to the support of the nation, and even Muslim Americans were silently supportive or silent if critical. The country also displayed a not-altogether-expected tolerance for Muslim Americans (except for some local incidents), partly because the government and media pled for tolerance. As a result, the immediate story was one of consensus and a notable lack of contestation, which are such typical features of national traumas.

This unanimity and solidarity, however striking it has been, cannot last. At the very least the routinization of trauma, the return of "normal" conflicts based on economic interests and social division, and the reappearance of partisanship between the parties will diminish the solidarity and conflicts. Other, more dramatic countereffects may also make their appearance. It is difficult to predict these with confidence, but possibilities for darkening and souring the national mood are a) telling revelations about our lack of preparedness for the September 11 attacks; b) repeated, successful terrorist attacks, which may lead to criticism and opposition to a government "expected" to be prepared because of the last attacks; c) government overreactions, which may encourage domestic scapegoating of opposition and compromises of civil liberties; and d) killing of civilians in military operations or significant loss of American lives in combat. No trauma, however heroically it is experienced, can maintain indefinitely the delicate equilibrium between enthusiasm and excess, between solidarity and internal conflict.

## The Blend of Negative and Positive

In chapter 2 I made two general points—first that cultural traumas are characterized primarily by negative affects, and second, finding positive elements in traumatic situations might be read as defenses against or ways of coping with negative affects. In reflecting on the diagnoses made in this epilogue, I conclude that these points are only partially correct. At the very least the balance between positive and negative must be regarded as more complex, according to the nature of the trauma at hand. Consider the following.

The outpouring of collective solidarity, goodwill toward others, and the celebration of America after September 11 cannot be written off as so many strategies of coping with shock, fear, and disgust. The positive reactions were an integral part of the reaction, and explicable by reference to the primordial elements in American culture considered above.

Some traumas begin as joyous celebrations and accumulate negative elements in the course of trauma work and routinization. Two notable instances are the end of communism in Eastern European countries in 1989–90, as analyzed by Sztompka (see ch. 5), and the reunification of West and East Germany.

Some traumas are so negative on their face that it is difficult to sustain consistent positive interpretations about them. The obvious example is the Nazi Holocaust, which, despite various attempts at "progressive narratives" (Alexander, ch. 4) and other positive modes of coping, has continued to reassert its essence as a negative blight on Germany and on humanity.

In a word, we need to adopt a more complicated view of the contra-

puntal relations between the positive and negative and between the
heroic and the tragic in the theory of collective trauma.

## The Centrality of Responsibility and Guilt in Trauma

In reviewing the stories of the various cultural traumas analyzed in this
volume and in assessing the events following September 11, it is evident
that the answers to the questions of who are the victims and who is
responsible for the victimizing are always central. No traumatic story can
be told without tracing these themes of suffering and blame. In most
cases the stories reflect vicissitudes of these ingredients and a great deal of
contestation among groups about who is designated and what that des-
ignation means. In the case of September 11, the fact that both the victim
and the guilty were so immediately and unequivocally established in the
public mind goes far in contributing to my diagnosis of the event as a
"simple" trauma. We cannot expect such simplicity to endure indefinitely, however, as new actors, groups, events, and situations emerge in
the nation's longer-term response to international terrorism. In all events,
the critical significance of suffering and guilt in all cultural traumas guarantees that these kinds of historical events invariably reach into the
moral depths of the human condition.[1]

NOTES

    1. Many of the ideas and reflections in this essay were generated in the course
of my work, begun weeks after September 11, with the collective activities on terrorism and counterterrorism undertaken by the National Academy of Sciences,
the Institute of Medicine, and the National Academy of Engineering. In particular, I was a member of the panel created by these bodies on Science and Technology in Countering Terrorism, and chair of its subpanel on Behavioral, Social, and
Institutional Aspects of Terrorism. I thank colleagues in those activities who
helped my thinking, but record here that I am speaking only for myself in this
essay, and not representing the National Academies in any way.

# Bibliography

Abzug, Robert H. 1985. *Inside the Vicious Heart: Americans and the Liberation of Nazi Concentration Camps.* New York: Oxford University Press.

Adorno, Theodore. W. 1992. *Negative Dialektik.* Frankfurt am Main: Suhrkamp.

Albrow, Martin. 1996. *The Global Age.* Cambridge: Polity Press.

Alexander, Jeffrey C. 1992. "Citizen and Enemy as Symbolic Classification: On the Polarizing Discourse of Civil Society." In *Cultivating Differences: Symbolic Boundaries and the Making of Inequality,* ed. M. Lamont and M. Fournier. Chicago: The University of Chicago Press.

———. 1987. *Twenty Lectures: Sociological Theory since World War II.* New York: Columbia University Press.

Alexander, Jeffrey C., and P. Smith. 1993. "The Discourse of American Civil Society: A New Proposal for Cultural Studies." *Theory and Society* 22: 151–207.

Alexander, Jeffrey C., Bernhard Giesen, Richard Munch, and Neil Smelser. 1987. *The Micro-Macro Link.* Berkeley: University of California Press.

Alexander, Jeffrey C., and Piotr Sztompka, eds. 1990. *Rethinking Progress.* Boston: Unwin and Hyman.

Allen, William, Charles Ware, and Lucy Garrison. 1867. *Slave Songs of the United States.* Bedford, Mass.: Applewood Books.

American Psychiatric Association. 1994. *Diagnostic and Statistical Manual of Mental Disorders.* 4th ed. Washington, D.C.: American Psychiatric Association.

Anderson, Benedict. 1991. *Imagined Communities.* London: Verso.

Angelou, Maya. 1976. *Singin' and Swingin' and Gettin' Merry Like Christmas.* New York: Bantam.

———. 1974. *Gather Together in My Name.* New York: Random House.

Archer, Margaret. 1986. *Culture and Agency*. Cambridge: Cambridge University Press.

Arendt, Hannah. 1950. "The Aftermath of Nazi Rule: Report from Germany." *Commentary* 10: 342–53.

Aristotle. 1987. *Poetics I*. Translated by Richard Janko. Indianapolis: Hacket.

Assmann, Jan. 1999. "Monotheismus, Gedächtnis und Trauma: Sigmund Freuds archäologische Lektüre der Bibel." *Internationale Zeitschrift für Philosophie* 2: 227–44.

Austin, John L. 1962. *How to Do Things with Words*. Oxford: Clarendon Press.

Baer, A. "Visual Testimonies and High-Tech Museums: The Changing Embodiment of Holocaust History and Memorialization." Unpublished manuscript, Departmento de Sociologia IV, Universidad Complutense de Madrid.

Banfield, Edward C. 1967 (1958). *The Moral Basis of a Backward Society*. New York: Free Press.

Barlow, William. 1999. *Voice Over: The Making of Black Radio*. Philadelphia: Temple University Press.

Barthes, Roland. 1996. *Mythen des Alltags*. Frankfurt am Main: Suhrkamp.

Barton, Craig Evan, ed. 2001. *Site of Memory: Perspectives on Architecture and Race*. New York: Princeton Architectural Press.

Bauman, Zygmunt. 1989. *Modernity and the Holocaust*. Cambridge: Polity Press.

———. 1989. *Legislators and Interpreters: On Modernity, Post-Modernity, and Intellectuals*. Cambridge: Polity Press.

Bellah, Robert. 1975. *The Broken Covenant: American Civil Religion in a Time of Trial*. New York: The Seabury Press.

Bellah, Robert, et al. 1985. *Habits of the Heart: Individualism and Commitment in American Life*. Berkeley: University of California Press.

Benn, D. W. 1995. "Perceptions of the Holocaust: Then and Now." *World Today* 51: 102.

Berenbaum, Michale, and Abraham J. Peck, eds. 1998. *The Holocaust and History: The Known, the Unkown, the Disputed, and the Reexamined*. Bloomington: Indiana University Press.

Berlin, Ira., et al., eds. 1998. *Remembering Slavery*. New York: The New Press.

Blight, David. 1997. "Reunion and Race." In *Union and Emancipation*, ed. D. Blight and B. Simpson. Kent: Kent State University Press.

Boime, Albert. 1990. *The Art of Exclusion*. Washington: Smithsonian Institution Press.

Böll, Heinrich. 1972. *Wo warst Du, Adam?* München: DTV.

Boltanski, Luc. 1999. *Distant Suffering*. New York: Cambridge University Press.

Bradford, Sarah H. 1901 (1886). *Harriet, the Moses of her People*. New York: J. J. Little.

Braun, R. 1994. "The Holocaust and Problems of Historical Representation." *History and Theory* 33 (2): 172–97.

Brown, J. F. 1997. "Goodbye (and Good Riddance?) to De-Communization." *Transition* 2: 28–34.

Browning, Christopher. 1992. *Ordinary Men: Reserve Police Battalion 101 and the Final Solution in Poland*. New York: Harper Collins.

Buck, Pearl S. 1947. "Do You Want Your Children to Be Tolerant?" *Better Homes and Gardens* 25 (February): 33ff.

Carter, Hodding. 1947. "How to Stop the Hate Mongers in Your Home Town." *Better Homes and Gardens* 26 (November): 45ff.

Caruth, Cathy. 1996. *Unclaimed Experience: Trauma, Narrative, and History.* Baltimore: Johns Hopkins University Press.

Caruth, Cathy, ed. 1995. *Trauma Exploration in Memory.* Baltimore: Johns Hopkins University Press.

*CBOS Bulletin,* a periodical of the Center for the Study of Social Opinions, Warsaw.

*Central and Eastern Eurobarometer,* a periodical of the Commission of European Communities, Brussels.

Chang, Iris. 1997. *The Rape of Nanking: The Forgotten Holocaust of World War II.* New York: Penguin.

Charcot, Jean M. 1887. *Leçons sur les maladies du système nerveux faites à la Salpêtrière.* Vol. 3. Paris: M Progrès Médical en A. Delahaye and E. Lecrosnie.

Christian, Charles. 1995. *Black Saga.* Boston: Houghton Mifflin.

Clendinnen, Inga. 1999. *Reading the Holocaust.* Cambridge: Cambridge University Press.

Cohen, R. 1999. "Berlin Holocaust Memorial Approved." *New York Times,* June 26, A3.

Connerton, Paul. 1989. *How Societies Remember.* Cambridge: Cambridge University Press.

Courtois, Stéphane. 1997. *Le livre noir du communisme: Crimes, terreur et répression.* Paris: Laffont.

Cunningham, Michael. 1999. "Saying Sorry: The Politics of Apology." *The Political Quarterly* 70 (3) 285–93.

Darden, Norma J., and Carole Darden. 1994. *Spoonbread and Strawberry Wine.* New York: Doubleday.

Dawidowicz, Lucy. 1982. *On Equal Terms: Jews in America, 1881–1981.* New York: Holt, Rinehart, and Winston.

Dean, Eric T. 1992. *Shook over Hell: Post-Traumatic Stress, Vietnam, and the Civil War.* Cambridge, Mass.: Harvard University Press.

de Grazia, Sebastian. 1948. *The Political Community.* New York: Columbia University Press.

Deutscher, Isaac. 1968. "The Jewish Tragedy and the Historian." In *The Non-Jewish Jew and Other Essays,* ed. Tamara Deutscher. London: Oxford University Press.

de Vries. 1996. "Trauma in Cultural Perspective." Pp. 398–413 in *Traumatic Stress: The Effects of Overwhelming Experience on Mind, Body, and Society,* ed. Bessell A. van der Kolk, Alexander C. McFarlane, and Lars Weisaeth. New York: The Guildord Press.

Diamond, Sander A. 1969. "The Kristallnacht and the Reaction in America." *Yivo Annual of Jewish Social Science* 14: 196–208.

Dilthey, Wilhelm. 1976. "The Construction of the Historical World in the Human Sciences." Pp. 168–245 in *Dilthey: Selected Writings.* Cambridge: Cambridge University Press.

Diner, Dan. 2000. *Beyond the Conceivable: Studies on Germany, Nazism, and the Holocaust.* Berkeley: University of California Press.

——. 1988. *Zivilisationsbruch. Denken nach Auschwitz.* Frankfurt am Main: Fischer Taschenbuch-Verlagubiel.

Diner, Dan, ed. 1987. *Ist der Nationalsozialismus Geschichte? Zu Historisierung und Historikerstreit.* Frankfurt am Main: Fischer Taschenbuch-Verlagubiel.

Dinnerstein, L. 1981–82. "Anti-Semitism Exposed and Attacked, 1945–1950." *American Jewish History* 71 (September-June): 134–49.

Dodson, D. W. 1946. "College Quotas and American Democracy." *The American Scholar* 15 (3): 267–76.

Doneson, Judith E. 1987. "The American History of Anne Frank's Diary." *Holocaust and Genocide Studies* 2 (1): 149–60.

Drake, St. Clair, and Horace Cayton. 1945. *Black Metropolis.* New York: Harper and Row.

Drinan, R. F. 1987. "Review of Ann Tusa and John Tusa, The Nuremberg Trial." *Holocaust and Genocide Studies* 3 (2): 333–34.

Dubiel, Helmut. 1999. *Niemand ist frei von der Geschichte: Die nationalsozialistische Herrschaft in den Debatten des Deutschen Bundestages.* München: Hanser.

Du Bois, W. E. B. 1999. "The Conservation of Races," a speech before the American Negro Academy delivered in 1897. In *The Oxford Du Bois Reader,* ed. Eric Sundquist. New York: Oxford.

——. 1997. *John Brown.* Armonk, N.Y.: M. E. Sharpe.

——. 1903. *The Souls of Black Folk.* Chicago: A. C. McClurg.

Durkheim, Emile. 1982. *The Rules of Sociological Method.* New York: Free Press.

——. 1951. *Suicide.* New York: Free Press.

Early, Emmett. 1993. *The Raven's Return: The Influence of Psychological Trauma on Individuals and Culture.* Wilmette, Ill.: Chiron Publications.

Ebihara, May, and J. Ledgerwood. 2002. "Aftermaths of Genocide: Cambodian Villagers." In *Annihilating Difference: The Anthropology of Genocide,* ed. Alexander Hinton. Berkeley: University of California Press.

Eisenstadt, Shmuel N. 1998. *Die Antinomien der Moderne: Die jakobinischen Grundzüge der Moderne und des Fundamentalismus; Heterodoxien, Utopismus und Jakobinismus in der Konstitution fundamentalistischen Bewegungen.* Frankfurt am Main: Suhrkamp.

——. 1982. "The Axial Age: The Emergence of Transcendental Visions and the Rise of Clerics." *Archives Europeennes de Sociologie* 23 (2): 294–314.

Ekiert, G., and J. Kubik. 1997. "Collective Protest and Democratic Consolidation in Poland, 1989–93." In *Pew Papers on Central Eastern European Reforms and Regionalism,* No.3, ed. A. Seleny and E. Suleiman. Princeton: Center of International Studies, Princeton University.

Elder, Glenn H., Jr. 1974. *Children of the Great Depression.* Chicago: University of Chicago Press.

Emerson, Ralph Waldo. 1922 [1851]. *Representative Men.* Girard, Kans.: Haldeman-Julius Co.

Engler, Wolfgang. 1999. *Die Ostdeutschen. Kunde von einem verlorenenland.* Berlin: Aufbau Verlag.

Epstein, Arnold L. 1992. *In the Midst of Life: Affect and Ideation in the World of the Tolai.* Berkeley: University of California Press.

Erikson, Kai. 1994. "Notes on Trauma and Community." Pp. 183–99 in *Trauma: Explorations in Memory,* ed. Cathy Caruth. Baltimore: Johns Hopkins University Press.

———. 1976. *Everything in Its Path.* New York: Simon and Schuster.

Erlanger, Steven. 2001. "After the Arrest: Wider Debate about the Role of Milosevic, and of Serbia." *New York Times,* April 2, A8.

Essien-Udom, E. U. 1962. *Black Nationalism.* Chicago: University of Chicago Press.

Eyerman, Ron, and Andrew Jamison. 1994. *Social Movements: A Cognitive Approach.* Cambridge: Polity Press.

Feingold, Henry L. 1974. *Zion in America: The Jewish Experience from Colonial Times to the Present.* Boston: Twayne.

Foster, Gaines. 1987. *Ghosts of the Confederacy.* New York: Oxford University Press.

French, Howard W. 2000."Japanese Veteran Testifies in War Atrocity Lawsuit." New York Times, December 21, A1–6.

Freud, Sigmund. 1964 (1939 [1934–38]). "Moses and Monotheism." Pp. 7–237 in *The Standard Edition of the Complete Psychological Works of Sigmund Freud,* vol. 23, ed. J. Strachey. London: Hogarth Press.

———. 1963 (1916–17). "Introductory Lectures on Psycho-analysis." Pp. 243–463 in *The Standard Edition of the Complete Psychological Works of Sigmund Freud,* vol. 16, ed. J. Strachey. London: Hogarth Press.

———. 1962a (1896). "Heredity and the Aetiolgy of the Neuroses." Pp. 143–56 in *The Standard Edition of the Complete Psychological Works of Sigmund Freud,* vol. 3, ed. J. Strachey. London: Hogarth Press.

———. 1962b (1896). "Further Remarks on the Neuro-psychoses of Defense." Pp. 162–85 in *The Standard Edition of the Complete Psychological Works of Sigmund Freud,* vol. 3, ed. J. Strachey. London: Hogarth Press.

———. 1961 (1930). "Civilization and Its Discontents." Pp. 59–148 in *The Standard Edition of the Complete Psychological Works of Sigmund Freud,* vol. 21, ed. J. Strachey. London: Hogarth Press.

———. 1959 (1926 [1925]). "Inhibitions, Symptoms, and Anxiety." Pp. 77–172 in *The Standard Edition of the Complete Psychological Works of Sigmund Freud,* vol. 10, ed. J. Strachey. London: Hogarth Press.

———. 1959 (1908). "Hysterical Phantasies and Their Relation to Bisexuality." Pp. 159–66 in *The Standard Edition of the Complete Psychological Works of Sigmund Freud,* vol. 9, ed. J. Strachey. London: Hogarth Press.

———. 1957 (1917 [1915]). "Mourning and Melancholia." Pp. 243–58 in *The Standard Edition of the Complete Psychological Works of Sigmund Freud,* vol. 14, ed. J. Strachey. London: Hogarth Press.

———. 1956 (1895). "Project for a Scientific Psychology." Pp. 195–287 in *The Standard Edition of the Complete Psychological Works of Sigmund Freud,* vol. 1, ed. J. Strachey. London: Hogarth Press.

———. 1956 (1893). Sketches for the "Preliminary Communication" of 1893. Pp. 146–54 in *The Standard Edition of the Complete Psychological Works of Sigmund Freud,* vol. 1, ed. J. Strachey. London: Hogarth Press.

————. 1956 (1887–88). "Extracts from Freud's Footnotes to His Translation of Charcot's Tuesday Lectures." Pp. 137–43 in *The Standard Edition of the Complete Psychological Works of Sigmund Freud*, vol. 1, ed. J. Strachey. London: Hogarth Press.

————. 1955 (1923 [1922]). "Two Encyclopedia Articles." Pp. 235–59 in *The Standard Edition of the Complete Psychological Works of Sigmund Freud*, vol. 18, ed. J. Strachey. London: Hogarth Press.

————. 1953 (1900). "The Interpretation of Dreams" (second part). Pp. 339–621 in *The Standard Edition of the Complete Psychological Works of Sigmund Freud*, vol. 5, ed. J.Strachey. London: Hogarth Press.

Freud, Sigmund, and Josef Breuer. 1955 (1893–95). "Studies in Hysteria." Pp. 1–335 in *The Standard Edition of the Complete Psychological Works of Sigmund Freud*, vol. 2, ed. J. Strachey. London: Hogarth Press.

Friedlander, Saul. 1992. "Trauma, Transference, and 'Working through' in Writing the History of the Shoah." *History and Memory* 4 (1): 39–59.

————. 1979. When Memory Comes. New York: Farrar, Strauss, and Giroux.

Frieske, Kazimierz. 1996. "Porzadek spoleczny i jego zagrozenia." Pp. 116–34 in *Podstawy zycia spolecznego w Polsce* (The Foundations of Social Life in Poland), ed. M. Marody and E. Gucwa-Leny.Warszawa: Instytut Studiów Spoecznych.

Frye, Northrop. 1971. *The Anatomy of Criticism*. Princeton: Princeton University Press.

Furet, François. 1989. *1789: Jenseits des Mythos*. Hamburg: Junius.

————. 1981. *Interpreting the French Revolution*. Cambridge: Cambridge University Press.

Fussell, Paul. l975. *The Great War and Modern Memory*. New York: Oxford Universty Press.

Garber, Zev, and B. Zuckerman. 1989. "Why Do We Call the Holocaust 'The Holocaust'? An Inquiry into the Psychology of Labels." *Modern Judaism* 9 (2): 197–211.

Garvey, Marcus. 1994. "Africa for Africans." In *The Portable Harlem Renaissance Reader*, ed. David Lewis.

*Gazeta Wyborcza*, a popular Polish daily, edited by A.Michnik.

Geyer, M. 1996. "The Politics of Memory in Contemporary Germany." Pp. 169–200 in *Radical Evil*, ed. Joan Copjec. London: Verso.

Gibson, James W. 1994. *Warrior Dreams: Violence and Manhood in Post-Vietnam America*. New York: Hill and Wang.

Giesen, Bernhard. 2004. *Triumph and Trauma*. Boulder: Paradigm Press.

————. 1999. *Kollektive Identität. Die Intellektuellen und die Nation II*. Frankfurt am Main: Suhrkamp.

————. 1998. *Intellectuals and the Nation*. Cambridge: Cambridge University Press.

Gill, M. 1961. "Topography and Systems in Psychoanalytic Theory." *Psychological Issues* 3 (2): Monograph #10.

Giza-Poleszczuk, A. 1991. "Stosunki miedzyludzkie i zycie zbiorowe" (Interpersonal Relations and Collective Life). In *Co nam zostalo z tych lat* (What Has Remained of Those Years), ed. M. Marody. London: Aneks.

Glazer, Nathan. 1996. "Monuments in an Age without Heroes." *The Public Interest* (Spring): 22–39.

Gleason, P. 1981. "Americans All: World War II and the Shaping of American Identity." *The Review of Politics* 43 (4): 483–518.

Goldhagen, Daniel J. 1996. *Hitler's Willing Executioners: Ordinary Germans and the Holocaust.* New York: Knopf.

Greene, J. M., and S. Kumar. 2000. "Editors' Introduction." Pp. xxi–xxix in *Witness: Voices from the Holocaust,* ed. J. M. Greene and S. Kumar. New York: Free Press.

Greenfeld, Liah. 1992. *Nationalism: Five Roads to Modernity.* Cambridge, Mass.: Harvard University Press.

Grinker, Roy R., and J. P. Spiegel. 1945. *Men Under Stress.* Philadelphia: Blakiston.

Gross, Jan T. 2001. *Neighbors: The Destruction of the Jewish Community in Jedwabne, Poland.* Princeton, N.J.: Princeton University Press.

Gucwa-Lesny. E. 1996. "Zmiany poziomu zycia i ich ocena." Pp. 100–115 in *Podstawy zycia spolecznego w Polsce* (The Foundations of Social Life in Poland), ed. M. Marody and E. Gucwa-Leny. Warszawa: Instytut Studiów Spoecznych.

Habermas, Jürgen. 1987a. "Vom öffentlichen Gebrauch der Historie." Pp. 243–55 in *Historikerstreit: Die Dokumentation der Kontroverse um die Einzigartigkeit der nationalsozialistischen Judenvernichtung.* München: Piper.

———. 1987b. "Eine Art Schadensabwicklung." Pp. 62–76 in *Historikerstreit: Die Dokumentation der Kontroverse um die Einzigartigkeit der nationalsozialistischen Judenvernichtung.* München: Piper.

———. 1987c. "Geschichtsbewußtsein und posttraditionale Identität: Die Westorientierung der Bundesrepublik." Pp. 159–79 in *Eine Art Schadensabwicklung: Kleine politische Schriften VI.* Frankfurt am Main: Suhrkamp.

———. 1985. "Die Krise des Wohlfahrtstaates und die Erschöpfunutopischer Energien." Pp. 141–63 in *Die neue Unübersichtlichkeit.* Frankfurt am Main: Suhrkamp.

———. 1984. *The Theory of Communicative Action.* Boston: Beacon Press.

Halbwachs, Maurice. 1992. *On Collective Memory.* Chicago: University of Chicago Press.

Hale, Grace. 1998. *Making Whiteness.* New York: Vintage.

Haley, Alex. 1965. *The Autobiography of Malcolm X.* New York: Grove.

Hammacher, W. 1996. "Working through Working." *Modernism* 3 (1): 23–55.

Hammon, Briton. 1994 (1760). *A Narrative of the Uncommon Sufferings, and Surprizing Deliverance of Briton Hammon.* Fairfield, Wash.: Ye Galleon Press.

Hart, W. R. 1947. "Anti-Semitism in N.Y. Medical Schools." *The American Mercury* 65 (July): 53–63.

Hartman, Geoffrey H. 1996. *The Longest Shadow: In the Aftermath of the Holocaust.* Bloomington: Indiana University Press.

Hayes, P., ed. 1999. *Memory, Memorialization, and Denial.* Vol. 3 of *Lessons and Legacies.* Evanston: Northwestern University Press.

Heer, Hanes, and K. Naumann, eds. 1995. *Vernichtungskrieg: Verbrechen der Wehrmacht 1941–1944.* Hamburg: Hamburg Institüt für Soziolforschüng.

Hegel, Georg W. F. 1927. "Phänomenologie des Geistes." In *Sämtliche Werke, Bd2.* Stuttgart: Frommanns.

Herf, Jeffrey. 1997. *Divided Memory: The Nazi Past in the Two Germanys.* Cambridge, Mass.: Harvard University Press.

Higham, John. 1984. *Send These to Me.* Baltimore: Johns Hopkins University Press.

Hillgruber, Andrew. 1987. "Für die Forschung gibt es kein Frageverbot." Pp. 232–42 in *Historikerstreit: Die Dokumentation der Kontroverse um die Einzigartigkeit der nationalsozialistischen Judenvernichtung.* München: Piper.

Hinton, Alexander. Forthcoming. "The Dark Side of Modernity." In *Annihilating Difference: The Anthropology of Genocide,* ed. Alexander Hinton. Berkeley: University of California Press.

Holton, J. 1990. "Crisis and Progress." In *Rethinking Progress,* ed. J. Alexander and P. Sztompka. Boston: Unwin and Hyman.

Horowitz, Mardi J. 1976. *Stress Response Syndromes.* New York: Jason Arons.

Hyde, Margaret O. 1977. *Brainwashing and Other Forms of Mind Control.* New York: McGraw-Hill.

Igartua, Juan José, and Darío Paez. 1997. "Art and Remembering Collective Events." In *Collective Memory of Political Events,* ed. James Pennebaker, Darío Paez, and Bernard Rimé. Mahwah, N.J.: Lawrence Erlbaum Associates.

Ignatieff, Michael. 1999. "Human Rights: The Midlife Crisis." *New York Review of Books,* May 20: 58–62.

Institut für Demoskopie Allensbach. 1950. *Warum kam das Dritte Reich?* Rückblick: Allensbach.

Jacobs, Harriet A. 1988 (1861). *Incidents in the Life of a Slave Girl.* New York: Oxford University Press.

Jelin, Elizabeth, and Susana Kaufman. "Layers of Memories: Twenty Years After in Argentina." In *Memory and Narrativity.* Unpublished.

Johnson Charles S. and the Chicago Commission on Race Relations. 1919. *The Negro in Chicago: A Study of Race Relations and a Race Riot.* Chicago: University of Chicago Press.

Kahn, Charlotte. 1998. "Introduction." Pp. 1–9 in *Children Surviving Persecution: An International Study of Trauma and Healing,* ed. Judith S. Kestenberg and Charlotte Kahn. Westport, Conn.: Praeger.

Kampe, N. 1987. "Normalizing the Holocaust? The Recent Historians' Debate in the Federal Republic of Germany." *Holocaust and Genocide Studies* 2 (1): 61–80.

Kant, Immanuel. 1960. *Religion within the Limits of Reason Alone.* Translated by Theodore M. Greene and Hoyt H. Hudson. New York: Harper.

King, Martin Luther, Jr. 2003. *A Testament of Hope: The Essential Writings and Speeches of Martin Luther King Jr.* San Francisco: Harper.

Klein, Melanie. 1986 (1940). "Mourning and Its Relation to Manic-Depressive States." In *The Selected Melanie Klein.* Harmondsworth: Penguin Books.

Kleinman, Arthur, Veena Das, and Margaret Lock, eds. 1997. *Social Suffering.* Berkeley: University of California Press.

Klotman, Phyllis, and Janet Cutler. 1999. *Struggles for Representation.* Bloomington: Indiana University Press.

Koralewicz, J., and M. Ziolkowski. 1990. *Mentalnosc Polakow* (The Mentality of the Poles), Poznan: Nakom.

Kornai, Janos. 1992. *The Socialist System*. Princeton: Princeton University Press.

Krystal, H. 1988. *Integration and Self Healing: Affect, Trauma, and Alexithymia*. Hillsdale, N.J.: Analytic Press.

———. 1978. "Trauma and Affects." *Psychoanalytic Study of the Child* 33 (8) 91–116.

Kuper, Leo. 1981. *Genocide: Its Political Use in the Twentieth Century*. New Haven: Yale University Press.

LaCapra, Dominick. 1994. *Representing the Holocaust: History, Theory, Trauma*. Ithaca: Cornell University Press.

Langbein, Herman, ed. 1965. *Der Auschwitz-Prozess: Eine Dokumentation*. Frankfurt am Main: Europäische Verlagsanstalt.

Langer, Lawrence L. 2000. "Forward." Pp. xi–xx in *Witness: Voices from the Holocaust*, ed. J. M. Greene and S. Kumar. New York: Free Press.

Laqueur, Walter. 1980. *The Terrible Secret: Suppression of the Truth about Hitler's "Final Solution."* Boston: Little, Brown.

Lara, Maria Pia. 1999. *Feminist Narratives in the Public Sphere*. Berkeley: University of California Press.

Leggewie, Claus. 1998. *Vom Schneider zu Schwerte: Das ungewöhnliche Leben eines Mannes, der aus der Geschichte lernen wollte*. München: Hanser.

Lepsius, M. Rainer. 1993. "Nationalstaat oder Nationalitätenstaat als Modell für die Weiterentwicklung der Europäischen Gemeinschaft." Pp. 265–85 in *Demokratie in Deutschland*, ed. M. Rainer Lepsius. Göttingen: Vandenhoeck und Ruprecht. New York: Simon and Schuster.

———. 1989. "Das Erbe des Nationalsozialismus und die politische Kultur der Nachfolgestaaten des 'Großdeutschen Reiches.' Pp. 247–64 in *Kultur und Gesellschaft. Verhandlungen des 24, Deutschen Soziologentages, des 11. Österreichischen Soziologentags und des 8*, ed. Max Haller et al. Kongresses der Schweizerischen Kongresses für Soziologie in Zürich 1988. Frankfurt am Main: Campus-Verlag.

Lifton, Robert. 1973. *Home from the War: Vietnam Veterans, Neither Victims nor Executioners*. New York: Simon and Schuster.

Lindemann, Erich. 1944. "Symptomatology and Management of Acute Grief." *American Journal of Psychiatry* 101: 141–48.

Linenthal, Edward T. 1995. *Preserving Memory: The Struggle to Create the Holocaust Museum*. New York: Viking.

———. 1989. *Symbolic Defense: The Cultural Significance of the Strategic Defense Initiative*, with a foreword by Paul Boyer. Urbana: University of Illinois Press.

Lipstadt, D. E. 1996. "America and the Memory of the Holocaust, 1950–1965." *Modern Judaism* 16: 195–214.

Lischer, Richard. 1995. *The Preacher King: Martin Luther King, Jr. and the Word that Moved America*. New York: Oxford University Press.

Locke, Alain, ed. 1997 (1925). *The New Negro*. New York: Simon and Schuster.

Loewald, Hans. 1980 (1962). "Internalization, Separation, Mourning, and the Superego." Pp. 221–57 in *Papers on Psychoanalysis*. New Haven: Yale University Press.

Loshitzky, Yosefa, ed. 1997. *Spielberg's Holocaust: Critical Perspectives on Schindler's List.* Bloomington: Indiana University Press.

Lübbe, Hermann. 1981. *Zwischen Trend und Tradition. Überfordert uns die Gegenwart?* Zürich: Edition Interforum.

Maier, Charles. 1997. *The Unmasterable Past: History, Holocaust, and German National Identity.* Cambridge, Mass.: Harvard University Press.

Maillot, A. 2000. "Shaping New Identities: The Peace Process and Post-Conflict Reconciliation." Unpublished manuscript, presented at City College Dublin, May.

Mannheim, Karl. 1952. *Essays in the Sociology of Culture.* London: Routledge.

Manz, Beatriz. 2002. "Terror, Grief, and Recovery: Genocidal Trauma in a Mayan Village in Guatemala." Pp. 292–309 in *Annihilating Difference: The Anthropology of Genocide,* ed. Alexander Hinton. Berkeley: University of California Press.

Marody M. 1987. "Antynomie spolecznej podswiadomosci" (Antinomies of Social Subconsciousness). *Odra* 1: 4–9. Reprinted in *Studia Socjologiczne* 2.

Marody, M., ed. 1996. *Oswajanie rzeczywistosci* (Taming the Reality). Warszawa: Instytut Studiów Spoecznych.

McCann, Lisa I., and Laurie Anne Pearlman. 1990. *Psychological Trauma and the Adult Survivor: Theory, Therapy, and Transformation.* New York: Bruner/Mazel.

McMurry, Linda. 1998. *To Keep the Waters Troubled.* New York: Oxford University Press.

Mead, Margaret. 1965 (1942). *And Keep Your Powder Dry: An Anthropologist Looks at America.* New York: William Morrow and Company.

Merton, Robert. K. 1996 (1938). "Social Structure and Anomie." In *Robert K. Merton on Social Structure and Science,* ed. P. Sztompka. Chicago: University of Chicago Press.

Michnik, A. 1998. "Hero or Traitor?" *Transitions* 9: 26–33.

Minow, Martha. 1998. *Between Vengeance and Forgiveness: Facing History after Genocide and Mass Violence.* Boston: Beacon.

Mishkin, Tracy. 1998. *The Harlem and Irish Renaissances.* Gainesville: University Press of Florida.

Miszalska, Anita. 1996. *Reakcje spoleczne na przemiany ustrojowe* (Social Reactions to Regime Change). Lódz: Lodz University Press.

Mitscherlich, Alexander, and M. Mitscherlich. 1994. *Die Unfähigkeit zu trauern: Grundlagen kollektiven Verhaltens.* München: Piper.

Mokrzycki, Edmund. 1995. "A New Middle Class?" Pp. 219–38 in *Democracy, Civil Society, and Pluralsim,* ed. C. Bryant and E. Mokrzycki. Warsaw: IFIS PAN.

Mommsen, Hans. 1983. "Die Realisierung des Utopischen. Die 'Endlösung der Judenfrage' im 'Dritten Reich.'" *Geschichte und Gesellschaft* 19: 381–420.

Mommsen, Hans, and D. Obst. 1988. "Die Reaktion der deutschen Bevölkerung auf die Verfolgung der Juden 1933–1943." In *Herrschaftsalltag im Dritten Reich: Studien und Texte,* ed. H. Mommsen and S. Willems. Düsseldorf: Schwann.

Moses, William. 1978. *The Golden Age of Black Nationalism.* Hamden, Conn.: Archon Books.

Naimark, Norman M. 1995. *The Russians in Germany: A History of the Soviet Zone of Occupation 1945–1949.* Cambridge, Mass.: Belknap.

———. 1997. *The Problem of Ethnic Cleansing in Modern Europe.* Greenville, N.C.: East Carolina University Press.

Neal, Arthur G. 1998. *National Trauma and Collective Memory: Major Events in the American Century.* Armonk, N.Y.: M. E. Sharpe.

Niethammer, Lutz, et al., eds. 1983. *Lebensgeschichte und Sozialkultur im Ruhrgebiet 1930–1960.* Berlin: Dietz.

Nisbett, Richard E., and Dov Cohen. 1996. *Culture of Honor: The Psychology of Violence in the South.* Boulder, Colo.: Westview.

Nolte, Ernst. 1987. *Der europäische Bürgerkrieg 1917–1945: Nationalsozialismus und Bolschewismus.* Frankfurt am Main: Propyläen-Verlag.

Nora, Pierre. 1992. *Les lieux de mémoire.* Paris: Gallimard.

Norich, A. 1998–99. "Harbe sugyes/Puzzling Questions: Yiddish and English Culture in America during the Holocaust." *Jewish Social Studies* 1, 2 (Fall-Winter): 91–110.

Novick, Peter. 1999. *The Holocaust in American Life.* New York: Houghton Mifflin.

———. 1994. "Holocaust and Memory in America." In *The Art of Memory: Holocaust Memorials in History,* ed. James E. Young. Munich: Prestel-Verlag.

Nussbaum, Martha. 1992. "Tragedy and Self-Sufficiency: Plato and Aristotle on Fear and Pity." Pp. 261–90 in *Essays on Aristotle's Poetics,* ed. A. O. Rorty. Princeton, N.J.: Princeton University Press.

*OBOP Bulletin,* a periodical of the Center for the Study of Public Opinion, Warsaw.

Okolski, M. 1996. "Przemiany ludnosciowe w Polsce w XX wieku." Pp. 17–38 in *Podstawy zycia spolecznego w Polsce* (The Foundations of Social Life in Poland), ed. M. Marody and E. Gucwa-Leny. Warszawa: Instytut Studiów Spoecznych.

Painter, Nell. 1976. *Exodusters.* New York: Norton.

Parsons, Talcott. 1978 (1974). "Religion in Postindustrial America: The Problem of Secularization." Pp. 300–322 in *Talcott Parsons: Action Theory and the Human Condition.* New York: Free Press.

Parsons, Talcott, and Edward A. Shils, eds. 1951. *Toward a General Theory of Action.* Cambridge, Mass.: Harvard University Press.

Patterson, Orlando. 1998. *Rituals of Blood.* Washington, D.C.: Civitas.

Pearlman, Laurie A., P. S. MacIan. 1995. "Vicarious Traumatization: An Empirical Study of the Effects of Trauma Work on Trauma Therapists." *Professional Psychology: Research and Practice 26,* no. 66: 558–65.

Pennebaker, James W., and Banasik, Becky L. 1997. "On the Creation and Maintenance of Collective Memories: History as Social Psychology." In *Collective Memory of Political Events: Social Psychological Perspectives,* edited by J. W. Pennebaker, D. Paez, and B. Rime. Mahwah, N.J.: Erlbaum.

Perlez, J. 2001. "Milosoevic Should Face Trial by Hague Tribunal, Bush Says." *The New York Times,* April 2, A6.

Perry, G. S. 1948. "Your Neighbors: The Golombs." *Saturday Evening Post 221* (November 13): 36ff.

*Poland: An International Economic Report, 1993/1994.* Warsaw: Warsaw School of Economics.

Polanyi, Karl. 1944. *The Great Transformation.* Boston: Beacon Press.

*Polityka,* a leading political and cultural weekly published in Poland.

Prager, Jeffrey. 1998. *Presenting the Past: Psychoanalysis and the Sociology of Misremembering.* Cambridge, Mass.: Harvard University Press.

Prince, R. 1998. "Historical Trauma: Psychohistorical Reflections on the Holocaust." Pp. 43–55 in *Children Surviving Persecution: An International Study of Trauma and Healing,* ed. Judith S. Kestenberg and Charlotte Kahn. Westport, Conn.: Praeger.

Przeworski, Adam, et al. 1995. *Sustainable Democracy.* Cambridge: Cambridge University Press.

Puvogel, Ulrike. 1989. *Gedenkstätten für die Opfer des Nationalsozialismus: Eine Dokumentation.* Bonn: Bundeszentrale für politische Bildung.

Pynoos, Robert S., and S. Eth. 1985. "Children Traumatized by Witnessing Acts of Personal Violence." Pp. 19–40 in *Post-Traumatic Stress Disorder in Children,* ed. Spencer Eth and Robert S. Pynoos. Washington, D.C.: American Psychiatric Press.

Radley, Alan. 1990. "Artefacts, Memory, and a Sense of the Past." In *Collective Remembering,* ed. David Middleton and Derek Edwards. London: Sage.

Rampersad, Arnold. 1976. *The Art and Imagination of W. E. B. Du Bois.* Cambridge: Harvard University Press.

Rampersad, Arnold, and Deborah E. McDowell, eds. 1989. *Slavery and the Literary Imagination.* Baltimore: Johns Hopkins University Press.

Rapoport, David. 1951. *Organization and Pathology of Thought: Selected Sources.* New York: Columbia University Press.

Reisinger, W. M., A. H. Miller, V. L. Hesli, and K. H. Maher. 1994. "Political Values in Russia, Ukraine, and Lithuania: Sources and Implications for Democracy." *British Journal of Political Science,* 24 (2) (April) 183–224.

Riesman, David. 1961. *The Lonely Crowd.* New Haven: Yale University Press.

Ritzer, G. 1993. *The McDonaldization of Society.* Newbury Park, Calif.: Pine Forge Press.

*Rocznik Statystyczny,* a yearbook of the Central Statistical Office, Warsaw.

Rolde, David. 1999. "The Visitor: Wiesel, a Man of Peace, Cites Need to Act." *The New York Times,* June 2, A1.

Rorty, Amélie O. 1992. "The Psychology of Aristotelian Tragedy." Pp. 1–22 in *Essays on Aristotle's Poetics,* ed. A. O. Rorty. Princeton: Princeton University Press.

Rosenfeld, A. H. 1995. "The Americanization of the Holocaust." *Commentary* 90 (6): 35–40.

Rosenthal, Alan. 1995. *Writing Docudrama: Dramatizing Reality for Film and TV.* Boston: Focal Press.

Savage, Kirk. 1994. "The Politics of Memory: Black Emancipation and the Civil War Monument." In *Commemorations,* ed. John Gillis. Princeton: Princeton University Press.

Schafft, Gretchen E., and Zeidler, G. 1996. *Die KZ-Mahn und Gedenkstätten in Deutschland.* Berlin: Dietz.

Schudson, Michael. 1989. "The Present in the Past versus the Past in the Present." *Communication* 11: 105–13.

Schuman, Howard, and Jacqueline Scott. 1989. "Generations and Collective Memory." *American Sociological Review* 54: 359–81.

Schuman, Howard, Robert F. Belli, and Katherine Bischoping. 1997. "The Generational Basis of Historical Knowledge." Pp. 47–77 in *Collective Memories of Political Events: Social Psychological Perspectives,* edited by J. W. Pennebaker, D. Paez, and B. Rime. Mahwah, N.J.: Erlbaum.

Schwartz, Barry. 1982. "The Social Context of Commemoration: A Study in Collective Memory." *Social Forces* 61 (2): 374–97.

Scruggs, Jan, with Joel Swerdlow. 1985. *To Heal a Nation: The Vietnam Veterans Memorial.* New York: Harper and Row.

Searle, John. 1969. *Speech Acts.* London: Cambridge University Press.

Shapiro, E. S. 1992. *A Time for Healing: American Jewry since World War II.* Baltimore: Johns Hopkins University Press.

Short, K. R. M. 1981. "Hollywood Fights Anti-Semitism, 1945–47." In *Feature Films as History,* ed. K. R. M. Short. Knoxville: University of Tennessee Press.

Silk, M. 1986. "Notes on the Judeo-Christian Tradition in America." *American Quarterly* 36 (Spring): [[pages?]].

Simmons, Charles A. 1998. *The African American Press.* Jefferson, N.C.: McFarland.

Singh, Amritjit, Joseph Skerrett Jr., and Robert Hogan, eds. 1994. *Memory, Narrative, and Identity.* Boston: Northeastern University Press.

Smelser, Neil J. 1998. *The Social Edges of Psychoanalysis.* Berkeley: University of California Press.

———. 1987. "Depth Psychology and the Social Order." Pp. 267–86 in *The Macro-Micro Link,* ed. Jeffrey C. Alexander, Bernhard Giesen, Richard Münch, and Neil J. Smelser. Berkeley: University of California Press.

———. 1974. "Growth, Structural Change, and Conflict in California Public Higher Education, 1950–1970." Pp. 9–142 in *Public Higher Education in California,* ed. N. J. Smelser and G. Almond. Berkeley: University of California Press.

———. 1962. *Theory of Collective Behavior.* New York: The Free Press of Glencoe.

Soeffner, Hans-Georg. 1992. *Die Ordnung der Rituale: Die Auslegung des Alltags 2.* Frankfurt am Main: Suhrkamp.

Sorokin, Pitirim. 1967 (1928). *The Sociology of Revolution.* New York: Howard Fertig.

———. 1962. *Society, Culture, and Personality.* New York: Cooper Square Publishers.

Stember, Charles H. l966. *Jews in the Mind of America.* New York: Basic Books.

Stocking, G. 1993. "The Turn-of-the-Century Concept of Race" *Modernism/modernity* 1 (1): 4–16.

Stovall, Tyler. 1996. *Paris Noir: African Americans in the City of Light.* Boston: Houghton Mifflin.

Sztompka, Piotr. 1999. *Trust: A Sociological Theory.* Cambridge: Cambridge University Press.

———. 1996. "Looking Back: The Year 1989 as a Cultural and Civilizational Break." *Communist and Post-Communist Studies* 29 (2): 115–29.

———. 1993a. *The Sociology of Social Change*. Oxford: Blackwell.

———. 1993b. "Civilizational Incompetence: The Trap of Post-Communist Societies." *Zeitschrift fur Soziologie* 2 (April): 85–95.

———. 1991a. *Society in Action: The Theory of Social Becoming*. Cambridge: Polity Press.

———. 1991b. "The Intangibles and Imponderables of the Transition to Democracy." *Studies in Comparative Communism* 3: 295–312.

Thomas, William I., and Znaniecki, Florian. 1974 (1927). *The Polish Peasant in Europe and America*. New York: Octagon Books.

Thompson, Kenneth. 1998. *Moral Panics*. London: Routledge.

Thompson, Michael, Richard Ellis, and Aaron Wildavsky. 1990. *Cultural Theory*. Boulder: Westview Press.

Tischner, Józet. 1991. *Polski mlyn* (Polish Melting Pot). Krakow: Nasza Przeszlosc.

Tocqueville, Alexis de. 1945 (1835). *Democracy in America*. Vols.1 and 2. New York: Knopf.

Tönnies, Ferdinand. 1955 (1877). *Community and Association*. London: Routledge.

*Transitions,* a monthly journal, Prague.

Turner, Victor. 1969. *The Ritual Process*. Chicago: Aldine.

Van Deburg, William. 1997. *New Day in Babylon and Black Camelot*. Chicago:University of Chicago Press.

van der Kolk, Bessel A. 1996. "The Complexity of Adaptation to Trauma: Self-Regulation, Stimulus Discrimination, and Characterological Development." Pp. 182–213 in *Traumatic Stress: the Effects of Overwhelming Experience on Mind, Body, and Society,* ed. Bessel A. van der Kolk, Alexander C. McFarlane, and Lars Weisaeth. New York: The Guilford Press.

van der Kolk, Bessel A., Lars Weisaeth, and Onno van der Hart. 1996. "History of Trauma in Psychiatry." Pp. 47–74 in *Traumatic Stress: The Effects of Overwhelming Experience on Mind, Body, and Society,* ed. Bessel A. van der Kolk, Alexander C. McFarlane, and Lars Weisaeth. New York: The Guilford Press.

van der Kolk, Bessel A., Alexander C. McFarlane, and Lars Weisaeth, eds. 1996. *Traumatic Stress: The Effects of Overwhelming Experience on Mind, Body, and Society*. New York: The Guilford Press.

Wagner-Pacifici, Robin, and Barry Schwarz. 1991. "The Vietnam Veterans Memorial: Commemorating a Difficult Past." *American Journal of Sociology* 97: 376–420.

Washington, Booker T. 1901. *Up from Slavery*. New York: Penguin.

Watson, Paul. 2001. "War's Over in Yugoslavia, but Box-Office Battles Have Begun." *Los Angeles Times,* January 3, A1–6.

Watson, Steven. 1995. *The Harlem Renaissance*. New York: Pantheon.

Weber, Max. 1958 (1904). *The Protestant Ethic and the Spirit of Capitalism*. Translated, with an introduction by Talcott Parsons. New York: Charles Scribner's Sons.

———. 1968. *Economy and Society.* Berkeley: University of California Press.

Weiss, Johannes. 1998. *Handeln und Handeln lassen: Über Stellvertretung.* Opladen: Westdeutscher Verlag.

Welles, Sumner. 1945. "New Hope for the Jewish People." *The Nation* 160 (May 5): 511–13.

White, Hayden V. 1987. *The Content of the Form.* Baltimore: Johns Hopkins University Press.

Whitman, H. 1949. "The College Fraternity Crisis." *Collier's* 123 (January 8): 34–35.

Wiesel, E. 1978. "Trivializing the Holocaust." *New York Times,* April 16, 2:1.

Wilkinson, I. 1999. "Where Is the Novelty in Our Current Age of Anxiety?" *The European Journal of Social Theory* 2: 445–67.

Williams, George Washington. 1882. *History of the Negro Race in America.* New York: G. P. Putnam's Sons.

Williams, Robin M. Jr. 1970 (1951). *American Society: A Sociological Interpretation.* New York: Knopf.

Wilson, John P., and Terence M. Keane, eds. 1997. *Assessing Psychological Trauma and PTSD.* New York: The Guilford Press.

Wines, M. 1999. "Two Views of Inhumanity Split the World, Even in Victory." *New York Times,* June 13, Section 4: 1.

Wintz, Cary. 1988. *Black Culture and the Harlem Renaissance.* Houston: Rice University Press.

Wittrock, B. 1991. "Cultural Identity and Nationhood: The Reconstitution of Germany or the Open Answer to an Almost Closed Question." Pp. 76–87 in *University and Society,* ed. M. Trow and T. Nybom. London: Jessica Kingsley Publishers.

Wnuk-Lipinski, E. 1990. "Freedom or Equality: An Old Dilemma in a New Context." Pp. 317–31 in *Philosophy of Social Choice,* ed. P. Ploszajski. Warsaw: Institute of Philosophy and Sociology Publishers.

Wodak, Ruth. 1990. "Wir sind alle unschuldige Täter." In *Diskurstheoretische Studien zum Nachkriegsantisemitismus.* Frankfurt am Main: Suhrkamp.

Wolfenstein, Martha. 1957. *Disaster: A Psychological Essay.* Glencoe, Ill.: The Free Press and the Falcon Wing's Press.

Yehuda, Rachel, ed. 1998. *Psychological Trauma.* Washington, D.C.: American Psychiatry Press.

Young, Allan. 1995. *The Harmony of Illusions: Inventing Post-Traumatic Stress Disorder.* Princeton: Princeton University Press.

Young, James E. 1993. *The Texture of Memory: Holocaust Memorials and Meaning.* New Haven: Yale University Press.

Young, James E., and M. Baigell, eds. 1994. *Mahnmale des Holocaust: Motive, Rituale und Stätten des Gedenkens.* München: Prestel.

Zaslavsky, Victor. 1994. *The Neo-Stalinist State.* Armonk, N.Y.: M. E.Sharpe.

Zelizer, Barbie. 1998. *Remembering to Forget: Holocaust Memory through the Camera's Eye.* Chicago: University of Chicago Press.

# Index

| | |
|---|---|
| Compositor: | BookMatters, Berkeley |
| Text: | 10/13 Sabon |
| Display: | Sabon |